1998

ANTHONY & BERRYMA

Magistrates' Court Guide

1998

ANTHONY & BERRYMAN'S

Magistrates' Court Guide

T G Moore

BA, Solicitor

Clerk to the Justices, Woodspring Magistrates' Court

Butterworths

London, Edinburgh, Dublin

1998

United Kingdom	Butterworths a Division of Reed Elsevier (UK) Ltd, Halsbury House, 35 Chancery Lane, LONDON WC2A 1EL and 4 Hill Street, EDINBURGH EH2 3JZ
Australia	Butterworths, SYDNEY, ADELAIDE, BRISBANE, CANBERRA, MELBOURNE and PERTH,
Canada	Butterworths Canada Ltd, TORONTO and VANCOUVER
Ireland	Butterworth (Ireland) Ltd, DUBLIN
Malaysia	Malayan Law Journal Sdn Bhd, KUALA LUMPUR
New Zealand	Butterworths of New Zealand Ltd, WELLINGTON and AUCKLAND
Singapore	Reed Elsevier (Singapore) Pte Ltd, SINGAPORE
South Africa	Butterworths Publishers (Pty) Ltd, DURBAN
USA	Michie, CHARLOTTESVILLE, Virginia

A CIP Catalogue record for this book is available from the British Library.

ISBN 0 406 89897 9

Printed by Mackays of Chatham plc, Chatham, Kent

Preface

I, like many other commentators, made a plea last year, in this preface, for a respite from new legislation. As it's turned out, 1997 has been a year of new legislation. Acts brought into force include the Knives Act 1997, the Firearms (Amendment) Act 1997, the Sexual Offences (Protected Material) Act 1997, the Dangerous Dogs (Amendment) Act 1997, the Road Traffic (New Drivers) Act 1995, the Protection from Harassment Act 1997, the Criminal Proceedings and Investigations Act 1996, the Crime (Sentences) Act 1997, the Family Law Act 1996 and the Sex Offenders Act 1997. In addition, there have been a number of deregulation orders in respect of betting, gaming and licensing.

The Sex Offenders Act 1997 has not been included in the text, as the requirement is imposed on the offender convicted or cautioned for specific sexual offences to notify the police of their name and address. Section 5 of the Act merely requires a court to state in open court that a person has been so convicted and that they may then wish to remind the offender of their obligations under the Act.

References to most of the other statutes are included in this year's text and in some cases major new sections have been added. Examples of this are the Family Law Act, which has resulted in a completely new section on domestic violence, covering non-molestation orders, undertakings, occupation orders and breach provisions. A new section has been included to cover the Protection from Harassment Act and the offences created under those provisions.

Yet another Dangerous Dogs Act is in force and the amendments to that section now make it one of the longest in the book! The provisions themselves act to mitigate the previously strict provisions concerning the destruction of dangerous dogs in certain circumstances.

Procedurally, the new mode of trial provisions and committal provisions have finally been enacted. In essence they mean that a defendant is now asked to intimate his plea to the court in respect of an either-way offence without the need to hear representations from the defence or the prosecution. If the plea is one of guilty, then the court will proceed to hear the case summarily. If no plea is entered or a not guilty plea is intimated, then the court will proceed by hearing mode of trial representations and deciding whether the case is heard in a magistrates' or a Crown Court. The sentencing section has also been amended to include the new s 38A of the Magistrates' Courts Act 1980 which now allows for related offences to be committed along with cases which are sent to Crown Court for sentence under s 38.

The 'old-style' committal is finally dead, with a decision to commit or not being made purely on the basis of written statements.

Some items still remain *in italics* to mark the fact they are not yet in force. An example of this is the secure training order; this remains in the text as the present government has indicated a desire to continue to build and open secure training centres.

Some of the newer initiatives in the Crime (Sentences) Act 1997 are in force – such as the removal of the need for the court to require the consent of the defendant to such orders as probation and community service (an exception being the imposition of a condition of mental, drug or alcohol treatment, when the defendant's agreement is still required). Other provisions have not been included in the main body of the text as they are being implemented as pilot schemes only. However, readers in Norfolk and Greater Manchester will be interested to know that for an 18-month period from January 1998 community service orders, curfew orders and driving disqualification will be available as a disposal for fine defaulters. Additionally, driving disqualification will be available for any offender, curfew orders for young (10–15-year-old) offenders will be available in Greater Manchester from 1 April 1998, and those courts will have the ability to use curfew orders with electronic monitoring as a condition of court bail.

On the subject of disqualification, the New Drivers Act is now fully noted and, although technically not a disqualification, newly-qualified drivers who collect penalty points in their first two years of driving will find themselves with a provisional driving licence awaiting a retest.

There are many new cases included in the text to assist the reader where appeal court decisions have substantially clarified statutory provisions.

As always, I am indebted to Michael Harris for his work on the licensing section of the book, a section in which there are a number of minor changes this year. The most substantial changes affect applications to the licensing committee for occasional permissions. The statutory provisions in this respect have been considerably relaxed to allow for more applications and for those applications to be made by members as well as officers of organisations, and indeed in the absence of those persons where they have made a previous successful application before the same committee.

Once again I take this opportunity to thank those readers who take the trouble to write with suggested amendments to the text. And I also thank my wife Karen for painstaking work on the computer, making amendments and inserting whole new sections into the text.

As is customary, every attempt have been made to ensure that the law is stated accurately as at 1 October 1997, which this year was the commencement date for much of the new legislation.

November 1997

TG Moore
North Somerset

Contents

Contents

Section one

Criminal offences dealt with in magistrates' courts

Index to criminal offences and table of maximum penalties

Set out below are a number of maximum penalties for some common offences. If an offence is dealt with more fully in this book the relevant page is stated.

† Penalty on summary conviction of an offence triable either way.

For index and penalties for road traffic offences, see p 251

Absconding level 5 and 3 months 458

Abusive words or behaviour level 5 and 6 months 138

Actual bodily harm level 5 and 6 months 12

Affray level 5 and 6 months† 16

Aggravated vehicle-taking level 5 and 6 months 18

Air gun in public place (FA 1968, s 22(5)) level 3 forfeiture 20

Airports (Aviation Security Act 1982)
False statements relating to baggage, cargo, etc (s 21A) level 5
False statements in connection with identity documents (s 21B) level 5
Unauthorised presence in restricted zone (s 21C) level 5
Unauthorised presence on board aircraft (s 21D) level 5
Intentionally obstructing an authorised person (s 21E(1)(a)) level 5†
Impersonating an authorised person (s 21E(1)(b)) level 5

Ammunition (FA 1968, s 1) (*See* Firearms) level 5 and 6 months, forfeiture† 73

Animal (cruelty to) level 5 and 6 months 36

Animals straying on highway level 3

Article with blade or point in public place (CJA 1988, s 139) level 5 and 6 months 21

Assault (*See* Actual bodily harm, Common assault, Indecent assault, Grievous bodily harm, Wounding)

Assault on police constable or person assisting police constable level 5 and 6 months 23

Avoiding customs duty (*See* Customs duty) 41

Bankrupt (undischarged, obtaining credit) level 5 and 6 months†

Begging level 3

Blade, article with, in public place (CJA 1988, s 139) level 5 and 6 months 21

Breach of peace (*See* Insulting words, and *see* p 173 for Binding over) 138

Brothel level 3 and 3 months; level 4 and 6 months (second or subsequent offence in relation to a brothel)

Builder's skip
depositing on highway level 3
not complying with a condition level 3
unlit on roadway level 3

Burglary level 5 and 6 months† 25

Car dumping (*See* Litter) 104

Children (cruelty to) level 5 and 6 months† 38

Chimes level 5 65

Common assault level 5 and 6 months 28

Computers (Computer Misuse Act 1990)
unauthorised access to computer material (s 1) level 5 and 6 months
unauthorised access with intent to commit or facilitate further offences (s 2) level 5 and 6 months†
unauthorised modification of computer material (s 3) level 5 and 6 months†

Contempt of court level 4 and 1 month 445

Controlled drugs Penalty varies with classification of drug 58

Copying false instrument level 5 and 6 months† 80

Court security officer
assault level 5 and 6 months 23
obstruction level 3 112

Criminal damage Penalties vary with value of property 31

Crossbow (draw weight 1.4kg or more) (Crossbows Act 1987)
sell or lease to person under 17 level 5 and 6 months, forfeiture
buying or hiring by person under 17 level 3 forfeiture
possession of by person under 17 level 3 forfeiture

Cruelty to animals level 5 and 6 months 36

Cruelty to children level 5 and 6 months† 38

Customs duty (avoiding) 3 times value of goods or £5000 and 6 months† 41

Damaging property Penalty varies with value of damage 31

Dangerous dog 43

Dangerous drugs (*See* Controlled drugs) 58

Dangerous machinery level 5† 47

Deception (obtaining by) level 5 and 6 months† 49 & 52

Dishonestly handling level 5 and 6 months† 91

purchasing, possession, etc, without certificate level 5 and 6 months† (s 1) 72
trespassing in a building level 5 and 6 months 75
trespassing on land level 4 and 3 months 77

Food (selling food not of quality demanded) (Food Safety Act 1990, s 14) £20,000 and 6 months†

Football spectators 78
throwing of missiles level 3
indecent or racialist chanting level 3
going onto the playing area level 3

Forgery level 5 and 6 months† 80

Found on enclosed premises level 3 or 3 months 83

Fraud (*See* Obtaining pecuniary advantage by) 49

Game (trespassing on land in daytime in search of game) level 3; level 5 if 5 or more trespassers (Game Act 1831, s 30) 118

Glue sniffing, supplying level 5 and 6 months 85

Going equipped to steal level 5 and 6 months† 86

Grievous bodily harm level 5 and 6 months† 88

Gross indecency level 5 and 6 months†

Handling stolen goods level 5 and 6 months† 91

Harassing residential occupier (Protection from Eviction Act 1977, s 1) level 5 and 6 months†

Harassment (Protection from Harassment Act 1997, s 1 and s 4) level 5 and 6 months† 94

Harassment, alarm or distress (Public Order Act 1986, s 5) level 3 54

Highway
builder's skip (depositing or leaving unlit) level 3
straying animals on level 3
wilful obstruction level 3

Housebreaking implements (*See* Going equipped to steal) 86

Indecency (gross between males) level 5 and 6 months†

Indecency with child level 5 and 6 months† 96

Indecent assault level 5 and 6 months† 98

Indecent display level 5

Indecent exposure level 3 or 3 months (Vagrancy Act 1824, s 4); level 3 or 14 days (Town Police Clauses Act 1847, s 28) 101

Obstructing or resisting a constable (or a person assisting a constable) level 3 and one month 112

Obstructing highway level 3 114

Obtaining evasion of liability by deception level 5 and 6 months† 49

Obtaining pecuniary advantage level 5 and 6 months† 49

Obtaining property by deception level 5 and 6 months† 52

Obtaining services by deception level 5 and 6 months† 49

Offensive letters level 4

Offensive weapon level 5 and 6 months, forfeiture† 115

Offices, shops, railway premises, and factories
Occupier of unclean premises
Occupier allowing dirt etc to accumulate
Occupier failing to clean floors
Employer failing to
  keep premises warm
  allow employee to warm himself
Employer failing to provide
  sanitary conveniences
  washing facilities
  adequate ventilation
  adequate lighting
  drinking water
  cloakroom
  sitting facilities
  eating facilities (shops)
  first-aid equipment
  fire alarm
Dangerous machinery unfenced
Floor opening unfenced
Untrained person
  using dangerous machine
  in charge of first aid box
Employer exposing person under 18 to risk from cleaning machinery
Committing dangerous act
Interfering with machinery, equipment
Employing person in premises, no fire certificate in force
Employer breaching terms of fire certificate
— level 5† (Health and Safety at Work etc Act 1974, s 33(3))
Employer failing to keep fire certificate on premises level 3
Obstructing Inspector (Health and Safety at Work Act 1974) level 5

Payment, making off without level 5 and 6 months† 49

Smuggling 3 times value of goods or £5000 and 6 months† 41

Social security
false statement to obtain level 5 and 6 months (Social Security Administration Act 1992, s 112)
persistently refusing or neglecting to maintain oneself or a dependant level 4 and 3 months (Social Security Administration Act 1992, s 105)

Soliciting by prostitutes level 2 /level 3

Soliciting women for prostitution level 3 102

Solvent, supplying for intoxication level 5 and 6 months 85

Sporting event
exclusion order 207
intoxicating liquor, possessing at/on the way to level 3 and 3 months 127
drunk at/on the way to level 2 127

Statutory nuisance (noise) 109

Stealing level 5 and 6 months† 134

Taking motor vehicle or conveyance level 5 and 6 months, disqualification 130

Tattooing a minor level 3

Telephone (Telecommunications Act 1984)
fraudulent use of public telephone (s 42) level 5 and 6 months†
indecent or false calls (s 43) level 3

Television licence level 3 132

Theft level 5 and 6 months† 134

Threatening to damage or destroy property level 5 and 6 months† 35

Threatening letters level 4

Threats or intimidation of witnesses level 5 and 6 months 140

Threatening words or behaviour (Public Order Act 1986, s 4) level 5 and 6 months 138

Trade description
applying false trade description level 5† 67
supplying goods with false description level 5† 67

Trespassing on land during daytime in search of game, etc level 3/level 5 (if 5 or more trespassers) (Game Act 1831, s 30) 118

Trespassing with firearm in a building level 5 and 6 months (†if not an air weapon) forfeiture 75

Trespassing with firearm on land level 4 and 3 months, forfeiture 77

Actual bodily harm

Charge

Assault occasioning actual bodily harm

Offences against the Person Act 1861, s 47

Maximum penalty - Fine level 5 and 6 months. Triable either way.

Crown court - 5 years imprisonment and unlimited fine.

Mode of trial

Consider first the general guidelines on p 446.

In general, except for the presence of one or more of the following factors, an offence of assault occasioning actual bodily harm should be tried summarily.

(a) Use of a weapon which was likely to cause or which did cause serious injury.
(b) Serious injury caused by kicking or headbutting.
(c) Victim in the 'front line', eg police officer, taxi driver, bus driver.
(d) Victim particularly vulnerable.
(e) The offence has a clear racial motivation.

The same considerations apply to assaults in a domestic setting.

Owing to the nature of charges of assault it is particularly important that magistrates hear an outline of the facts before making their decision.

Legal notes and definitions

Assault. See under 'Common assault' on p 28.

Intent. The defendant must intend to cause his victim to apprehend immediate and unlawful violence, or be reckless whether such apprehension be caused (*R v Venna* (1975)). This constitutes an assault. The offence of assault occasioning actual bodily harm is made out upon proof of an assault together with proof of the fact that actual bodily harm was occasioned by the assault. The prosecution are not obliged to prove that the defendant intended to cause some actual bodily harm or was reckless as to whether such harm would be caused (*R v Savage, R v Parmenter* (1991)).

In *DPP v K (a minor)* (1990), a schoolboy who put acid in a hot air dryer recklessly but in a mindless panic rather than with any intention to cause harm was nonetheless guilty of assault.

Actual bodily harm. This is less serious than grievous bodily harm. There need not be permanent injury. Any hurt or injury calculated to interfere with health or comfort can be actual bodily harm, so can an assault causing unconsciousness or an hysterical or nervous condition (*R v Miller* (1954)), ie some psychiatric damage and not just distress or panic (*R v Chand and Fook* (1993)). Significant psychological symptoms caused by a series of telephone calls, followed by silence can constitute an assault causing actual bodily harm (*R v Ireland* (1996)). Where a victim suffered great pain immediately and for some time thereafter suffered tenderness and soreness, that was sufficient for the court to infer that there was actual bodily harm notwithstanding that no physically discernible injury had been occasioned. Where there is evidence that a blow was struck, the justices are entitled if they see fit to infer that some bodily harm, however slight, has resulted.

Provocation. Is not a defence but can be taken into consideration when deciding sentence.

Self-defence. A person must not use force in attacking or retaliating, or revenging himself. But it is permissible to use force not merely to counter an actual attack but to ward off an attack honestly believed to be imminent. The reasonableness or otherwise of the belief is only relevant in ascertaining whether he actually held the belief or not (*Beckford v The Queen* (1987)).

Proof that the accused tried to retreat or call off the fight might be a cast-iron method of rebutting the suggestion that he was an attacker or retaliator or trying to revenge himself. It is to be stressed, however, that this is not the only method of doing so, and it depends on the circumstances of the particular case (*R v Bird* (1985)).

A man who is attacked can defend himself but can only do what is reasonably necessary to effect such defence. However when a person, in a moment of unexpected anguish, does only what he honestly and instinctively thought was necessary, that is most potent evidence that reasonable defensive action had been taken (*R v Whyte* (1987)). But a man cannot rely on a belief of fact which was induced by voluntary intoxication (*R v O'Grady* (1987)).

Misadventure
Consent
Lawful sport
Defence of property
Execution of legal process

see these headings on pp 29ff

Reduction of charge. The court cannot reduce this charge to common assault but, if a separate charge of common assault is preferred, a conviction for that may be possible. The clerk should be consulted.

Sentencing

Structure of the sentencing decision. See p 157.

Available sentences. See Table A on p 154

In considering sentence a helpful starting point is to consider factors which are relevant to the mode of trial decision. Aggravating factors include:

(a) the use of a weapon;
(b) kicking or headbutting;
(c) assaults on public servants doing their duty or members of the public going to their aid when attacked, eg assaults on police officers and traffic wardens usually merit an immediate custodial sentence (eg *R v Robertson* (1990)). 'Public servants' include such people as bus drivers, taxi drivers or publicans;
(d) vulnerable victim, eg an old person;
(e) aggressors outnumbering the victim;
(f) unprovoked assault;
(g) racial violence or motivation.

Apart from general mitigation such as previous good character the court might consider whether the accused was provoked by the victim and also the absence of any aggravating features.

Custodial sentence. See p 151.

Community sentence. See p 153.

Fines. See p 209.

Compensation. This may be ordered in respect of the victim's injuries or any other loss he may have suffered (eg broken dentures). Maximum is £5000. It may be ordered in addition to another sentence, or as a substantive penalty by itself. If a monetary penalty is appropriate and the defendant's means are limited, preference must be given to ordering compensation instead of a fine.

Licensed premises

An assault committed on licensed premises will enable the court to make an exclusion order. See p 207.

Husband and wife

These cases present especial difficulty. There has been a tendency amongst police and magistrates to treat the violent husband with leniency. This was probably based on a general reluctance to interfere in matrimonial disputes. However, a wife, like a policeman, is entitled to the protection of the law from those most likely to assault her. When wives are murdered it is usually by their husbands. When there are children in the family the effect of paternal violence should be considered and so should the ramifications of children seeing a violent father go unpunished by the law.

In a case decided in 1986 Mr Justice Michael Davies said that it was high time that the message was understood in clear terms by courts, by police forces, by probation officers and, above all, by husbands and boyfriends of women, that it was no mitigation of a serious assault that it had occurred in a domestic scene. That did not mean of course that for every tiff in which a slap was exchanged or given by one to another the involvement of the police and prosecution ought to follow. That would be taking what their Lordships had just said out of its context and out of proportion. The idea that in some way serious assaults were rendered trivial because of a relationship of marriage or friendship was completely outdated (*R v Cutts*). The Home Office has now encouraged the police to become more responsive to cases of domestic violence (August 1990).

Affray

Charge

Using or threatening unlawful violence towards another such that the conduct would cause a person of reasonable firmness present at the scene to fear for his personal safety

Public Order Act 1986, s 3

Maximum penalty - Fine level 5 and 6 months. Triable either way.

Crown court - 3 years imprisonment and unlimited fine.

Mode of trial

Consider first the general guidelines on p 446.

In general, except for the presence of one or more of the following factors, affray should be tried summarily:

(a) the violence was organised;
(b) significant injury to victims;
(c) a racial element;
(d) violence towards people called to the scene, eg ambulancemen or policemen.

Legal notes and definitions

The charge. Only one offence is created.

Using or threatening. Where two or more persons use or threaten the violence, it is the conduct of them taken together that must be considered for the purpose of the offence.

Threats. Cannot be made by way of words alone, there must be at least a physical gesture.

Person of reasonable firmness need not actually be or be likely to be present at the scene, it is the hypothetical reasonable bystander who has to be put in fear for his personal safety, not just the victim himself (*R v Sanchez* (1996)).

Violence. Violence does not include violence justified in law (self-defence or prevention of crime).The violence must be directed towards another, ie not property - such as kicking a door. However, the violence is not restricted to violence causing or intended to cause injury and includes violent conduct such as throwing a missile of a kind capable of causing injury even though it misses or falls short.

Intent. The accused must intend to use or threaten violence or be aware that his conduct may be violent or threaten violence.

Intoxication. See under the offence of violent disorder, p 143. Affray can be committed in a public or private place.

Sentencing

Structure of the sentencing decision. See p 157.

Available sentences. See Table A on p 154.

In assessing the gravity of the offence the court may consider the factors which are relevant to mode of trial. Affray was formerly considered to be a more serious offence than now. More serious offences are charged as violent disorder, p 143.

Custodial sentence. See p 151.

Community sentence. See p 153.

Fines. See p 209.

Compensation. See p 183.

Aggravated vehicle-taking

Charge

Taking a mechanically propelled vehicle without the owner's consent or other lawful authority (or driving, or allowing oneself to be carried in or on it, knowing it to have been taken without the owner's consent etc) and at any time after it had been unlawfully taken and before it was recovered:

> **the vehicle was driven dangerously on a road or public place;**
> **owing to the driving of the vehicle an accident occurred by which (injury was caused to any person) (damage was caused to property other than the vehicle);**
> **damage was caused to the vehicle.**

Theft Act 1968, s 12A(1)

Maximum penalty - Fine level 5 and 6 months imprisonment. Mandatory disqualification for one year and endorsement. Penalty points 3-11.

Crown court - 2 years imprisonment (5 years where death has been caused) and unlimited fine.

Mode of trial

Where no allegation is made other than damage to property or the vehicle concerned, the offence is triable only before magistrates where the total value of the damage concerned does not exceed £5000. The value of the damage to property other than the vehicle involved in the offence is what it would probably have cost to buy the property in the open market at the time of the offence. The value of the damage to the vehicle taken is assessed in a similar manner to that where property has been damaged (p 32). Otherwise the offence is triable either way.

For the procedure where it is not clear whether the damage is above or below £5000, see p 31. Although no mode of trial guidance has been issued it is apparent that these will be serious offences by their nature and that justices will accept jurisdiction only after careful consideration. Cases involving death should go to the crown court for trial.

Seriousness factors, such as prolonged high speed chases with the police, disregard for passenger pleas to stop and alcohol, may indicate a custodial sentence outside the powers of a magistrates' court for a single offence (*R v Bird* (1993)) and (*R v Ore and Tandy* (1995)).

Legal notes and definitions

Mechanically propelled vehicle ie a vehicle intended or adapted for use on a road.

Vehicle recovered ie when it is restored to its owner or to other lawful possession or custody.

Owner includes a person in possession under a hiring or hire purchase agreement.

Dangerous driving ie driven in a way which falls far below what would be expected of a competent and careful driver and it would be obvious to a competent and careful driver that driving the vehicle in that way would be dangerous.

Road or public place. See p 288.

Defence. The defendant is not guilty of this offence if he proves that the driving accident or damage occurred before he committed the basic offence or that he was neither in, nor on, nor in the immediate vicinity of the vehicle when that driving etc occurred. The defendant does not have to establish one of these defences beyond reasonable doubt. He need only establish that it was probably true.

Sentencing

Structure of the sentencing decision. See p 157.

Available sentences. See Table A on p 154.This offence was created to deal with the spate of offences of taking vehicles without consent accompanied by dangerous driving and damage to property or injury to persons.

Custodial sentences. See p 151.

Community sentences. See p 153.

Fines. See p 209.

Disqualification is mandatory for a minimum period of one year unless special reasons exist (see p 260). However the fact that the defendant did not drive the vehicle at any particular time or at all cannot amount to a special reason for not disqualifying (Road Traffic Act 1988, s 34(1A)).

Air guns

Charge

Being a person under 17 having with him in a public place an air weapon not being an air gun or air rifle which was so covered with a securely fastened gun cover that it could not be fired

Firearms Act 1968, s 22(5)

Maximum penalty - Fine level 3 or any other adjudication to which a young person is liable, bearing in mind the offence is not punishable with imprisonment.

Forfeiture of the air weapon or ammunition can be ordered.

Legal notes and definitions

With him ie more than mere possession, a close physical link and immediate control over the firearm but not necessarily that he had been carrying it.

Air weapon means an air rifle, air gun or air pistol of a type which has not been declared to be specially dangerous in rules made by the Home Office.

Public place includes any highway or premises or place to which at the material time the public had access whether for payment or otherwise.

A person between 14 and 17 years of age having in his possession in a public place an air weapon commits an offence unless it is so covered and fastened with a gun cover that it cannot be fired.

He does not commit an offence if he is engaged in target practice as a member of a club approved by the Home Office or if the weapon and ammunition are being used at a shooting gallery where only air weapons or miniature rifles of 0.23 calibre or less are used (s 23(2)).

Sentencing

Available sentences. See Table C on p 156.

Fines. See p 209.

Article with blade or point in public place

Charge

Having an article which has a blade (or is sharply pointed) namely a . . . in a public place or on school premises

Criminal Justice Act 1988, s 139 and s 139A

Maximum penalty - Fine level 5 and 6 months. Triable either way.

Legal notes and definitions

For other provisions concerning the carrying of offensive weapons in public places see p 115. This is an arrestable offence.

For the offence described here, the prosecution merely has to prove that the accused had an article to which this offence applies and it is then up to the accused to justify its possession. The prosecution has a lesser burden of proof, than in the offence described on p 115. The defendant does not discharge this burden merely by providing an explanation uncontradicted by prosecution evidence if the justices disbelieve his explanation (*Godwin v DPP* (1992)).

Mode of trial . Consider the general guidelines on p 446. In general the offence will be tried summarily.

Exceptions. This offence does not apply to a folding pocket knife except if the cutting edge of its blade exceeds 3 inches. Folding knife does not include a knife where the blade is secured in the open position by a locking device (*Harris v DPP* (1992)).

Public place includes any place to which at the material time the public have or are permitted access, whether on payment or otherwise.

School premises includes any land used for the purposes of a school but excludes a dwelling occupied by a person employed at the school.

Defences. It is a defence for the accused to prove that he had good reason or lawful authority for having the article with him in a public place. The defendant does not have to prove this beyond all reasonable doubt, only that it is more probable than not.

Good reason or lawful authority includes cases where the accused had the article with him:

(a) for use at work;
(b) for religious reasons (eg a Sikh); or

(c) as part of any national costume (eg a Scotsman's dirk).The defendant cannot rely on forgetfulness as constituting a good reason for having a weapon with him even where at an earlier period he was in lawful possession of the article (*DPP v Gregson* (1992));
or, in the case of the school offence
(d) for educational purposes.

Sentencing

Available sentences. See Table A on p 154.

This offence is punishable with imprisonment and so sentences such as a detention in a young offender institution, community service or attendance centre are available.

Structure of the sentencing decision. See p 157.

Custodial. See p 151.

Community sentence. See p 153.

Fine. See p 209.

Assaulting a police constable (or a person assisting the police)
Assaulting a court security officer

Charge

Assaulting a constable in the execution of his duty

OR

Assaulting a person assisting a constable in the execution of his duty

Police Act 1996, s 89

AND

Assaulting a court security officer in the execution of his duty

Criminal Justice Act 1991, s 78

Maximum penalty - Fine level 5 and 6 months. Triable only summarily.

Legal notes and definitions

Assault. See under Common assault on p 28.

Constable. Includes a special constable and any member of the police irrespective of actual rank.

Court security officer. A person employed by a magistrates' court's committee as a result of a contract with another person for the employment by him of persons to act as such officers.

In the execution of his duty. The constable must be carrying out his duty at the time of the assault. If he goes beyond his duty, for example by catching hold of a person whom he is not arresting, then this offence is not committed by a person resisting him with reasonable force. The line between duty and what lies beyond is not easily discernible. This needs reference to many decided cases in the higher courts - see, for example, *Donnelly v Jackman* (1970).

A court security officer shall not be regarded as acting in the execution of his duty unless he is readily identifiable by a badge or uniform (powers of court security officers are found in the Criminal Justice Act 1991, s 77).

The burden of proof that the constable was acting in the execution of his duty rests on the prosecution but the prosecution does not have to prove that the defendant knew that the constable was a constable, nor that the defendant knew that the constable was acting in the execution of his duty. The offence may be established even if the court accepts that the defendant (who must take his victim as he finds him) did not know that his victim was a police officer. Where the accused is unaware that his victim is a police officer and believes there are circumstances which would justify the use of force, eg self-defence, he should have a defence (*Blackburn v Bowering* (1995)) (see p 29 for defences).

If a police officer touches a person to draw his attention that contact must be acceptable by ordinary standards and for no longer than necessary to remain within the execution of the officers duty (*Mepstead v DPP* (1996)).

Reduction of charge. The court cannot reduce this charge to common assault, but if a separate charge for common assault is preferred, a conviction for that may be possible.

Sentencing

Structure of the sentencing decision. See p 157.

Available sentences. See Table B on p 155.

This is a serious offence and will frequently attract a custodial sentence. The Court of Appeal has upheld immediate custodial sentences for deliberate assaults on police officers, even where the offender has been of previous good character. An aggravating feature appears to be assaults on officers in order to prevent them arresting other offenders, particularly in the context of violent disorder (*R v Coote* (1992)). Gang attacks will invariably attract a custodial sentence if the policy of the Court of Appeal is followed.

Conversely, some police assaults may be more technical than injurious, no actual bodily harm may have been caused and sometimes the defendant may not have been aware that the victim was a police officer.

The surrounding facts must be considered carefully when deliberating on the seriousness of the offence.

Custodial sentence. See p 151.

Community sentence. See p 153.

Fines. See p 209.

Compensation. This may be ordered up to £5000 in respect of the victim's injuries or other loss he has suffered as a result of the assault. It may be ordered as part of a wider sentence, or by itself as a substantive penalty. If a monetary penalty is appropriate and the offender's means are limited, preference must be given to ordering compensation instead of a fine.

Licensed premises. If the offence takes place on licensed premises an exclusion order may be made. See p 207.

Burglary

Charge

Entering a building (or part of a building) as a trespasser with intent to steal therein (or with intent to do unlawful damage)

OR

Having entered a building (or part of a building) as a trespasser stole (or attempted to steal)

Theft Act 1968, s 9(1)(a) and s 9(1)(b) respectively

Maximum penalty - Fine level 5 and 6 months. Triable either way.

Crown court - 14 years imprisonment (for burglaries involving a dwelling), 10 years (other premises) and unlimited fine.

Mode of trial

Aggravated burglary is the commission of a burglary whilst armed with a firearm or other weapon of offence and is triable only at the crown court.

Burglary comprising the commission of, or an intention to commit, an offence of rape or grievous bodily harm may only be heard at the crown court.

If the building is a dwelling-house the magistrates' court can try the case unless it is alleged that the defendant used, or threatened, violence to someone in the dwelling-house.

Where the offence is triable either way consider first the guidelines on p 446.

Having considered these, then in general, **except** for the presence of one or more of the following factors, a burglary may be tried summarily:

Burglary in a dwelling-house

(a) day time when the occupier is present;
(b) night time when the house is normally occupied (whether or not it is actually occupied);
(c) a series of similar offences;
(d) soiling, vandalism or ransacking;
(e) offence has professional hallmarks;
(f) unrecovered property of high value.

Burglary (non dwelling-house)

(a) premises are a pharmacy or doctor's surgery;
(b) fear caused or violence offered to a person lawfully on the premises;

(c) offence has professional hallmarks;
(d) vandalism on a substantial scale;
(e) unrecovered property of high value.

Legal notes and definitions

Entering. Whether the defendant can properly be described as entering or having entered the building is a question of fact for the magistrates. They will have to decide whether the accused had made an effective entry into the building (*R v Brown* (1985)). An effective entry can be made by the burglar putting his hand through a broken shop window and stealing therefrom. It can be sufficient for only a part of the burglar's body to enter the premises.

Building. The offence is committed by one who is lawfully in part of a building but trespasses into another part.

An inhabited vehicle (eg a caravan) or vessel is within the section notwithstanding that the occupant is absent at the time of the offence.

Stealing is dishonestly appropriating another person's property with the intention of permanently depriving the other person of it. See p 135.

Trespass. Accidental trespass would not be an offence. The defendant must know, or be reckless as to whether, he is trespassing (*R v Collins* (1972)). If there is doubt whether the defendant was trespassing, consult the clerk.

Sentencing

Structure of the sentencing decision. See p 157.

Available sentences. See Table A on p 154.

This is a serious offence especially when committed during the hours of darkness. Amongst the factors to be taken into account when fixing sentence would be those referred to under mode of trial above and in addition:

(a) if a dwelling-house is involved was it occupied by a young or old person, or by a single person, who might be in fear for some time to come as a result of this experience?
(b) if commercial premises are involved were they likely to contain valuable or readily disposable property?
(c) the defendant operates in such a way as to suggest that he is a professional burglar.

Confirming sentences of borstal training on two teenagers for burglary in 1978 Lord Justice Lawton said:

> 'It may be necessary to set out and stress the reasons why at the present time offences of this kind should be dealt with severely and usually by a custodial sentence. It is within the knowledge of this court, and the criminal statistics bear it out, that one of the growth criminal industries in this country is burglary. The particular type of burglary which is becoming very common

> indeed is breaking into other people's homes ... This court knows that when there is a burglary in a house great distress is caused. Not only is there a loss of property, but there is induced a feeling of insecurity. This court knows that when householders are women they sometimes worry a great deal about what has happened to them. It has been said, and rightly said, that when a house has been burgled it never seems the same again. This court for some months has been pointing out to trial judges, and it does so again, that burglary in the form of housebreaking is a very serious crime indeed. The public are entitled to be protected against burglars. In the opinion of this court they are not likely to be protected if lenient sentences are passed. Unfortunately it is a matter of experience that nowadays a large number of housebreakers are adolescents and that when they break into houses ... the house is frequently turned upside down. Adolescents have got to be discouraged from housebreaking and, in our judgment, they are not likely to be discouraged by sentences which do not involve loss of liberty.'

The Court of Appeal has also stressed that long custodial sentences (3 years, in one case on a youth of 18 years) were appropriate for those who travel in pairs or gangs to commit burglary and similar offences.

The present trend towards short prison sentences does not extend to burglary of a dwelling-house. Many such cases will fall outside the magistrates' sentencing powers particularly if they are associated with other indictable offences. For example, in a Court of Appeal decision in 1991 the defendants had driven to a rural area during daylight and gained access to a house which was unoccupied at the time. They left without stealing anything when the burglar alarm sounded. Mr Justice Owen said that the defendant, who had no previous convictions, should be sentenced to the shortest possible sentence - 12 months imprisonment. Although a custodial sentence is appropriate in the great majority of cases the court should nevertheless be alert to mitigating circumstances which may indicate that the offence is not 'so serious' that only custody may be imposed. See *R v Edwards* (1996) suggesting the need for custodial sentences in the case of repeat offenders.

Custodial sentence. See p 151.

Community sentences. See p 153.

Fines. See p 209.

Compensation. This may be ordered up to £5000 either as part of a wider sentence or by itself as a substantive penalty. If the offender's means are limited and a monetary penalty is appropriate, preference must be given to ordering compensation instead of a fine. Compensation may also be ordered for similar offences taken into consideration.

An order may be made depriving the defendant of any property used in the commission of the offence; this would include, for example, a motor vehicle used to carry away stolen property. Such an order may be made notwithstanding that the property concerned did not belong to the defendant, but in such cases the clerk should be consulted.

Common assault

Charge

Did assault [ ]

Contrary to the Criminal Justice Act 1988, s 39

Maximum penalty - Fine level 5 and 6 months. Triable only by magistrates.

Legal notes and definitions

The offence is triable only by magistrates but may be alleged as an alternative charge at a trial at the crown court if the prosecution chooses with a maximum penalty of £5000 and 6 months.

Intent. The defendant must intend to cause his victim to apprehend immediate and unlawful violence, or be reckless whether such apprehension be caused (*R v Venna* (1975)). 'Reckless' means that the accused foresaw the risk and went on to take it (*R v Cunningham* (1957)).

Assault. Does not require any contact between the two parties, a threatening gesture is enough. Words, however insulting, are probably not an assault but any attempt to commit a battery, even if the blow does not connect, can be an assault. It is not necessary that the other party should receive an actual injury, but there must have been a hostile intent. In modern usage the term assault will now include a battery, ie the actual application of force as opposed to its threatened use, and this is how it is used in most statutes. But if a charge alleges 'did assault and batter' then 'assault' will be taken to mean assault in its pure form and the charge will be as bad as being duplicitous. If anything other than 'did assault' is to be alleged it should be 'did assault by beating' (*DPP v Taylor and Little* (1991)). A reckless act which causes injury will suffice, for example a man who having fallen to the ground when struggling with the police lashed out wildly with his legs, striking the officer and fracturing a bone in his hand, was held to have been properly convicted. Just placing a hand on someone's shoulder to call his attention to something is not an assault. Throwing something at a person, even if it misses, may be an assault.

If a man strikes at another but at such a distance that it would be quite impossible for it to connect then it is not an assault. If the other person is actually touched then it is a battery which includes an assault.

Misadventure. If a horse out of control strikes a person that is not an assault. In an old decision a soldier drilling in the ranks fired his gun as a man was passing unexpectedly and this was held not to be an assault.

Accidental jostling. In a crowd is not an assault as there is an implied consent to the physical contacts of ordinary life.

Consent. Consent of the victim is a defence but there are limits to this. The test is whether it is in the public interest to allow the activity complained of. In 1981 the Lord Chief Justice decided consent was irrelevant where two youths settled an argument in a public street by agreeing to have a fight. It was not in the public interest for people to cause each other actual bodily harm for no good reason. A similar principle has been applied by the House of Lords to assault which took place in the course of sado-masochistic activities (*R v Brown* (1992)).

However consensual activity between husband and wife in the privacy of the matrimonial home was held not to be a proper matter for criminal investigation in *R v Wilson* (1996). Lawful sport or reasonable chastisement would be unimpeachable as being in the public interest and the exercise of a legal right.

Defendants who maintained that they had been engaged in rough and undisciplined horseplay, had not intended any harm, and had thought that the victims were consenting to what had occurred, were entitled to have their defence considered by the court (*R v Muir* (1986)).

Lawful sport. Players in games which involve some risk of injury in play must be taken to accept that risk. So a player who injures another in a fair tackle would not be guilty of an offence. Even where the accused infringes the 'rules of the game' he might still not be acting unreasonably although it might be otherwise if he was guilty of serious and dangerous foul play which showed a reckless disregard for the victim's safety and fell far below the standards which might reasonably be expected in anyone pursuing the game. Where one player offers violence to another otherwise that in actual pursuit of the game this would be an assault.

Self-defence. A person must not use force in attacking or retaliating, or revenging himself. But it is permissible to use force not merely to counter an actual attack but to ward off an attack honestly believed to be imminent. The reasonableness or otherwise of the belief is only relevant in ascertaining whether he actually held the belief or not (*Beckford v The Queen* (1987)).

Proof that the accused tried to retreat or call off the fight might be a cast-iron method of rebutting the suggestion that he was an attacker or retaliator or trying to revenge himself. It is to be stressed, however, that this is not the only method of doing so and it depends on the circumstances of the particular case (*R v Bird* (1985)).

A man who is attacked can defend himself but can only do what is reasonably necessary to effect such defence. However when a person, in a moment of unexpected anguish, does only what he honestly and instinctively thought was necessary, that is most potent evidence that reasonable defensive action had been taken (*R v Whyte* (1987)). A a man cannot rely on a belief of fact which was induced by voluntary intoxication (*R v O'Grady* (1987)).

Defence of property. A trespasser should first be asked to leave the house or land. If he refuses, as much force as is reasonably necessary to remove him can be used. Similarly, such reasonable force can be used to prevent another person taking or destroying one's goods.

Execution of legal process. An officer of justice acting on a court order can, if he is resisted, use whatever force is necessary to carry out the order of the court.

Justification or triviality. In a case of common assault where the information was preferred by or on behalf of the party aggrieved, if the court finds that an assault has been committed but that either it was justified or that it was so trifling as not to merit any punishment, they may dismiss the charge and issue a certificate of dismissal.

Certificate of dismissal. If, after hearing such a case, the magistrates decide to dismiss the case the defendant can apply for a certificate of dismissal which will protect him from being subsequently prosecuted or sued for damages for the same assault.

Provocation. This is not a defence but may be put forward to mitigate the penalty.

Sentencing

Structure of the sentencing decision. See p 157.

Available sentences. See Table B on p 155.

In addition to any penalty the court may decide to inflict, the magistrates have the power to bind over, with or without sureties for any reasonable period. See p 173.

Where a case of common assault involves injury or serious injury the court should take those injuries into account in sentencing (*R v Nottingham Crown Court, ex p DPP* (1995)). Lesser cases can often be adequately met by binding over the defendant but this must be in addition to the sentence. A prosecution witness may also be bound over but not before he has been warned that the court has this course in mind and has been given the opportunity to address the court. Caution should be exercised in such cases.

Custodial sentence. See p 151.

Community sentence. See p 153.

Fines. See p 209.

Compensation. This may be ordered up to £5000, either as part of a wider sentence or by itself as a substantive penalty. If the offender's means are limited and a monetary penalty is appropriate, preference must be given to ordering compensation instead of a fine.

1 Criminal damage

Charge

Without lawful excuse destroyed (or damaged) property namely [ ] belonging to [ ] intending to destroy (or damage) it or being reckless as to whether such property would be destroyed or damaged

Criminal Damage Act 1971, s 1

Maximum penalty and venue for trial - Where the damage or destruction is caused by fire (arson) the offence is triable either way without regard to the value of the damage caused and the maximum penalty is a fine on level 5 and 6 months imprisonment. If it is alleged in the charge that the accused intended to endanger life, or was reckless as to whether life would be endangered, the offence is triable only on indictment and is punishable in the crown court with life imprisonment.

Where the value of the damage (see note below) is not more than £5000 the offence is punishable with a fine on level 4 and 3 months imprisonment and is triable as if it were a summary offence. There is no power to commit to the crown court for sentence.

Where the value of the damage (see note below) is more than £5000 the offence is triable either way and is punishable in the magistrates' court with a fine on level 5 and 6 months imprisonment.

Where it is not clear to the court whether the value of the damage is more than £5000 or not the court must decide whether the value is more or less than that sum (it is not necessary to decide what the value is, simply whether it is above £5000. If the court decides that the value of the damage exceeds £5000 (and it may hear representations from the prosecution and defence to assist in arriving at a decision) then the offence is triable either way as in the preceding paragraph. Likewise if the court reaches a decision that the value of the damage does not exceed £5000 the offence is triable summarily, as above. In those cases where the court is unable to decide whether the value is more or less than £5000 the accused must be told that if he wishes he may consent to be tried summarily, and if he does he will be so tried and will be liable to a maximum penalty on level 4 and 3 months. If the accused then consents, the trial will proceed summarily.

If he does not consent, the court proceeds as for an ordinary either way offence.

Assessing the value of the damage. Unless the damage was caused by fire, where property has been destroyed the mode of trial depends upon its value. This means what it would probably have cost to buy in the open market at the material time.

If the allegation is one of damage (excluding damage caused by fire) the mode of trial depends upon the value of the damage. If, immediately after the damage was caused, the property was capable of repair (eg a car windscreen) then the value of the damage is the lesser of (a) what would probably have been the market price for the repair of the damage immediately after the damage was caused (this would, for example, not include the cost of repairing further deterioration since the offence) OR (b) what the property would probably have cost to buy in the open market at the material time, whichever is the less. Thus, if it would cost more to repair the property than its probable market value, then the value of the damage for the purposes of deciding the venue of trial would be the probable market price. If, immediately after the damage was caused, the property was beyond repair (eg a shattered crystal decanter) then the value for trial purposes is its probable cost in the open market at the time of the offence.

The use of the word 'probable' in the Act indicates that the court must make up its mind in the light of the available information.

Multiple offences. Where an accused is charged with a series of offences of damage or destruction the offences are only triable either way if their aggregate value is in excess of £5000.

Mode of trial considerations. See first the general guidelines on p 446. In general, except for the presence of one or more of the following factors, criminal damage should be tried summarily:

(a) deliberate fire raising;
(b) offence committed by a group;
(c) damage of high value (ie in excess of £10,000);
(d) there was an element of racial motivation.

Legal notes and definitions

Without lawful excuse. It is a defence if the defendant proves he had a lawful excuse for destroying or damaging the property. He only has to establish that this defence is probably true, he does not have to establish it beyond reasonable doubt. Section 5(2) provides that, inter alia, the following can be lawful excuses:

(a) that at the time he destroyed or damaged the property he believed that a person or persons entitled to consent to the destruction or damage had given consent; or that person or persons would have consented if he or they had known of the destruction or damage and the circumstances; or
(b) that at the time he destroyed or damaged the property he believed that property belonging to himself or another was in immediate need of

protection and that the adopted or proposed means of protection were reasonable in all the circumstances.

Provided that the defendant honestly held such a belief, it is immaterial whether the belief was justified or not (even if the defendant was drunk) (*Jaggard v Dickinson* (1981)).

Destroy or damage. Where a defendant was initially unaware that he had done an act that in fact set in train events which, by the time he became aware of them, would make it obvious to anyone who troubled to give his mind to them that they presented a risk that property belonging to another would be damaged, he would be guilty if he did not try to prevent or reduce the damage because he gave no thought to the possibility of such a risk or having done so he decided not to prevent or reduce the risk. An example would be the man who, unawares, drops a lighted cigarette down a chair and later, on discovering the chair is smouldering, leaves the room not caring whether the chair catches light or not.

Property is defined at length in s 10(1). It means property of a tangible nature and includes money. It also includes wild creatures which have been tamed or are ordinarily kept in captivity. It does not include mushrooms, fungus, flowers, fruit or foliage of a plant, shrub or tree which are growing wild on any land.

Damage. Defendants who had painted graffiti on a pavement with a water-soluble whitewash in the expectation that the graffiti would be washed away by rainwater, were guilty especially since expense and inconvenience had been caused to the local authority which removed the marks before it rained. 'Damage' may be used in the sense of mischief to property. The 'temporary functional derangement' of a police officer's cap by the defendant stamping on it constituted damage although it could be pushed back into shape. Accordingly the erasure of a computer program on a plastic circuit card was damage and although it could be restored, this necessitated time, labour and expense (*Cox v Riley* (1986)).

Belonging to another person (s 10(2)). In addition to an ordinary owner this includes a person who had the custody or control of the property, or a proprietary right or interest in the property (except for an equitable interest arising only from an agreement to transfer or grant an interest), or who had a charge on the property.

As far as trust property is concerned, it can be treated for the purposes of this offence as belonging to any person having the right to enforce the trust (s 10(3)).

Intending. The court must decide whether the defendant intended the damage by considering all the evidence and drawing from it such inferences as appear proper in the circumstances.

Reckless. A person is reckless if (a) he commits an act which creates an obvious risk that the property would be destroyed or damaged, and (b) when he commits the act he either gives no thought to the possibility of there being any such risk or, having recognised that there is some risk involved, he nevertheless goes on to commit the act (*R v Caldwell* (1981)).

Sentencing

Structure of the sentencing decision. See p 157.

Available sentences. For an offence triable either way see Table A on p 154, for a purely summary offence see Table B on p 155.

Reference might usefully be made to the factors relevant to deciding mode of trial (p 446).

Imprisonment can be ordered as well as a fine, and should be considered whenever the offence is serious or made so by its prevalence.

Custodial sentence. See p 151.

Community sentence. See p 153.

Fines. See p 209.

Compensation. This may be ordered up to £5000 either as part of a wider sentence or by itself as a substantive penalty. If the offender's means are limited and a monetary penalty is appropriate, preference must be given to ordering compensation instead of a fine.

2 Threatening to destroy or damage property

(Criminal Damage Act 1971, s 2(a))

Charge

Without lawful excuse made to [ ] a threat to destroy (or damage) property belonging to that other person (or belonging to a third person), intending that the other person would fear it would be carried out

Maximum penalty - Fine level 5 and 6 months. Triable either way.

The legal notes and definitions relating to the previous offence on pp 31-34 also apply here, except for the reference to compensation and mode of trial. The threats can be spoken or in writing.

Crown court - 10 years imprisonment and unlimited fine.

3 Possessing anything with intent to destroy or damage property

(Criminal Damage Act 1971, s 3(a))

Charge

Had in his custody (or under his control) a . . . intending without lawful excuse to use it to destroy (or damage) property belonging to another person

Maximum penalty - Fine level 5 and 6 months. Triable either way.

The legal notes and definitions relating to offence no. 1 on p 31 also apply here except for mode of trial.

Crown court - 10 years imprisonment and unlimited fine.

Cruelty to animals

Charge

Cruelly beating, kicking, ill treating, over-loading, torturing, infuriating, terrifying or causing by act or omission any unnecessary suffering to an animal or tethering any horse, ass or mule under such conditions as to cause that animal unnecessary suffering

Protection of Animals Act 1911, s 1, as amended

Maximum penalty - Fine level 5 and 6 months - triable only summarily.

Legal notes and definitions

Each of the types of cruelty listed above is a separate offence and a charge should only allege one of them.

Ill treatment of a number of animals. If the defendant ill treated a number of animals on the same occasion there may be one charge in respect of all the animals.

Abandonment. If the animal's owner or any person having charge or control of an animal abandons it permanently or temporarily, without reasonable cause or excuse in circumstances likely to cause unnecessary suffering, then an offence has been committed.

Necessary purpose. If pain is inflicted for a necessary purpose (eg branding) then no offence has been committed.

Animal. Means any domestic or captive animal. Wild mammals are proteceted from any unnecessary suffering or ill treatment under the Wild Mammals (Propection) Act 1996. Maximum penalty: fine level five.

Domestic animal. Means any horse, ass, mule, bull, sheep, pig, goat, dog, cat, fowl or any other animal of whatever kind or species whether a quadruped or not, which is tame or which has been tamed or is being sufficiently tamed to serve some purpose for the use of man.

Captive animal. Means any animal (other than a domestic animal) of any kind or species, whether quadruped or not, and includes any bird, fish or reptile which is in captivity or confinement or which has been maimed, pinioned or subjected to any appliance or contrivance for the purpose of hindering or preventing its escape from captivity or confinement. However it does not include the maiming of wild animals whilst still in that state.

Owner of an animal. It is an offence for the owner of an animal to permit any of the listed kinds of ill treatment and an owner will be deemed guilty if he has failed to exercise reasonable care and supervision to protect the animal from ill treatment. Where an owner is deemed guilty in this way he cannot be sent to prison without the option of a fine.

Sentencing

Structure of the sentencing decision. See p 157.

Available sentences. See Table B on p 155.

The maximum penalty for this offence was doubled in 1987 to reflect concern at the gravity of some offences that had been committed and offences of this kind often arouse strong public feeling. Magistrates should therefore be careful to maintain some relationship with penalties for assaulting persons, lest a criticism may be sustained that a more serious view has been taken of cruelty to an animal than of cruelty to a human being.

Custodial sentence. See p 151.

Community sentence. See p 153.

Fines. See p 209.

Deprivation of ownership. If the court comes to the conclusion that leaving the animal in the ownership of the defendant is likely to expose the animal to further cruelty either because of a previous conviction for this offence or because of evidence of the owner's character or otherwise, it can deprive the defendant of ownership and make such order for the animal's disposal as it thinks fit.

Destruction of animal. After conviction the court, if satisfied that it would be cruel to keep the animal alive, can order the destruction of the animal and order the defendant to pay the costs involved.

Disqualification. The court may disqualify the defendant for any period it thinks fit from having custody of an animal of the kind ill treated or the disqualification may embrace all kinds of animals. The court may suspend the order pending an appeal or to allow time for arrangements to be made for the handing over of the animal to someone else. A disqualification may only be imposed in the defendant's absence if the case has been adjourned after conviction and the defendant given an opportunity to attend and make representations.

After the disqualification has been in force for 12 months the defendant can apply for its removal and if refused can re-apply at intervals of 12 months.

If the disqualification order is disobeyed the maximum penalty is a fine on level 3 and 3 months.

Cruelty to children

Charge

Having responsibility for a child or young person under the age of 16 and wilfully assaulting, ill treating, neglecting, abandoning, or exposing him in a manner likely to cause him unnecessary suffering or injury to health

Children and Young Persons Act 1933, s 1, as amended

Maximum penalty – Fine level 5 and 6 months. Triable either way.

Crown court – 10 years imprisonment and unlimited fine.

Mode of trial

Consider first the general guidelines on p 446.

In general, except for the presence of one or more of the following factors, offences of cruelty to children should be tried summarily:

(a) substantial injury caused;
(b) the neglect or assault repeated over a long period of time even if the harm is slight;
(c) deliberate sadistic injury.

Legal notes and definitions

All or any of the types of cruelty listed in the charge above can be included in a single information but on conviction one penalty must cover the lot.

The offence of cruelty can only be committed by a person over the age of 16.

Exemptions. The Act expressly stipulates that a parent or teacher or other person having lawful control of a child or young person is not guilty of this offence if the child is punished by them moderately and reasonably.

A child. Means someone under 14 years of age.

A young person. Means for this offence someone aged 14 or 15 years.

Wilfully. Means deliberately (as opposed to accidentally or by mistake or inadvertence) or because the defendant knew there was a risk or he was unaware of the risk because he did not care that the treatment of the child was likely to cause him unnecessary suffering etc. The clerk should be consulted on this concept and it appears that in a case of assault whether the force used was moderate and reasonable is to be decided by the magistrates. The prosecution only has to prove that the defendant intended to use *force*.

Assaulting. See under the charge of 'Common assault', p 28.

Ill treating. Actual assault or battery need not be proved. Bullying or frightening or any course of conduct calculated to cause unnecessary suffering or injury to health will suffice.

Neglecting. Means omitting to take such steps as a reasonable parent would take and can including failing to apply for state benefits. Failure to obtain medical care can amount to neglect. It is a question of fact which the magistrates have to determine in each case.

Abandoning. Means leaving the child to his fate. In one case a child was carefully packed in a hamper and sent by train to the father's address and although the child came to no harm it was held that the child had been abandoned.

In another case a child had been left on his doorstep and the father knew it was there and he permitted the child to remain there during an October night for six hours. It was held that he had abandoned the child.

Leaving children at a youth court has been held not to be an offence under this section.

Exposing. It is not necessary to prove that the defendant intended to cause suffering or injury to health. The requisite is that the defendant exposed the child or young person in a manner which was likely to cause unnecessary suffering or injury to health.

In a manner likely to cause him unnecessary suffering or injury to health. This part of the offence must be proved in addition to wilfully assaulting, ill treating, neglecting, abandoning or exposing as set out in the charge.

Presumption of guilt. A parent or person legally liable to maintain a child or young person will be presumed to have neglected the child or young person in a manner likely to cause injury to health if he has failed to provide adequate food, clothing, medical aid or lodging. If the parent has been unable to provide any of these things he will still be presumed to have neglected him if he fails to apply for them under state benefits. (However the prosecution must still establish that this neglect was 'wilful'.)

Dealing with the children. As the defendant is almost always over the age of 18 this offence is usually tried in the adult court.

Either before the charge is heard in the adult court or concurrently it is often the practice that the ill treated child or young person is brought before the family proceedings court as in need of care and the family proceedings court can make a care order placing the child or young person in the care of a local authority.

The court may direct that nothing may be published or broadcast which would identify any child concerned; the clerk should be consulted.

Sentencing

Structure of the sentencing decision. See p 157.

Available sentences. See Table A on p 154.

If two or more children are concerned in the same occasion then all of them can be included in one charge and if this is done then only one penalty can be imposed for the one collective charge and not a penalty for each child (s 14).

If the prosecution has brought a separate charge for each child, then a separate penalty can be ordered for each charge.

As mentioned above, if in the case of an individual child one information is laid alleging assault, ill treatment, neglect, etc, only one penalty may be imposed.

The court may usefully consider the factors referred to under 'Mode of trial' above.

An isolated assault on a child caused perhaps by loss of temper will attract a less severe penalty than a course of conduct covering a period of time. Lord Roskill has drawn attention to the difficulties of sentencing in cases of assault on or ill treatment of children:

> 'There are few cases which cause more difficulty to a court in assessing the appropriate sentence than cases of ''child bashing''. At one extreme they reveal utter brutality which must be dealt with very severely both as a punishment and as a deterrent and, up to a point, in order to assuage outraged public feeling. At the other extreme one gets cases of undoubted maltreatment, but where the explanation is to be found in social inadequacy or momentary loss of temper where a parent is utterly unable to control his feelings when he becomes angry.'

Custodial sentence. See p 151.

Community sentence. See p 153.

Fines. See p 209.

Customs and excise duty

Charge

Knowingly and with intent to defraud Her Majesty of the duty payable was concerned in carrying, removing, depositing, harbouring, keeping or concealing or dealing with goods, namely, ... , which were chargeable with a duty which had not been paid

OR

Knowingly and with intent to defraud Her Majesty of the duty payable acquired possession of goods namely, ... , which were chargeable with a duty which had not been paid

OR

Knowingly was concerned in a fraudulent evasion (or attempt at evasion) of any duty chargeable on certain goods, namely ...

Customs and Excise Management Act 1979, s 170

Maximum penalty – Three times the value of the goods or £5000 fine whichever is the greater and 6 months. Triable either way.

Crown court – 7 years imprisonment and unlimited fine.

Drugs – Different penalties will apply in both the magistrates' and the crown court if drugs are involved and in the crown court where there is the import or export of counterfeit money. The clerk or judge will advise.

Mode of trial

See general notes on p 446.

Legal notes and definitions

Knowing. If it is proved that dutiable goods were in the defendant's possession there is a presumption that he knew they were in his possession. Recklessness is not sufficient (*R v Panayi* (1988)).

Intent to defraud. The intention of defrauding the crown of duty can be inferred from the circumstances of the case. It has been held that telling a lie to a customs officer can be evidence of an intention to defraud.

The prosecution. Must be authorised by HM Customs and Excise. Neither the police nor a private citizen can instigate proceedings on their own authority.

Death of informant. If the informant (or person authorised by HM Customs and Excise) dies, is dismissed or is absent then the Customs and Excise can nominate another person to proceed with the case.

Presumptions against the defendant. The Act is so worded that it gives to the prosecution a number of advantages in presuming certain points to be in the prosecution's favour.

For example, if a defendant claims that the goods were lawfully imported or lawfully unloaded from a ship or aircraft the burden of proving these points rests on the defendant. However, the burden of proof is not to establish his defence beyond all reasonable doubt but to satisfy the magistrates that on the balance of probabilities his defence is true.

Mistake. If the customs officer makes a mistake and undercharges the duty, no offence is committed by a person who pays the duty realising the mistake, provided that he has not given false information or induced the error.

Sentencing

Structure of the sentencing decision. See p 157.

Available sentences. See Table A on p 154.

The value of the goods, for the purpose of determining the penalty, shall be the price they might reasonably be expected to have fetched on the open market, after duty has been paid, at or about the time of the commission of the offence.

Custodial sentence. See p 151.

Community sentence. See p 153.

Fines. See p 209.

Dangerous dogs

Offences under the Dangerous Dogs Act 1991

Charge

Being the owner (person for the time being in charge) of a dog which on [ ] was dangerously out of control in a public place namely [ ] (and which injured a person)

Dangerous Dogs Act 1991, s 3(1)

Maximum penalty – Fine level 5 and 6 months imprisonment. Triable only by magistrates.

Where it is alleged and proved that the dog injured a person (an 'aggravated offence') the offence is triable either by magistrates (with the penalties as above) or at the crown court where the maximum penalty is 2 years imprisonment and an unlimited fine.

Legal notes and definitions

Owner. Includes, where the dog is owned by a person who is less than sixteen years old, the head of the household of which that person is a member.

Dangerously out of control. Is defined to include any occasion on which there are grounds for reasonable apprehension that the dog will injure any person, whether or not it actually does so (exception is made inter alia for police dogs). The Act imposes strict liability on the owner (*R v Bezzina* (1994)).

The offence (under s 3(3)) of allowing the dog to enter a place, not being a public place, where it injures someone, can be committed by omission, ie where the dog escapes from an enclosed area (*Greener v DPP* (1996))

Public place. Any street, road or other place (whether or not enclosed) to which the public have or are permitted to have access whether for payment or otherwise and includes the common parts of a building containing two or more separate dwellings.

It is an offence under s 3(3) to allow a dog to enter a place which is not a public place where it is not permitted to be and while there it injures a person or there are grounds for reasonable apprehension that it will do so.

If this type of dog is in a car which is parked in a public place then the dog itself is in a public place (*Bates v DPP* (1993)).

Sentencing

Structure of the sentencing decision. See p 157.

Available sentences. See Table B on p 155; for aggravated offences see Table A on p 155.

Order for destruction. Where a person is convicted of an offence under s 3(1) or s 3(3) the court may order the destruction of the dog and must do so in the case of an aggravated offence, unless the court is satisfied the dog does not constitute a danger to public safety. A court should not make an order for destruction without giving the dog's owner an opportunity to be heard (*R v Ealing Magistrates, ex p Fanneran* (1996)). Any person having custody of the dog may be required to deliver it up to a person appointed by the court to undertake its destruction which will be suspended pending the determination of any appeal. Note that disobedience of a court order to deliver up for destruction is a criminal offence. The maximum penalty under these provisions is a fine on level 5.

Additional powers. A person convicted under s 3(1) or (3) may be ordered to keep the dog under proper control or failing that the dog shall be destroyed. The court may also specify measures for keeping the dog under proper control such as muzzling, keeping on a lead or excluding the dog from entering specific places. The court may also order a male dog to be neutered.

Disqualification. Whether or not there is an order for destruction of the dog the court may disqualify the person convicted (ie not necessarily the owner) for having custody of a dog for a period specified in the order. A person disqualified for having custody of a dog may apply to the court after one year to terminate the disqualification having regard to his character, conduct and any other circumstances. Where an application is refused, no further application can be considered for a further year. Costs may be awarded.

Having custody of a dog in contravention of a disqualification is an offence, maximum penalty a fine on level 5.

Right to appeal to the crown court. A person convicted of an offence has an automatic right to appeal to the crown court against his conviction, sentence or any order made. In addition, where an order has been made for the destruction of a dog owned by a person other than the offender, then, unless the order was one which the court was required to make the owner may appeal to the crown court against the destruction order.

Other offences

The Dangerous Dogs Act 1991 creates a number of offences in connection with 'fighting dogs' which are defined as pit bull terriers, Japanese Tosas and other dogs specified by the Secretary of State. It is unlawful to breed, sell, exchange, advertise for sale or to make a gift of such a dog. Accordingly, these dogs will decline in numbers with the effluxion of time. Those persons who already possess such dogs must obtain a certificate of exemption and comply with the stringent conditions attached thereto. It is an offence for an owner to have such a dog which is not registered, or to abandon it. The most common charge is for the owner or person for the time being in charge of such a dog to allow it to stray or to be in a public place without being muzzled and kept on a lead: maximum penalty 6 months imprisonment and a level 5 fine – triable only by magistrates. It should be noted that a dog 'of the type known as a pit bull terrier' is not to be taken as being synonymous with the definition breed (*R v Knightsbridge Crown Court, ex p Dunne* (1993)). The provisions relating to destruction and disqualification apply as for 'aggravated offences' under s 3 of the 1991 Act. Except that where no destruction order is made in the case of a designated dog, the court must order that unless a certificate of exemption is obtained for the dog within two months of the date of the order the dog shall be destroyed. If a certificate is not obtained the court has a discretion to extend the two-month period.

Control or destruction order

(Dogs Act 1871, as amended)

As an alternative to prosecution under the Dangerous Dogs Act 1991 the pre-existing civil remedy under the Dogs Act 1871 is still available and is not confined to public places nor where the dog has injured a person.

Legal notes and definitions

Application for dangerous dog to be kept under control or destroyed. Application may be made to a magistrates' court for an order that the dog be destroyed or kept under proper control by the owner. The magistrates may in their discretion make a destruction order without the option of a control order. A dog is not allowed his 'one bite' although in most cases a control order is sufficient for the first transgression. Costs can be awarded by the court to the successful party.

The proceedings must be in the form of a **complaint** and not as an **information** for an offence.

The court must be satisfied (a) that the dog *is* dangerous and (b) that it *is* not kept under proper control. The dog need not be dangerous to mankind. It is sufficient if it is proved that the dog injured cattle or chased sheep. At the other end of the scale, a dog which on only one occasion killed two pet rabbits was not dangerous, it being in the nature of dogs to chase, wound and kill other small animals. It need not be proved that the owner knew his dog was dangerous. Moreover the dog need not be dangerous by temperament if he is shown to have been dangerous on one occasion. Evidence of the temperament of the animal, however, is admissible if it shows the likelihood of its being dangerous on a particular occasion.

Change of ownership. If the owner of the dog establishes in court that he is no longer the owner of the dog but has made a bona fide transfer of the dog to some other person no order can be made against him for the dog's destruction or its proper control; but the order can be made against the new owner provided that a complaint is made against the new owner within 6 months from the date of the cause of the complaint.

Procedure at the hearing. If the **complaint** is accompanied by an **information** alleging some additional offence (such as worrying livestock) then the **information** should be dealt with first and the **complaint** afterwards. The clerk should be consulted in such cases.

Control order. The court may specify the measures to be taken for keeping the dog under proper control, whether by muzzling, keeping on a lead, excluding it from specified places, or otherwise. Where the dog is male, the court may order it to be neutered if thereby it would be less dangerous.

Destruction order. Any person having custody of the dog may be required to deliver it up to a person appointed by the court to undertake its destruction which will be suspended pending the determination of any appeal.

Disqualification. A court which makes a destruction order may disqualify the owner for having custody of a dog for a period specified in the order. Disqualification may also be imposed on conviction of an offence of failure to comply with a court order (either to keep the dog under proper control or deliver it up for destruction), maximum penalty a fine on level 3.

A person disqualified for having custody of a dog may apply to the court after one year to terminate the disqualification having regard to his character, conduct and any other circumstances. Where an application is refused, no further application can be considered for a further year. Costs may be awarded.

Disobedience of a court order for control or to deliver up for destruction is a criminal offence, maximum penalty a fine on level 3 .

Having custody of a dog in contravention of a disqualification is an offence, maximum penalty a fine on level 5.

Right to appeal to the crown court. If an order is made for control or destruction, the owner can appeal to the crown court. Appeal against conviction and sentence for the criminal offences lie to the crown court in the normal way.

Dangerous machinery

Charge

Having a dangerous part of machinery not being securely fenced

Factories Act 1961, s 14;
Health and Safety at Work Act 1974, s 33(3)

Maximum penalty – Fine £5000 (company); level 5 (individual). Triable either way.

Crown court – Unlimited fine.

Mode of trial

See general notes on p 446.

Legal notes and definitions

Factory. The premises must be a factory which is defined at length in the Factories Act 1961 (Factories Act 1961, s 175); a submission that the premises are not a factory is rare.

Dangerous part of machinery. This means that the piece of machinery could be reasonably anticipated to be dangerous unless fenced. There is an absolute duty to fence such machinery and it is no defence that an employee disobeyed instructions or caused the accident by undue haste, carelessness or laziness. Nor is it a defence that the machinery was used in that condition over a long period of time without an accident occurring and without complaint from HM Inspector of Factories.

Securely fenced. This means so securely fenced as to prevent the body of the employee using the machine from coming into contact with the machinery. If the machine has been found to be not securely fenced it is not a defence to allege that the best known type of fencing was used. Nor is it a defence that to fit secure fencing would render the machine commercially unprofitable.

Exemptions. *Prime movers* and *transmission machinery* are exempt from this offence, but two other sections of the same Act require prime movers and transmission machinery to be securely fenced. A failure to fence either securely would be contrary to s 12 or 13 of the Factories Act 1961.

Prime mover. Means every engine, motor or other appliance which provides mechanical energy derived from steam, water, wind, electricity, the combustion of fuel or other source of power (s 176).

Transmission machinery. Means every shaft, wheel, pulley, system of pulleys, couplings, clutch, driving belt or other device by which motion of a prime mover is transmissible to or received by any machine or appliance (s 176).

Sentencing

Unlike most either way offences this does not carry imprisonment (and therefore sentences such as community service are not available). For this reason, and because the defendant in these cases is usually a company, the most common penalty is a fine.

Where the court is of the opinion that the offence or the combination of the offence and other offences associated with it was so serious that greater punishment should be inflicted for it than the court has power to impose, the defendant, whether an individual or a company, may be committed to the crown court for sentence. See p 176.

Those whose work brings with it a familiarity with machinery notoriously become indifferent to safety precautions and will sometimes take the most appalling risks. It may be appropriate to take into account any contribution a worker may have made to his own misfortune in accident cases, but employers must be expected to know the nature of their workers and take and maintain measures to protect workers not only from dangerous machines but from themselves.

Deception: obtaining by deception (a) pecuniary advantage, (b) services, (c) evasion of liability Making off without payment

Charges

1 (a) Dishonestly obtaining for himself [or for . . .] a pecuniary advantage, namely [ ], by a deception

Theft Act 1968, s 16

(b) dishonestly obtained services namely [ ] from [ ] by deception

Theft Act 1978, s 1

(c) dishonestly secured the remission of [part of] an existing liability to make a payment to [ ] by deception

Theft Act 1978, s 2(1)(a)

(d) with intent to make permanent default in whole or part of an existing liability to make a payment dishonestly induced [ ] to wait for [or forgo] payment by deception

Theft Act 1978, s 2(1)(b)

(e) dishonestly obtained an exemption from [or abatement of] a liability to make a certain payment to [ ] by deception

Theft Act 1978, s 2(1)(c)

2 Knowing that payment on the spot for certain goods supplied [or service done] was required or expected dishonestly made off without having paid as required or expected and with intent to avoid payment of the amount due

Theft Act 1978, s 3

Maximum penalty – Fine level 5 and 6 months. Triable either way.

Crown court –
Charges 1 (a)–(e): 5 years and unlimited fine.
Charge 2: 2 years and unlimited fine.

Mode of trial

Consider first the general guidelines on p 446. In general, offences of deception should be tried summarily except for the presence of one or more of the following factors:

(a) breach of trust by a person in a position of substantial authority or in whom a high degree of trust has been placed;
(b) there has been sophisticated hiding or disguising of the offence;
(c) the offence has been committed by an organised gang;
(d) the victim was particularly vulnerable;
(e) there is unrecovered property of high value.

Legal notes and definitions

Some dishonest activities may be caught by more than one current statutory provision and for this reason the offences shown above are included in one section in this book.

The basis of this offence is deception and dishonesty. Dishonesty can be inferred from the surrounding circumstances.

It is an offence whether the advantage is obtained for the defendant or for someone else.

Dishonesty. The test of dishonesty is (a) whether the accused's actions were dishonest according to the ordinary standards of reasonable and honest people and, if so, (b) whether the accused himself had realised that his actions were, according to those standards, dishonest (*R v Ghosh* (1982)).

Obtaining a pecuniary advantage. Includes the following:

(a) Where a defendant is allowed to borrow by way of overdraft, or to take out an insurance policy or annuity contract, or has obtained improved terms for any of those arrangements. OR
(b) Where a defendant is given the opportunity to earn remuneration or greater remuneration in an office or employment, or to win money by betting.

Deception means any deception (whether deliberate or reckless) by words or conduct as to a fact or as to a point of law. It also includes a deception as to the **present** intentions of the defendant or someone else.

Obtaining services. This includes where another is induced to confer some benefit by doing an act, or causing or permitting an act to be done, on the understanding that the benefit has been or will be paid for. An example would be having a free roadside repair of one's car by the AA or RAC by dishonestly pretending to be a member.

Liability means a legally enforceable liability.

Payment by cheque. A person induced to accept a cheque or other security (eg a credit card) by way of conditional satisfaction of a pre-existing liability is to be treated as being induced to wait for payment, and not as having been paid.

Obtains includes obtaining for a third party and enabling a third party to obtain.

Payment on the spot includes payment at the time of collecting goods on which work has been done, or in respect of which a service has been provided, eg collecting one's car from a garage after repair.

With intent to avoid payment of the amount due. This means with intent *never* to pay the sum due. An intent merely to defer or delay payment is not enough for a 'making off' offence (*R v Allen* (1985)).

Sentencing

Structure of the sentencing decision. See p 157.

Available sentences. See Table A on p 154.
Reference might usefully be made to the factors relevant to deciding mode of trial.

Custodial sentence. See p 151.

Community sentence. See p 153.

Fines. See p 209.

Compensation. This may be ordered up to £5000 either as part of a wider sentence or by itself as a substantive penalty. If the offender's means are limited and a monetary penalty is appropriate, preference must be given to ordering compensation instead of a fine.

Compensation should be awarded only when it can easily be assessed. Otherwise it might be better to leave it to the county court to deal with it as a civil matter. If in doubt consult the clerk.

If compensation is to be awarded in respect of offences taken into consideration, consult the clerk as to the maximum amount.

Deception: obtaining property

Charge

Dishonestly obtaining from [ ] property, namely [ ], with the intention of permanently depriving the said [ ] of it by deception

Theft Act 1968, s 15

Dishonestly obtaining a money transfer by deception

Theft Act 1968, s 15A

Maximum penalty – Fine level 5 and 6 months. Triable either way.

Crown court – 10 years imprisonment and unlimited fine.

Mode of trial

Consider first the general guidelines on p 446. In general, offences of deception should be tried summarily except for the presence of one or more of the following factors:

(a) breach of trust by a person in a position of substantial authority or in whom a high degree of trust has been placed;
(b) there has been sophisticated hiding or disguising of the offence;
(c) the offence has been committed by an organised gang;
(d) the victim was particularly vulnerable;
(e) there is unrecovered property of high value.

Legal notes and definitions

The defendant must have acted dishonestly. Dishonesty may be inferred from the surrounding circumstances.

It is an offence whether the property is obtained for himself or someone else. The offence also includes the case of enabling another person to obtain or retain the property.

Dishonesty. The test of dishonesty is (a) whether the accused's actions were dishonest according to the ordinary standards of reasonable and honest people and, if so, (b) whether the accused himself had realised that his actions were, according to those standards, dishonest (*R v Ghosh* (1982)).

Obtaining property. The defendant need only obtain possession or control of the property. It is not essential that he obtained ownership.

Deception. Means every deception (whether deliberate or reckless) by words or conduct as to a fact or as to a point of law. It also includes a deception as to the present intentions of the defendant or someone else. The prosecution must establish that the deception induced the person deceived to part with the property.

With the intention of permanently depriving the other person of it. The court must be satisfied that the defendant had this intention, or that he intended treating the property as his own regardless of the owner's rights. The court must decide the defendant's intention by considering all the evidence and drawing from it such inferences as appear proper in the circumstances.

Borrowing or lending. Obviously ordinary borrowing or lending are not offences, but borrowing or lending can amount to intending to deprive the other person permanently if the borrowing or lending were for a period and the circumstances show that the borrowing or lending were equivalent to an outright taking or disposal of the property.

Fraudulent letters from abroad. In a decided case the defendant posted fraudulent letters from abroad addressed to football pool promoters in England. The Court of Appeal upheld his conviction for attempting to commit this offence even though the letters were posted from abroad.

Sentencing

See the notes under this heading on p 51.

Disorderly conduct

(Harassment, alarm or distress)

Charge

Using threatening, abusive or insulting words or behaviour or disorderly behaviour (or displaying any writing, sign or other visible representation which is threatening, abusive or insulting) within the hearing or sight of a person likely to be caused harassment, alarm or distress thereby

Public Order Act 1986, s 5

Maximum penalty – Fine level 3. Triable only by magistrates.

Legal notes and definitions

This offence is designed to deal with such cases as groups of youths persistently shouting abuse and obscenities, rowdy behaviour in the street late at night, hooligans causing disturbances in the common parts of flats, banging on doors, knocking over dustbins and throwing items down stairs.

The charge. Only one offence is created.

Threatening; abusive; insulting. See p 140.

Another person. The defendant's behaviour must be within the hearing or sight of a person likely to be caused harassment etc. The prosecution must identify the person who was likely to have been alarmed etc though he need not be called as a witness. In *Chambers and Edwards v DPP* (1996) demonstrators made it difficult for a surveyor to carry out his work. Although the surveyor was in no fear for his safety, his annoyance and inconvenience were sufficient to meet the requirements of the section.

Intent. The accused must intend his words or behaviour etc to be, or be aware that his words etc may be threatening, abusive or insulting, or intend his behaviour to be or is aware that it may be disorderly.

Intoxication. See under the offence of violent disorder, p 143. Disorderly conduct may be committed in a public or private place. For offences committed in dwelling-houses see under the offence of threatening behaviour below, p 138.

Defences. Where the accused proves—

(a) that he had no reason to believe that there was any person within hearing or sight who was likely to be caused harassment, alarm or distress, or

(b) that he was inside a dwelling and had no reason to believe that the words or behaviour used, or the writing, sign or other visible representation displayed, would be heard or seen by a person outside that or any other dwelling, or

(c) that his conduct was reasonable,

he must be acquitted. He does not have to establish his defence beyond a reasonable doubt, but only on the balance of probabilities.

Power of arrest. A police officer has power to arrest an accused for this offence where he engages in offensive conduct after an officer has warned him to stop such conduct. 'Offensive conduct' means conduct a constable reasonably suspects to constitute this offence.

Sentencing

Available sentences. See Table C on p 156.

This offence is not imprisonable and therefore sentences such as detention in a young offender institution, community service or attendance centre are *not* available.

Fines. See p 209.

Dog worrying livestock

Charge

Being the owner of (or being in charge of) a dog worrying livestock namely [ ] on agricultural land situated at [ ]

Dogs (Protection of Livestock) Act 1953, s 1, as amended

Maximum penalty – Fine level 3.

Legal notes and definitions

A dog's owner or the person in charge of a dog commits an offence if the dog worries livestock on agricultural land. A prosecution for livestock worrying can only be brought by or with the consent of the chief officer of the police, or by the occupier of the agricultural land or the owner of the livestock.

Worrying livestock means:

(a) attacking livestock; or
(b) chasing livestock in such a way as may reasonably be expected to cause injury or suffering to the livestock, or abortion or loss or diminution in their produce; or
(c) being at large in a field where there are sheep except a dog owned by or in the charge of the occupier or the owner of the sheep or a person authorised by them or a police dog, guidedog, trained sheep dog, working gun dog or pack of hounds.

Livestock is extensively defined by s 3 of the Act and means cattle, sheep, goats, swine, horses or poultry.

Possible lines of defence.

(a) That the livestock were trespassing and the dog in question was owned by or in the charge of the occupier of the land on which the livestock were trespassing or the dog was in the charge of a person authorised by the occupier of the land.
This defence is not available if the dog was deliberately set on the livestock.
(b) The owner of the dog is not liable if at the time of the attack on the livestock the dog was in the custody of a person whom the owner considered to be a fit and proper person to have charge of the dog.
(c) That the worrying took place on land that was not agricultural land.

A street or a private garden is not therefore agricultural land and some moors and heaths are excluded from the definitions of agricultural land.

(d) That the Ministry of Agriculture, Fisheries and Food has directed that this offence shall not apply to the land in question.

Compensation. This may be ordered up to a maximum of £5000 on each charge, eg for the loss of livestock, either as part of a wider sentence or by itself as a substantive penalty. If the offender's means are limited and a monetary penalty is appropriate, preference must be given to ordering compensation instead of a fine.

Drugs

The misuse of drugs is made unlawful by the Misuse of Drugs Act 1971, which introduced the term 'controlled drugs' (ie drugs, the use of which is controlled by the Act). The second schedule of the Act allocates controlled drugs to Classes A, B or C and maximum penalties vary according to the class to which a controlled drug belongs.

The second schedule can be varied by an order in council. Magistrates will be able to ascertain full details from their clerk; the following table sets out the class of some of the commoner controlled drugs.

The sections mentioned below are sections of the Act.

CLASS A

Cocaine, heroin, LSD, morphine, opium, and ecstacy (MDA).

CLASS B

Amphetamines, cannabis, cannabis resin, codeine, dexedrine, methadrine, some derivatives of morphine, and preludin.

CLASS C

Lucofen, mandrax and villescon. The text below concerns two drug offences which seem likely to be among the most frequently committed offences created by the Act. These are the offences created by s 5(2) and 5(3).

1 Possessing a controlled drug

(Section 5(2))

Charge

Having a quantity of a controlled drug, namely . . . , in his possession

Maximum penalty – £5000
Class A level 5 and 6 months
Class B £2500 and 3 months
Class C £1000 and 3 months

Court can order forfeiture but see 'Forfeiture' below.

Crown court –

Class A 7 years and fine
Class B 5 years and fine
Class C 2 years and fine

Triable either way in respect of any class of drug.

Mode of trial

See the general notes on p 446.

Possession or supply of Class A drugs should go to the crown court unless the offence is possession and the amount small and consistent with personal use. See *R v Cox* (1993) – possession of 16 ecstasy tablets and 1.5 grammes of crack cocaine, sentence reduced to 3 months imprisonment by the Court of Appeal.

Supply of Class B drugs should go to the crown court unless the supply was of small scale and not for payment; possession should only be committed when the amount involved is substantial.

Legal notes and definitions

Quantity. The charge should state the quantity involved. If it is a diminutive quantity consult the clerk. Scrapings from a pocket can be enough. A few droplets in a tube only discernible microscopically are not enough; the court must be satisfied that there is sufficient there to amount to something. If the quantity is very small it may be relevant to the question of the accused's knowledge that it was in his possession.

Expert examination. The court should be satisfied that an expert has confirmed that the substance is the controlled drug alleged. In a contested case this would have to be proved by the prosecution or admitted by the defendant.

Possession. In many cases this may be established by proving that the defendant had the drug in his custody. Possession can also be established by showing that the drug was in someone else's custody, but subject to the defendant's control (s 37(3)). A drug which has changed its nature by digestion would not be a drug for the purposes of prosecution but evidence of digestion might go towards proving possession prior to consumption.

Defences. Each of the following defences is expressly provided by the Act, but a defendant is also entitled to rely on other defences.

(a) Authorised by regulation (s 7). After consulting the Advisory Council on the Misuse of Drugs, the Home Secretary is empowered to introduce regulations exempting certain persons (eg doctors, dentists, veterinary surgeons, pharmacists) and controlled drugs (in certain circumstances) from the scope of this offence.

or

(b) Knowing or suspecting it was a controlled drug, the defendant took possession of it to prevent another person from committing or continuing to commit an offence with it; and further that as soon as possible after taking possession of it he took all reasonable steps to destroy it or to deliver it to a person lawfully entitled to take it (s 5(4)(a)).

or

(c) Knowing or suspecting it was a controlled drug, the defendant took possession of it to deliver it to a person lawfully entitled to it and as soon as possible he took all reasonable steps to deliver it to that person (s 5(4)(b)).

or

(d) The defendant neither knew nor suspected, nor had reason to suspect, the existence of any fact (except whether the article was a controlled drug, see (e) below) which the prosecution must prove if the defendant is to be convicted (s 28(2)) eg he did not know he possessed anything (this is where quantity might be relevant). Possession is not dependent on the accused *recollecting* that he has it. Where a man had knowingly placed some cannabis in his wallet and had later forgotten it was there, he was still in possession of it. Of course it would be otherwise if a third party had slipped it in his pocket unawares so that he never knew it was there (*R v Martindale* (1986)). Where the defendant knew he possessed something but denies he knew it was a controlled drug the next defence is appropriate.

or

(e) In cases where the prosecution must prove that the substance or product was the controlled drug alleged in the charge and has done so, the defendant shall not be acquitted by reason only of proving that he neither knew or suspected that the substance was the particular drug alleged but shall be acquitted if he proves either:
   (i) that he neither believed nor suspected nor had reason to suspect that the substance or product was *any kind* of controlled drug, ie not just that it was not the controlled drug referred to in the charge; or
   (ii) that he believed it to be a controlled drug and that he also believed the circumstances were such that he would not be committing any offence (s 28(3)).

Burden of proof upon the defendant. A defendant relying upon one of the above defences does not have to establish it beyond reasonable doubt. He need only establish it was more probable than not.

Cannabis. Means the whole or any part of the plant except cannabis resin or the separated mature stalk, fibre produced from the mature stalk or the seed.

Sentencing

Structure of the sentencing decision. See p 157.

Available sentences (Class A, B and C drugs). See Table A on p 154.

The gravity of this offence will be appreciated from the maximum penalties which may be inflicted. A difference may properly be made between 'hard' and 'soft' drugs and between possession of a large quantity of drugs for distribution (which would normally attract a custodial sentence) and a small quantity for private consumption. Heroin will almost always attract a custodial sentence.

Possession of cannabis. Where only small amounts are involved for personal use a fine is often appropriate. Imprisonment may become necessary for a persistent flouting of the law (*R v Aramah* (1982)). In 1981 for 3.2 grammes of cannabis a fine of £50 was considered appropriate (*R v Jones*), whereas in 1982 a defendant with six previous convictions for the same offence received three months (*R v Osborne*).

The different maxima in the crown court should be noted and magistrates should be careful in deciding whether to deal summarily with cases involving Class A drugs and the supply of drugs on a large scale because offences of that kind will attract substantial periods of imprisonment at the crown court. Many of those who commit sexual offences, assaults, robberies and burglaries do so when they are under the influence of drugs or alcohol, and many offences of dishonesty are committed by those desperate to obtain money to buy drugs.

Custodial sentence. See p 151.

Community sentence. See p 153.

Forfeiture (s 27). The court can order the controlled drugs, or anything proved to relate to the offence, to be forfeited and either destroyed or otherwise dealt with as the court may order.

However, if a person claims to be owner of the drug or item to be forfeited, or to be otherwise interested in it, he must first be given an opportunity to show cause why a forfeiture order should not be made.

2 Possessing a controlled drug with intent to supply it to another

(Section 5(3))

Charge

Having in his possession a quantity of [ ] a controlled drug of Class [ ] with intent to supply it to another person

Maximum penalty –
Class A £5000 and 6 months
Class B £5000 and 6 months
Class C £2500 and 3 months

Court can order forfeiture, but see 'Forfeiture' above.

Crown court –
Class A life imprisonment and fine
Class B 14 years and fine
Class C 5 years and fine

Triable either way in respect of any class of drug.

Mode of trial

See general notes on p 446.

Legal notes and definitions

The notes in respect of the previous offence starting on p 59 also apply here except that the defences numbered (b) and (c) on p 60 are not applicable.

Intent to supply to another person. In deciding whether or not the defendant had this intention, the court must consider all the evidence drawing such inferences from it as appear proper in the circumstances.

Sentencing

Structure of the sentencing decision. See p 157.

Available sentences (Class A, B and C drugs). See Table A on p 154.

The notes in respect of the previous offence on p 61 also apply here.

The gravity of this offence will be appreciated from the penalties which can be inflicted. Normally prison will be considered for the supply of heroin, cocaine and ecstacy (*R v Warren* (1995)).

Supplying cannabis. The only cases likely to be heard in the magistrates' court are those of supplying small amounts gratis to a friend. Where there is a commercial motive (for example, where cannabis is supplied at a party) the offence may well be serious enough to justify a custodial sentence (*R v Aramah* (1982)). Those who have supplied on a regular basis have generally received custodial sentences.

Custodial sentence. See p 151.

Community sentence. See p 153.

Forfeiture. See p 61.

Drug trafficking. For the power of the crown court to make a confiscation order in respect of the proceeds of drug trafficking offences, see p 187.

Drunkenness

Charges

1 Being found drunk in any highway, public place, or on licensed premises

Licensing Act 1872, s 12

Maximum penalty – Fine level 2.

2 In a public place namely [ ] was guilty while drunk of disorderly behaviour

Criminal Justice Act 1967, s 91

Maximum penalty – Fine level 3.

Legal notes and definitions

Found. Means 'ascertained to be', not 'discovered'.

Drunk. Typical evidence of drunkenness is strong smell of drink, falling over, swaying, stumbling, showing evidence of incoordination, slurred thick speech, rapid pulse, redness in the face, glazed expression, drowsiness or semi-coma and no evidence of any other cause for these symptoms. A person exhibiting these symptoms as a result of 'glue sniffing' is not drunk for the purposes of this offence or the offence of being drunk and disorderly.

The offence is constituted by the state of drunkenness. The inability of the defendant to take care of himself simply confers a power for a constable to arrest the defendant.

Public place. Includes buildings and any place to which the public has access whether on payment or otherwise, as well as buses or taxis. The entrance hall of a block of flats where admission was controlled by an intercom and a security lock was not a public place (*Williams v DPP* (1992)).

Licensed premises. This not only includes normally licensed premises for the sale of liquor but also premises given an occasional licence and includes any part of licensed premises hired out to a private party.

Sentencing

A fine or discharge will normally be appropriate.

Excessive noise

(Prosecution)

Problems caused by noise amounting to a nuisance, eg caused by noisy neighbours, are dealt with by proceedings for a nuisance order, see p 111.

Night time charge

Operating a loudspeaker in a street between 9 p.m. and 8 a.m.

Control of Pollution Act 1974, s 62

Maximum penalty – Fine level 5 (and a further fine not exceeding £50 for each day on which the offence continues after the conviction).The notes which follow only apply to proceedings brought under the Control of Pollution Act 1974, s 62 and magistrates should confirm with their clerk that the proceedings are in fact being brought under that Act.

Legal notes and definitions

In certain circumstances loudspeakers are exempt from prosecutions as follows:

(a) those used by the police, fire, ambulance, water authority or local authority;
(b) those used for communicating with a vessel to direct it or any other vessel;
(c) those forming part of the public telephone system;
(d) those fitted to vehicles solely for the entertainment of persons in the vehicle or for communicating with persons in the vehicle or for giving warning to other vehicles if the loudspeaker forms part of the vehicle's horns or warning system but all such loudspeakers fitted to vehicles must not operate so loudly that they give reasonable cause for annoyance to persons in the vicinity or the exemption is forfeited;
(e) transport undertakings may use loudspeakers off the highways to make announcements to passengers, prospective passengers and staff;
(f) a travelling showman may use a loudspeaker on his fairground;
(g) loudspeakers may be used in an emergency.

Except for the above exemptions there is a complete ban on the use of loudspeakers in a street between 9 p.m. and 8 a.m.

Loudspeaker. Includes a megaphone and any other device for amplifying sound.

Street. Means any highway, road, footway, square or court which is for the time being open to the public.

Day time charge

Operating a loudspeaker in a street between 8 a.m. and 9 p.m. for the purpose of advertising an entertainment, a trade or a business

Control of Pollution Act 1974, s 62

Maximum penalty – Fine level 5 (and a further fine not exceeding £50 for each day on which the offence continues after the conviction).

Legal notes and definitions

See under this heading on p 65.

Defences. It is permissible to use a loudspeaker in a street between the hours of 8 a.m. and 9 p.m. except as outlined above for advertising. However, there is an exception to this ban on advertising in the following circumstances. Where the loudspeaker is:

(a) fixed to a vehicle conveying a perishable commodity for human consumption; and
(b) is used solely to inform the public (otherwise than by words) that the commodity is on sale from the vehicle; and
(c) is so operated as not to give reasonable cause for annoyance to persons in the vicinity,

it may be operated between the hours of noon and 7 p.m. on the same day. This is the provision, for example, under which ice cream vans are allowed to use chimes to advertise their wares.

Sentencing

Noise amounting to a statutory nuisance. If a noise is persistent and seriously affects persons in an area then the local authority may serve a noise abatement notice or the person affected can lay a complaint alleging that the noise or vibration amounts to a statutory nuisance. See p 109.

False trade description

Charge

In the course of a trade or business applying a false trade description, namely [ ], to goods, namely

OR

In the course of a trade or business supplying (or offering to supply) to [ ] goods, to which a false trade description is applied; namely

Trade Descriptions Act 1968, s 1(1)(a) and (b) respectively

Maximum penalty – Fine level 5 (individual). Triable either way.

Crown court – Unlimited fine and 2 years imprisonment.

Mode of trial

See general notes on p 446.

Legal notes and definitions

Applying a false trade description, supplying and offering to supply are three separate offences and only one of them should be alleged in one charge.

The defendant must have acted in the course of a trade or business, ie for instance, he was not merely indulging in a hobby.

Applying (s 1(1)(a)). This includes affixing the description to the goods, or marking it on the goods themselves or on, in or with anything with which the goods are supplied. It is also enough if the defendant used the description in any manner likely to be taken as referring to the goods. An oral trade description is sufficient.

Offering to supply (s 1(1)(b)). This includes exposing goods for supply as well as having goods in one's possession for supply.

Section 1(1)(a) offences usually deal with the dishonest trader and s 1(1)(b) with the careless trader, although that would not aways be the case: *R v Southwood* (1987).

Trade description. This too is widely defined and includes an indication as to quantity, size, composition, strength, performance, accuracy, results of any testing, place or date of manufacture, person by whom manufactured, history of the goods including previous ownership and use, etc.

Disclaimer. Where a false trade description has been applied or goods supplied to which a false trade description has been applied certain defences may be open to the accused (see below). However the defendant may deny that there is a false trade description at all. For example, the odometer (or mileometer) of a motor vehicle is a trade description. A dealer charged with an offence under s 1(1)(b) (supplying) may rely on a suitable and effective disclaimer (such 'disclaimers' often take the form of a label glued over the mileometer reading).

False trade description. This means a trade description which is false or misleading to a material degree. 'Showroom condition throughout' has been held to be a false trade description when the vehicle had mechanical defects. In that case a judge commented that even if the word 'throughout' had been omitted the remaining words would be taken to refer to the exterior, interior and mechanical condition of the vehicle.

Advertisements. If an advertisement contains a false trade description, it can be treated as having referred to all goods of the class mentioned in the advertisement. This can also be the position even though the goods did not exist at the time when the advertisement was published.

If the person whose business it is to publish or to arrange for the publication of advertisements is prosecuted, he may be able to rely upon the defence of innocent publications.

Where a case turns on the meaning which is to be attributed to an advertisement, consult the clerk for rules of interpretation.

Partners. A partner of a firm may be convicted of selling goods for which a false trade description has been attached even though the sale was affected without his knowledge by another partner. The clerk should be consulted if this situation arises.

Defences of mistake or accident. As far as any of the above three offences are concerned, it is a defence for the defendant to prove:

(a) that the commission of the offence was due to a mistake or to reliance on information supplied to him or to the act or default of another person, an accident or some other cause beyond his control. 'Another person' can be an employee. Whether or not one of the defence points mentioned in this paragraph applies appears to be a question of fact for the court to decide in each case; and

(b) that the defendant took all reasonable precautions and exercised all due diligence to avoid the commission of the offence by himself or any person under his control. Again this appears to be a question of fact for the court to decide in each case. The House of Lords has ruled that a large company had fulfilled the requirements of this paragraph by instructing superior employees to supervise inferior employees whose acts might otherwise lead to the commission of an offence. Where this defence takes the form of attributing fault to an employee, it will succeed only if the defendant proves on the balance of probabilities that he had done all that could reasonably be expected to discover who was the person responsible. It is not enough to show that one of several persons must have been at fault.

A defendant relying on the defence of a third person's default should at least 7 clear days before the hearing serve a notice on the prosecution giving certain prescribed information; if the defendant has not done this he must obtain the court's leave to dispense with the notice. If the court refuses leave, he cannot rely upon the above defences.

If the offence alleged is supplying or offering to supply goods it is also a defence for the defendant to prove that he did not know, and could not with reasonable diligence have ascertained, that the goods did not conform to the description or that the description had been applied to the goods.

Degree of proof required from the defendant. The defendant does not have to prove one of the above defences beyond reasonable doubt. It is enough for him to prove that one of those defences is probably right.

Offences by buyers. An offence can be committed by one who buys in the course of trade, eg a car dealer, antique dealer, etc. A car dealer was convicted when, after persuading a seller that a car was dangerous beyond repair and good only for scrap, he repaired it and offered it for sale.

Offence by a private individual. Where an offence committed by a trader under s 1 is due to the fault of another person, even an individual not acting in the course of trade of business, that other person commits the same offence by virtue of s 23 of the Act, eg an individual knowingly selling a car with a false odometer reading to a dealer who sells it in the course of his trade (*Olgeirsson v Kitching* (1986)).

Sentencing

Unlike most either way offences, this does not carry imprisonment on summary conviction. Therefore community penalties, with the exception of a probation order, are not available.

Compensation. This may be ordered up to £5000 either as part of a wider sentence or by itself as a substantive penalty. If the offender's means are limited and a monetary penalty is appropriate, preference must be given to ordering compensation instead of a fine.

Crown court. Prison is appropriate only where there has been deliberate dishonesty.

Firearm or loaded air gun or loaded shotgun in a public place

Charge

Without lawful authority or reasonable excuse having in a public place (a loaded shotgun), (a firearm and ammunition suitable for use in the said firearm)

Firearms Act 1968, s 19

Maximum penalty –

Firearm Fine level 5 and 6 months and forfeiture. Triable either way.

Air weapon Fine level 5 and 6 months and forfeiture. Triable only by magistrates.

Crown court – 7 years imprisonment and unlimited fine.

Mode of trial

See general notes on p 446.

Legal notes and definitions

Public place. Means any highway, premises or place to which the public at the material time has access whether on payment or otherwise.

Without lawful authority or reasonable excuse. The Act expressly places on the defendant the burden of proving that he had lawful authority or reasonable excuse. He only has to prove that on the balance of probabilities he had lawful authority or reasonable excuse. He does not have to prove this beyond all reasonable doubt.

(a) A certificate for a firearm was not in itself lawful authority under s 19 of the Firearms Act 1968 for the holder of the certificate to have the firearm and ammunition for it in a public place.

(b) The mistaken belief by the holder of an invalid firearm certificate that it was valid and that it was lawful authority under s 19 of the 1968 Act was not capable of being a reasonable excuse and therefore a defence under that section.

(*R v Jones* (1994).)

Shotgun. Although the firearm need not be loaded a shotgun must be loaded to establish this offence. A shotgun is a smooth bore gun whose barrel is 24 inches or longer with a bore not exceeding two inches and which is not a revolver nor has an illegal magazine, not being an air gun.

Air weapon. An air weapon must be loaded to establish this offence. An air weapon is an air gun, air rifle or an air pistol of a type which has not been declared by the Home Office to be specially dangerous (see p 73).

Firearm. Means any lethal barrelled weapon of any description from which any shot, bullet or other missile can be discharged but for this offence excludes shotguns and air weapons as described above. A lethal weapon includes one capable of inflicting injury although not designed to do so, eg a signal pistol. An imitation firearm which is so constructed or adapted as to be readily converted into a firearm is to be treated as a firearm even though it has not been so converted.

A starting pistol which can be adapted to fire bullets if the barrel was drilled is a firearm.

An offence is committed whether the firearm is loaded or not but the defendant must have with him ammunition suitable for use in that firearm.

Sentencing

Structure of the sentencing decision. See p 157.

Available sentences. See Table A on p 154 (firearms) and Table B on p 155 (air weapons).

Custodial sentence. See p 151.

Community sentence. See p 153.

Fines. See p 209.

Forfeiture. The court can order the firearm (or shotgun or air weapon) to be forfeited to the police or to be disposed of as the court thinks fit. The court can also cancel any firearm or shotgun certificate held by the defendant.

Firearm (purchasing etc without certificate)

Charge

Purchasing or acquiring or possessing a firearm (or ammunition) without certificate

Firearms Act 1968, s 1

For shotguns see p 127

Maximum penalty – Fine level 5 and 6 months and forfeiture. Triable either way.

Crown court – 5 years imprisonment and unlimited fine.

Mode of trial

See general notes on p 439.

Legal notes and definitions

Purchasing, acquiring and **wrongly possessing.** These are three separate offences and the charge should only include one of these allegations. Possession can include where a person has a firearm in his custody for another for the purpose of cleaning it.

Excessive ammunition. It is also an offence to have in one's possession more ammunition than the quantity authorised by a firearms certificate.

Certificate. This is granted by the police. It may specify conditions. Failure to observe such conditions is an offence. The certificate may bear a photograph of the holder and, unless revoked or cancelled, remains in force for the period specified which may be up to 3 years.

Firearm. This means any lethal barrelled weapon of any kind from which any shot, bullet or missile can be discharged. A lethal weapon includes one capable of inflicting injury although not designed to do so, eg a signal pistol. An imitation firearm which is so constructed or adapted as to be readily converted into a firearm is to be treated as a firearm even though it has not been so converted.

A smooth bore shotgun with a barrel of 24 inches or more with a bore not exceeding two inches and which is not a revolver nor has an illegal magazine is not a firearm as far as this offence is concerned; nor normally are air guns, air rifles or air pistols unless the Home Secretary declares them to be of a specially dangerous type. This now includes high powered air weapons and all disguised weapons including those designed for use only when submerged in water. The Court of Appeal has ruled that a starting pistol which could be adapted to fire bullets if the barrel was drilled was a firearm. In this case the barrel was partly drilled (*Read v Donovan* (1947)).

Ammunition. Means ammunition for any firearm as defined above. It also means grenades, bombs and other similar missiles. It also includes ammunition containing or adapted to contain any noxious liquid, gas or other noxious thing.

Exemptions. If a defence is raised that a weapon or ammunition is not covered by the Act the clerk should be consulted.

Certain persons and organisations are exempted from having to hold firearms certificates such as the following:

(a) A registered dealer and his staff, an auctioneer, carrier or warehouseman in the course of his business, a licensed slaughterer in respect of his slaughtering instruments, ships and aircraft (ss 8–10 and 13).
(b) A person may carry a firearm or ammunition for another person who does hold a firearms certificate if he is acting under that other person's instructions and if that other person is to use the firearm or ammunition for sporting purposes only. Sporting purposes does not include the shooting of rats (s 11(1)).
(c) Members of rifle clubs, miniature rifle clubs and cadet corps in possession of Home Office approval do not require certificates for club or corps activities such as drilling or target practice (s 11(3) and Firearms (Amendment) Act 1988, s 15).
(d) A certificate is not necessary for weapons at a miniature rifle range if the miniature rifles do not exceed 0.23 calibre or if the weapons are air guns, air rifles or air pistols which have not been declared as dangerous by the Home Office (s 11(4)).
(e) Persons participating in a theatrical performance or rehearsal or in producing a film may have a firearm without a certificate (s 12).
(f) Starters at athletic meetings may have a firearm without a certificate (s 11(2)).
(g) A person who has obtained a permit from the police may have a firearm and ammunition, as authorised by that permit without holding a firearms certificate. The permit will usually be for short periods such as one month to allow, for example, the next of kin of the holder of a firearms certificate time to sell the weapons and ammunition after the holder has died (s 7).
(h) A person may borrow a shotgun or, if over 17 years, a rifle from the occupier of private premises (which includes land) and use it on those premises in the occupier's presence (s 11(5) and Firearms (Amendment) Act 1988, s 16).
(i) A person visiting Great Britain may have in his possession a firearm or shotgun without a certificate where he has been granted a visitor's permit.

Such permits are granted by the police and may continue in force for up to 12 months (Firearms (Amendment) Act 1988, s 17).

(j) A person temporarily in Great Britain purchasing weapons for export (F(A) Act 1988, s 18).

(k) Museums granted a licence by the Secretary of State (F(A) Act 1988, Sch).

Degree of proof. A defendant wishing to establish one of the above exemptions does not have to satisfy the court beyond reasonable doubt; he need only satisfy the court that on the balance of probabilities his defence is true.

Antique firearms. The legislation does not apply to an antique firearm sold, transferred, purchased, acquired or possessed as a curiosity or ornament (s 58(2)).

Sentencing

Structure of the sentencing decision. See p 157.

Available sentences. See Table A on p 154.

Custodial sentence. See p 151. See *R v Clarke* (1996) on use of imprisonment.

Community sentence. See p 153.

Fines. See p 209. **Forfeiture.** The court can order the firearm and ammunition to be forfeited to the police or disposed of as it thinks fit.

The court can cancel any firearm or shotgun certificate held by the defendant.

Firearm (trespassing in a building)

Charge

Whilst having a firearm or imitation firearm with him, entering or being in any building or part of a building, as a trespasser and without reasonable excuse

Firearms Act 1968, s 20(1)

Maximum penalty –

Firearm Fine level 5 and 6 months and forfeiture. Triable either way.

Air weapon or imitation firearm Fine level 5 and 6 months and forfeiture. Triable only by magistrates.

Crown court – 7 years imprisonment and unlimited fine.

Mode of trial

See general notes on p 440.

Legal notes and definitions

Trespasser. The court must be satisfied that the defendant was a trespasser which means that the defendant was personally within the domain of another person without his consent.

With him. The prosecution must establish more than mere possession, namely, a close physical link and immediate control over the firearm, but not necessarily that he had been carrying it (*R v Kelt* (1977)).

Reasonable excuse. The onus of establishing reasonable excuse for his presence, when a trespasser, in a building and in possession of a firearm rests on the defendant. He does not have to prove reasonable excuse beyond all reasonable doubt. He has only to prove that on the balance of probabilities he had reasonable excuse.

Firearm. Means any lethal barrelled weapon of any description from which any shot, bullet or other missile can be discharged. A lethal weapon includes one capable of inflicting injury although not designed to do so, eg a signal pistol. An imitation firearm which is so constructed or adapted as to be readily converted into a firearm is to be treated as a firearm even though it has not been so converted. The Court of Appeal has ruled that a starting pistol which could be adapted to fire bullets if the barrel was drilled was a firearm. In this case the barrel was partly drilled.

Shotguns and air weapons count as firearms for the purpose of this offence. An air weapon is an air rifle, air gun or air pistol of a type which has not been declared by the Home Office to be specially dangerous.

Sentencing

Structure of the sentencing decision. See p 157.

Available sentences. See Table A on p 154 (firearms) and Table B on p 155 (air weapons).

Custodial sentence. See p 151.

Community sentence. See p 153.

Fines. See p 209.

Forfeiture. The court can order the weapon and ammunition to be forfeited to the police or disposed of as the court thinks fit.

The court can also cancel any firearm or shotgun certificate held by the defendant.

Firearm (trespassing on land)

Charge

Whilst having a firearm or imitation firearm with him entering or being on any land as a trespasser and without reasonable excuse

Firearms Act 1968, s 20(2)

Maximum penalty – Fine level 4 and 3 months and forfeiture.

Legal notes and definitions

Firearms. As defined in the previous charge of 'trespassing with firearm in a building' (see p 75). For the purpose of this offence firearm includes a shotgun or air weapon.

With him. See notes on p 75.

Trespasser. As defined in the previous charge of 'trespassing with a firearm in a building'.

Land. The Act provides that 'land' includes 'land covered by water'.

Reasonable excuse. As defined in the adjacent charge of 'trespassing with firearm in a building'.

Sentencing

For structure of the sentencing decision. See p 157.

For available sentences. See Table B on p 155.

In practice this offence is generally not so serious as the offence of trespassing in a building.

See notes on p 76.

Football spectators

Charges

1 Being a person at a designated football match and throwing anything at or towards (the playing area, or any area adjacent to the playing area to which spectators are not generally admitted) (any area in which spectators or other persons are or may be present) without lawful authority or lawful excuse

Football (Offences) Act 1991, s 2

2 Taking part at a designated football match in chanting of an indecent or racialist nature

Football (Offences) Act 1991, s 3

3 At a designated football match going onto the playing area, or any area adjacent to the playing area to which spectators are not generally admitted, without lawful authority or lawful excuse

Football (Offences) Act 1991, s 4

Maximum penalty (for each offence) – Fine level 3.

Legal notes and definitions

The creation of these offences follows the recommendations of the Taylor report into the Hillsborough Disaster. They can be committed only in respect of matches in England and Wales.

Designated football match. Means any association football match where one of the participating clubs is a member (full or associate) of the Football League or Premier League; it also includes international matches, and those which involve a team representing a club in a country outside England and Wales, and matches in a competition organised by UEFA.

In addition, the match must take place on a ground occupied by a Football (or Premier League) League Club or which is designated under the Safety of Sports Grounds Act 1975.

Being or taking part at. The offence may be committed in a period beginning two hours before the start of the match or, if earlier, two hours before the time it is advertised to start and ending one hour after the end of the match. Where a match is postponed or cancelled, the period includes the two hours before and one hour after the advertised starting time.

Without lawful authority or lawful excuse. The defendant must establish this but he only has to establish that his defence is probably true, he does not have to establish it beyond reasonable doubt.

Charge 1: Throwing an object. The prosecution only has to prove that the object was thrown, not that a particular person was aimed at or caused alarm or distress thereby.

Charge 2: Indecent or racialist chanting. 'Chanting' means the repeated uttering of any words or sounds in concert with one or more others. 'Racialist nature' means consisting of or including matter which is threatening, abusive or insulting to a person by reason of his colour, race, nationality (including citizenship) or ethnic or national origins.

Sentencing

Available sentences. See Table C on p 156.

None of these offences carries imprisonment and therefore penalties such as community service and attendance at an attendance centre are not available. However, in addition to any sentence it may impose, the court may make an **exclusion order** (p 207), or a **restriction order** (p 239), or both. These orders prevent the defendant from attending football matches in England and Wales (exclusion orders) or outside England and Wales (restriction orders).

Forgery

Charge

1 Unlawfully making a false instrument with the intention that he (or another) should use it to induce somebody to accept it as genuine, and, by reason of so accepting it to do, or not to do, some act to that person's or some other person's prejudice

Forgery and Counterfeiting Act 1981, s 1

2 Unlawfully using a false instrument, which is and which he knows or believes to be false, with the intention of inducing somebody to accept it as genuine, as above

Forgery and Counterfeiting Act 1981, s 3

3 Unlawfully using a copy of a false instrument, which is and which he knows or believes to be false, as above

Forgery and Counterfeiting Act 1981, s 4

Maximum penalty – Fine level 5 and six months. Triable either way.

Crown court – 10 years imprisonment and unlimited fine.

Mode of trial

Consider first the general guidelines on p 446. In general, forgery offences should be tried summarily except for the presence of one or more of the following factors:

(a) breach of trust by a person in a position of substantial authority or in whom a high degree of trust has been placed;
(b) there has been a sophisticated hiding or disguising of the offence;
(c) the offence has been committed by an organised gang;
(d) the victim was particularly vulnerable;
(e) there is unrecovered property of high value.

Legal notes and definitions

Instrument. Means any document whether of a formal or informal character, any stamp issued or sold by the Post Office, any Inland Revenue stamp and any disc, tape, soundtrack or other device on or in which information is recorded is stored by mechanical, electronic or other means.

False. This is extensively defined in the Act. The essence of falsity in this connection is that the document should tell a lie about itself.

Make. A person makes a false instrument if he alters it so as to make it false in any respect, whether or not it is false in some other respect apart from that alteration. There is no further element of dishonesty required.

Intention. In a case decided in 1985 (*R v Tobierre*) on an offence under s 3 it was held that the prosecution must prove both that the accused intended to induce somebody to accept the forgery as genuine *and* intended that by so doing he should act, or not act, to his etc prejudice.

Prejudice. An act or omission intended to be induced is to be regarded as being to a person's prejudice only if it is one which *will* result (and not merely which has the *potential* to result (*R v Garcia* (1987)):

(a) in his temporary or permanent loss of property;
(b) in his being deprived of the opportunity to earn remuneration, or greater remuneration;
(c) in his being deprived of an opportunity to gain a financial advantage otherwise than by way of remuneration; or would result in someone being given an opportunity;
(d) to earn remuneration, or greater remuneration from him; or
(e) to gain a financial advantage from him otherwise than by way of remuneration;

or

(f) would be the result of his having accepted a false instrument as genuine, or a copy of a false instrument as a copy of a genuine one, in connection with the performance of a duty.

In deciding whether to deal summarily with an offence of forgery the court will have regard, amongst other things, to the harm intended to be caused, or which potentially would be caused by the offence and will compare the very different levels of maximum penalty available at the crown court.

Sentencing

Structure of the sentencing decision. See p 157.

Available sentences. See Table A on p 154.

Reference might usefully be made to the factors relevant to deciding mode of trial on assessing seriousness.

Custodial sentence. See p 151.

Community sentence. See p 153.

Fines. See p 209.

Compensation. This may be ordered up to £5000 either as part of a wider sentence or by itself as a substantive penalty. If the offender's means are limited and a monetary penalty is appropriate, preference must be given to ordering compensation instead of a fine.

Found on enclosed premises

Charge

Being found in or upon any dwelling-house, warehouse, outhouse, or in any enclosed yard, garden or area for an unlawful purpose

Vagrancy Act 1824, s 4

Maximum penalty – For a first offence fine level 3 or 3 months. For a subsequent offence the accused may sometimes be committed to the crown court as an incorrigible rogue for sentence.

Legal notes and definitions

Found. The defendant must have been found there although his arrest happened elsewhere.

Enclosed. The yard may still rate as being enclosed even if there is access through spaces in surrounding buildings, an archway, open gate, etc.

Yard. Would not include a very large area, such as a shipyard or railway sidings, the essential feature of a yard is that it should be a relatively small area ancillary to a building.

Unlawful purpose. Means that the defendant was there for the purpose of committing a criminal offence. In deciding whether the defendant had such a purpose, the court must consider all the evidence drawing such inferences from it as appear proper in the circumstances.

Sentencing

Structure of the sentencing decision. See p 157.

Available sentences. See Table B on p 155.

Custodial sentence. See p 151.

Community sentence. See p 153.

Fine. See p 209.

Committal for sentence. For a subsequent offence, as long as the previous offence was **not** dealt with by absolute or conditional discharge the court may commit the defendant to the crown court for sentence on bail or in custody as an incorrigible rogue. The crown court can impose imprisonment for up to 1 year.

Even if there is no previous conviction for a similar offence but there is evidence of previous convictions under the Vagrancy Act 1824, then this procedure may still be available to the magistrates.

Glue sniffing: supplying substances which cause intoxication when inhaled

Charge

Supplied or offered to supply a substance other than a controlled drug to a person knowing or having reasonable cause to believe to be under the age of 18 (or to a person acting on behalf of such a person knowing or having reasonable cause to believe to be so acting) and knowing or having reasonable cause to believe that the substance was, or its fumes were, likely to be inhaled by the person under the age of 18 for the purpose of causing intoxication (Intoxicating Substances (Supply) Act 1985, s 1(1))

Maximum penalty – Fine level 5 and 6 months. Triable only by magistrates.

Legal notes and definitions

Controlled drug. The supplying of controlled drugs is controlled by other legislation, see p 58.

Supply. Includes not only a seller but also an adult who gives such a substance to a young person for the purpose of intoxication.

Knowing or having reasonable cause to believe. The shopkeeper who makes an honest mistake and sells in good faith to a youngster who unknown to him subsequently abuses it, is not liable.

Defence. It is a defence for a defendant himself under the age of 18 that at the time he made the supply or offer he was acting otherwise than in the course or furtherance of a business. It is not an offence for one youngster to pass solvents to another to sniff. The Act is aimed at the adult who exploits the addicts.

Other offences. There is no specific offence of 'glue sniffing' but a 'glue sniffer' can commit the offence of entering or remaining on the railway whilst in a state of intoxication (however caused) contrary to the Railway Byelaws 2 and 16 (maximum penalty £50 fine) or causing a nuisance on school premises contrary to the Local Government (Miscellaneous Provisions) Act 1982, s 40 (maximum penalty fine level 2).

Sentencing

Available sentences. See Table B on p 155.

Fines. See p 209.

Going equipped for stealing

Charge

Having, when not at his place of abode, an article, namely a [ ], for use in the course of burglary, theft or cheat

Theft Act 1968, s 25

Maximum penalty – Fine level 5 and 6 months. Triable either way.

Crown court – 3 years imprisonment and unlimited fine.

Motor vehicles. If the defendant intended to steal or take a motor vehicle the offence is not endorsable nor are penalty points applicable but disqualification may be ordered.

Mode of trial

See general notes on p 446.

Legal notes and definitions

Theft includes taking a conveyance without the owner's consent.

Cheat means an offence of obtaining by deception.

If the article was made or adapted for use in committing a burglary, theft or obtaining property by deception, the court can treat that as evidence that the defendant had the article with him for such use.

The offence can be committed by day or night. The offence cannot take place at the defendant's place of abode. It must be proved that he had the articles with him for the purpose of using them in connection with burglary, theft or obtaining property by deception though it is not necessary for the prosecution to prove that the defendant intended to use them himself. An intention to use the item if the opportunity arose would be sufficient to convict the accused, but it would not be sufficient where he had not actually decided whether to use the item if the opportunity presented itself.

More than one article may be specified in the charge without offending the rule against duplicity.

Sentencing

Structure of the sentencing decision. See p 157.

Available sentences. See Table A on p 154.

The relative gravity of this offence will vary with the circumstances in each case but by convicting the defendant of this offence the court is saying that it believes the defendant had placed himself in a position to commit a serious offence. Absolute or conditional discharge therefore would not usually be appropriate.

Custodial sentence. See p 151.

Community sentence. See p 153.

Fines. See p 209.

Forfeiture. The court may deprive the defendant of any property in his possession which was, or was intended to be, used for committing a crime, see Forfeiture order, p 218.

Grievous bodily harm and malicious wounding

(Offences Against the Person Act 1861, s 20)

Charges

Unlawfully and maliciously inflicting grievous bodily harm

Unlawfully and maliciously wounding

Offences against the Person Act 1861, s 20

Maximum penalty – Fine level 5 and 6 months. Triable either way.

Crown court – 5 years and unlimited fine.

Mode of trial

In general, cases should be tried summarily unless the court considers that one or more of the features below is present in the case and that its sentencing powers are insufficient:

(a) the use of a weapon likely to cause serious injury;
(b) a weapon is used and serious injury is caused;
(c) more than minor injury is caused by kicking, head butting or similar forms of assault;
(d) serious violence is caused to those whose work has to be done in contact with the public, eg police officers, bus drivers, taxi drivers, publicans and shopkeepers;
(e) violence to vulnerable people, eg the elderly and infirm;
(f) the offence has clear racial motivation.

The same considerations apply to cases of domestic violence.

For guidance on mode of trial see notes on p 446.

Legal notes and definitions

Intent. 'Maliciously' means intentionally or recklessly (*R v Mowatt* (1967)) and 'recklessly' means that the accused foresaw the particular risk and yet went on to take it (*R v Cunningham* (1957)). In offences under s 20 what must be intended or foreseen is that some physical harm might occur, not necessarily amounting to grievous bodily harm or wounding. An intention to frighten is not enough.

Grievous bodily harm. Means really serious bodily harm. The injuries caused do not have to be permanent or dangerous, but they have to be more severe than actual bodily harm. (See p 12.)

Provocation. Is no defence, but can be taken into account when sentencing.

Misadventure
Consent
Lawful sport
Defence of property
Execution of legal process

} See pp 28ff

Reduction of charge. The court cannot reduce this charge to a less serious one (eg actual bodily harm or common assault); but if a separate charge for a lesser offence has been preferred there could be a conviction for that. Consult the clerk.

Sentencing

Structure of the sentencing decision. See p 157.

Available sentences. See Table A on p 154.

Although the maximum penalty for these offences is the same as that for 'Actual bodily harm' (p 12), offences under s 20 are regarded as more serious. The factors set out under 'Sentencing' on p 14 will be relevant here. Guidelines on the mode of trial decision encourage magistrates to accept jurisdiction in more serious cases. However where aggravating features such as a gang attack or the use of a weapon exist the magistrates must be prepared to use the full range of their powers which include up to 6 months imprisonment or, in appropriate cases, committal for sentence.

Decided cases in the Court of Appeal have been mainly concerned with sentences for offences too serious to be heard by magistrates, but occasionally in cases which might now be within the jurisdiction of justices, sentences of up to 6 months immediate custody have been imposed.

Compensation. This may be ordered up to £5000 either as part of a wider sentence or by itself as a substantive penalty. If the offender's means are limited and a monetary penalty is appropriate, preference must be given to ordering compensation instead of a fine.

The court may deprive the defendant of any property in his possession which was used or intended to be used to commit the offence.

Custodial sentence. See p 151.

Community sentence. See p 153.

Fines. See p 209.

Husband and wife. See the notes on p 14 under this heading.

Licensed premises. If the offence took place on licensed premises an exclusion order may be made. See p 207.

Handling stolen goods

Charge

Handled stolen goods, namely [ ], knowing or believing them to have been stolen

Theft Act 1968, s 22

Maximum penalty – Fine level 5 and 6 months. Triable either way.

Crown court – 14 years imprisonment and unlimited fine.

Mode of trial

Consider first the general guidelines on p 446. In general, handling offences should be tried summarily except for the presence of one or more of the following factors:

(a) the handler commissioned the offence;
(b) the offence has professional hallmarks;
(c) the property is of high value (ie over approximately £10,000).

Legal notes and definitions

The prosecution must prove that the goods were:

(a) stolen; or
(b) obtained by deception; or
(c) obtained by blackmail.

Also that the defendant knew or believed the goods had been obtained by one of those methods (see below).

Handling. Any of the following actions can constitute handling:

(a) dishonestly receiving the goods; or
(b) dishonestly undertaking the retention, removal, disposal or realisation of the goods by or for the benefit of another; or
(c) dishonestly assisting in the retention, removal, disposal or realisation of the goods by or for the benefit of another; or
(d) arranging to do (a) or (b) or (c).

Thus a defendant who has not himself personally handled goods can be convicted for this offence.

As far as (c) is concerned failure to reveal stolen goods during a police search does not amount to 'dishonestly assisting in the retention of stolen goods'. 'Assisting' means helping or encouraging, amongst other things. It would be otherwise where deliberate lies were told to the police.

If the only evidence against the defendant is that of the thief, it may be unsafe to convict and the clerk should be consulted.

Goods include money and every kind of property except land. The term also includes things severed from land by stealing.

Knowledge or belief. Mere suspicion which does not amount to knowledge or belief is not sufficient to justify conviction. The state of the defendant's mind must be judged subjectively, ie what did *this* defendant know, or believe, not what did he suspect.

The word 'believe' has its ordinary meaning of holding something to be true.

In a case decided in 1985 (*R v Hall*), the Lord Chief Justice presided in a court which gave some examples of what might amount to knowledge and what might amount to belief. A man might be said to *know* that goods were stolen when he was told by someone with first-hand knowledge, such as the thief, that such was the case. *Belief* was something short of knowledge. It might be said to be the state of mind of a person who said to himself: 'I cannot say I know for certain that those goods are stolen, but there can be no other reasonable conclusion in the light of all the circumstances of all I have heard and seen.' It was enough for belief even if the person said to himself: 'Despite all that I have seen and heard, I refuse to believe what my brain tells me is obvious.'

What was insufficient was a mere suspicion: 'I suspect that these goods may be stolen but on the other hand they may not be stolen.' That state of mind does not fall within the words 'knowing or believing'.

Sentencing

Structure of the sentencing decision. See p 157.

Available sentences. See Table A on p 154.

The gravity of this offence varies with the circumstances but it should be regarded at least as seriously as theft. It is sometimes said that handling is a more serious offence than theft, because without handlers there would not be thieves. The maximum penalties on indictment reflect this: 14 years imprisonment for handling and 7 years for theft. But this is only true to a certain extent, that is, where the handler is a professional fence who makes the activities of thieves or burglars profitable.

In the magistrates' court the situation is usually different. The handler often plays a minor role, for example, he has been given an item which has been stolen by the thief.

Having said this, there might be situations dealt with summarily where thieves only operate because they know they have a ready market. An instance of this might be the theft of video recorders for resale in public houses. The courts would tend to view offences which offer encouragement to thieves as more serious and which might justify a custodial sentence.

Custodial sentence. See p 151.

Community sentence. See p 153.

Fines. See p 209.

Compensation. This may be ordered up to £5000 either as part of a wider sentence or by itself as a substantive penalty. If the offender's means are limited and a monetary penalty is appropriate, preference must be given to ordering compensation instead of a fine. The defendant may be deprived of any property in his possession which was used or intended for use in the commission of the offence.

Harassment

Charge

1. Did pursue a course of conduct amounting to harassment of another which he knew or ought to have known amounted to harassment

Protection from Harassment Act 1997, s 1

Maximum penalty – Fine level 5 and 6 months summary only.

2. Did pursue a course of conduct on two or more occasions, causing another to fear that violence would be used against him, which he knew or ought to have knownwould cause that other person to fear violence would be used against him

Protection from Harassment Act 1997, s 4

Maximum penalty – Fine level 5 and 6 months. Triable either way.

Crown court – 5 years imprisonment and unlimited fine.

Mode of trial

Consider first the general guidlines on p 446. In general trial before the magistrates will be appropriate except for the presence of one or more of the following factors:

(a) the victim was typically vulnerable;
(b) there was a racial motivatiuon;
(c) the course of conduct complained of took place over a long period of time.

Note that the Crown Court can bring in an alternative verdict under s 2 but the magistrates cannot.

Legal notes and definitions

Course of conduct denotes actions taking place on at least two occasions. In the case of a s 4 offence the victim must have been put in fear that violence would have been used against him on at least two of those occasions.

Knows or ought to know in the case of the defendant means that he will be presumed to have that knowledge in a reasonable person in possession of the same information would think the course of conduct would amount to harassment or cause the other person to fear violence would be used against him.

Defences. The statute gives three possible defences if the defendant can show:

(a) his course of conduct was pursued for the purposes of preventing or detecting crime;
(b) that it was pursued under an enactment or rule of law;
(c) that in the particular circumstances the course of conduct was reasonable and in the case of a s4 offence that it was reasonable for the protection of himself or another or his or another's property.

Sentencing

Structure of the sentencing decision. See p 157.

Available sentences. See table A on p 154.

The relative gravity of this offence will vary with the circumstances in each case, but by convicting the defendant of this offence the court is saying that it believes the defendant had harassed or put another in fear of violence and consequently an absolute or conditional discharge will usually be inappropriate.

Restraining orders. On conviction under s 2 or s 4 the court can (in addition to any other sentencing disposal) make a restraining order to protect the victim or any named person from further conduct which would amount to harassment or which would cause the fear of violence.

Custodial sentence. See p 151.

Community sentence. See p 153.

Fines. See p 209.

Compensation. This may be ordered for terror or distress caused (*Bond v Chief Constable of Kent* (1983)): see p 183.

Indecency with a child

Charge

Committing an act of gross indecency with or towards a child under 14 or inciting such a child to an act of gross indecency

Indecency with Children Act 1960, s 1

Maximum penalty – Fine level 5 and 6 months. Triable either way.

Crown court – 10 years imprisonment and unlimited fine.

Mode of trial

See general notes on p 446.

Legal notes and definitions

Gross indecency. This offence covers cases where the child has not strictly speaking been assaulted but has been persuaded or incited by the defendant to touch him in an indecent manner. In some circumstances inactivity can amount to an invitation.

Consent by the child is no defence.

Evidence of children

The evidence of children (ie those persons under 14 years) must be given unsworn (Criminal Justice Act 1988, s 33A). Such evidence need not be corroborated only because it is unsworn (*R v Hampshire* (1995)).

A court may not refuse to admit the evidence of a child complainant by reason of age only. The court should assess whether the child is capable of giving intelligible testimony either by watching a video of the child or by questioning the complainant themselves (*DPP v M* (1997)).

Trials on indictment and proceedings in youth courts. In cases of assault, cruelty or neglect and sexual offences, a video recording of a child witness' evidence may be admitted with the leave of the court. A 'child witness' for the purpose of assault or cruelty etc is a person under 14 years, and for sexual offences, under 17 years (Criminal Justice Act 1988, s 32A). A defendant may not cross-examine a child witness in person; this must be done by his solicitor or counsel (Criminal Justice Act 1988, s 34A).

Adult magistrates' courts may consider such a video even though the child is not called to give evidence. In trials before magistrates a screen may be used so that the witness may not feel intimidated by the presence of the accused (*R v X* (1989)).

Privacy

Clearing the court. The magistrates can order the court to be cleared (except for those directly concerned with the case and the press) whilst the child or young person is testifying (Children and Young Persons Act 1933, s 37).

Anonymity of victim. The general prohibition on the revealing of the identity of the victim of a sexual offence applies (see p 97). In the case of persons under 18 the existing power under the Children and Young Persons Act 1933 is preserved. The court may direct that any press, radio or television report of the case must not reveal the name, address, school or identity of any child or young person concerned in the proceedings (Children and Young Persons Act 1933, s 39).

Corroboration

The evidence of a complainant in sexual cases is no longer required.

Sentencing

Structure of the sentencing decision. See p 157.

Available sentences. See Table A on p 154.

Custodial sentence. See p 151.

Community sentence. See p 153.

Fines. See p 209.

Indecent assault

Charge

Indecently assaulting a female

Sexual Offences Act 1956, s 14

OR

Indecently assaulting a male

Sexual Offences Act 1956, s 15

Maximum penalty – Fine level 5 and 6 months. Triable either way.

Crown court – (Man or woman) 10 years imprisonment and unlimited fine.

Mode of trial

Consider first the general guidelines on p 446. In general, except for the presence of one or more of the following factors, offences of indecent assault should be tried summarily:

(a) there is a substantial disparity in age and the assault was not trivial;
(b) the assault was accompanied by violence or threats;
(c) trust between victim and offender;
(d) there were several offences and they were not trivial;
(e) serious nature of the assault;
(f) the victim was particularly vulnerable.

Legal notes and definitions

Indecently assaulting. The accused must intentionally assault the victim. The assault, or the assault and the circumstances accompanying it, must be capable of being considered by right-minded persons as indecent and the accused must intend to commit an assault of such kind.

An accused's explanation for the assault, whether or not it reveals an indecent motive, is admissible to support or negative that the assault was indecent and was so intended by the accused (*R v Court* (1988)).

Defences. Consent of the alleged victim is a defence except if obtained by force or fraud. The following two categories of persons cannot give consent:

Persons under 16. A person under the age of 16 years is incapable in law of consent in these circumstances and therefore it is no defence that a person under 16 consented; nor that the defendant reasonably believed the person was over 16.

Mental defectives. If the person assaulted was a mental defective he or she cannot give consent; the defendant can only be convicted if he knew or had reason to suspect that the person was a mental defective.

Indecency with children. If a child under the age of 14 was not actually assaulted but was persuaded or incited to commit an act of indecency upon the defendant's own body it becomes an offence under the Indecency with Children Act 1960. See p 94

Evidence of children. See under this heading on p 94.

Anonymity of victim. Where an allegation has been made or a person is accused of this offence neither the name or address nor any moving or still picture of the victim shall be published or broadcast during his lifetime if it is likely to lead members of the public to identify him as the victim of the offence (Sexual Offences (Amendment) Act 1992). Before the trial a magistrate may direct that the prohibition does not apply where he is satisfied the direction is necessary to induce witnesses to come forward, or the applicant's defence is otherwise likely to be substantially prejudiced. The restriction may also be lifted during the trial to such an extent as is necessary in the public interest.

The existing power under the Children and Young Person's Act 1933, in respect of persons under 18, to direct that any press, radio or television report of the case must not reveal his name, address, school or identity is preserved.

The magistrates can order the court to be cleared (except for those directly concerned with the case and the press) whilst the child or young person is testifying (Children and Young Persons Act 1933, s 37).

Corroboration. The Criminal Justice and Public Order Act 1994 removes any requirement for corroboration in sexual offences.

Sentencing

Structure of the sentencing decision. See p 157.

Available sentences. See Table A on p 154.

A 28 day immediate prison sentence was held to be wrong in the case of a 42 year old man of previous good character who indecently assaulted a young woman on an underground train. The Court of Appeal was of the view that such cases could be dealt with by a fine. The court imposed a fine of £300 and a compensation order of £250 was left unchanged (*R v Neem* (1992)).

However, with aggravating factors an indecent assault can require a custodial sentence to be passed (*R v Townsend* (1994)).

In the youth court. It should be noted that indecent assault may be treated as a grave crime in the youth court and committed to the Crown Court for trial. See p 390.

Custodial sentence. See p 151.

Community sentence. See p 153.

Fines. See p 209.

Compensation. This may be ordered up to £5000 either as part of a wider sentence or by itself as a substantive penalty. If the offender's means are limited and a monetary penalty is appropriate, preference must be given to ordering compensation instead of a fine.

Indecent exposure

Charges

Wilfully, openly, lewdly and obscenely exposing one's person with intent to insult a female

Vagrancy Act 1824, s 4

Maximum penalty – Fine level 3 or 3 months for a first offence. For a subsequent offence the accused may be committed to the crown court as an incorrigible rogue for sentence.

In a street wilfully and indecently exposing one's person to the annoyance of residents or passengers

Town Police Clauses Act 1847, s 28

Maximum penalty – Fine level 3 or 14 days imprisonment.

Legal notes and definitions

An offence under the 1824 Act may be committed on private premises.

Evidence. In certain circumstances evidence may be admitted of other indecent exposures.

Person. This means penis for the purpose of this charge.

Sentencing

Offences under the Vagrancy Act 1824

See Table B on p 155 for available sentences.

If a subsequent offence is committed and the first offence was not dealt with by absolute or conditional discharge the magistrates may commit the defendant on bail or in custody to the crown court as an incorrigible rogue. The crown court can impose imprisonment up to one year.

This procedure also applies, even to a first offence of this kind, where there is an antecedent history of other convictions under the Vagrancy Act 1824.

Offences under the Town Police Clauses Act 1847

See Table B on p 155 for available sentences except that a sentence of detention in a young offender institution is not available.

Kerb crawling and soliciting women for prostitution

Charges

Being a man, soliciting a woman (or different women) for the purpose of prostitution

(a) from a motor vehicle while it is in a street or public place or
(b) in a street or public place while in the immediate vicinity of a motor vehicle that the accused has just got out of or off

persistently (or in such a manner or in such circumstances as to be likely to cause annoyance to the woman (or any of the women) solicited, or nuisance to other persons in the neighbourhood)

Sexual Offences Act 1985, s 1(1)

Being a man in a street or public place persistently soliciting a woman (or different women) for the purpose of prostitution

Sexual Offences Act 1985, s 2(1)

Maximum penalty – (for either offence) Fine level 3. Triable only by magistrates.

Legal notes and definitions

The words in brackets in s 1 enable proceedings to be taken where the soliciting was likely to cause annoyance etc to the woman or nuisance to other persons in the neighbourhood, eg to local residents who are annoyed at their district becoming a 'red light' area.

Soliciting a woman for the purpose of prostitution means soliciting her for the purpose of obtaining her services as a prostitute. The accused must have given some indication, by act or word, to the woman that he required her services as a prostitute (*Darroch v DPP* (1990)).

Woman includes girl. These offences can only be committed by a man and for this act 'man' includes 'boy'.

Street includes any bridge, road, lane, footway, subway, square, court, alley or passage, whether a thoroughfare or not, which is for the time being open to the public; and the doorways and entrances of premises abutting on a street and any ground adjoining and open to a street are to be treated as forming part of the street.

Persistently means a degree of repetition, of either more than one invitation to one person or a series of invitations to different people.

Likely to cause annoyance. No persons need be present witnessing the incident for the offence to be made out; it is sufficient if there is a likelihood of nuisance to other persons in the neighbourhood. Justices may use their local knowledge that an area is a frequent haunt of prostitutes with a constant procession of cars there (*Paul v DPP* (1989)).

Sentencing

Since neither of these offences is punishable with imprisonment, a fine will be the usual penalty. The court might consider the amount of distress caused to the victim. When a prosecution is brought on the basis of annoyance to a neighbourhood, an element of deterrent sentencing may be necessary.

Fines. See p 209.

Binding over orders

Complaints for bindover are sometimes included by the prosecution or brought as an alternative remedy to the above charges. Magistrates may use their common law powers to bind over the offender where a future breach of the peace is anticipated (see p 173).

Litter (including dumping articles and car dumping)

Under the general term of **litter** there are three different offences: car dumping, dumping objects other than vehicles, and depositing general litter.

Charge 1

Without lawful authority abandoning on land in the open air or on land forming part of a highway a motor vehicle

Refuse Disposal (Amenity) Act 1978, s 2(1)(a)

Maximum penalty – Fine level 4 and 3 months in prison.
A removal charge can also be imposed if the local authority applies.

Legal notes and definitions

It is also an offence to abandon on such land a part of a motor vehicle if the vehicle was brought to that land and there dismantled and some part of the vehicle abandoned there.

Motor vehicle. This is defined in the Act as a mechanically propelled vehicle intended or adapted for use on roads whether or not it is in a fit state for such use. It includes a trailer, a chassis or body with or without wheels appearing to have formed part of a motor vehicle or trailer and anything attached to a motor vehicle or trailer.

Burden of proof. If the vehicle (or part of a vehicle) was left on the land in such circumstances or for such a period that it may be reasonably assumed that the defendant had abandoned it then he shall be deemed to have abandoned the vehicle (or part of a vehicle) unless he can prove the contrary. The degree of proof required of the defendant is not such as is necessary to establish this point beyond all reasonable doubt but only such as establishes that on the balance of probabilities it is true.

Land. The land must be land in the open air or land which forms part of the highway.

Sentencing

Prison will rarely be appropriate but a fine will in most cases need to be such as to reflect the seriousness of the offence.

On application by police or local authority, a removal charge can also be imposed.

Charge 2

Without lawful authority abandoning on land in the open air (or on land forming part of the highway) property namely . . . which he brought to the land for the purpose of abandoning it there

Refuse Disposal (Amenity) Act 1978, s 2(1)(b)

Maximum penalty – Fine level 4 and 3 months in prison.

Legal notes and definitions

Although this offence does not apply to motor vehicles it does apply to a part of a motor vehicle which was dismantled elsewhere and then brought and abandoned. If the motor vehicle was dismantled on the land then the charge should have been the previous one on p 104.

Land. Means land in the open air or land forming part of a highway.

Sentencing

The position is the same as for the previous charge on p 104 except that ordering a removal charge is limited to removing motor vehicles.

Charge 3

Throwing down (or dropping or depositing) [in a public open place] [in a place to which this section applies] and there leaving certain articles namely . . . in such circumstances as to tend to lead to defacement by litter

Environmental Protection Act 1990, s 87

Maximum penalty – Fine level 4.

Legal notes and definitions

The charge should allege one or other of the following:

Throwing down; dropping; depositing. If two or more of these words are included in the charge then it may be defective.

Public open place. Means a place in the open air to which the public are entitled or permitted to have access without payment. Any covered place open to the air on at least one side and available for public use is to be treated as a public open place.

Place to which the section applies. Includes publicly maintained highways and motorways, local authority open spaces, certain Crown lands and land belonging to certain designated statutory undertakers and educational establishments. Also included is land designated by a local authority as a 'litter control area', eg a shopping mall.

Time limit. Proceedings must be commenced within six months of the litter being thrown down or dropped or deposited. If litter is left for a considerable period then the time limit of six months still commences from the time the litter was deposited.

Leaving. No offence is committed if the litter is not left; thus prompt clearing up can be a defence.

Consent of the owner. If the owner, occupier or person having control of the place consented to the depositing of the litter then no offence is committed.

Sentencing

Aggravating factors which the court may have regard to may include the defacement by litter, but also the nature of the litter and any resulting risk of injury to persons or animals or of damage to property.

Whatever the circumstances the fine will usually need to be such as to reflect the prevalence of the offence in an area.

Fines. See p 209.

National Insurance contributions

Charge

Being an employer and failing to pay a National Insurance contribution which he is liable to pay in respect of an employee

OR

Being a self-employed or non-employed person who fails to pay a National Insurance contribution which he is liable to pay

Social Security Administration Act 1992, ss 114, 115, 116, 119, 120

Maximum penalty – £1000 (corporate defendant) level 3 (individual) plus costs and arrears for two years.

Legal notes and definitions

It is no defence for an employer to say he delegated the task of making these contributions to somebody who failed to do so.

The prosecutor. Any person authorised by the Secretary of State in that behalf may conduct the proceedings before a magistrates' court although not qualified as a barrister or solicitor.

Time limits. Proceedings must be started (ie an information laid) within 12 months of the date of the offence or within 3 months from the date on which evidence sufficient in the opinion of the Secretary of State to justify a prosecution came to his knowledge, whichever is the later.

Evidence of non-payment may be given by certificate if certain provisions are complied with.

Those liable to contribute. From school age to age 60 for a woman and to 65 for a man. Whether or not a person is liable to pay these contributions, and whether he is to be classified as self-employed, non-employed, or employed are matters decided by the Department of Social Security subject to a right of appeal to the High Court. The department's decision on these matters is binding on the court.

Arrears. If the defendant has been served with a notice stating that the Department of Social Security intends claiming for the unpaid contributions that arose during the preceding two years then on conviction the court must order the defendant to pay such arrears. This power exists even if the sentence is an absolute or conditional discharge.

If more than two years' contributions are in arrears the department can enforce such arrears by civil proceedings.

If a court has ordered arrears which are not paid, there is no power at a subsequent means enquiry to remit arrears, in the same way that fines can be remitted.

Exemption. Self-employed and non-employed persons whose gross income is less than £3480 (in the tax year 1997-98) per annum can apply to the department for exemption from paying National Insurance contributions. This provision can also apply to full-time students and unpaid apprentices. If a defendant falls into one of these categories he could be asked why he had not applied for such exemption.

Weekly. The week is a period of seven days starting with midnight between Saturday and Sunday. The law requires payment to be made no later than the last day of a contribution week. Intent to avoid payment is not a necessary ingredient of the offence nor is it a defence to be paid up by the time of a court appearance (*R v Highbury Magistrate* (1987)).

Employed by two employers. If an employee is employed by two persons during a week both employers will be liable to pay secondary contributions (provided the employers are not carrying on business in association with each other), and the employee will be liable to pay primary contributions on each employment.

Company directors etc. If it is proved that a director, secretary or other officer of a limited company or body corporate consented to or connived at the offence he can be prosecuted personally.

The same applies if the offence was attributable to his negligence.

Sentencing

Order for payment of arrears. The court can order the arrears to be paid to the court or direct to an appropriate office of the department the address of which must be made known to the defendant.

A prosecution used often to be brought against a bankrupt company with the purpose of asking the court to order an absolute discharge and an order for payment of the arrears. If the arrears were not paid by the company, the Department of Health and Social Security would take proceedings against the directors of the company for recovery of the amount owing provided they knew, or could reasonably be expected to have known, of the failure to pay the contribution. (Note this was not a *prosecution* against the directors as in the example given above of connivance or negligence in the commission of the offence.) However, although the Department is still entitled to take such civil proceedings, as a matter of policy it has decided that it will no longer do so.

Nuisance

In addition to the remedies which the law affords in respect of nuisances in civil proceedings before the county court and the High Court, local authorities and private persons may bring proceedings for the abatement or restriction of a statutory nuisance before the magistrates' court.

Statutory nuisance

(Environmental Protection Act 1990, s 79)

The following matters constitute statutory nuisances where they are such as to be prejudicial to health or a nuisance:

(a) the state of any premises;
(b) the emission of smoke from premises;
(c) the emission of fumes or gases from private dwellings;
(d) any dust, steam, smell or other effluvia arising on industrial, trade or business premises;
(e) any accumulation or deposit;
(f) the manner or keeping in such a place of any animal;
(g) noise emitted from premises;

and also

(h) any other matter declared by any enactment to be a statutory nuisance.

Prejudicial to health. Means injurious, or likely to cause injury to health.

Noise. Includes vibration.

Exceptions are made to the definitions of a statutory nuisance given above. These include activities of the armed forces, smoke emissions covered by the Clean Air Acts (excluding bonfires), dark smoke from trade or industrial premises, smoke and steam from steam locomotives and noise from aircraft.

Premises. Includes land and any vessel (except one powered by steam reciprocating engines).

Proceedings by the local authority

(Environmental Protection Act 1990, s 82)

The local authority must from time to time cause its area to be inspected to detect the existence of any statutory nuisance and, where a complaint has been made, take such steps as are reasonably practicable to investigate the complaint (s 79).

Abatement notice. Where the local authority are satisfied that a statutory nuisance exists or is likely to occur or reoccur, the local authority must serve a notice requiring abatement or prohibiting or restricting its occurrence together with the taking of any steps necessary for this purpose and any times within which the required action is to be taken.

Appeal. The person served with the notice may appeal within 21 days to the magistrates' court.

Offence. Contravention of or failure to comply with the terms of a notice without reasonable excuse is an offence triable only by magistrates. The maximum penalty is a fine of £5000 and £500 per day for each day the offence continues after conviction. For an offence on industrial, trade or business premises the fine is £20,000.

Defence. It is a defence for the defendant to prove that the best practicable means were used to prevent, or to counteract the effects of, the nuisance. This defence is not available:

(a) in paras (a), (d), (e), (f) and (g) on p 109 except where the nuisance arose on trade, industrial or business premises;
(b) in para (b) except where the smoke is emitted from a chimney.

Certain other defences are available where it is alleged that the activity is in conformity with consents or notices under control of pollution legislation.

Appeal. A person convicted of an offence may appeal against conviction and sentence to the crown court in the usual way.

Complaint by person aggrieved by a statutory nuisance

(Environmental Protection Act 1990, s 82)

A private individual may complain to the local authority about an alleged statutory nuisance and it will be the duty of the authority to take such steps as are reasonably practicable to investigate the complaint and if they consider it appropriate to serve an abatement notice as described above (Environmental Protection Act 1990, s 79).

However, a person may also lay a complaint before the magistrates on the ground that he is aggrieved by the existence of a statutory nuisance. Proceedings are normally brought against the person responsible for the nuisance; where he cannot be found it will be the owner or occupier of the premises.

Notice of intention to bring proceedings and the matters complained of should be served not less than 3 days before, in respect of noise, and 21 days before, in respect of any other allegation.

Magistrates' order. If the court is satisfied that the alleged nuisance exists or that, although abated, it is likely to reoccur, the court must make either or both of the following orders:

(a) to abate the nuisance, within a time specified in the order, and to execute any works necessary for that purpose;
(b) prohibiting a recurrence of the nuisance, and requiring the defendant, within a time specified in the order, to execute any works necessary to prevent the recurrence.

The court may also impose a fine not exceeding £5000 (level 5).

Where the nuisance renders premises unfit for human habitation, the order may prohibit their use for this purpose until the court is satisfied they are fit for such use.

Offence. See p 110 and below for private premises.

Defence. See p 110. The 'best practicable means' defence is not available for a nuisance which is such as to render the premises unfit for human habitation.

Costs. Where the alleged nuisance is proved to have existed at the making of the complaint then whether or not at the date of the hearing it still exists or is likely to recur the court shall order the defendant to pay the complainant's proper costs.

Local authority. Where a person has been convicted of failing to comply with an order the court, after allowing the local authority an opportunity to be heard, may direct the authority to do anything which the person convicted was required to do by the order. Similarly, where the defendant cannot be found the court may direct the local authority to do that which it would have ordered him to do.

(Noise Act 1996)

If a warning notice has been served under this Act, in respect of noise emitted from a dwelling, any person who is responsible for such a breach is liable to a fine not exceeding level 3.

Defence. It is open to the defendant to show he has reasonable excuse.

Forfeiture. Magistrates may direct the forfeiture of any equipment related to a noise conviction.

Before doing so the court must have regard:

(a) to the value of the equipment; and
(b) to the likely financial and other effects on the offender of the making of the order.

Obstructing or resisting a constable in the execution of his duty
Obstructing a court security officer in the execution of his duty

Charges

1 **Resisting a constable in the execution of his duty**

2 **Resisting a person assisting a constable in the execution of his duty**

3 **Wilfully obstructing a constable in the execution of his duty**

4 **Wilfully obstructing a person assisting a constable in the execution of his duty**

Police Act 1996, s 89(2)

Maximum penalty – Fine level 3 and one month.

5 **Wilfully obstructing a court security officer in the execution of his duty**

Criminal Justice Act 1991, s 78(2)

Maximum penalty – Fine level 3.

Legal notes and definitions

The offences of resisting and wilfully obstructing will usually involve some other activity than an assault on the police or a court security officer (which would constitute a different charge). A person exercising their right to silence does not commit the offence of obstructing a police officer.

Resisting. Means striving against, opposing or trying to impede. For the intention which the defendant must have to commit the offence see p 23 (police assault).

Wilfully means that there must be an intention to bring about a state of affairs whereby, judged objectively, the constable is obstructed in the sense of making it more difficult for him to carry out his duty. The accused need not be hostile to the police, motives are irrelevant. Two examples may make this clear:

(a) The defendant sees the constable trying to arrest a robber. With the intention of helping the officer, the defendant intervenes but he is so clumsy that the villain escapes. He is not guilty of obstruction because the state of affairs that he *intended* to bring about was that the officer would be helped to effect the arrest.

(b) The defendant sees the constable about to arrest what he considers to be the wrong man. He intervenes to stop the arrest. The arrest was in fact lawful. He is guilty because, objectively, the officer has been obstructed in his duty and this was the intention of the accused. It is irrelevant that his motives for doing so were good (otherwise the police would be in peril of all sorts of interruptions whilst exercising their duty).

Unlike a charge of assaulting a police officer, it may be that the defendant must know that the person he is obstructing is a police officer. A defendant who honestly believes the complainant is *not* a police officer, is not guilty of the offence.

Obstructing. Deliberately causing a physical obstruction is an offence and so is shouting a warning to a person committing an offence or about to commit an offence. It is not a wilful obstruction if a person refuses to answer questions which he is not legally obliged to answer.

Constable. A constable includes a special constable and member of the police force of any rank however high.

In the execution of his duty. Sometimes the defendant claims that the constable was not acting in the course of his duty and if the court accepts this defence then the charge must be dismissed.

This type of defence sometimes raises difficult questions of law as to whether, for example, a constable had a right to be on private premises when not in possession of a search warrant, or whether a constable had a right to detain a person without there being in force a warrant for arrest.

The burden of proof that the constable was acting in the execution of his duty rests on the prosecution.

See p 23.

Court security officer. See p 23 for definitions.

Sentencing

Structure of the sentencing decision. See p 157.

Available sentences. See Table B on p 155.

Custodial sentence. See p 151.

Community sentence. See p 153.

Fines. See p 209.

Obstructing the highway

Charge

Without lawful authority or excuse wilfully obstructing the free passage along a highway

Highways Act 1980, s 137

Maximum penalty – Fine level 3.

Legal notes and definitions

This offence can be committed in a number of different ways apart from leaving a motor vehicle. It should not be confused with the offence of causing an unnecessary obstruction on a road with a motor vehicle or with a breach of parking regulations. See p 316.

The correct approach for magistrates dealing with an offence of obstruction is as follows:

(a) Was there an obstruction? Unless within the *de minimis* rule, any stopping on the highway is prima facie an obstruction.
(b) Was it wilful, ie deliberate?
(c) Have the prosecution proved that the obstruction was without lawful authority or excuse? Lawful authority includes permits and licences granted under statutory provision; lawful excuse embraces activities otherwise lawful in themselves which may or may not be reasonable in all the circumstances, including the length of time the obstruction continues, the place where it occurs, the purpose for which it is done and whether it does in fact cause an actual obstruction as opposed to a potential obstruction (*Hirst and Agu v The Chief Constable of West Yorkshire* (1986)).

Highway. A highway means the whole or part of a highway. Only a part of a highway needs to be obstructed to commit this offence and the highway, available to the general public, may be a wide road or a narrow passageway, only suitable for pedestrians. Bridges and tunnels used by the public are also highways.

Offensive weapon

Charge

Having, without lawful authority or reasonable excuse, an offensive weapon in any public place

Prevention of Crime Act 1953, s 1

Maximum penalty – Fine level 5 and 6 months. Triable either way.

Crown court – 4 years' imprisonment and unlimited fine.

Mode of trial

See general notes on p 446.

Legal notes and definitions

General. The possession of offensive weapons is also controlled by several other statutes. The Crossbows Act 1987 regulates the sale or hire of crossbows to persons under 17 years, and the purchase or possession of crossbows by such persons. The Firearms Act 1968 controls the possession and use of airguns, shotguns and firearms and the possession of articles with blades or sharp points is governed by the Criminal Justice Act 1988 (see p 21).

Controls are also imposed on the manufacturers of and dealers in or persons who lend or give 'flick knives' by the Restriction of Offensive Weapons Act 1959 and the Criminal Justice Act 1988 extends such controls to offensive weapons specified by the Home Office such as weapons used in martial arts and stun guns. Selling a knife to a person under the age of 16 is an offence by virtue of amendments brought into force in January 1997. The maximum penalty for contravention of such regulations is a fine on level 5 and 6 months imprisonment.

Offensive weapon. A police constable may arrest without warrant anyone carrying or suspected of carrying an offensive weapon in a public place. In order to convict the prosecution must first prove that the defendant was in possession of an offensive weapon. An offensive weapon means any article either

(a) made or adapted for use for causing injury to the person; or
(b) intended by the person having it with him for such use by him or by some other person.

Articles in category (a), such as knuckledusters and flick knives, are always offensive weapons. An article in category (b), such as for example a milk bottle, only becomes an offensive weapon when the person carrying it has the intention of using it to cause injury to the person. The prosecution must prove this intention.

With him. The prosecution must prove secondly that the defendant was carrying the offensive weapon with him. 'Carrying' would not include the situation where the accused seized a clasp knife, which he had not been carrying, for instant use on his victim.

Knowledge of possession. The accused must have acquired the weapon knowingly (eg it was not slipped into his pocket unawares) (*R v Cugullere* (1961)). But he still has it if he subsequently forgets it is there (*R v McCalla* (1988)) until he or another does something to rid him of it. A person who has forgotten that he has an offensive weapon is unlikely to have a 'reasonable excuse' (see below) for having it with him, but it might be otherwise where the original possession was lawful, eg picking up a policeman's truncheon intending to take it to the police station and then forgetting to do so (*R v McCalla* (1988)).

In a public place. This includes any highway and any other premises or place to which at the material time the public have or are permitted to have access, whether on payment or otherwise.

Without lawful authority or reasonable excuse. If the prosecution has established that an offensive weapon was carried in a public place then the onus shifts to the defendant to prove that lawful authority or reasonable excuse existed. The degree of proof is not to establish this beyond all reasonable doubt but that on the balance of probabilities it is true. A police officer's truncheon is an offensive weapon per se, but a police officer has lawful authority or reasonable excuse for carrying it. In a case decided in 1986, a person who was carrying a truncheon as part of a fancy dress costume was held to have reasonable excuse for doing so (there were no suspicious circumstances, eg he was not under the influence of alcohol nor was he a member of a gang).

The common excuse put forward is that the article was carried for use in self-defence. As the authority or excuse relates to the reason for carrying the offensive weapon, not to a use for which it is subsequently employed, one has to look at the situation when the defendant was carrying it. Accordingly, fear of being attacked, arising from the experience of friends and general violence in the neighbourhood, has been held not to be a reasonable excuse for carrying a metal ball and chain for self-protection. Self-protection from an actual or imminent attack might provide a 'reasonable excuse'. There would be no excuse or authority for a bouncer at a dance carrying an offensive weapon.

Sentencing

Structure of the sentencing decision. See p 157.

Available sentences. See Table A on p 154.

Custodial sentence. See p 151.

Community sentence. See p 153.

Fines. See p 209.

Forfeiture. The court may order the weapon to be forfeited.

Poaching

1 Day time offence

Trespassing by entering or being in the day time upon any land in search or pursuit of game, or woodcocks, snipes or conies

Game Act 1831, s 30, as amended

Maximum penalty – Fine level 3. Triable only by magistrates.

Note – Where it is alleged that there were five or more persons together trespassing in pursuit of game the maximum penalty is a fine set at level 5 for each defendant.

Legal notes and definitions

A prosecution must be commenced within three calendar months after the commission of the offence (s 41). The charge creates only one offence, that of trespass, and the summons may refer to pursuit of more than one species.

Claim of right. The magistrates' jurisdiction is ousted if the accused contends that he had a right to act as he did. However, this claim must be bona fide and made on reasonable grounds. The magistrates may decide on the reasonableness and sufficiency of the evidence to support it.

Trespassing is a complicated concept. However, for this offence the accused must himself have been personally entering on the land and 'constructive' trespass, eg sending a dog into the land, would not be sufficient.

Day time commences at the beginning of the last hour before sunrise and concludes at the expiration of the first hour after sunset (s 34).

Game means hares, pheasants, partridges, grouse, heath or moor game, and black game (s 2).

Game licence. A conviction of this offence renders a licence to kill game void (Game Licences Act 1860, s 11).

Hunting. This offence does not apply to hunting or coursing in fresh pursuit of deer, hare, or fox (s 35).

2 Night time offences

(a) Unlawfully taking or destroying any game or rabbits by night in any land, open or enclosed

or by night unlawfully entering or being on any land, whether open or enclosed, with any gun, net, engine, or other instrument for the purpose of taking or destroying game

Night Poaching Act 1828, s 1, as amended

Maximum penalty – Fine level 3 (offence under s 2 where violence is offered to gamekeepers etc with the weapons described in charge (b) the maximum is a fine on level 4 and 6 months). Triable only by magistrates.

(b) Three or more persons together by night unlawfully entering or being on any land, whether open or enclosed, for the purpose of taking or destroying game or rabbits, any of such persons being armed with gun, cross bow, firearms, bludgeon or any other offensive weapon

Night Poaching Act 1828, s 9, as amended

Maximum penalty – Fine level 4 and 6 months. Triable only by magistrates.

Legal notes and definitions

Claim of right. See above, p 118.

Game includes hares, pheasants, partridges, grouse, heath or moor game, black game and bustards (s 13).

Land includes public roads, highways, or paths, or the sides thereof or at the opening, outlets, or gates, from any such land into any such road, highway or path.

Charge. Section 1 creates two offences and any information must allege only one offence.

Unlawfully entering or being. See above, p 118. This offence does not relate to the taking or destroying of rabbits.

Night time commences at the expiration of the first hour after sunset and concludes at the beginning of the last hour before sunrise.

Three or more together. It is not necessary for all the persons actually to enter provided they are associated together on a common purpose, some entering while others remain near enough to assist.

3 Pursuing game without a licence

Taking, killing, pursuing, or using any dog, gun, net or other engine for the purpose of taking, killing, or pursuing any game, or any woodcock, snipe or any coney, or deer, without a proper licence

Game Licences Act 1860, s 4, as amended

Maximum penalty – Fine level 2. Triable only by magistrates.

Legal notes and definitions

Game licences are granted by local authorities.

Exceptions. Include taking woodcocks and snipe with nets or springs; taking or destroying conies by proprietors or tenants of lands; pursuing and killing of hares by coursing with greyhounds or hunting with beagles or other hounds; a person assisting a licence holder in his company or presence; a person authorised under the Hares Act 1848 to kill hares without a game certificate.

Sentencing

Where the police have arrested a person for an offence under the Night Poaching Act or Game Act they may search him and may seize and detain any game or rabbits, or any gun or cartridges or other ammunition, or any nets, traps, snares or other devices of a kind used for the killing or taking of game or rabbits, which are found in his possession.

If convicted the court may order any of these items to be forfeited (whether or not the offence of which he was convicted concerned that game, rabbit etc) (Game Laws Amendment Act 1960, s 4).

Police (Property) Act 1897

Application for order for delivery of property in possession of the police in connection with their investigation of a suspected offence

Legal notes and definitions

While this proceeding is a civil case of a kind that is more usually dealt with at a county court, nevertheless it can be dealt with at a magistrates' court. Clearly it will be cheaper and more expeditious if the magistrates' court deals with the matter fairly soon after the hearing of a criminal charge, thus saving a hearing in the county court or High Court. Sufficient notice of the date of hearing should be given to each claimant of the property to enable him to prepare for the hearing before the magistrates.

When applicable. This procedure applies when the police have in their possession property which has come into their hands during investigation into a suspected offence. It is not necessary that the person has been charged with any offence.

Often there is no such difficulty as stolen property can be restored direct to the rightful owner. In other cases where the defendant has been convicted for several stealing offences, at the end of the case the police may be in possession of a large sum of money taken from the defendant. The various losers may each claim part or all of this money as being stolen from them or arising from the sale by the thief of the stolen property.

The police, any claimant or even the defendant can lay a complaint or make an application asking the magistrates to decide to whom the money should be delivered.

At the hearing the police or a claimant has the right to call witnesses, cross-examine the other party's witnesses and to address the magistrates.

Powers of the magistrates. Having heard all the parties the magistrates may make an order for delivery of the property to the person who appears to the court to be the owner or if he cannot be ascertained they may make such order as they think meet.

This gives the magistrates wide powers of discretion. If, for instance, the magistrates are not impressed by any of the claims then they can order the money or the money the police obtain from selling the stolen property (eg a stolen motor vehicle) to be paid to the Police Property Act Fund which is administered by the Police Authority. The money is invested and the income is used (a) to defray the expenses in handling and storing such property; (b) for compensating the persons who deliver such property to the police; (c) for charitable purposes.

If there are several claimants the magistrates might find in favour of one claimant and order his claim to be paid and find against the other claimants and then order the balance of the money to be delivered to the fund.

Deliver. It is to be noted that the word used in disposing of the money is 'delivered'. The magistrates have not made any ruling on the ownership of the money or property.

An unsuccessful claimant can sue the authority or person to whom the magistrates order delivery, but must do so within six months from the date of the hearing.

Case unsuitable for magistrates' courts. The High Court has ruled that magistrates should hesitate to deal with a claim of a similar kind if the value of the property is substantial or if difficult matters of law are likely to arise. For example, a motor car which was stolen whilst subject to a hire-purchase agreement led to there being several claimants.

If the magistrates feel that either of the above points arise the best course is to adjourn the hearing *sine die* and to invite the claimant or claimants to commence proceedings in the county court or the High Court.

Criminal Damage Act 1971

The above provisions also apply if the police have possession of property following the execution of a search warrant granted under s 6 of the above Act.

Costs. Where proceedings are commenced by way of an 'application' there is no power to award costs. Where proceedings have begun by way of a complaint it is inappropriate to order costs against the police where they do not object to the order sought (*R v Uxbridge JJ, ex p MPC* (1981)).

Railway offences

Charge 1

Travelling on a railway without having previously paid the fare with the intention of avoiding payment

OR

Having paid a fare knowingly and wilfully travelling beyond the distance paid for without previously paying for an additional distance with the intention of avoiding additional fare

Regulation of the Railways Act 1889, s 5(3)(a) and (b) respectively

Maximum penalty - Fine level 3 or 3 months (British Railways or London Transport).

Legal notes and definitions

A fare must be paid to the railway authority or one of its employees.

The prosecution must satisfy the magistrates that the defendant intended to avoid paying the fare or additional fare (if he paid for part of the journey). If the magistrates believe that the defendant genuinely forgot to pay his fare then the case must be dismissed. It is sufficient for a conviction if the defendant's intention was to avoid paying until payment was demanded; there is no need to prove an intention permanently to avoid payment.

The prosecution has only to establish the intention to avoid paying the fare, not the intention to defraud.

It has been held that the offence of 'without having previously paid the fare with the intention of avoiding the fare' has been committed if the defendant uses the return half of a ticket issued to another person. It is not necessary to show that the offender knew that the ticket was non-transferable.

Travelling. This includes the time between leaving the railway carriage and proceeding to the exit barrier. Thus an offence is committed if a passenger decides to avoid the fare at that stage of the journey.

Wilfully. This means deliberately.

Sentencing

See Table B on p 155 for available sentences.

Charge 2

Having failed to pay the fare, when asked by an officer of the railway authority, gives a false name or address

Regulation of the Railways Act 1889, s 5(3)(c)

Maximum penalty - Fine level 3 or 3 months (British Railways or London Transport).

Legal notes and definitions

The request for a traveller's name and address must be made by an officer of the railway authority.

Sentencing

The position is the same as for the previous offence.

Shotgun (purchasing etc without shotgun certificate)

Charge

Possessing, or purchasing or acquiring a shotgun without holding a shotgun certificate

Firearms Act 1968, s 2(1)

Maximum penalty - Fine level 5 and 6 months. Triable either way.

Crown court - 5 years imprisonment and unlimited fine.

Mode of trial

See general notes on p 446.

Legal notes and definitions

Purchasing, possessing, acquiring. Are three separate offences and the charge should only allege one of these.

Shotgun. Means a smooth bore gun with a barrel of 24 inches or longer with a bore not exceeding two inches and which is not a revolver nor has an illegal magazine, which is not an air gun.

Certificate. This is granted by the police and it may contain conditions. Failure to observe the conditions is an offence which is also punishable with a fine of level 5 and 6 months imprisonment (s 2(2)) and is only triable before magistrates. The police can revoke the certificate if they are satisfied that it entails danger to public safety or peace.

Exemptions. These include visitors to Great Britain who are holders of a visitor's shotgun permit; persons using shotguns on occasions and at places approved by the police; a person who borrows a shotgun and uses it on the lender's private premises, in the presence of the lender; persons holding a Northern Ireland firearm certificate which authorises holders to possess shotguns. See also p 73.

The degree of proof required from the defendant is to establish that on the balance of probabilities he was exempt. He does not have to establish this beyond reasonable doubt.

Sentencing

Structure of the sentencing decision. See p 157.

Available sentences. See Table A on p 154.

Custodial sentence. See p 151.

Community sentence. See p 153.

Fines. See p 209.

Forfeiture. The court can order the shotgun to be forfeited to the police or disposed of as it thinks fit.

The court can also cancel any firearm or shotgun certificate held by the defendant.

Sporting events (control of alcohol etc)

Charges

1(a) Being the operator (or hirer) (or his servant or agent) knowingly causing or permitting intoxicating liquor to be carried on a public service vehicle which was being used for the principal purpose of carrying passengers for the whole or part of a journey to or from a designated sporting event

OR

(b) Possessing intoxicating liquor whilst on such a vehicle

OR

(c) Being drunk on such a vehicle

Sporting Events (Control of Alcohol etc) Act 1985, ss 1(2), 1(3) and 1(4)

2(a) Possessing intoxicating liquor (or an article specified by the Act namely) at a time during the period of a designated sporting event when in an area of a designated sports ground from which the event might have been directly viewed (or while entering or trying to enter such an event)

OR

(b) Being drunk in a designated sports ground at a time during the period of a designated sporting event (or, being drunk while entering or trying to enter such an event)

Sporting Events (Control of Alcohol etc) Act 1985, ss 2(1) and 2(2)

Maximum penalties -

Offences under s 1(2) - Fine level 4
ss 1(3) and 2(1) - Fine level 3 and 3 months
ss 1(4) and 2(2) - Fine level 2

Legal notes and definitions

These offences were created in an attempt to deal with rowdy behaviour at football matches primarily where teams belonging to the Football (or Premier) League are involved (including their reserve and youth teams) but generally not at games exclusively concerning 'non league' or amateur clubs. In addition, the Act provides for a total ban on the sale of alcohol at such matches although there is the opportunity for the club to apply to the magistrates for an order modifying this prohibition (see p 417).

Public service vehicle means a motor vehicle adapted to carry more than eight passengers for hire or reward. (For this and the definition of 'operator' see the Public Passenger Vehicles Act 1981, ss 1 & 81.) This offence also applies to a person who knowingly causes or permits intoxicating liquor to be carried in these circumstances on a railway passenger vehicle which he has hired. Section 1A makes provision for offences similar to those under s 1(a), (b) and (c) for drivers and keepers of a minibus, ie not a public service vehicle, but one which is adapted to carry more than 8 passengers, and is being used for the principal purpose of carrying two or more passengers for the whole or part of a journey to or from a designated sporting event.

Designated sporting event means any association football match where one of the participating clubs is a member (full or associate) of the Football (or Premier) League. It also includes all international association football matches and matches in competition for the European Champion Clubs Cup, European Cup Winner's Cup or UEFA Cup (whether or not either of the teams concerned is a member of the Football (or Premier) League eg where a final is played in England between two foreign teams). Also included are events in Scotland designated under the equivalent Scottish legislation (all Scottish League Clubs are designated as well as rugby internationals at Murrayfield). A match is also designated if it takes place outside Great Britain where either the team represents the Football Association or is a Football (or Premier) League Club or where a Football Association Club (not necessarily being a 'league' club) participates in one of the three European competitions. Accordingly, persons on a journey to Scotland or to Europe for a designated event are subject to the provisions of the Act whilst they are in England.

Period of the event. The prohibitions apply to a period beginning two hours before the start of the event or, if earlier, two hours before the time it is advertised to start and ends one hour after the end of the event. Where a match is postponed or cancelled, the period includes the two hours before and one hour after the advertised start of the event. A shorter restricted period starting 15 minutes before and ending 15 minutes after the event applies to private boxes overlooking the ground.

Exceptions. Apart from those clubs or matches not covered by the designation, eg games exclusively concerning 'non league' clubs, the Act does not apply to matches where all competitors take part without reward *and* all spectators are admitted free of charge.

Prohibited articles. As well as intoxicating liquor this includes any article capable of causing injury to a person struck by it being a bottle, can or other portable container (including such a container when crushed or broken) which is for holding *any* drink and which when empty is of a kind normally discarded or returned to the supplier, or part of such a container eg a beer glass. Thus a vacuum flask containing tea would be exempt. Also exempted are containers for holding medicinal products.

Prohibited articles also include under s 2A any article or substance whose main purpose is the emission of a flare for purposes of illuminating or signalling (as opposed to igniting or heating) or the emission of smoke or visible gas, eg distress flares, fog signals, pellets for fumigating, but not matches, lighters, or heaters; fireworks are also prohibited. It is a defence if the accused proves that he was in possession of an article under s 2A with lawful authority.

Designated sports ground. These are the home grounds of all Football Association clubs (ie not necessarily just those clubs in the Football (or Premier) League) including any ground used occasionally or temporarily by such a club, Wembley Stadium and any ground used for any international association match. However, it should be noted that all the restrictions apply only to a designated sporting event and so where, for example, a boxing match is held on a Football League ground the provisions of the Act do not apply.

Sentencing

For the non-imprisonable offences see Table C on p 156 and for the offences contrary to ss 1(3) and 2(1) see Table B on p 155.

For the power to make exclusion orders on persons convicted of certain offences in relation to football matches see p 207.

Fines. See p 209.

Taking motor vehicle (or other conveyance)

Charge

Without the owner's consent or other lawful authority taking a conveyance, namely a . . . for his own use (or for another person's use)

Theft Act 1968, s 12(1)

Note – It is also an offence to drive a conveyance, or allow oneself to be carried in or on it, if one knows the conveyance has been taken without such authority; the penalty for such offences is the same as for the offence of unauthorised taking.

Maximum penalty – Fine level 5 and six months. Triable only by magistrates.

Motor vehicles. The defendant may be disqualified but no endorsement or penalty points are applicable.

Legal notes and definitions

Pedal cycles. Section 12(5) of the Theft Act 1968 applies a special provision if the conveyance is a pedal cycle. The maximum penalty is a fine up to level 3.

If the circumstances amounted to theft and theft is alleged, the notes on p 134 will apply.

Taking. An offence is committed if the conveyance is taken. 'Driving away' does not have to be proved but there must be evidence of some movement and that the vehicle was used as a conveyance. Accordingly, the moving of a motor car round the corner as a practical joke to lead the owner to believe it had been stolen was not an offence as it was not established that anyone rode inside it (*R v Stokes* (1983)). But where a defendant allowed a vehicle to roll down a hill by climbing in it and releasing the handbrake, he was guilty of the offence (*R v Bow* (1977)). It would be otherwise if he did not get inside the vehicle. It is not a defence that the conveyance was stolen, as opposed to being taken. Nor is it a defence that the vehicle had been previously taken (*DPP v Spriggs* (1993)).

Conveyance. Means a conveyance constructed or adapted for carrying one or more persons by land, water or air. It does not include a conveyance which can only be controlled by a person not carried in or on it.

Motor vehicle. A motor vehicle is a mechanically propelled vehicle intended or adapted for use on a road.

Owner. Includes a person in possession of the conveyance under a hiring or hire-purchase agreement.

Owner's consent. Where the owner is induced by fraud to part with possession of his vehicle, no offence under this section has been committed (*Whittaker v Campbell* (1983)). The owner has in fact consented even though in the civil law he may have a remedy against the fraudster.

No offence was committed where consent was obtained by a false pretence as to the destination and purpose of the journey (*R v Peart* (1970)). Nor where consent of an owner to allow a vehicle to be hired was obtained by the fraudulent misrepresentation of the hirer as to his identity and the holding of a full driving licence.

Reduction of charge from theft of conveyance. If a defendant is tried in a magistrates' court for stealing a conveyance, the court cannot reduce the charge to this offence of taking the conveyance.

Successful defence. If the court is satisfied the defendant acted in the belief that he had lawful authority, or that the owner would have consented if the owner knew the circumstances, then he must be acquitted. The defendant only has to raise the defence. The absence of lawful authority or the owner's consent is an essential ingredient of the offence and it remains the prosecutor's duty to prove the allegation.

Aggravated vehicle-taking. See p 18.

Sentencing

Structure of the sentencing decision. See p 157.

Available sentences. See Table B on p 155.

Custodial sentence. See p 151.

Community sentence. See p 153.

Fines. See p 209.

Disqualification may be ordered in the case of a motor vehicle.

Compensation. This may be ordered up to £5000 either as part of a wider sentence or by itself as a substantive penalty. If the offender's means are limited and a monetary penalty is appropriate, preference must be given to ordering compensation instead of a fine.

Television licence

Charge

Using (or installing) apparatus for wireless telegraphy, namely a television receiver without a licence

Wireless Telegraphy Act 1949, s 1

Maximum penalty – Fine level 3.

Legal notes and definitions

The charge should allege either that the apparatus was used or was installed.

Using should be given its natural and ordinary meaning. This might create problems for enforcing authorities. They would if necessary have to persuade the court to draw the inference that the apparatus in question had been used by the defendant during the relevant period. If, for example, a television set in working order was found in the sitting-room of a house occupied by the defendant, it would not be difficult for a court to draw the necessary inference in the absence of some credible explanation by the defendant to the effect that it was not being used (*Rudd v Secretary of State for Trade and Industry* (1987)) and (*Whiley v DPP* (1995)) in respect of a radio scanner.

A user does not have to be an owner or hirer. Therefore where a set belonged to a husband but the wife switched it on, she was convicted of using it (*Monks v Pilgrim* (1979)).

Licence. Applies to the person named on the licence, his family and domestic staff living with him on the premises.

Applies to the premises named on the licence and covers any number of sets. Also covers members of family living away as full time students at educational establishments using a portable television set (black and white or colour as described in the licence) in any other place provided

(a) they normally reside at the licence holder's address and
(b) the equipment is powered by internal batteries and
(c) is not permanently installed.

There are concessions for touring caravans.

Duration. Normally one year. If the licence is paid for by a subsequently dishonoured cheque, it continues in force until it is properly revoked. It may be short-dated if it is not renewed immediately on the expiry of the previous licence.

Wireless telegraphy. This technical expression is defined in the Wireless Telegraphy Act 1949.

A licence is required where a television set is used to receive BBC, ITV, satellite or cable television programmes, whether or not it is used for other purposes such as a home computer. No licence is required for closed circuit television or a set which reproduces a signal only from a recorder.

Concessions and exemptions are made under regulations for particular categories of persons.

Sentencing

Although a conditional or absolute discharge may occasionally be appropriate the most usual penalty is a fine but the court cannot order confiscation of the set, nor can the court order 'arrears' of the licence fee.

Any fine will be fixed in accordance with the seriousness of the offence, ie duration of unlicensed use and the means of the offender (see p 209). However, in order to indicate that it is cheaper to buy a licence, the court may increase the amount of any fine by the amount exceeding the cost of the relevant licence. This is subject to the overall maximum fine fixed on level 3.

Theft

Charge

Stealing

Theft Act 1968, s 1(1)

Maximum penalty – Fine level 5 and 6 months. Triable either way.

Crown court – 7 years imprisonment and unlimited fine.

Motor vehicles. See p 130.

Mode of trial

Consider first the general guidelines on p 446. In general, offences of theft should be tried summarily except for the presence of one or more of the following factors:

(a) breach of trust by a person in a position of substantial authority or in whom a high degree of trust has been placed;
(b) there has been sophisticated hiding or disguising of the offence;
(c) the offence has been committed by an organised gang;
(d) the victim was particularly vulnerable;
(e) there is unrecovered property of high value.

Legal notes and definitions

Theft or **stealing** means dishonestly appropriating property belonging to another person with the intention of permanently depriving the other person of it. It does not matter whether the purpose of the theft was gain or not. Nor does it matter if the theft was for the benefit of the defendant or another person.

The prosecution does not have to prove that the property was appropriated without the owner's consent. However, if the defendant believed he had the owner's consent that could be relevant in deciding whether the defendant acted dishonestly.

1 Dishonestly

The appropriation can be dishonest even though the defendant was willing to pay for the property.

The general test of dishonesty is: first, whether the accused's actions were dishonest according to the ordinary standards of reasonable and honest people and, if so, whether the accused himself had realised that his actions were, according to those standards, dishonest. (Thus a genuine belief by the accused that he was morally justified in acting as he did is no defence if he knew that ordinary people would consider such conduct to be dishonest (*R v Ghosh* (1982).)

The Act provides that appropriation in the following circumstances is not 'dishonest':

(a) if the defendant believed he had the legal right to deprive the other of the property, either for himself or a third party; or
(b) if the defendant believed the other person would have consented had the other person known of the appropriation and the circumstances of the appropriation; or
(c) if the defendant believed the person to whom the property belonged could not be discovered by taking reasonable steps (but this defence is not available if the property came to the defendant as a trustee or a personal representative).

2 Appropriates

Any assumption of the rights of an owner amounts to appropriation. If the defendant came by the property (innocently or otherwise) without stealing it and later assumed a right to it by keeping it or dealing with it as an owner, he has appropriated it.

The following are examples of dishonest appropriation:

(a) a parent whose child has brought home someone else's property and who retains the property, or
(b) a person who has found property (but see (1)(c) above), or
(c) a person who has acquired property through another person's mistake and has taken advantage of the error,
(d) a person who switches price labels in a supermarket in order to obtain the goods at a price lower than the original marked price.

Repentance. It is important in some cases to appreciate the moment when the offence is complete. Sometimes, for example, the shoplifter decides either to put the goods back or to pay for them. Once the offence is completed such action is evidence of repentance only and may affect the sentence, but it does not establish innocence.

Acquiring in good faith. If the defendant in good faith gave value for the property and later found that the vendor (or other person from whom he acquired the property) had no right to the goods, then the defendant is not guilty of theft in the event of his keeping or disposing of the property.

3 Property

Includes money, stocks and shares, bills of exchange, insurance policies and all kinds of goods and property.

Land. Land or anything forming part of land cannot be stolen except in the following circumstances:

(a) dishonest appropriation by trustees, personal representatives, liquidators of companies, persons holding a power of attorney and certain similar persons; or
(b) dishonest appropriation of something forming part of land by a person not in possession of the land (eg removing soil); or
(c) dishonest appropriation by tenants of fixtures let to be used with land.

Attempting the impossible. A person may be guilty of an attempt to steal even though the facts are such that the commission of the offence of theft is impossible, for example by placing one's hand into an empty pocket.

Things growing wild. If mushrooms, flowers, fruit or foliage from a plant which is growing wild are picked, that only amounts to theft if it is done for reward, or for sale or any other commercial purpose.

Wild creatures. Appropriating a wild creature can only amount to theft if it has been reduced into the possession of someone else who has not lost or abandoned such possession of the creature; or if someone else is in the course of reducing it into his possession.

4 Belonging to another

The property must be treated as belonging to anyone having possession or control of it or having any proprietary right or interest in it. Petrol ceases to belong to another when it is put in a vehicle's petrol tank at a self-service filling station. When goods in a supermarket are for convenience or hygiene bagged, weighed and priced by an assistant they remain the property of the supermarket until paid for, and may therefore be the subject of the theft.

Trust property. Must be treated as belonging to anyone having a right to enforce the trust. An intention to defeat the trust shall be treated as an intention to deprive the person entitled to enforce the trust of the property.

Being entrusted with property. If a defendant (eg the treasurer of a holiday fund or Christmas club) has received property and is under an obligation to retain it or deal with it in a particular way, the property shall be treated as belonging to the beneficiary and not to the defendant.

Getting property by mistake. If the defendant obtained property by a mistake on the part of another person, and is under a legal (as opposed to a moral or social) obligation to restore it, then the property must be treated as belonging to the other person.

If the court considers the defendant formed an intention not to restore the property, he must be deemed to have intended to deprive the other person of the property.

5 With the intention of permanently depriving

The court must be satisfied that the defendant had this intention; or alternatively that he intended treating the property as his own to dispose of regardless of the owner's rights. The court must decide the defendant's intention by considering all the evidence and drawing from it such inferences as appear proper in the circumstances.

Borrowing or lending. Can be used to establish that the defendant had the intention of permanently depriving the owner if, and only if, the borrowing or lending were for a period and the circumstances of the case make it equivalent to an outright taking or disposal. Ordinary borrowing or lending would not have this effect.

Reduction of the charge (motor vehicles). If the property is a motor vehicle a magistrates' court cannot reduce the charge of theft to one of 'taking a conveyance', see p 130.

Proof of stealing one article enough. If the charge alleges the theft of several articles, the court can convict of theft if it decides that only one of the articles was stolen. The announcement of decision and court register should make the decision clear.

Partnership property. A partner can be convicted of stealing property which he and another or other partners own.

Sentencing

Structure of the sentencing decision. See p 157.

Available sentences. See Table A on p 154.

Custodial sentence. See p 151.

Community sentence. See p 153.

Fine. See p 209.

Compensation. This may be ordered up to £5000 either as part of a wider sentence or by itself as a substantive penalty. The court may deprive the defendant of any property in his possession when arrested if it was used, or intended for use, in the commission of a crime.

Motor vehicles. If the property was a motor vehicle (defined as a mechanically propelled vehicle intended or adapted for use on a road) the court may disqualify but there is no endorsement or penalty points.

Threatening behaviour or intentional harassment, alarm or distress

Charge 1

Using towards another threatening, abusive or insulting words or behaviour (or distributing or displaying to another person any writing, sign or other visible representation being threatening, abusive or insulting) intending to cause that other person to believe that immediate unlawful violence would be used against him or another by any person, or to provoke the immediate use of unlawful violence by that person or another or whereby that other person was likely to believe that such violence would be used or it was likely that such violence would be provoked

Public Order Act 1986, s 4(1)

Maximum penalty – Fine level 5 and 6 months. Triable only by magistrates.

Charge 2

A person is guilty of an offence if with intent to cause a person harassment, alarm and distress, he

(a) uses threatening, abusive or insulting words or behaviour, or
(b) displays any writing, sign or visible representation which is threatening, abusive or insulting,

thereby causing that or another person harassment, alarm or distress

Public Order Act 1986, s 4A

Maximum penalty – Fine level 4 and 6 months imprisonment.

Legal notes and definitions

The charge. Only one offence is created.

Threatening; abusive; insulting. (The following comments are based on repealed legislation but still seem applicable.) The High Court has described these as being 'all very strong words'. If the evidence shows that the words or behaviour used fell short of being abusive, insulting or threatening but merely annoying then the case should be dismissed. The words 'f... off' shouted at a police officer who was trying to prevent a breach of the peace have been held to be 'insulting'. Shouting encouragement to a gang throwing stones at another gang is sufficient for a conviction under this section.

Violence does not include violence justified by law (eg self-defence or prevention of crime). The violence apprehended must be immediate which does not mean 'instantaneous' but connotes proximity in time and causation (*R v Horseferry Rd JJ* (1990)). For what is included see under the offence of violent disorder p 141.

Intent. The accused must *intend* his words or behaviour etc to be, or be aware that his words etc may be threatening, abusive or insulting and intend the apprehension of unlawful violence etc.

Intoxication. See under the offence of violent disorder.

Threatening etc behaviour may be committed in a public or private place. If the threatening etc words or behaviour are used inside a dwelling-house, the offence can only be committed if the other person is not inside that or another dwelling-house, but parts of a dwelling not occupied as a person's house or living accommodation do not count as a dwelling for this purpose, eg the shop underneath the owner's flat. A tent, caravan, vehicle, vessel or other temporary or movable structure may be a dwelling for this purpose where it is occupied as a person's house or as other living accommodation.

Sentencing

Structure of the sentencing decision. See p 157.

Available sentences. See Table B on p 155.

Custodial sentence. See p 151.

Community sentence. See p 153.

Fines. See p 209.

Bind over. The court can bind over the defendant, with or without sureties. The prosecution or witnesses may also be bound over if they are first warned and given the chance to address the court; the clerk should be consulted in such cases.

Threats or intimidation of witnesses

Charge 1

Did intimidate (...) knowing or believing (...) is assisting an investigation/ is a witness or potential witness in proceedings with the intention that the investigation/course of justice would be interefered/perverted/obstructed

Criminal Justice Act 1994, s 51(1)

Charge 2

Did threaten (..) with harm intending to harm him knowing or believing that (...) has assisted in an investigation or has given evidence in proceedings for an offence because he believes/ knows that assistence or evidence was given

Criminal Justice Act 1994, s 51(2)

Maximum penalty – Fine level 5 and 6 months imprisonment. Triable either way. Crown Court maximum 5 years imprisonment

Legal notes and definitions

A person does an act to another person with the intention of intimidating/ harming not only when it is done directly but also when it is done to a third party with the same intention. The threat may be at a distance, eg over the telephone (*DPP v Mills* (1996)).

Harm may be financial/physical to a person or property

Intention the intention or motive required for the two charges need not be the only or predominant motive or intention with which the act is done or threatened. If the prosecution can prove the act /threat and the defendants knowledge/belief in the circumstances then the resultant motive/intention shall be presumed unless the contrary is proven.

Witness includes jurors or potential jurors in the Crown court.

Investigation into an offence means an investigation by police or such other person charged with the duty of investigating offences or charging offenders.

Offence includes an alleged or suspected offence.

Sentencing

Generally this will be considered a serious offence and if committed in respect of a juror at the Crown Court will be dealt with by that court.

Structure of the sentencing decision. See p 157.

Available sentences. See table B on p 155.

Custodial sentences. See p 151.

Community sentences. See p 153.

Fines. See p 209.

Vehicle interference

Charge

Interfered with a motor vehicle or anything carried in or on the same with the intention that an offence of theft of the said motor vehicle or part of it or of anything carried in or on the said motor vehicle or an offence of taking and driving it away without consent should be committed

Criminal Attempts Act 1981, s 9(1)

Maximum penalty – Fine level 4 and 3 months.

Legal notes and definitions

This offence applies to trailers. A trailer means a vehicle drawn by a motor vehicle.

Interfere. It will be for the court to decide whether a particular activity amounts to interference; simply keeping a vehicle under observation in the hope that an opportunity will arise to commit an offence would not be interference. In many cases the alleged activity would support a charge of attempting to steal which, unlike this offence is triable either way but this offence may be easier to prove because of the provision regarding 'intent'.

Intent. There must be evidence of an intention to commit theft of the vehicle, trailer, any parts of them or anything carried in or on them, or to commit the offence of unauthorised taking of the vehicle or trailer. But the prosecution does not have to prove precisely which of these offences the accused intended. In some cases, for example, the prosecution would be unable to prove whether the intention was to take the vehicle, steal it, or steal goods from inside it.

Motor vehicle. Means a mechanically propelled vehicle intended or adapted for use on the road.

Sentencing

See Table B on p 155 for available sentences.

Violent disorder

Charge

Being one of three or more persons present together and using or threatening unlawful violence so that the conduct taken together is such as would cause a person of reasonable firmness present at the scene to fear for his personal safety

Public Order Act 1986, s 2(1)

Maximum penalty – Fine level 5 and 6 months. Triable either way.

Crown court – 5 years imprisonment and unlimited fine.

Mode of trial

Cases of violent disorder should generally be considered for trial on indictment and see general guidelines p 446.

Legal notes and definitions

The charge. Only one offence is created.

Three or more persons. The defendants need not be using or threatening violence simultaneously.

Violence does not include violence justified by law (eg self-defence or prevention of crime) but apart from that includes violent conduct towards property or persons and is not restricted to conduct causing or intended to cause injury or damage but includes any other violent conduct (for example, throwing at or towards a person a missile of a kind capable of causing injury which does not hit or falls short).

Person of reasonable firmness need not actually be or be likely to be, present at the scene. See p 16.

Intent. A person may be guilty only if he intends to use or threaten violence, or is aware that his conduct may be violent or threaten violence.

Intoxication. A person whose awareness is impaired by intoxication shall be taken to be aware of that of which he would be aware if not intoxicated, unless he shows that his intoxication was not self-induced, or that it was caused solely by the taking of a substance in the course of medical treatment. 'Intoxication' may be caused by drink, drugs or other means.

Violent disorder may be committed in a public or private place.

Sentencing

Structure of the sentencing decision. See p 157.

Available sentences. See Table A on p 154.

Custodial sentence. See p 151.

Community sentence. See p 153.

Fines. See p 209.

Compensation. See p 183.

Section two

Sentencing

Index to sentencing

Remission to another court

If the following conditions are met a magistrates' court may remit an offender to another magistrates' court (Magistrates' Courts Act 1980, s 39). The conditions are:

(a) The court proposing to remit has convicted the offender of an offence which is punishable by either imprisonment or disqualification.
(b) The offender has attained 18 years of age.
(c) The court to which the convicting court proposes to remit has convicted the offender of another such offence but has not sentenced him nor committed him to the crown court to be dealt with.
(d) The receiving court consents to the remission.

The offender may be remitted on bail or in custody. He is not required to consent to the remission neither has he any right of appeal against it.

Juveniles. A magistrates' court which has found a juvenile offender (under 18) guilty of an offence must remit the juvenile to a youth court unless satisfied that it is undesirable to do so (Children and Young Persons Act 1933, s 56) and must exercise that power unless it is of the opinion that the case is one which can properly be dealt with by means of

(a) an absolute or conditional discharge;
(b) a fine;

The court to which he is remitted will normally be the youth court for the area in which he resides. If the court finding the juvenile guilty is itself a youth court it may remit to another youth court or deal with him as it thinks fit.

■ Available sentences according to age of offender. For full details refer to pages following, on sentencing.

Age	10	11	12	13	14	15	16	17	18	19	20	21 and over	Notes
Imprisonment												■	restrictions on custodial sentences:
Suspended												■	offence 'so serious' etc, pre-sentence
Detention in young offender inst.*△						■	■	■	■	■	■		report, legal representation
Detention (One Day)*												■	
Community Service*△							■	■	■	■	■	■	
Probation△							■	■	■	■	■	■	Community Orders
Combination Order*△							■	■	■	■	■	■	offence 'serious enough'
Supervision△	■	■	■	■	■	■	■	■					pre-sentence report
Attendance Centre*△	■	■	■	■	■	■	■	■	■	■	■		
Fine	■	■	■	■	■	■	■	■	■	■	■	■	u 14 max £250; 14–17 £1000
Compensation/Deprivation Order□	■	■	■	■	■	■	■	■	■	■	■	■	see pp 181 and 216
Discharge (Abs/Cond)	■	■	■	■	■	■	■	■	■	■	■	■	
Hospital Order*△	■	■	■	■	■	■	■	■	■	■	■	■	Medical recommendation
Guardianship Order*△	■	■	■	■	■	■	■	■	■	■	■	■	
Committal for sentence s 38									■	■	■	■	Either way offences
Committal for sentence s 37△						■	■	■					
Deferred sentence	■	■	■	■	■	■	■	■	■	■	■	■	Court to give reasons

Notes

(1) Sentences marked with an asterisk * can only be imposed if the offence is punishable with imprisonment when committed by an adult over 21 years.

(2) As far as defendants aged under 18 are concerned a magistrates' court (as opposed to a youth court) cannot impose any of the penalties marked with a △. The magistrates' court must remit such juveniles on bail or in care to a youth court which will usually be the youth court for the area in which he lives.

(3) □Under PCCA 1973, s 43, see p 216.

Custodial sentences

There are three main forms of custodial sentence: imprisonment, detention in a young offender institution and secure training orders.†

Imprisonment (p 225) is confined to defendants over the age of 21 years. The minimum period is 5 days and the maximum is that fixed by statute. There is one other form of imprisonment – the suspended sentence.

Detention in a young offender institution (p 200) is the equivalent of imprisonment for those under 21. The minimum age is 15 years for both males and females.

The minimum term is not less than two months for 15, 16 and 17 year olds. The general minimum for 18–21 year olds is 21 days. In the case of detention in a young offender institution imposed for breach of a supervision order made on release from such an institution a term not exceeding 30 days may be imposed.

The maximum term is generally the maximum term that an adult could receive for the offence and for offenders aged 15, 16 or 17. The maximum is 12 months for two indictable offences.

Secure training orders.† Available for 12 to 14 year olds inclusive. The court may order a period between 6 months and 2 years, half of which will be detention in a secure training centre.

Presence of the accused. Imprisonment (or its equivalent) cannot be imposed in the absence of the accused.

Legal representation. A person shall not be sentenced to a custodial sentence of any form (whether suspended or not) unless he is legally represented. There is an exception where he has either applied for legal aid which was refused on financial grounds or he was informed of his right to apply for legal aid and he failed to apply for it.

Restrictions on imposing custodial sentences. A court may not pass a custodial sentence in any form on an offender of any age unless it is satisfied:

(a) that the offence, or the combination of the offence and one or more offences associated with it, was so serious that only such a sentence can be justified for the offences; or
(b) where the offence is a violent or sexual offence, that only such a sentence would be adequate to protect the public from serious harm from him.

In forming such an opinion a court must take into account all such information about the circumstances of the offence (including any associated offences and any aggravating or mitigating factors) as is available to it, which will almost invariably include information in a pre-sentence report (see below). In the case of (b) above a court may also take into account any information about the offender which is before it. The effect of the 1993 Criminal Justice Act is that the court may take into account previous convictions and previous failures to respond to sentences when assessing the seriousness of current offending.

Exceptionally the court may impose a custodial sentence where the defendant refuses to give his consent to a community sentence proposed by the court which requires his consent.

Apart from the exceptional case, the court must state in open court that it is of the opinion that either or both of the criteria (a) and (b) apply and why it is of that opinion. In any case, the court must explain to the offender in ordinary language why it is imposing a custodial sentence on him.

Length of custodial sentences

A custodial sentence passed by a court shall be for such term (not exceeding the permitted maximum) as in the opinion of the court is commensurate with the seriousness of the offence, or a combination of the offence and other offences associated with it.

In the case of a violent or sexual offence the sentence may instead be for such longer term (not exceeding the maximum) as in the opinion of the court is necessary to protect the public from serious harm from the offender. This situation is unlikely to occur in the magistrates' court and, if it should, the court must state its opinion and reasons in open court and give an explanation to the offender in ordinary language.

In forming an opinion on the appropriate length of sentence the court must take into account all such information about the circumstances of the offence (including any associated offences and any aggravating or mitigating factors) as is available to it (such as a pre-sentence report) and also where a longer sentence in respect of a violent or sexual offence is contemplated, any information about the offender which is before it.

Pre-sentence report

This means a report in writing which is made by a probation officer (or social worker) with a view to assisting the court in determining the most suitable method of dealing with an offender and contains such information as to such matters as may be prescribed by the Secretary of State.

Before forming an opinion on the necessity for, and appropriate length of, a custodial sentence the court should obtain a pre-sentence report. Although a custodial sentence is not invalidated by the court's failure to obtain such a report, magistrates will no doubt continue to wish to meet the statutory requirement in all cases where an offender is in jeopardy of losing his liberty despite the 'let out' clause 'unless the court is of the opinion that it is unnecessary to obtain a pre-sentence report'.

Mentally disordered offenders

Where the offender is, or appears to be, mentally disordered, the court must, unless in the circumstances of the case it appears unnecessary to do so, obtain a medical report made orally or in writing by a doctor approved under the Mental Health Act 1983 as having special experience in the diagnosis or treatment of mental disorder.

Where a court is considering a custodial sentence in such circumstances it must consider:

(a) any information before it which relates to his mental condition (whether given in a medical report, a pre-sentence report or otherwise); and
(b) the likely effect of such a sentence on that condition and on any treatment which may be available for it.

Community sentences

The Criminal Justice Act 1991 introduced the concept of a 'community sentence', ie a sentence which consists of or includes one or more community orders:

a probation order;
a community service order;
a combination order;
a curfew order;
a supervision order;
an attendance centre order.

Restrictions on imposing a community sentence

A court may not impose a community sentence unless:

(a) it is of the opinion that the offence was serious enough to warrant such a sentence taking into account all such information about the circumstances of the offence (including any associated offences or any aggravating or mitigating factors) as is available to it;
(b) the particular order or orders comprising or forming part of the sentence are such as in the opinion of the court is, or taken together are, the most suitable for the offender taking into account any information about the offender which is before it (such as a pre-sentence report, see below);
(c) the restrictions on liberty imposed by the order or orders are such as in the opinion of the court are commensurate with the seriousness of the offence, or the combination of the offence and other offences associated with it, taking into account information about the circumstances etc as in (a) above.

The effect of the Criminal Justice Act 1993 means that when considering seriousness of the current offence or offences previous convictions and previous failures to respond to court orders may be taken into account.

A community sentence shall not consist of or include both a probation order and a community service order (but may, of course, consist of a combination order, p 175).

Pre-sentence report

Before forming an opinion as to the suitability for an offender of one or more of a probation or supervision order with additional requirements, a community service order or a combination order, the court should obtain and consider a pre-sentence report unless it is of the opinion that it is unnecessary to obtain one.

TABLE A

■ Available sentences for either way offences punishable with imprisonment on summary conviction. See p 145 for page references.

Age	10	11	12	13	14	15	16	17	18	19	20	21 and over	Notes
Imprisonment												■	restrictions on custodial sentences: offence 'so serious' etc. pre-sentence report, legal representations
Suspended												■	
Detention in young offender inst.						■	■	■	■	■	■		
Detention (One Day)												■	
Community Service							■	■	■	■	■	■	Community Orders offence 'serious enough' pre-sentence report
Probation							■	■	■	■	■	■	
Combination Order							■	■	■	■	■	■	
Supervision	■	■	■	■	■	■	■	■					
Attendance Centre	■	■	■	■	■	■	■	■	■	■	■		
Fine	■	■	■	■	■	■	■	■	■	■	■	■	u 14 max £250; 14–17 £1000
Compensation/Deprivation Order	■	■	■	■	■	■	■	■	■	■	■	■	see pp 181 and 216
Discharge (Abs/Cond)	■	■	■	■	■	■	■	■	■	■	■	■	
Hospital Order	■	■	■	■	■	■	■	■	■	■	■	■	Medical recommendation
Guardianship Order	■	■	■	■	■	■	■	■	■	■	■	■	
Committal for sentence s 38									■	■	■	■	
Committal for sentence s 37						■	■	■					
Deferred sentence	■	■	■	■	■	■	■	■	■	■	■	■	Court to give reasons

TABLE B

■ Available sentences for purely summary offences punishable with imprisonment. See p 145 for page references.

Age	10	11	12	13	14	15	16	17	18	19	20	21 and over	Notes
Imprisonment												■	restrictions on custodial sentences:
Suspended												■	offence 'so serious' etc, pre-sentence
Detention in young offender inst.						■	■	■	■	■	■		report, legal representations
Detention (One Day)												■	
Community Service							■	■	■	■	■	■	
Probation							■	■	■	■	■	■	Community Orders
Combination Order							■	■	■	■	■	■	offence 'serious enough'
Supervision	■	■	■	■	■	■	■	■					pre-sentence report
Attendance Centre	■	■	■	■	■	■	■	■	■	■	■		
Fine	■	■	■	■	■	■	■	■	■	■	■	■	u 14 max £250; 14–17 £1000
Compensation/Deprivation Order	■	■	■	■	■	■	■	■	■	■	■	■	see pp 181 and 216
Discharge (Abs/Cond)	■	■	■	■	■	■	■	■	■	■	■	■	
Hospital Order	■	■	■	■	■	■	■	■	■	■	■	■	Medical recommendation
Guardianship Order	■	■	■	■	■	■	■	■	■	■	■	■	
Committal for sentence s 38	■	■	■	■	■	■	■	■	■	■	■	■	
Committal for sentence s 37													
Deferred sentence	■	■	■	■	■	■	■	■	■	■	■	■	Court to give reasons

TABLE C

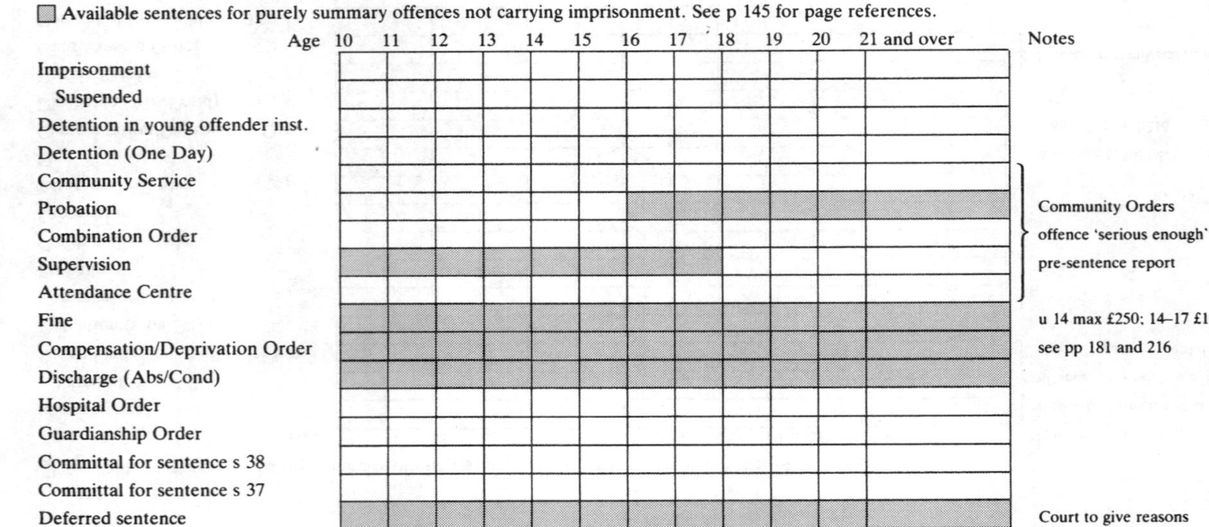

■ Available sentences for purely summary offences not carrying imprisonment. See p 145 for page references.

Age	10	11	12	13	14	15	16	17	18	19	20	21 and over	Notes
Imprisonment													
Suspended													
Detention in young offender inst.													
Detention (One Day)													
Community Service													
Probation							■	■	■	■	■	■	Community Orders
Combination Order													offence 'serious enough'
Supervision	■	■	■	■	■	■	■	■					pre-sentence report
Attendance Centre													
Fine	■	■	■	■	■	■	■	■	■	■	■	■	u 14 max £250; 14–17 £1000
Compensation/Deprivation Order	■	■	■	■	■	■	■	■	■	■	■	■	see pp 181 and 216
Discharge (Abs/Cond)	■	■	■	■	■	■	■	■	■	■	■	■	
Hospital Order													
Guardianship Order													
Committal for sentence s 38													
Committal for sentence s 37													
Deferred sentence	■	■	■	■	■	■	■	■	■	■	■	■	Court to give reasons

The sentencing decision

Guidance

Guidance on the seriousness of an offence and the suitability and length of sentences is available from the following sources:
- Statutes
- Court of Appeal
- Mode of trial guidelines
- Magistrates' Association
- Pre-sentence reports (pp 152 and 153)

The clerk's advice on the use of these guidelines will be essential (p 160).

Determining seriousness

1 Consider the aggravating and mitigating features of the offence (pp 161–164).
2 Is the previous record or failure to respond relevant?
3 Are associated offences relevant?
4 Was the offence(s) commmitted whilst on bail? If so, this is an aggravating feature.

How serious is the offence? (p 163)

1 Inexpedient to inflict punishment – discharge.
2 Suitable for a financial penalty.
3 'Serious enough' to warrant a community sentence.
4 'So serious' that only a custodial sentence can be justified.

Personal mitigation (p 165)

Choice of sentence (p 167)

1 Availability of sentences (p 164):
   (a) offence imprisonable/non-imprisonable (pp 154–156);
   (b) age of offender (p 150);
   (c) seriousness of offence (p 163).
2 Financial penalty of restriction of liberty commensurate with seriousness of offence.
3 Community penalty suitable for offender.

Ancillary orders

Compensation p 183; costs p 188; disqualification and endorsement p 260; deprivation of property and forfeiture p 218; legal aid contribution order p 451; restriction p 239.

Pronouncement (p 168)

Statement accompanying sentence (p 167)
- Reasons
- Time to pay financial orders

The process of sentencing

Introduction

Sentencing is not and never will be an exact science; only rarely could a group of sentencers agree that a particular sentence was exactly right and even if they did, they would probably by agreeing only that it was right to show a particular level of leniency. The prerogative of saying what is 'right' in terms of sentencing levels belongs to the Court of Appeal and since they always consider sentencing in the atmosphere of an appeal against a specific sentence, they generally tend to express themselves in terms that the sentence was 'too excessive', or was 'not wrong'.

However, a degree of vagueness might be thought to be inevitable when there are so many variables to be considered before a sentencing decision is reached. Not only should this fact not discourage a proper study of the subject of sentencing, but it should positively encourage it and the area of study most profitable to the lay magistrate is that of the process of sentencing, the route to be followed in order to reach a sentence which, if it cannot be said to be exactly right, at least is unlikely to be disturbed on appeal if the offender's circumstances remain the same. The framework for a structured sentencing decision is given on p 157. This is amplified and explained in paragraphs 5 to 12 which follow. Paragraphs 1 to 4 deal with the determination of guilt and the factual basis for the sentencing decision.

1 Not guilty plea

When an accused person enters a not guilty plea, he is not necessarily proclaiming his innocence. This arises from two factors: firstly, it is not the function of the court to decide whether he is guilty or not, the court's function is to decide *whether the prosecutor has proved that he is guilty*. Secondly, there may be legal or procedural reasons why an accused should enter a not guilty plea as will be seen from the following circumstances. A plea of not guilty should be entered when:

(a) the accused disputes the facts;
(b) the accused hopes to show that some legal condition precedent to conviction has not been fulfilled, eg notice of intended prosecution;
(c) the accused believes that the prosecutor's witnesses will be incapable of establishing the facts beyond reasonable doubt, for example because
  (i) there is a question of legal competence;
  (ii) there is lack of corroboration in a case where the law requires it;
  (iii) evidence vital to the prosecution is legally inadmissible;
  (iv) the accused believes he can discredit a prosecution witness by cross-examination;
(d) the accused agrees the facts but wishes to show that as a matter of law they do not constitute the offence charged;
(e) the accused has a statutory defence;
(f) the accused has no recollection of the circumstances alleged by the

prosecutor and wishes to hear evidence before deciding whether he should plead guilty.

Whatever is the accused's reason for a not guilty plea, once he has entered it all the facts relevant to the proof of guilt are said to be 'in issue' which means that the prosecutor must either prove those facts beyond reasonable doubt or (in some few cases) must establish facts which then place the burden of proving his innocence on the accused. An example of this last situation occurs where the police allege the uninsured use of a motor vehicle. Once they establish that the accused used a motor vehicle on a road it becomes the responsibility of the accused to satisfy the court that his use of the vehicle was insured. The prosecutor will establish his facts by the oral testimony of witnesses who may then be cross-examined, and/or by the production of witness statements of which the accused will have had prior notice in order to object to them if he wishes, and/or by formal admissions from the accused which should be written down and signed by him. If the accused wishes to give evidence he may use all or any of these methods of doing so. The basis on which a not guilty plea is entered is important to the sentencer in some cases. It is often urged in mitigation that the accused pleaded guilty consequently saving stress and inconvenience to witnesses, court time and expense. The court must take account of the stage in proceedings that the guilty plea was entered and the circumstances in which it was given. If as a result the court imposes a punishment which is less severe than would otherwise have been the case, it must state, in open court, that it has done so. It should not be held against an accused that he pleaded not guilty if he clearly was justified in doing so. However, the clerk will advise that in some cases where the basis of a not guilty plea proves unjustified, the accused's proper course is to change his plea. An example of this would be where he wishes to plead a technical point and has been overruled.

2 Guilty plea

A guilty plea must be quite unequivocal; when an accused purports to admit an offence but then adds words or an explanation redolent of a defence the clerk should normally be left to deal with the matter. A guilty plea, however, is an admission of the offence charged and not necessarily of every fact which the prosecutor may allege as a circumstance of it. A guilty plea to assault, for example, would not indicate an acceptance of the prosecution's allegations of the number of blows struck or their severity. Where there is a dispute about an important circumstance of the offence either side may call evidence notwithstanding the guilty plea. Furthermore, evidence may be called if there is a dispute relating to an ancillary matter, such as the amount of compensation or liability for back duty. The evidence should be confined solely to deciding the issue in question and, if the prosecution cannot establish its version of the facts beyond a reasonable doubt, the defence version must be accepted. The other aspect of the question is that the court must sentence only on the basis of the case put forward by the prosecution and not on the basis of conclusions it might draw that the case is in reality more serious. For example, if a person is accused of two cases of theft from his employer the court must not infer that in fact this was a common occurrence and sentence accordingly. Sometimes the inference might be inescapable, the important thing is that it does not affect the sentence for the offence charged.

3 Advice from the clerk

The clerk (ie the court clerk) has a duty to advise on matters of law and matters of mixed law and fact. Justices who refuse to act on his advice in a straightforward matter (eg a driver's liability to disqualification) may find themselves ordered to pay the costs of a consequent appeal. The justices are entitled to invite the clerk to retire with them if they think that a matter may arise on which they will seek his advice. In a case of any complexity it is wise to invite the clerk so to retire in order to be able to give advice as the occasion may require during the justices' discussion. If the clerk has taken a full note of the evidence he may be called upon to refresh the justices' memory from it. However, so far as it is practical to do so the clerk should be asked to give his advice openly in court. This will not always be a practical way to give advice, especially in complicated matters, or where reference to books may be necessary, or where a discussion with one or more of the justices may be involved. Whispered advice tendered across the bench in court can be unsatisfactory; it may be partly heard by those in court and misunderstood or it may not be fully heard by those on the bench who may also feel inhibited from following it up with questions either because of hearing difficulties or because they fear being overheard by solicitors or defendants. The justices' clerk has the right to advise even though he is not sitting with them in court so that, if he is available, he may always be sent for if necessary. It should be noted, however, where representations have been made to the court which the justices' clerk has not heard they should be repeated in the presence of the justices' clerk before he gives his advice to the bench. It is especially useful to bear this in mind when sitting with an inexperienced court clerk.

For a fuller account of the role of the justices' clerk and his staff see Section 12 on p 473.

4 Consideration of guilt

The question for justices to ask themselves at this stage is, 'Has the prosecutor satisfied the majority of us beyond reasonable doubt that the accused committed the offence with which he has been charged?' A reasonable doubt must not be a fanciful doubt nurtured by prejudice. The burden of proof, that is the degree to which a court should be convinced of guilt, is a matter of law and one on which the clerk can advise.

When announcing the decision in court it is generally better to avoid using a reference to 'the case'. It is better to say, 'We find you guilty of theft' or as the case may be, rather than, 'We find the case proved'. The accused feels he has 'a case' too, and the latter expression of the decision sometimes creates the impression that 'the case' which the court has been concerned with has been the prosecution case. The former method of announcing the decision leaves nothing to doubt or prejudice and is especially to be recommended when there has been more than one charge or accused.

5 Reports etc

Whatever the plea, once the guilt of the accused has been established the court may hear further information about him relevant to sentence. The prosecutor will give information about previous convictions or the fact that there are none. He will also indicate if the accused has admitted other similar offences which he wishes the court to take into consideration when determining the sentence. These will have been written down and should be put one by one by the clerk and the accused should be asked to signify his admission of each such offence separately. This is important because 'TICs' as these offences are usually known may be significant in the sentencing decision and because (especially if there is a long list) it is very easy for the police to include in a list of outstanding offences some which a prisoner will admit through not giving the matter proper thought. Compensation may be ordered in respect of offences taken into consideration and this is another reason for being procedurally correct when dealing with them. The maximum amount of compensation depends on the number of substantive charges.

Also at this stage the prosecutor will ask for any appropriate ancillary orders such as costs or the forfeiture of a weapon or drugs, etc. The chairman should make a written note of such matters so that they are not overlooked when the final sentencing decision is made.

Pre-sentence report. The court may at this stage consider a pre-sentence report and if one is not available the question of an adjournment in order to obtain one should not be overlooked. Although they need not do so if they are of the opinion that it is unnecessary, it is still a statutory requirement for a magistrates' court to consider a pre-sentence report before imposing any custodial sentence or a community sentence (except a probation order with no additional requirements, although the obtaining of a pre-sentence report is nevertheless still strongly advised).

The pre-sentence report is to assist the court in determining the most suitable method of dealing with an offender. The responsibility for determining the seriousness of an offence remains solely with the magistrates. However, the pre-sentence report will contain impartial advice and information and will balance the aggravating and mitigating factors in the case. The report may give advice in support of a particular sentence although it will bear in mind the ultimate responsibility of the sentencer. The Crown Prosecutor may make reperesentations on matters contained in the pre-sentence report.

Medical report. Where the offender is, or appears to be, mentally disordered, the court must, if it is considering a custodial sentence, obtain a medical report. Such a report is made orally or in writing by a doctor approved under the Mental Health Act 1983 as having experience in the diagnosis or treatment of mental disorder.

Reports from other sources may be available, for example, a reference from an offender's employer or educational establishment etc. In any case where the court thinks fit it may adjourn and call upon the maker of a report to attend for questioning upon its contents.

The court must give the accused or his solicitor and the Crown Prosecutor a copy of the pre-sentence report. In the Youth court the report will be given to a parent or guardian. It is very important, however, that the accused is aware of the contents of any written report submitted to the court. It is not considered entirely satisfactory simply to hand a written report to an unrepresented defendant in court. He may have difficulty in reading, especially in the stressful situation of court proceedings, so that he may not absorb the contents of the report at all, or he may not have finished reading it by the time he is invited to comment on it. Furthermore, he may not understand the meaning of everything he reads and he almost certainly will have had inadequate time to gather his thoughts and to express a useful opinion about anything contained in the report. The better practice, therefore, is that the probation officer has discussed the contents of the report, and especially the implications of any proposal therein, with the offender before the case is dealt with in court.

6 Mitigation

There are two particular objectives of mitigation: to draw to the attention of the court any factors relevant to mitigating the seriousness of the *offence*, and to highlight mitigation personal to the *offender*.

The first consideration for the court in determining sentence is the seriouness of the offence. Except in the case of a violent or sexual offence, where the court may be of the view that only a custodial sentence is adequate to protect the public from serious harm by the offender, the seriousness of the offence will determine whether the court must impose a custodial sentence or the offence warrants the making of a community sentence.

In addressing the seriousness of the offence, the circumstances of the offence should be examined to see whether they disclose any mitigating circumstances. Guidance on what may amount to a mitigating (or aggravating) feature of an offence is given by the Court of Appeal, the National Mode of Trial Guidelines and the Magistrates' Association. Such guidance is noted where appropriate in the articles on particular offences in Section 1 and 3 of *Anthony and Berryman's*. An example would be an offence of assault. The court would be concerned to know whether a weapon was used, whether the victim was subjected to kicks, and if the offender was provoked. An offence committed under considerable provocation will obviously be treated differently from one for which elaborate plans were made in advance. Considerations in an offence of theft might include the value of the property stolen, was any or all of the property recovered and was the offender in a position of trust? An offence committed whilst on bail must be treated as an aggravating circumstance.

The seriousness of the offence will broadly determine which range of sentencing options are open to the court: custody, community, financial or a discharge. Where the court is concerned with a violent or sexual offence and is considering a custodial sentence to protect the public, the personal circumstances and history will become relevant. However, personal mitigation is usually more relevant at the second stage when the general level of seriousness has been determined, where mitigation will affect the final choice of sentence and the impact it will have on the offender. While no sentence may be more severe than is justified by the defendant's offence, personal mitigation may serve to reduce his punishment or suggest that a more individualised approach may be appropriate. In forming an opinion, whether a particular community order or orders comprising a community sentence is or are the most suitable for the offender, the court may take into account any information about the offender which is before it. Mitigating factors which have commonly been considered by the courts are referred to under 'Consideration of sentences' on p 165.

7 The offence

An important principle of sentencing contained in the Criminal Justice Act 1991 is that a sentence should not be more severe than is warranted by the seriousness of the offence and other offences associated with it. When considering the seriousness of the current offence or offences, previous conviction and failure to respond to previous sentences may be taken into account where relevant. Custodial sentences are reserved for offenders who have committed an offence 'so serious' that only a custodial sentence can be justified for it, and community sentences are only available where the offence is 'serious enough' to warrant such a sentence.

Where the circumstances of a violent or sexual offence and information about the offender cause the court to be of the opinion that only a custodial sentence would be adequate to protect the public from serious harm by him, the sentence may be for such longer term (not exceeding the maximum) which would be necessary to protect the public from such harm.

A custodial sentence may also be imposed where the offender has refused to consent to a community sentence.

Otherwise any sentence imposed will generally be commensurate with the seriousness of the offence, although the court, having considered all the mitigation, may take this into account in mitigating an offender's sentence.

Determining seriousness

The facts. The court must be satisfied that the facts of the offence or offences for which sentence is to be passed have been proved or agreed.

In determining the seriousness of an offence the court must take into account all information about the circumstances of the offence, any aggravating or mitigating factors as are available to it, and information in a pre-sentence report.

Associated offence. In considering whether an offence is 'serious enough' to warrant a community sentence, or 'so serious' that only a custodial sentence can be justified, the court may consider the combination of the offence and other offences associated with it. An 'associated offence' is in essence another offence for which the offender is to be sentenced at that time or is to have taken into consideration.

Guidance on the seriousness of offences and aggravating and mitigating features is given by decisions of the Court of Appeal, the National Mode of Trial guidelines and guidelines issued by the Magistrates' Association.

Parliament also gives broad guidance to the courts by prescribing the maximum penalties available. For example, many minor offences are punishable only by a fine on level 1 (max £200) and level 5 (max £5000). Other, more serious, offences are also punishable with imprisonment of up to 6 months.

8 Availability of sentences

Available sentences are determined by the maximum penalties prescribed by Parliament and by the court's assessment of the gravity of the offence.

As mentioned above the maximum penalty for an offence is fixed by statute as being a fine, or a fine and imprisonment. Some sentences and orders of the court are available only where an *offence* is punishable in the case of an adult with imprisonment (the defendant himself does not need to be liable to imprisonment). A comparison of Tables A and C on pp 154 and 156 will make this apparent. Furthermore some sentences are only available to offenders of a certain age – see p 150.

By a systematic process of noting whether an offence is punishable with imprisonment and the age of the offender, the sentencing options available to the court can be progressively narrowed.

Criminal Justice Act 1991. This further categorises sentences and orders into four broad divisions: discharges (instead of sentencing), financial, community and custodial. In addition there are orders providing for the medical treatment of mentally disturbed offenders.

Discharges (absolute/conditional). These are available to all offenders and for all offences where the court is satisfied that having regard to the circumstances of the offence and the offenders it is inexpedient to inflict punishment. See p 203.

Financial penalties. These include fines (p 209), compensation (p 183) and deprivation of property (p 218) and are available to all offenders and for all offences.

Community orders (see p 153). These are:

probation order (p 232);
community service order (p 179);
combination order (p 175);
curfew order (p 192);
supervision order (juveniles only) (p 242);
attendance centre (p 171).

The court may only impose a community sentence which consists of one or more community orders (except that a probation order and community service order may only be combined in the form of a combination order) where it considers the offence, or a combination of the offence and other 'associated offences' to be 'serious enough' to warrant such a sentence. The fact that an offence is 'serious enough' does not mean that the court must pass a community sentence, only that it may do so.

Custodial sentences (see p 151). The custodial sentences available to the magistrates are imprisonment (p 225) and for offenders under 21, detention in a young offender institution (p 198) and secure training orders for offenders aged 12–14 inclusive.† They are only available where statute defines an offence as being punishable with imprisonment.

A custodial sentence may generally only be imposed where the offence or a combination of the offence and 'associated offences' is 'so serious' that only such a sentence can be justified for it. This means an offence which would make right thinking members of the public, knowing all the facts, feel that justice had not been done by the passing of any sentence other than a custodial one (*R v Bradbourne* (1985)). However, although this criterion may be satisfied the court may nevertheless, in the case of a mentally ill defendant, make a hospital or guardianship order.

Exceptionally a custodial sentence may be imposed in two further situations: where the offence is a violent or sexual offence, and only such a sentence would be adequate to protect the public from serious harm by him, or where the offender has refused to consent to a community sentence.

9 Consideration of sentences

When the court has ascertained the range of sentences appropriate for the seriousness of the offence, it must then proceed to select the particular sentence appropriate for the case. In this task it will be assisted by its appreciation of the seriousness of the offence but also by mitigation personal to the offender, any pre-sentence report and the court's objective in sentencing.

Mitigation. Nothing shall prevent a court from mitigating an offender's sentence by taking into account any such matters as, in the opinion of the court, are relevant in mitigation of sentence. Mitigating factors which have commonly been considered by courts include the following.

1 The youth of the offender. This may operate as mitigation and will usually indicate a lower level of sentence (eg a smaller fine or shorter period of custody) than would be appropriate otherwise. The mitigating effect of youth, however, may be cancelled out by other factors, such as a record of previous convictions which is serious having regard to the offender's age, or which shows a proclivity for crime beyond what one would expect for his age.

2 Older offenders who have not previously offended would receive credit for a previous blameless life especially when receiving a more serious penalty such as a community sentence or custody.

3 Effect of previous convictions. Previous convictions may be taken into account and make an offence more serious. Within the range of sentences appropriate to the seriousness of the offence good character is almost always strong mitigiation and the worse an offender's previous record is, the less 'discount' he can expect for good character. Occasionally, the record of previous convictions may show a significant gap since the last conviction and might be taken as evidence of a genuine effort to keep out of trouble. The record may also show that the present offence is out of character, for example, when a man with a long record of petty theft appears on a charge of indecent assault.

4 Plea of guilty. Remorse or contrition should usually mitigate the sentence particularly when there is real evidence of it. A ready admission of guilt, a willingness to assist the police, and voluntary efforts to make compensation can all be interpreted as evidence of contrition. Particularly in cases involving sexual offences a plea of guilty will spare witnesses, especially young persons, from the ordeal of giving evidence even though the law now provides more sympathetic means for the reception of such evidence. Where the court does reduce the sentence because of the circumstances and stage at which the guilty plea is entered it must state in open court that it has done so.

5 Loss of employment etc. An offender must generally be taken to have foreseen the normal consequences of conviction and so factors such as distress to his family, loss of job, pension, good character, etc will usually have little mitigating value. Where consequences follow which could not have been reasonably foreseen, for example, where the offence was unconnected with the offender's employment but he nevertheless finds himself dismissed, or where the offence was committed on the spur of the moment under provocation with no opportunity to consider the consequences, some allowance may be made if those consequences turn out to be disastrous. The person who is especially vulnerable must be expected to take special care. So, for example, the person whose employment depends upon his having a driving licence must be expected to take particular care not to commit endorseable offences. People such as doctors, nurses and solicitors, from whom a high ethical standard is expected, must expect the consequences of conviction for an offence which amounts to a breach of those standards and cannot claim professional disciplinary action in mitigation.

Unrepresented defendant. The court has a duty itself to seek out mitigating factors before finally arriving at a sentence. It should be especially careful not to assume that there are none in the case of the inarticulate unrepresented defendant.

10 The totality of sentencing

Sentencing objectives must now be understood in the light of the provisions of the Criminal Justice Act 1991. It has already been seen that the choice of available sentences is limited by the seriousness of the offence(s). In some cases where the offence(s) is(are) 'so serious', a custodial sentence is the only option. For community sentences the offences must be 'serious enough'. There is accordingly a link between the sentences for an offence and its seriousness. The general principle is that the term of a custodial sentence, the restriction of liberty imposed by a community sentence or the amount of a fine must be commensurate with the offence or associated offences, ie all the offences for which the defendant is being sentenced. This is referred to as the 'totality' principle of sentencing. An important consequence of that is that the sentence may not, with the exception of custodial sentences for violent or sexual offences, exceed that which is justified by the offence(s).

Protection of the public. Exceptionally the court may impose a sentence of custody where the offence is a violent or sexual offence and only such a sentence would be adequate to protect the public from serious harm by the offender. The sentence may be for such longer term than is commensurate with the seriousness of the offence (not exceeding the maximum) as is necessary to protect the public from serious harm. Such instances are likely to be rare in magistrates' courts.

11 Choice of sentence

The deliberations of the court will have brought into focus more than one form of sentence. For example, it may be that the offence is 'serious enough' to warrant a community sentence. The pre-sentence report may have considered a range of community orders. The probation officer will have considered the seriousness of the offence and have proposed a sentence which is commensurate with the seriousness of the offence and takes into account the circumstances of the offender. The court will need to be clear that the sentence adequately reflects the seriousness of the offence while (in the case of a community penalty) also being the most suitable for the offender. It does not mean that if an offence is serious enough to warrant a community sentence, that is the only sentence which may be imposed. If there is mitigation which allows the court to impose a fine then the fine must reflect the seriousness of the offence and the financial circumstances of the offender.

The advice of the clerk will be essential to ensure that all the statutory criteria which must be satisfied before sentence can be passed and the correct ancillary orders made.

The good chairman will have noted during the hearing such matters as applications for costs, or forfeiture of drugs, etc and will have noted also the position with regard to a possible contribution towards legal aid costs. Liability for endorsement and disqualification will also have occupied attention and after the substantive sentence has been agreed by (at least) a majority of the justices, the chairman will deal with each of these matters in turn. Save in the simplest cases, the chairman will make a written note of the total decision so that no error or omission is made.

12 Statement accompanying the sentence

For many years magistrates have been advised not to give reasons for their decisions when they sentence defendants, 'your decision may be right, but your reasons for it may be wrong' was the oft-quoted dictum. Opinion has changed and the effect – not to say the benefit – of a sound sentencing decision can sometimes be lost because the defendant does not understand the reasoning behind it, or because the public do not.

When a particular sentence might be described as 'normal' for the kind of offence and offender – when it is the sort of sentence the defendant probably expected to receive – there will seldom be justification for garnishing it with reasons. However, when the court imposes a sentence which might be unexpected the reasons for this departure from normal sentencing habits might be explained. Likewise when different types of sentence are imposed on co-accused whose circumstances may appear to be similar. The needs of the public as well as those of the defendant and any victim of his offence should be borne in mind. If the court decides that the chairman should give reasons for its decision, the clerk should be consulted and the chairman might care to make some notes to assist him when he speaks from the Bench.

In the following circumstances the law requires reasons to be given and before giving them the chairman should consult the clerk:

1 when sentencing an offender to imprisonment or detention in a young offender institution (except where he has refused to consent to a community sentence);
2 when not requiring the subject of a suspended sentence to serve that sentence after committing a further offence;
3 when declining to endorse or disqualify for special reasons;
4 when not disqualifying for the minimum period where 12 penalty points have accumulated;
5 when deferring sentence an indication should be given to the offender as to what is expected of him during the period of deferment, ie the reason for the deferment;
6 in the youth court the court should indicate in advance what it has in mind to order;
7 when refusing bail or in certain circumstances granting bail for murder, manslaughter or rape;
8 when deciding not to award compensation when otherwise empowered to do so;
9 when refusing to grant a justices' licence it is good practice for the licensing committee to give its reasons.

Very rarely indeed will it be advisable to deliver a lecture or homily or offer any other words of worldly wisdom to a defendant who is being sentenced. Research has shown that most prisoners could not remember even a short time after sentence not so much what the judge had said but whether he said anything at all.

13 Pronouncement of sentence

The chairman should announce the sentence(s) in a way which leaves no one in court in any doubt as to the court's decision. In the following pages each possible sentence is considered and a form of words is provided as a guide to the way in which the sentence may be announced. It is not suggested that the chairman should read the sentence from this book but that a glance at the wording suggested here will assist in ensuring that all the necessary legal points have been covered. Where an offender is to be sentenced for more than one offence it is advised that each sentence is related to each offence by description. It is bad practice to sentence in such terms as, 'For the first offence you will be fined £50. For the second offence you will be fined £100 and your licence endorsed. For the third offence etc.' Bear in mind that the offender has no idea of the order in which offences appear on the list and therefore has no way of relating the penalties with the offences if they are announced in this fashion. The better practice is exemplified as follows: 'For the burglary and theft at Jacksons, the butchers, you will go to prison for 20 days; for using the credit card to obtain a camera from Browns, you will go to prison for 15 days which will be in addition to the first sentence, which means you will go to prison for a total of 35 days.' Whenever there are several sentences to be announced, the chairman should totalise the effect of them, that is, the total amount of a monetary penalty, the total period of imprisonment or of disqualification should be stated. Words such as *concurrent* or *consecutive* need not be used if other words are used which make it clear what the total effect of the sentence is, as in the example above.

When offences have been taken into consideration in arriving at a sentence that fact should be stated as a preamble to the sentence.

Where relevant the chairman should announce that the sentence has been reduced by virtue of the defendant's guilty plea.

Duplicity of charges

Sometimes a defendant faces more than one charge stemming from the same circumstances and while this is generally unobjectionable there are occasions when the court feels that the prosecution is having two bites at the cherry. Some courts impose the appropriate penalty on one charge and mark the other 'No separate penalty'. Another practice is to decide the appropriate penalty and divide it between the two offences but this may result in penalties which appear inadequately low.

Power to review decisions

It occasionally happens that information reaches a court after a case is disposed of which, if it had been known earlier, might have affected the court's decision. Sometimes, for example, it is simply the realisation by a clerk that one of his staff failed to advise the justices that they had no power to make a particular decision. Or it may be that for some compelling reason, where the defendant was convicted after a not guilty plea, the verdict should be reconsidered (eg after a conviction for driving without insurance, a valid insurance certificate is discovered). The test as to whether a court should reopen a case is whether it would be in the interests of justice to do so.

The court has power to vary or rescind a sentence or order and may substitute some other sentence or order. If, however, the decision has already been subject to an appeal to a higher court, the power to reopen no longer applies.

The provisions may operate against a defendant, for example where the court has omitted to impose penalty points or an endorsable road traffic offence. Note, however, the power does not extend to overturing an aquittal (*R v Gravesend JJ, ex p Dexter* (1977)).

When the court alters a sentence or order under this procedure, and substitutes another, that other will take effect from the date of the first sentence or order, unless the court otherwise directs.

Attendance centre

(Criminal Justice Act 1982, ss 16–19)

Limitations

Offence must be punishable with imprisonment (even though the individual offender may not be).

Age limits – 10–under 21 years.

Maximum period – 12 hours unless the court thinks that would be inadequate in which event the maximum periods are:

offender under 16: 24 hours
offender aged 16–under 21: 36 hours

Note: A further order may be made during the currency of a previous one, in which case the period of the later order may be determined as above without regard to the unexpired part of the previous order.

Minimum period – If defendant is under 14 the normal minimum of 12 hours does not apply if the court is of opinion that 12 hours would be excessive. If the defendant is 14 or older, the minimum period is 12 hours.

Availability. Court must have been notified of the availability of a centre for persons of the offender's age and sex.

Regard must be paid to the accessibility of the centre to the offender.

Juveniles. A magistrates' court may not make this order but must remit him to a youth court.

Community sentences. Note the restrictions on imposing a community sentence, see p 151.

Ancillary orders

Compensation, p 183
Costs, p 188
Disqualification, p 260
Endorsement, p 260
Deprivation of property and forfeiture, p 218
Legal aid contribution order, p 449
Restitution, p 238

How to announce

We shall order you to attend the attendance centre at for a total of hours starting on . You will be given a copy of the order which will show the date and time of your first attendance. After that you will attend as directed by the officer in charge. You will make up the period of hours by attending on Saturday afternoons (or as the case may be) **for two** (or three, as the case may be) **hours at a time. If you arrive late the officer in charge may not count that day's attendance. If you fail to attend without a very good excuse, or if you fail to carry out the officer's instructions properly, he will bring you back here and we shall deal with you. Do you understand?**

General considerations

The aims of the attendance centre have been described by the Home Office as follows:

(a) to vindicate the law by imposing loss of leisure, a punishment that is generally understood by children;
(b) to bring the offender for a period under the influence of representatives of the authority of the state; and
(c) to teach him the constructive use of leisure and to guide him, on leaving, towards organisations or activities where he may use what he has learned. Centres usually require attendance for two-hour (juveniles) or three-hour (young offenders) periods on alternate Saturday afternoons. Only one period of attendance may be required in any one day. The court must take into account the availability of suitable transport and the journey time from home to the centre. A distance of 10 miles or a journey time of 45 minutes is roughly the limit for boys up to 14, but for boys of that age or above, 15 miles or a 90 minutes journey would be the limit.

The court must announce for how many hours the defendant must attend. The court should also tell the defendant the date, time and place of the first attendance.

Binding over

Limitations

None.

Age limits – None. However, a refusal to enter a recognizance (see below) will result in imprisonment and as those under 21 may not be imprisoned the court would be powerless to enforce an order to enter a recognizance.

Maximum period – None, but generally no more than one year or two years at the most.

Minimum period – None.

Ancillary orders

Costs, p 188.

How to announce

We are going to order you to enter a recognizance – that is a binding promise – that you will be of good behaviour and keep the peace for the next (period)**. The amount of that recognizance will be** (amount) **and that means that if you repeat the kind of behaviour we have heard about today, or commit any breach of the peace during the next** (period) **we will order you to pay that amount. Do you understand? Do you agree to making that promise and to guaranteeing to pay the** (amount) **if you break that promise?**

General considerations

One or more sureties may also be required if the court thinks fit. This order is commonly and conveniently referred to as a bind over order but this tends to disguise its real form. The court orders the defendant to enter a recognizance in terms chosen by the court as to the duration and amount. If the defendant so agrees, he is said to be bound over to keep the peace. If he refuses to enter the recognizance the only course left to the court is to send him to prison from which he will be released after a term fixed by the court of up to six months or when he enters the recognizance, whichever is the sooner. Great care should therefore be exercised before making such an order especially if there is any possibility of refusal to comply with it.

Before a court has any power to order a person to enter a recognizance to keep the peace, it must have grounds for believing that there is a possibility of a future breach of the peace.

Sometimes the court is asked to make this order by an applicant who has taken out a summons for that purpose. In addition to this, the court may on its own initiative consider the need to make the order when dealing with an offender. Moreover, a witness or complainant may also be ordered to enter a recognizance. Whenever the court takes the initiative it should explain to the person concerned what it has in mind to do and offer an opportunity to address the court before it is decided whether to make the order or not.

The procedure for binding over a complainant or witness must be followed punctiliously, and if this is in contemplation, the advice of the clerk should be followed.

There is no power generally to impose any conditions, but an order may be made in terms 'to keep the peace towards all Her Majesty's subjects, and especially towards A.B'. Also it appears that there may be a condition not to possess, carry or use firearms (FA 1968, s 21(3)).

Breach of the order will be dealt with by forfeiting the recognizance, or any part of it. The defendant may be given time to pay and in default, after a means enquiry, he may be committed to prison, as if he owed a fine.

Binding over a parent

Either a magistrates' court or a youth court may require the parent of a young person (or an 18 year old who was 17 when the proceedings commenced) who has been found guilty of an offence to enter a recognizance to take proper care of him and to exercise proper control over him. The court must exercise these powers where the juvenile has not attained 16 years if it is satisfied, having regard to the circumstances of the case, that it would be desirable in the interests of preventing the juvenile committing further offences. If the court does not exercise the powers it must say so and give its reasons in open court. The court's *duty* to bind over the parent is replaced by a *power* where the juvenile has attained 16 years. In such a case the maximum amount of the recognizance is £1000 and the maximum period is 3 years or until a young person attains 18, whichever is the shorter.

The parent must consent to the order, an unreasonable refusal is punishable by a fine of up to £1000. The parents may appeal to the crown court against the bind over.

Combination order

Although a community sentence (see p 153) may be composed of one or more community orders, the Criminal Justice Act 1991 only permits the combining of probation and community service in the form of a 'combination order'. This places a limit on the court's powers in that the period of supervision is restricted to a minimum period of one year and a maximum of 3 years and the number of hours of community service to a range of 40 to 100 hours in aggregate. Subject to these limitations the two elements of the order are treated as if they were a probation order and a community service order respectively.

How to announce

We propose to make what is known as a Combination Order.

This means you will be under the supervision of a probation officer for a period of . . . and we hope you will accept this advice and regard him as a friend. You will be required to be of good behaviour and notify the probation officer immediately of any change of your address (or employment), and comply with his instructions.

Also in your spare time for a total of (between 40–100 hrs) during the next year you must undertake unpaid work for the benefit of the local community. You will be required to perform such work at such times as the officer instructs you.

If during the period of this order you fail to comply with any of the requirements I have mentioned you will be liable to be brought back to the court and dealt with for the breach of the order or the order may be revoked and you can be dealt with again for the offence(s) for which we are dealing with you today.

You or the officer may at any time ask for the court to review the order and if the court thinks fit may revoke the order and deal with you for the offence(s).

Do you understand all I have said about the order?

Committal to crown court for sentence

(Magistrates' Courts Act 1980, s 38, s 38A)

(**Note** – There are a few circumstances in which a person may be committed to the crown court which are mentioned at the end of this section. The following notes are intended to refer to committal for sentence after conviction for an either way or related offence.)

Limitations

A magistrates' court when dealing with an either way offence (excluding criminal damage where the value makes the offence triable only by magistrates) to commit on bail or in custody an offender aged at least 18 to be sentenced by the judge with all the powers available to the crown court.

The court must be satisfied that the offence (or combination of the offence and any associated offences of which he is convicted) was so serious that the magistrates' powers of sentence are inadequate. The power under s 38A can be used to commit an offence or offences to the Crown Court which are related to other offences which are to be dealt with in the Crown Court for trial.The court may use this power to commit a company for sentence (although there will be no question of bail or custody).

Alternatively, the court may use the same powers in the case of an offender who has committed an offence of violence or a sexual offence, where the court considers it is necessary that a sentence longer than it has power to impose is necessary to protect the public from serious harm by him.

Ancillary orders

Disqualification pending sentence, but this would be unusual since committal for sentence is almost always in custody. It may be, however, that the reason for the committal is that the offence calls for a larger fine than the magistrates have power to impose.

How to announce

We feel that our powers to deal with you are not adequate. You will be committed in custody (or bail) **under the provisions of section 38 of the Magistrates' Courts Act 1980 to be sentenced at the** (name) **crown court.**

General considerations

The power to commit for sentence is used where a custodial sentence is likely to be imposed which would exceed the maximum available to the magistrates' court. The maximum period of custody which a magistrates' court may impose for an offence triable either way is six months. If an offender is convicted of more than one such offence, the maximum custodial sentence is 12 months. Magistrates may acquaint themselves with the sentences imposed in their local crown court either by sitting there, or through the liaison judge.

The Bail Act does not apply and although there is power to commit for sentence on bail the Divisional Court has said that committal in custody is usually appropriate (*R v Coe* (1969)).

An offender committed for sentence under the procedure described here may be dealt with by the crown court in any manner as if he had been convicted on indictment at the crown court.

The clerk should always be consulted if a committal to the crown court is contemplated.

An offender committed for sentence under the procedure described here may also be committed to be dealt with in respect of another offence of which he has been convicted by the committing court and which that court could have dealt with (Criminal Justice Act 1967, s 56). Section 38A of the Magistrates Courts Act 1980 is used to commit offences where a guilty plea has been indicated but those offences are related to matters which are to be dealt with at Crown Court for trial.

Committal for sentence

(Magistrates' Courts Act 1980, s 37)

A committal for sentence under s 38 applies only to a defendant aged 18 or older convicted of an either way offence.

Where a defendant aged 15 and under 18 years is convicted of an offence punishable on conviction on indictment with a term of imprisonment exceeding six months and the court considers he should be sentenced to a greater term of detention than it has power to impose, it may commit him to the crown court for sentence.

The following points should be noted:

(a) It is a power analogous to that of committal for sentence under s 38 and many of the same considerations apply but note:
(b) Juveniles are usually (except for homicide) tried summarily even if the offence in the case of an adult is triable purely on indictment therefore the section applies to either way and purely indictable offences.
(c) Although the accused may be convicted before an adult magistrates' court, the power to commit for sentence may only be exercised by the youth court to which he has been remitted.

(d) The accused may be committed on bail or in custody. If the remand is in custody he will be detained in a prison or remand centre if one is available.
(e) The power to commit for sentence is useful as the maximum sentence of detention in a young offender institution which can be imposed by the crown court on 15, 16 and 17 year old defendants is 24 months. Where the youth court are dealing with two either way or purely indictable offences, they may impose a sentence of 12 months in aggregate if appropriate.

Committals for sentence under other provisions

Other circumstances in which an offender may be committed to the crown court to be dealt with:

– where the offender has failed to surrender to bail (Bail Act 1976, s 6);
– where the offender is in breach of an order or sentence of the crown court, eg probation, suspended sentence (Criminal Justice Act 1991, Sch 2 and Powers of Criminal Courts Act 1973, s 24);
– where a prisoner subject to early release commits an imprisonable offence during the original period of a custodial sentence and is liable to be returned to prison to serve more than six months (Criminal Justice Act 1991, s 40);
– where the offender has been convicted of an offence under the Vagrancy Act which renders him liable to be sentenced as an incorrigible rogue (Vagrancy Act 1824, s 5).

Community service order

(Powers of Criminal Courts Act 1973, ss 14–17)

Limitations

Offender must have been convicted of an offence which is punishable with imprisonment (even if the offender is not personally liable to imprisonment).

Effect of the order must be explained to the offender. He must keep in touch with the relevant officer in accordance with instructions he may be given and must also notify any change of address to the officer in charge of him. He must perform the allotted work in accordance with the instructions he receives.

Court must be satisfied after considering a pre-sentence report by a probation officer (or social worker), that the offender is a suitable person to perform unpaid work under a community service order.

Age limits – Offender must be 16 or over.

Maximum period – 240 hours.

Minimum period – 40 hours. The hours of work specified must normally be completed within 12 months.

Community sentence. For the restrictions on imposing a community sentence see p 153.

Ancillary orders

Compensation, p 183
Costs, p 188
Disqualification, p 260
Endorsement, p 260
Deprivation of property and forfeiture, p 218
Legal aid contribution order, p 449
Restitution, p 238

How to announce

We propose to make what is known as a Community Service Order. This means that for a total of (between 40 and 240) hours during the next year you must undertake unpaid work for the benefit of the local community. For this period you will be under the supervision of a probation officer or an officer involved with a particular scheme.

Under the terms of this order you must keep in touch with the officer and inform him of any change of your address. You will be required to perform such work at such times as the officer instructs you. The work you will be required to do will normally be undertaken during the evenings or at weekends having regard to your normal working hours and your availability for the work.

If during the period of this order you fail to comply with any of the requirements I have mentioned you will be liable to be brought back to the court and dealt with for the breach of the order or the order may be revoked and you can be dealt with again for the offence(s) for which we are dealing with you today. This includes any failure to perform the work you have been instructed to do in a satisfactory manner. You or the officer may at any time ask the court to review the order and if the court thinks fit may then revoke the order and deal with you again for the offence(s).

Do you understand all I have said about this order?

We make a Community Service Order on these terms.

General considerations

The choice of work and the environment in which it is performed is that of the community service officer and not the court. Even if an indication is given to the court of the type of work available for the offender the community service officer is not bound to allocate the offender to that work, or to require him to perform it for the full period of the order.

Community service is a community sentence and is subject to the restriction on imposing community sentences that the offence etc is 'serious enough' to warrant such a sentence. It is a sentence in its own right and is not an 'alternative to imprisonment'. Community service is generally regarded as an onerous punishment which imposes a considerable restriction on the offender's liberty.

In determining the number of hours to be imposed magistrates might consider sentences of community service as 'short' (40–80 hours),'medium' (80–120 hours) and 'long' (120–180 hours), although it must be stressed that these are merely the suggestions of the editor and magistrates should seek the advice of their clerk. Orders of up to 240 hours might indicate a case more appropriate to the crown court.

The permitted number of hours represent, broadly, a minimum of one working week (40 hours) and a maximum of 6 working weeks. The offender, whether in employment or not, is unlikely to be allowed to meet his obligations under the order in quite this way, but is more likely to be required to do several hours work each week. The weekly numbers of hours will depend on the nature of the work to be done and whether the offender is in gainful employment. Every precaution is taken by the community service officer to ensure that the offender is not put to temptation, nor the beneficiaries of the work put at risk when considering whether suitable work is available. Where appropriate the approval of relevant trade unions will have been obtained before any work is included in the scheme so there is little risk that the offender is putting or keeping out of work an honest man by his community service.

Where the offender is convicted of more than one offence, consecutive community service orders may be made provided that the total does not exceed 240 hours.

Where the offender is liable to more than one sentence at the same time, a suspended prison sentence should not be imposed at the same time as a community service order (*R v Starie* (1979)).

The Court of Appeal has approved the use of community service for some quite serious offences, eg burglary, where the trial judge imposed custodial sentences. It has done so, however, only when there has been real evidence of remorse and circumstances indicating a significant hope that the offender will not offend again, such as a marriage or similar relationship which is proving to be supportive.

When varying a custodial sentence to one of community service, the Court of Appeal has frequently reduced the number of hours to reflect the period already spent in custody. Therefore it would be right in principle, if magistrates were to make some small reduction when an offender has been in custody on remand.

Breach of requirements of order

An offender who fails without reasonable excuse to comply with the requirements of a community service order, if it was made by a magistrates' court, may be either fined up to £1000 or made subject to further community service up to 60 hours (or a total liability of 240 hours whichever is the less), when the order remains in force, or be dealt with for the original offence. If the order was made by the crown court a magistrates' court may commit him on bail or in custody to the crown court to be dealt with.

Unacceptable and violent behaviour towards a Community Service Officer can amount to a failure, without reasonable excuse, to comply with the requirements of the order (*Caton v CSO* (1995)).

Insofar as a court deals with an offender by substituting a different sentence for the original offence, this would not affect any order for endorsement, disqualification or compensation which may have been made at the same time as the community service order. The court should have information concerning the circumstances of the original offence before substituting a sentence and should take account also of the extent to which the offender has complied with the community service order and compensation order if there was one. However, it would not be necessary for the court sentencing for the original offence for which the community service order was made to have a fresh pre-sentence report (*R v Meredith* (1993)).

An offender who has wilfully and persistently fails to comply with the requirements of the order may be subject to a revocation of the order and the court may then substitute a custodial sentence (see p 151).

An alleged breach may be dealt with by the magistrates notwithstanding that the defendant has lodged a notice of appeal, if it is right to do so in all the circumstances (*Greater Manchester Probation v Bert* (1996)).

Compensation order

(Powers of Criminal Courts Act 1973, ss 35–38)

Compensation order. Either as a sentence in its own right or in addition to another sentence, the court may order the defendant to pay compensation to a person who has suffered as a consequence of the defendant's crime. Compensation orders are intended to be used in simple, straightforward cases where no great amount is at stake. A compensation order can only be made when sentence is being passed and therefore cannot be made when committing for sentence or deferring sentence. The court shall give its reasons, on passing sentence, if it does not make a compensation order where it is empowered to do so. Examples of such reasons will be the defendant's lack of means, or that the loss is difficult to quantify (see below).

For what may compensation be ordered? For any personal injury, loss or damage (or to make payments for funeral expenses or bereavement in respect of a death resulting from any such offence, other than a death due to an accident arising out of the presence of a motor vehicle on a road (ie the only such situation likely to arise in a magistrates' court, death arising from careless driving, is not covered)) resulting from the offence or any offences taken into consideration. Personal injury need not be physical injury, compensation may be ordered for terror or distress caused by the offence (*Bond v Chief Constable of Kent* (1983)).

In the case of an offence under the Theft Act 1968, if the property is recovered but is damaged, a compensation order may be made against the defendant no matter how the damage was caused provided it was caused while the property was out of the owner's possession.

Exceptions

(a) Loss caused to the dependants of a victim who has died (except funeral expenses etc in the circumstances referred to above).

(b) Injury, loss or damage due to an accident arising out of the presence of a motor vehicle on a road (but compensation may be awarded

 (i) for damage caused *to* a motor vehicle stolen or taken without the owner's consent but not damage caused *by* the vehicle, eg to another car on the road; and

 (ii) in cases where the defendant's use of the vehicle was uninsured and no compensation is payable under the Motor Insurers' Bureau scheme (see p 310).

The amounts ordered under (i) and (ii) may include payment to cover loss of a 'no claims' bonus).

Proof of loss. As a result of amendments made to the law in 1982 it was considered that the approach to establishing the amount of the loss was not so strict as it was formerly. However, in 1985 the judges of the Divisional Court reaffirmed that (unless the amount was admitted by the accused at the outset) it was the duty of the prosecution to establish the loss and its amount, and make it clear to the defendant by means of evidence. If, after this, there was any real dispute as to the loss suffered by the victim, a compensation order should not be made and the victim should be left to resort to civil remedies to obtain compensation (*R v Horsham JJ, ex p Richards* (1985)).

Fixing the amount

(a) The amount of the loss should be established after proof or agreement.
(b) Where the loss is not determined the court cannot fix an arbitrary amount at a figure below that which is in dispute. Either the lowest amount admitted should be adopted or no order made at all.
(c) Compensation for personal injury may be ascertained having regard to guidelines issued by the Criminal Injuries Compensation Board (see p 186).
(d) The maximum compensation that may be awarded is £5000 for each offence against each defendant. For the maximum where offences are to be taken into consideration the clerk should be consulted.
(e) Having ascertained what the loss is, and what the maximum amount is that can be ordered, the court must have regard to the defendant's ability to pay. He may be allowed to pay by instalments but generally such instalments should not extend beyond two years (*R v Olliver and Olliver* (1989), a case in the crown court where a large sum was to be paid) although in the magistrates' courts simple straightforward orders will probably be paid within a shorter period. Where the defendant is of limited means and would be unable to pay both compensation and a fine, preference must be given to the award of compensation.
(f) If the defendant cannot afford to pay for the whole amount of the loss, then this lower amount, which he can afford, must be ordered.
(g) The circumstances in which a court may subsequently vary a compensation order are limited. Accordingly, an unrealistically high order for compensation may result in the defendant being committed to prison for default; this is wrong in principle. (See p 185 'appeal and review'.)

Making an order. When deliberating whether to make an order, the court should bear in mind that the wealthy offender should never be allowed to buy his way out of prison by offering compensation. Also the court should be wary of an accused mitigating for a suspended sentence on the basis of extravagant promises to pay compensation.

On the other hand, when a custodial sentence is imposed, compensation should be ordered only if the offender has the means to pay immediately or out of existing resources. He should not have to face the payment of compensation upon his discharge from a custodial sentence unless it is clear that he will then have the means to pay, eg by being able to return to gainful employment immediately.

The court should announce the amount of compensation for each offence and for each defendant. Where there are competing claims for compensation, the court may make an order for one compensatee in preference to another, eg a private individual in preference to a financial institution (*R v Amey* (1983)).

In all cases where a compensation order is contemplated, the clerk should be consulted.

Compensation and deprivation orders. Where a court makes a deprivation order (see p 218) in a case where a person has suffered personal injury, loss or damage but a compensation order for the full loss cannot be made because of the offender's inadequate means, it may direct that the proceeds arising from the disposal of the forfeited goods be paid to the victim to make good the deficiency. The amount to be paid is a sum not exceeding the amount of compensation that the court would have ordered were it not for the offender's lack of means. See also p 187 for confiscation orders.

Appeal and review

The entitlement of the victim is suspended for 21 days to allow the defendant time to appeal if he wishes, or until after the appeal is heard. But the enforcement of the order against the offender is not suspended; the obligation to pay arises immediately. Accordingly, where an appeal is successful, the court will have to repay to the appellant any monies that he has already paid.

At any time before the order has been fully complied with, the court may discharge or reduce the order

(a) if a civil court determines an amount of damage or loss less than that stated in the order; or
(b) if the property or part of it is subsequently recovered; or
(c) where the defendant's means are insufficient to satisfy in full the compensation order and a confiscation order made in the same proceedings; or
(d) where he has suffered a substantial reduction in his means which was unexpected at the time the compensation order was made, and his means seem unlikely to increase for a considerable period.

The permission of the crown court is required where it made the original order, if the magistrates' court contemplates the action at (c) or (d).

Guidelines for compensation for personal injury

Guidelines are contained in Home Office circular 53/1993 for the assistance of magistrates. They were prepared by the Criminal Injuries Compensation Board and reflect the level of damages which would be awarded in the civil courts for the injuries described. The Criminal Injuries Compensation Board has no power to compensate for injuries attracting compensation under £750 and therefore guidelines for some of the more minor injuries commonly encountered in the magistrates' court are reproduced below.

In each example the victim is assumed to be in the age bracket 20–35 years but the age of the victim may materially affect the assessment, cf for example, the psychological effect of an assault on an elderly victim as opposed to a youth. Scarring is particularly problematical and reference should be made to the full circular for this and other injuries not referred to in the list below. Before making an award magistrates must also take into account the defendant's ability to pay any order made.

Type of injury

Less serious injury including:		*Suggested award*
Graze	depending on size	up to £50
Bruise	depending on size	up to £75
Black eye		£100
Cut (without permanent scarring	depending on size and whether stitched	£75–£500
Sprain	depending on loss of mobility	£100–£1000
Loss of a tooth (not a front tooth)	depending on position of tooth and age of victim	£250–£500
Minor injury	causing reasonable absence from work of about 3 weeks	£550–£850
More serious injury		
Loss of a front tooth		£1000
Nasal	undisplaced fracture of the nasal bone (see note)	£750
Nasal	displaced fracture of the bone requiring manipulation under general anaesthetic (see note)	£1000
Nasal	not causing fracture but displaced septum requiring a sub-mucous resection (see note)	£1750

Note Assuming that after the appropriate treatment there is no visible deformity of the nose and no breathing problem. If either of these factors is present, an increased award is appropriate and the amount of the increase will depend on the severity of the remaining problems. It is not uncommon for a fractured nasal bone to be manipulated and for the patient thereafter to have breathing problems which after some months require a sub-mucous resection – in this situation the suggested award would be £2000 assuming full recovery after a second operation.

Confiscation order

(Criminal Justice Act 1988, Part VI)

Confiscation orders are generally applicable in the crown court but a magistrates' court has the power to make such an order in certain limited circumstances. The power to make an order is in *addition* to dealing with the offender in any other way. The effect of a confiscation order is that the defendant is ordered to pay to the court an amount which represents the benefit he has obtained from the offence. The monies paid into the court will usually be paid to the government but where the court has also made a compensation order and it appears that the defendant will not have sufficient means to satisfy both orders in full, proceeds of the confiscation order may be used to 'top up' the compensation order. There are very wide-ranging powers to enforce the order. The defendant may be sent to prison in default of payment but perhaps a more effective sanction will be that orders may be made by the High Court to put a charge on the defendant's property which may be then realised and the proceeds used to satisfy the confiscation order. In order to prevent the defendant disposing of his property so as to defeat the order, there are special provisions for the High Court to make a restraining order preventing the disposition of the defendant's property and the recovery of property dissipated by means of gifts.

Salient points for magistrates to consider include:

(a) the defendant must have been found guilty of certain offences relating to sex establishments, supplying, or possessing for supply, unclassified video material, using unlicensed premises for an exhibition which requires a licence under the Cinemas Act 1985, copyright and trademark offences, and certain offences involving unlicensed entertainments (in particular 'Acid House' parties);
(b) he has benefited from such offences;
(c) the prosecutor has given a written notice to the court that, were it to consider such an order it would, in his opinion, be able to make such. In cases where the confiscation order is low the prosecution will exercise particular care before issuing a notice;
(d) the order should be made *before* proceeding to sentence the defendant for the offence;
(e) account must be taken of the making of a confiscation order before imposing a fine, ordering costs or making a forfeiture order, but not when deciding an appropriate non-financial penalty.

The occasions on which a confiscation order will be contemplated by a magistrates' court will necessarily be rare and the procedure is complex so that the advice of the clerk will be essential.

Costs

The award of costs is the exercise of a judicial discretion and any decision must always be made after taking each case on its merits, hearing each party and taking proper account of the law. As a general rule, the successful party in any proceedings can expect to be reimbursed for the costs he has incurred in conducting the proceedings. In civil proceedings, a successful party can only receive his costs from the other party. In criminal proceedings according to the circumstances of the particular case, it may be possible for costs to be awarded either against the unsuccessful party or from central funds, which are monies provided by Parliament to defray the costs of criminal proceedings.

Criminal proceedings

(Prosecution of Offences Act 1985, ss 16–19)

In a criminal case, the court's duty is firstly to consider what is the appropriate sentence. If that is a fine, the offender's means so far as they are known to the court must be taken into account. It is wrong in principle to reduce a fine in order to accommodate an order for costs. Costs should never be awarded as a disguised penalty and the offender's means should be taken into account as above (*R v Nottingham JJ, ex p Fohmann* (1986)). The costs awarded should bear some relationship to the level of any fine (*R v Jones* (1988)).

Prosecution costs

Central funds. Almost all criminal prosecutions are conducted by the Crown Prosecution Service or a public authority such as the Trading Standards Department of a local authority. The funding for these prosecutions is provided by national or local revenues, and so there is no power to award the costs of the prosecution to these authorities out of central funds, even where the prosecution is successful. This avoids the wasteful practice of transferring monies from one public fund to another.

Private prosecutors. The court may, in a case where an indictable offence is concerned, order the costs of the prosecutor to be paid out of central funds whether the prosecution is successful or not. An indictable offence includes an offence triable either way and also offences of criminal damage where the damage is under £5000 and is therefore triable only summarily.

There is no power to order costs from central funds to a prosecutor for purely summary offences. The costs to be awarded would normally be such amounts as the court considers reasonably sufficient to compensate the prosecutor for any expenses properly incurred by him and can include the costs of compensating a witness for the expense, trouble or loss of time properly incurred in his attendance at court. The amount payable to witnesses in respect of travelling expenses and loss of earnings is fixed by regulations and witnesses' expenses are dealt with in the clerk's office. A witness may be reimbursed even if he did not actually give evidence, if he was properly called to do so. Witnesses may be called, for example, in anticipation of a trial only to find that there is a last minute guilty plea. The cost of investigating offences is not included.

Making an order for the costs of a private prosecutor. The court may fix the amount to be paid to the prosecutor out of central funds at the hearing where the prosecutor is in agreement, or in any other case the amount of the costs can be assessed afterwards by the clerk.

Reducing the amount of the prosecutor's order. Where the court is prepared to order the prosecutor's costs out of central funds but is of the opinion that there are circumstances that make it inappropriate to order the full amount of costs, eg where the defendant is convicted of some offences and acquitted of others, the court can assess what in its opinion would be just and reasonable, and specify that amount.

Ordering the accused to pay the prosecution costs. Where a person has been convicted of an either way or purely summary offence, the court can order the accused to pay to the prosecutor (the Crown Prosecution Service, a public authority or a private prosecutor) such costs as it considers just and reasonable. The amount of the costs is specified by the court at the hearing and cannot be left to be assessed later.

Monetary penalty not exceeding £5.00. Where, on conviction of an offence, the court orders payment of any sum as a fine, penalty, forfeiture or compensation not exceeding £5.00, the court shall not order the accused to pay the prosecution costs unless in the particular circumstances of the case it considers it right to do so.

Juveniles. Where a person under 17 years of age is convicted of an offence before a magistrates' (or youth) court and he is ordered to pay the costs, the amount that is ordered shall not exceed the amount of any fine that is properly imposed on him. This restriction does not apply if his parents are ordered to pay the fine etc (p 216).

Defence costs

Where an accused is acquitted, or where the information is withdrawn, the court may order the defendant's costs to be paid out of central funds. This applies whether the charge is triable purely summarily or is an indictable offence. Apart from exceptional circumstances, a prosecutor cannot be ordered to pay an acquitted defendant's costs. The amount of the order will be such amount as the court considers reasonably sufficient to compensate him for any costs incurred in the proceedings and includes the expense of compensating any witness for the expense, trouble or loss of time properly incurred or incidental to his attendance, in a similar manner to that for prosecution witnesses. A defendant cannot claim any loss of earnings or income foregone by himself personally. He can claim defence *witness expenses* even where convicted.

A legally aided defendant can only claim those costs which cannot be covered by a legal aid order, eg his travelling expenses to court.

Reducing the amount of the defendant's order. An order in favour of a successful defendant, known as a 'defendant's costs order', would normally be made unless there are positive reasons for not making such an order, eg where the defendant's own conduct has brought suspicion on himself and has misled the prosecution into thinking that the case against him is stronger than it is or where there is ample evidence to support a conviction but the defendant is acquitted on a technicality which has no merit (*R v Dengie and Maldon JJ* (1988)). In these circumstances the court may make no order or a reduced order for costs.

Costs unnecessarily or improperly incurred

Where the court is satisfied that one party to criminal proceedings has incurred costs as a result of an unnecessary or improper act or omission, it may order the party responsible to pay the additional costs thereby incurred whatever the final result of the case. This enables the court to mark its displeasure at the unreasonable behaviour of a party, eg where one party has put the other to unnecessary expense by requiring an adjournment when they should have been ready to proceed. Before making such an order both parties should be invited to make representations to the court and the court should determine the sum to be paid.

Costs against legal representatives. The magistrates may disallow or order a legal representative to meet the whole or any part of any costs incurred by a party as a result of any improper, unreasonable or negligent act or omission of the representative or, where the conduct occurred after the incurring of the costs, the court considers it is unreasonable for the party to pay. Such orders are not common and the court must follow a detailed procedure before ordering costs against a legal representative. If such an order is in contemplation, the clerk should give detailed guidance.

Miscellaneous provisions

Medical reports. In criminal proceedings, where the court has required a medical practitioner to make a report to the court orally or in writing, for the purpose inter alia of determining the most suitable method of dealing with the offender, his costs may be ordered to be paid from central funds.

Interpreters. In any criminal proceedings provision is made for the payment of interpreters from central funds.

Proceedings for breach or revocation of probation or community service orders etc. The above provisions apply as if the court were dealing with the offence for which the order was originally made.

Civil proceedings

(Magistrates' Courts Act 1980, s 64)

On hearing a complaint (eg concerning a dangerous dog), the court may order the defendant to pay to the successful complainant such costs as it thinks just and reasonable and, where the complaint is dismissed, the complainant may similarly be ordered to pay the defendant's costs. However, where the complaint is for the revocation, revival, variation or enforcement of an order for the paying of maintenance, a court can order either party to pay the other's costs whatever order is made. In proceedings under the Children Act 1989 the court may at any time during the proceedings order that a party pay the whole or any part of the costs of any other party.

In civil cases, it is not usual to order one party to pay or contribute towards the other's costs if both are legally aided, but there is no reason why an order for costs should not be paid against a party who is not legally aided where the successful party is so aided, so that the legal aid fund will receive the benefit of the order.

Applications. There is no power to award costs where proceedings are begun by way of an application (eg an application under the Police Property Act 1897) except in family proceedings (see above).

Curfew order

The Criminal Justice Act 1991 introduced the 'curfew order' whereby the court may require an offender of or over 16 years of age who has been convicted of an offence to remain at a specified place during specified periods. However, these provisions have not been brought into force.

As this is a 'community sentence' the critéria for imposing such a sentence must be satisfied and the court must obtain and consider information about the place proposed to be specified in the order and as to the attitude of the persons likely to be affected by the offender's enforced presence with them.

The court must explain to him in ordinary language the effects of the order, the consequences of any breach of its requirements and the power to review the order.

The curfew must be for a period of at least 2 hours and not more than 12 hours in any one day and any curfew requirements may only have effect during a period of six months from the making of the order. As far as practicable the curfew should not conflict with the offender's religious beliefs, work or attendance at school.

Where arrangements are available, the court may require the electronic monitoring of the offender's whereabouts during the curfew periods.

However a court shall not make an order unless it has been notified by the Secretaty of State that arrangements for monitoring the offender's whereabouts are available in the area.

**Notification has currently been given to three areas of the country only:*

the City of Manchester;
the County of Berkshire; and
the County of Norfolk.

Deferment of sentence

(Powers of Criminal Courts Act 1973, s 1)

Limitations

The offender must consent.

Deferment may be used only once in respect of any one offence.

The court must be satisfied that it is in the interests of justice to defer sentence, having regard to the nature of the offence and the character and circumstances of the offender.

There are no limitations as to age or the nature of the offence.

Ancillary orders

None, because this is not a final disposal of the case, except that a restitution order may be made.

How to announce

We feel that it is not in the interests of justice that we impose a sentence on you today and we are considering deferring our decision for (state period, and give the reason, or state what is expected from the offender during the period of deferment). **Do you understand? We cannot defer sentence without your consent. Do you consent?** (If answered affirmatively) **Then you must attend court here on** (date) **when we shall consider what sentence to impose after hearing how you have progressed in the meantime.**

(**Note** – The essential ingredients of this announcement are the request for consent and the date when the case will be heard again. Consent must be obtained before the order is formally made and, as with any consent, has no value unless the offender understands exactly to what he is consenting. Accordingly the words above may be varied according to the circumstances and in the light of the general considerations below.)

General considerations

This power of the court might be less confusing if it were referred to as deferment of sentencing. There is no question, contrary to what is sometimes believed, that the court decides upon a sentence but postpones announcing it in case it changes its mind.

Only exceptionally may a custodial sentence be imposed after deferment; it is advised that where an offender is liable to be ordered to serve a suspended sentence it will rarely be appropriate to defer sentencing him for the offence which he has committed during the operational period.

Deferment is appropriate when some event may occur in the near future which, according to whether it occurred or not, would influence the court when imposing a sentence. It may be, for example, that the offender has an uncertain chance of employment upon which voluntary compensation depends. There should always be some reason for deferment which can be stated so that the offender knows what is expected of him and may, as he thinks fit, take steps to improve his situation from a sentencing point of view. Great care should be exercised, however, not to use this power as a threat or a coercion or to give an offender an opportunity to buy his way out of prison by making compensation (especially if he may do so by resorting to further offences).

The concern of a victim of the offence should be borne in mind when considering deferment; one effect of deferment, for example, may be to postpone the day when compensation is ordered.

The maximum period for which sentencing may be deferred is six months. The defendant shall not be remanded. A summons or warrant will be issued if he fails to appear.

Magistrates should never fall into the trap of deferring sentencing because they are unable to make up their minds as to the appropriate sentence. The court will obviously wish to be informed at the end of the period of deferment whether the offender has done what it was hoped he would do, or whether the event has taken place which was the reason for the deferment. In many cases it will be convenient to ask the probation officer to report, but in some cases only the offender or a third party will be able to satisfy the court. It is advised that the court when deferring sentence makes clear arrangements at that time as to how such information is to be provided.

The court might consider that a conditional discharge for six months but imposed immediately would achieve the court's objectives. It is not necessary, but may be desirable, that the same magistrates should impose the sentence as those who deferred sentence. Provided the reasons for deferment are explicitly stated, the clerk will note them and bring them to the attention of the sentencing court.

If the offender commits an offence during the period of deferment, the court convicting him of that offence may deal with the deferred case even though the period of deferment has not expired.

Deportation

> **'... a person who is not a British citizen shall be ... liable to deportation from the United Kingdom if, after he has attained the age of seventeen, he is convicted of an offence for which he is punishable with imprisonment and on his conviction is recommended for deportation by a court ...'**

Immigration Act 1971, s 3(6)

Recommendation. A magistrates' court cannot *order* deportation, but it can make a *recommendation* to the Home Secretary for the deportation of the convicted person.

Not a British citizen. The following categories of citizens cannot be deported:

(a) British citizens;
(b) Commonwealth citizens having a right of abode in the United Kingdom;
(c) Commonwealth citizens not included in (b) and citizens of the Republic of Ireland provided in either case they were such citizens at the time of the coming into force of the Immigration Act 1971 and were ordinarily resident in the United Kingdom and at the time of conviction had been ordinarily resident in the United Kingdom and Islands for the last five years.

The following may be deported:

(d) Commonwealth citizens not included in (b) or (c) above;
(e) aliens;
(f) aliens being citizens of countries which are members of the European Community.

Age of seventeen. A person shall be deemed to have obtained the age of seventeen at the time of his conviction, if on consideration of any available evidence, he appears to have done so to the court.

Convicted. Means found to have committed the offence.

Punishable with imprisonment. This means punishable with imprisonment in the case of a person over 21 years even though the defendant himself may not be liable to imprisonment.

Criteria for making a recommendation

General considerations

The court. In deciding whether to make a recommendation for deportation the court may consider:

(a) Would the offender's continued presence in the United Kingdom be detrimental. In considering this the court might take account of
   (i) the seriousness of the crime, eg a simple offence of shoplifting would not merit such a recommendation;
   (ii) the length of the defendant's criminal record.
(b) The effect of a deportation order on innocent persons such as the offender's family.

The court should not consider:

(c) The consequences to the offender of his being returned to his own country, eg persecution. This is generally a matter for the Home Secretary.
(d) The fact that the offender is in receipt of social security.

Home Secretary's considerations. In considering a recommendation the Home Secretary takes into account:

(a) the nature of the offence;
(b) the length of time he has spent in this country;
(c) the offender's criminal record;
(d) the strength of his connections with this country, his personal history and domestic circumstances (eg if the offender's wife or children are citizens of this country and resident here, it might be a great hardship to them to order deportation of the offender);
(e) any compassionate feature that may be present;
(f) any representation made by the offender.

The Home Secretary will not normally deport an offender sentenced to borstal training (now abolished and replaced by youth custody), or detention, or a first offender unless the offence was very grave or other offences were taken into consideration.

Citizens of EC countries

Before recommending the deportation of a national of a country in the EC the court must have regard to Community laws. Article 48 of the Treaty makes the following relevant provisions;

> '1. Freedom of movement for workers shall be secured within the Community by the end of the transitional period at the latest.
> 2. Such freedom of movement shall entail the abolition of any discrimination based on nationality between workers of the member states as regards employment, remuneration and other conditions of work and employment.
> 3. It shall entail the right, subject to limitations justified on grounds of public policy, public security or public health
> (a) to accept offers of employment actually made,
> (b) to move freely within the territories of member states for this purpose,
> (c) to stay in the member state for the purpose of employment in accordance

with the provisions governing the employment of nationals of that said state laid down by law, regulation or administrative action,

(d) to remain in the territory of a member state after having been employed in that state subject to conditions which shall be embodied in implementing regulations which shall be drawn up by the Commission.

4. The provisions of this Article shall not apply to employment in the public service.'

With regard to the references in paragraph 3 above to public policy or security, a directive has been issued (no. 64/221) which states:

> '(1) Measures taken on grounds of public policy or public security shall be based exclusively on the conduct of the individual concerned.
> (2) Previous criminal convictions shall not themselves constitute grounds for the taking of such measures.'

The European Court of Justice has ruled:

(a) that any action affecting the rights of persons covered by article 48 to enter and reside freely in a member state under the same conditions as nationals of that state constituted a 'measure' for the purposes of the directive quoted above;
(b) that a recommendation for deportation by a court of a member state according to its national law was such an action (ie the 'action' referred to in (a) above);
(c) that the directive must be interpreted to mean that previous convictions are relevant only insofar as the circumstances which gave rise to them are evidence of personal conduct constituting a present threat to the requirements of public policy;
(d) that the justification for restricting free movement provided in article 48 (above) presupposed the existence of a genuine and sufficiently serious threat affecting one of the fundamental interests of society additional to the disturbance of order which any infringement of the law involved.

It should be noted that not all EC nationals come within the ambit of the directive. In practice it covers those who come to the United Kingdom to take or seek work, to set up in business or in a self-employed capacity or to receive services for money, eg medical, educational or business.

Procedure

There should be a full inquiry into the case before a recommendation is made. A person who is likely to be the subject of an order must be given 7 clear days' notice of what may happen to him. The defendant should have legal aid and be represented. Solicitors should be asked to address the court specifically on the possibility of a recommendation for deportation being made.

What should *not* be done is to add a sentence as if by an afterthought at the end of observations about any sentence of imprisonment.

EC national within the scope of article 48

The recommendation can only be based on the grounds of public policy, public security or public health. The offender must be informed of the grounds on which the recommendation is based. A short statement in writing should be given to the offender and also attached to the written recommendation. It should include some indication of the extent to which the current and previous criminal convictions of the defendant have been taken into account and the light which such conviction or convictions threw on the likely nature of the defendant's personal conduct in the future. Of particular importance will be the court's assessment of the gravity of the conduct and the likelihood of reoffending.

EC national to which article 48 does not apply

It is desirable that the same procedure be followed.

Aliens

Similarly reasons, not necessarily in writing, should be given.

The effect of a recommendation. Where the court makes a recommendation and the defendant is not sentenced to imprisonment or is not liable to be detained in any other way he will be detained under the Immigration Act until he is deported. The court may, however, order his release subject to such restrictions as to residence and/or to reporting to the police as it may direct.

Detention for one day at the court or at a police station

(Magistrates' Courts Act 1980, s 135)

Magistrates may order the detention of a defendant

(a) aged 21 or more who has been convicted of an offence punishable with imprisonment; or
(b) aged 18 or more for default in paying a fine

at the court or at a police station for any period until 8.00 p.m. on the day of the hearing; but the offence must be punishable with imprisonment or alternatively the detention must be an alternative to payment of a fine. The magistrates should announce at what time the defendant can be released, taking into account that the defendant should be given the opportunity of returning home that day.

Detention in a young offender institution

(Criminal Justice Act 1982, s 1A)

General

Imprisonment is not available for offenders under the age of 21 years. The main custodial provision for these offenders is detention in a young offender institution. This is subject to the criteria restricting the use of custodial sentences imposed by the Criminal Justice Act 1991.

Limitations

Imprisonable offence. The offence of which the offender is found guilty must be punishable with imprisonment in the case of a person aged 21 or over.

Age of offender. The minimum age for male and female offenders is 15 years. In either case the offender must be under 21 years.

Criteria for imposing a custodial sentence. The court must be of the opinion:

(a) that the offence, or the combination of the offence and any other offence(s) associated with it, was so serious that only such a sentence can be justified for the offence;
(b) where the offence is a violent or sexual offence, that only such a sentence would be adequate to protect the public from serious harm from the offender.

Other circumstances in which custody may be imposed. Nothing in paragraphs (a) and (b) above prevents the court imposing a custodial sentence on an offender who refuses to consent to a community sentence proposed by the court which requires his willingness to comply with a proposed requirement. A court may also impose custody for a wilful and persistent breach of a community order.

Serious offence means the kind of offence which when committed by a young person would make right-thinking members of the public, knowing all the facts, feel that justice had not been done by the passing of any sentence other than a custodial one (*R v Bradbourne* (1985)). The court must take account of all the information about the circumstances of the offence including any aggravating or mitigating factors as are available to it (Criminal Justice Act 1991, s 3).

Associated offence. An offence of which the offender has been convicted in the same proceedings or for which he is sentenced at the same time, or an offence taken into consideration.

Violent offence. An offence which leads, or is intended or likely to lead, to a person's death or to physical injury to a person, and includes an offence which is required to be charged as arson.

Sexual offence such as indecent assault, indecency with children and offences relating to the protection of children. It does not include offences relating to prostitution and brothels. Nor does it include offences such as indecent exposure.

Protection from serious harm. This refers to protecting members of the public from death or serious personal injury, whether physical or psychological, occasioned by further such offences committed by the offender.

Pre-sentence report. Except where the court considers it unnecessary to do so, the court must obtain and consider a pre-sentence report before forming an opinion on:

(a) whether the offence etc was so serious;
(b) (violent or sexual offence) only custody would be adequate to protect the public etc;
(c) the length of term commensurate with the offence;
(d) (violent or sexual offence) the length of term necessary to protect the public etc.

In the case of an offender under 18 years the court may not form the opinion that a pre-sentence report is unnecessary unless a previous report prepared for the court is still available.

Failure to obtain pre-sentence report. Does not invalidate the sentence but the appeal court must obtain and consider such a report if the court below was not justified in forming an opinion that a report was unnecessary.

Mentally disordered offender. Where an offender is or appears to be mentally disordered, ie suffering from a mental disorder within the meaning of the Mental Health Act 1983, the court must additionally obtain and consider a medical report before passing a custodial sentence unless the court considers it unnecessary to do so. The court must take any such information into account and consider the likely effect of any custodial sentence on his condition and any treatment for it. Failure to obtain a medical report does not invalidate any sentence but one must be obtained and considered by an appeal court.

Legal representation. The offender must first be given the opportunity to be legally represented unless he has been refused legal aid for financial reasons. Note that the requirement is not that he should be represented, but that he should have an opportunity to be.

Offenders under 18 years. A magistrates' court (as opposed to a youth court) cannot commit defendants aged 15, 16 or 17 to a young offender institution. Such juveniles must be remitted on bail or in local authority accommodation to a youth court which will usually be the youth court for the area in which they reside.

The youth court is required to explain the general nature and effect of this penalty to the juvenile and his parent if present.

Passing sentence

Maximum length of sentence. 12 months or the maximum term of imprisonment available for the offence, whichever is the lesser term.

Minimum length of sentence

Two months for 15, 16 and 17 year olds, 21 days over 18 years of age, except for detention imposed where an offender has breached a supervision order made on his release.

Consecutive terms. Detention in a young offender institution may be ordered to be consecutive to an existing period of detention or, if more than one period of detention is imposed on the same occasion, one period of detention may be ordered to be consecutive to another, so, however, that the offender will not be liable to a period of more than 12 months in total. If a longer period is ordered the excess period will be treated as remitted.

Length of custodial sentence. Shall be for a term which is commensurate with the seriousness of the offence or the combination of the offence and other offences associated with it, or in the case of a violent or sexual offence for such longer term as is necessary to protect the public from serious harm from the offender.

Committal to crown court. The longest term of detention available to a magistrates' court in respect of an offender for a single indictable or either way offence is 6 months, however a youth court may commit offenders aged 15 and under 18 years to the crown court for sentence under s 37 of the Magistrates' Courts Act 1980 where the crown court may impose 24 months for the one offence, and an adult may be committed for sentence according to the provisions of s 38 (p 176).

Reasons for decisions

It is the duty of the court to state in open court:

(a) that it is of the opinion that either or both of paragraphs (a) and (b) on p 200 apply;
(b) that it is of the opinion that in the case of a violent or sexual offence it is necessary to pass a longer term than is commensurate with the seriousness of the offence to protect the public from serious harm from the offender;
(c) why it is of that opinion

and in all cases to explain to the offender in open court and in ordinary language why it is passing a custodial sentence on him or such longer term.

How to announce

We have decided to pass a sentence of detention in a young offender institution on the defendant and we are of the opinion that:

((a) the offence (or the combination of the offence and other associated offence(s) namely . . .) was so serious that only such a sentence can be justified for the offence; and/or
(b) this is a violent/sexual offence and only such a sentence would be adequate to protect the public from serious harm from him)

because (then explain why either or both of the paragraphs apply). (Violent/ sexual offence) **We are also passing a sentence of detention for a term longer than is commensurate with the seriousness of the offence as this is necessary to protect the public from serious harm from him because** (give reasons).

Accordingly (addressing the defendant) **you will be sent to a young offender institution for** (state period) **and this is because** (explain in ordinary language why he is receiving a custodial sentence and, where applicable, why he is receiving a term longer than is commensurate with the seriousness of the offence).

(**Note** – If there is more than one offence it should be clearly stated what the total period of detention is to be.)

Ancillary orders

Compensation, p 183
Costs, p 188
Disqualification, p 260
Endorsement, p 260
Deprivation of property and forfeiture, p 218
Legal aid contribution order, p 449
Restitution order, p 238

Early release

A juvenile offender subject to a term of detention in a young offender institution for 12 months or less will be automatically released after he has served one half of the term. (For adults see p 231.) In determining the period that has been served, time spent on remand in custody or secure accommodation is to be taken into account. However, additional days may be imposed under the prison rules where the offender has been guilty of disciplinary offences.

Supervision following release. An offender who is released and is under 22 years will be under the supervision of a probation officer or social worker for a period of three months or until he attains the age of 22 years, whichever is the shorter period.

Failure to comply with requirements as to supervision is punishable by custody of up to 30 days or a fine of up to £1000.

Further offences. Where an offender commits an imprisonable offence before he would (but for his release) have served his sentence in full, the court which deals with him for the later offence may return him to custody for the whole or part of the period which begins with the making of the order of return and is equal in length to the period between the date of commission of the new offence and the date of expiry of the original term.

Discharge (absolute or conditional)

(Powers of Criminal Courts Act 1973, s 1A)

Limitations

Absolute – none.
Conditional – minimum period, none,
maximum period, three years.

Special consideration – Before making either of these orders the court must be of opinion, having regard to the circumstances including the nature of the offence and the character of the offender, that it is inexpedient to inflict punishment.

Before making an order for conditional discharge the court must explain to the offender in ordinary language that if he commits another offence during the period of discharge he will be liable to be sentenced for the offence for which the conditional discharge is given. This is the court's duty and only in the most exceptional circumstances may it be delegated to another person, eg the accused's lawyer.

Ancillary orders

Compensation, p 183
Costs, p 188
Disqualification, p 260
Endorsement, p 260
Deprivation of property and forfeiture, p 218
Legal aid contribution order, p 449
Restitution, p 238

How to announce

Absolute discharge – **We have decided to discharge you absolutely. This means we have decided that it is not necessary to punish you.**

Conditional discharge – **We propose to discharge you on condition that you do not commit any other offence during the next month(s). This means that we have decided not to punish you for this offence today. Instead, we shall see if you can keep out of trouble for month(s) and if you can, we shall not punish you at all for this offence. But if you are convicted of**

another offence during that period then the court which deals with you will be told about this offence and may punish you for it. Do you understand?

Legal note

A defendant who is convicted of an offence while subject to a Crown Court conditional discharge may be committed to the Crown Court to be sentenced for the offence for which the conditional discharge was originally ordered, under s 1B(5), Powers of Criminal Courts Act 1973. S/he may also be committed to be dealt with for the new offence, under s 56, Criminal Justice Act 1967 (*R v Penfold* (1995)).

General considerations

It is most important to note that only after the court has decided that it is inexpedient to inflict punishment because of all the circumstances may it make an order for discharge. But magistrates are specifically empowered to make a deprivation order or order for costs and compensation where appropriate: Power of Criminal Courts Act 1973, s 12(4), as amended. Disqualification and endorsement may be ordered where appropriate.

No conditions or requirements may be added to either of these orders.

Period of conditional discharge. This must always commence on the pronouncement of sentence. There is no provision to make this period consecutive to any other period.

Exclusion orders

1 Licensed Premises (Exclusion of Certain Persons) Act 1980

When a person is convicted of an offence (of whatever nature) which was committed on licensed premises and the court which convicts him is satisfied that when he committed the offence he resorted to violence, or offered or threatened violence, the court may make an exclusion order prohibiting him from entering those licensed premises or any other licensed premises which the court may specify in the order. Such an order is made in addition to any sentence imposed, including a discharge. Licensed premises for this purpose are those in respect of which a full justices' on licence is in force but the term does not include off licences, registered clubs nor premises upon which the sale of liquor is authorised by an occasional permission. The court must state the period during which the defendant is to be excluded; the minimum period is 3 months and the maximum is 2 years. Any person who is subject to such an order and is in the specified premises otherwise than with the express consent of the licensee or one of his staff is guilty of an offence punishable with a fine on level 4 and one month's imprisonment. Thus, a person convicted of breach of an exclusion order who is also subject to a suspended sentence (which might be imposed for the offence which gave rise to the exclusion order) will be in jeopardy of having to serve that sentence. Courts would probably want to make this point to the defendant both in fairness to him and also perhaps the better to enforce the order. At the time of convicting a person for breach of an exclusion order the court may also determine whether to revoke the order or vary it by deleting the name of any specified premises.

The licensee or his staff may expel from his premises any person whom he reasonably suspects of having entered in breach of an exclusion order and a constable shall at the request of the licensee or his staff help to expel any person whom the constable reasonably suspects of being present in breach of such an order.

2 Public Order Act 1986, s 30 (football matches)

A court which convicts a person of certain offences may make an order prohibiting him from entering football grounds for the purpose of attending prescribed football matches.

Criteria. (a)(i) The defendant must have been convicted of an offence connected with a football match. This means an offence committed 2 hours before or 1 hour after a prescribed match, while at, entering or leaving the ground, or (ii) is either an offence of disorderly conduct, racial hatred or involves the use or threat of violence to another person or property and is committed on a journey to or from an association football match, or (iii) it is an offence under the Sporting Events (Control of Alcohol etc) Act 1985 (p 127).

(b) The court must be satisfied that the making of such an order in relation to the accused would help to prevent violence or disorder at or in connection with prescribed football matches.

Scope of the order. An exclusion order can only be made *in addition* to a sentence for the offence of which the accused has been convicted. The order may be of any duration specified by the court with a minimum period of 3 months or 3 months plus the unexpired period of any pre-existing exclusion order. For the period of the order a person who enters premises to attend a football match involving a Football League or Premier League team, or which is a European, European Cup Winners or UEFA cup match, in breach of the order commits an offence punishable only by magistrates with a fine of up to level 4 and 1 month imprisonment.

Photographs. On the application of the prosecutor, the court which makes the exclusion order may also make an order requiring a constable to take a photograph of the defendant and require the defendant to go to a specified police station within 7 days of the requirement being made and at a specified time of day.

Application to terminate order. Where a person has been the subject of an exclusion order for at least one year he may apply to the court which made the order to terminate it. The court will take into account the person's character, his conduct since the order was made, the nature of the offence which led to it and any other circumstances of the case. Where the application is refused a fresh application cannot be made for a further six months.

Fines

Limitations

Offences. The court may fine for any criminal offence.

Maximum fine. The power of magistrates' courts (unlike that of the crown court) to impose a fine is entirely controlled by statute. Therefore the maximum fine for the offence may not be exceeded.

The maximum fine for the vast majority of offences which are only triable by magistrates is expressed as being on one of five levels, each level representing a monetary limit. (The maximum for most offences triable either way is expressed as the 'statutory maximum' or 'prescribed sum'.)

Level 1: maximum fine is £200
Level 2: maximum fine is £500
Level 3: maximum fine is £1000
Level 4: maximum fine is £2500
Level 5: maximum fine is £5000

(Either way offences: prescribed sum is £5000.)

This is known as the standard scale of fines and it has been devised as an attempt to rationalise the maximum amounts of fines and to provide a simple means of increasing them in inflationary times.

Juveniles

Offender under 14 (a child). Maximum fine is the amount in the statute creating the offence or £250, whichever is less.

Offender 14 – under 18 (young person). Maximum fine is the amount in the statute creating the offence or £1000, whichever is the less.

Parental responsibility for payment

In the case of a person under 16 the court must order the parent or guardian to pay unless either he cannot be found or the court is satisfied that it would be unreasonable to order the parent to pay having regard to the circumstances of the case. Provided the parent has been given the opportunity to attend court, an order for payment may be made against him in his absence. If he is present, he must be given the opportunity of making representations about whether he should be ordered to pay.

Before exercising its power to make an order that a parent should pay a financial order in respect of an offence committed by a child the court must be satisfied that it is reasonable to do so (*A v DPP* (1996)).

Where the offender is aged 16 or 17, and it would not be unreasonable to do so, the court has a *power* to make the parent responsible for the financial order.

Where a local authority has parental responsibility (p 363) for a child in their care or accommodated by them, the local authority is responsible for payment, unless it has done everything reasonably and properly expected of it to protect the public from the young offender (*D v DPP* (1996)).

Determining the amount of any fine

In accordance with the sentencing principles of the Criminal Justice Act 1991 the court must ensure that any penalty is commensurate with the seriousness of the offence for which it is imposed. The court therefore must assess carefully the gravity of the offence having regard to the circumstances and to any mitigation. The court's assessment of the seriousness of the offence should then be reflected in the fine imposed. However, in fixing the amount of any fine the court must also inquire into the offender's financial circumstances and ability to pay before setting the level of the fine. This requirement to take the offender's financial circumstances into account in setting the amount of a fine also applies to compensation orders and to the financial circumstances of a parent or guardian who is ordered to pay the fine of a young offender. The court has power to make a financial circumstances order after conviction (ie an order requiring the defendant to provide the court with a statement of means within such period specified in the order) and before conviction where an offender has pleaded guilty by post. The court has the power to make such determination as it thinks fit of the financial circumstances of an offender where he has been convicted in his absence,or where the offender (or a parent or guardian who has been ordered to pay the fine of a young offender) has failed to comply with an order to give a statement of financial circumstances,or has in any other way failed to comply with the court's inquiry into his financial circumstances. Where the court has made a determination of the offender's financial circumstances in the absence of sufficient infomation it may, on subsequently inquiring into means, remit the whole or part of the fine, if it is of the opinion as a result of that inquiry that the original fine was too high. In making its determination of the offenders financial circumstances the court may take into consideration income , capital and outgoings and the fine may be increased as well as reduced to reflect the financial circumstances of the offender.

Most courts have a grid system showing both levels of seriousness and levels of disposable income, thus providing a starting point for fines imposition to meet most circumstances.

So, for example, if two offenders have committed the same offence for which they should receive the same punishment and are to be fined, the court will determine the same seriousness for each offender. However, the financial consequences for each may be widely differing because the monetary value of the unit will be assessed according to each offender's financial circumstances.

Announcing the fine and time to pay

We have taken into account the seriousness of this/these offence(s) and your financial circumstances and have decided to inpose a fine of £'X'. Can this be paid now?

Time to pay. When a fine is announced the court should rarely invite an application for time to pay unless it is already well informed about the offender's circumstances.

An immediate committal to prison in default of payment can only be ordered in the four types of cases mentioned below on p 211. In other cases the court must announce (and cause to be entered in the register) the time allowed for payment. This may be a fixed period, eg 14 days, or it may be an order that the defendant pays by instalments.

The court, when imposing a fine, may stipulate a date upon which if any part of the fine remains unpaid the defendant must appear before the court for a means enquiry. Instalments should be fixed at such a rate as will ensure that the fine (and costs, compensation if any) is paid within a reasonable period.

Costs and compensation. Costs against a defendant in criminal cases and compensation are enforceable in the same way as a fine.

Limited companies. In law a company is a person. Therefore a fine imposed against a company can only be enforceable against the company and not against any of its officials. For non-payment of a fine a distress warrant can be issued against the company and its property seized and sold to meet the fine and any costs involved in conducting the sale.

Payment of the fine can sometimes be enforced in the High Court or county court. Consult the clerk. In certain circumstances the clerk may apply to the High Court to have a company wound up under the Insolvency Act 1986.

Partnership firm. The conviction will have been against the partners personally and fines can be enforced against them personally in the usual way.

Searching. The court may order the defendant to be searched and any money found used to pay the fine, compensation and costs. If there is a balance this must be returned to the defendant.

Such money must not be taken if the court is satisfied that the money does not belong to the defendant or if the loss of money would be more injurious to his family than his detention.

Fine supervision order. Instead of the court fixing the time to pay or ordering fixed instalments, it may decide that the defendant is so incompetent or feckless that he will not put aside the money to meet the fine. In such circumstances the court can make a supervision order placing the defendant under the care of some person (often the probation officer) whose duty is not to collect the fine or decide the rate of payments, but to persuade the offender to pay so as to keep out of prison. When making such an order the rate of payment should be fixed by the court.

Imposing a fine and suspended imprisonment. If an offence is punishable both by a fine and imprisonment, a fine and a suspended prison sentence can be imposed.

Fine and immediate imprisonment. This combination is appropriate where the defendant has made a substantial profit from the offence. Generally, however, a fine should be imposed with an immediate custodial sentence only when the defendant has resources from which to pay the fine despite his imprisonment. The situation should be avoided which saddles a discharged prisoner with a fine.

Procedure for enforcing fines

Enforcement of a fine. This should begin the moment it is imposed. The chairman of the court should never invite an application for time to pay. The court should always enquire how much can be paid immediately (if the defendant cannot pay in full) and should consider requiring even a small sum to be paid forthwith. If instalments are allowed they should be within the defendant's means to pay and the defendant should be told precisely the date on which the first instalment is due. It is usually better to fix this by reference to his pay day rather than 7 days from the date of his conviction.

Immediate enforcement

When a fine is imposed the court can use the following methods to enforce immediate payment.

1 Search. The court can order the defendant to be searched for money to meet the fine. See above.

2 Immediate committal to prison. In the circumstances listed below the court may order imprisonment forthwith for a period determined in accordance with the following scale:

An amount not exceeding £200	7 days
An amount exceeding £200 but not exceeding £500	14 days
An amount exceeding £500 but not exceeding £1000	28 days
An amount exceeding £1000 but not exceeding £2500	45 days
An amount exceeding £2500 but not exceeding £5000	3 months
An amount exceeding £ 5000 but not exceeding £10,000	6 months
An amount exceeding £10,000	12 months

It must be borne in mind that these are the maximum periods applicable, the court is not obliged to impose the maximum period in default.

If part payments have been made then the period of imprisonment is calculated by taking the period of imprisonment considered appropriate for the whole sum and reducing that period by the proportion which the part payment bears to the original sum due. For example, if a defendant is fined £600 and over a period pays £400, the maximum period of imprisonment for that balance is one third of 28 days in band 4. Where a defendant is fined at one time for several offences, each fine must be calculated separately and the periods of imprisonment may be made consecutive. However, it is not appropriate to fix consecutive terms of imprisonment in respect of fines imposed for several offences arising out of the same incident. In every case where several fines are outstanding the court must look realistically at the total situation.

This table applies to monetary penalties (ie fines, costs, compensation and legal aid contributions) and not to arrears of maintenance for which the maximum period is 6 weeks. Nor does it apply to the community charge for which the maximum period is 3 months. (It may be convenient to note here that periods of imprisonment for more than one amount of unpaid community charge may not be made consecutive.)

An immediate committal to prison can only be ordered in the following cases:

(a) if the offence is punishable with imprisonment and the defendant appears to the court to have sufficient means to pay immediately; or
(b) if it appears to the court that the defendant is unlikely to remain at an address in the United Kingdom long enough for the fine to be enforced by other methods; or
(c) if the defendant is already serving a prison or detention sentence; or
(d) if the defendant is being sent to prison or detention on the same or another charge.

The court should announce its reasons (that is, (a), (b), (c) or (d) above) for making an immediate committal to prison and these reasons should be entered in the court register and on the committal warrant. Failure to comply may result in a challenge to the decision by judicial review (*R v Oldham JJ, ex p Cawley* (1996)). If the defendant has second thoughts about paying and tenders payment to the court staff, the police or the prison officials he is entitled to be released. If only part of the fine is paid then he is entitled to a proportionate remission of the prison sentence. This applies even if he offers part payment after he has served a part of the prison sentence.

The period of imprisonment for non-payment can be concurrent with or consecutive to another sentence already being served; or if more than one fine is being enforced, the periods of imprisonment for non-payment can be consecutive to each other subject to the overall restrictions on the aggregate length of sentences (see p 228). Consult the clerk.

3 Suspended committal order. The court can order a committal to prison under the scale on p 212 to be **suspended** for a definite period of time during which the defendant has to find the money for the fine or it may suspend the prison sentence whilst he pays instalments at a rate per week or per month decided by the court. Such a suspended committal order can only be ordered if the case falls into one of the categories listed above as (a), (b), (c), or (d). If more than one fine is being enforced in this way, the periods of imprisonment for non-payment can be concurrent with or consecutive to each other subject to the overall restrictions on the aggregate length of sentence (p 228). The defendant may apply subsequently to the court to vary the terms of the postponement. Where the defendant subsequently defaults in payment of the order, the court must give him notice that the warrant of commitment falls to be issued. He then has an opportunity to make representations orally or in writing as to why the warrant should not issue. Consult the clerk.

4 Detention for one day or overnight at a police station. The court can order the defendant to be detained for the remainder of the day within the precincts of the court or police station but must be released at a time which will allow him to get home the same day or at the latest by 8 p.m. The release time should be announced by the court. Similarly, overnight detention authorises the police to arrest the defendant and keep him until 8 a.m. on the morning following his arrest or if he is arrested between midnight and 8 o'clock in the morning, until 8 o'clock in the morning of the day on which he is arrested. The effect of this is to wipe out the fine.

5 Distress warrant. The magistrates can issue a distress warrant which orders the seizure of the defendant's property to meet the unpaid fine. Such an order may be suspended on terms that the defaulter pays as ordered by the court.

6 Supervision order. This means placing the **defendant** under supervision, usually of the probation officer, see p 212.

7 Fixing a means enquiry. When imposing a fine etc the court may fix a date on which the offender must appear in court for a means enquiry if at that time any part of the monetary penalty remains unpaid.

Enforcement as a result of a means enquiry

If the defendant fails to pay the fine within the time allowed by the court the clerk will arrange for the issuing of a summons or warrant to bring the defendant back before the court who will conduct a means enquiry to investigate the defendant's ability to pay the fine and may demand that the defendant produce documentary evidence of his financial resources, eg pay slips, account books, post office savings book, bank statements, etc. The court can order the defendant to produce a statement of means either before the enquiry or during the enquiry by a specified date and failure to produce such a statement is punishable with a fine up to level 3.

Power to remit whole or part of the fine. The magistrates are empowered to remit the whole or part of a fine having regard to any change of circumstances since the defendant's conviction. Arrears of national insurance (see p 109) cannot be remitted. The court may also remit or reduce the fine where the court fixed the fine in the absence of adequate information about the offender's means either because he was convicted in absence or failed to comply with an order to furnish a statement of means and the result was that the original fine was set too high.

For compensation see p 183.

If the fine was imposed by a higher court, magistrates can only remit the whole or part of the fine if the higher court consents.

At a means enquiry magistrates can enforce payment by the following methods:

1 Attachment orders. If the magistrates are satisfied that the defendant is being paid earnings they may make an attachment order directing that the employer make deductions from the defendant's wages and remit them to the court. If the magistrates have this course in mind they should first consult the clerk as he must obtain certain details about the defendant and his employment.

2 Distress warrants. See above.

3 Search. See p 212.

4 Immediate committal to prison. The magistrates can order an immediate committal to prison for a specified period according to the scale set out on p 212. For calculation of the term in default see p 213. Immediate committal to prison can only be ordered if:

(a) the offence for which he has been fined is also punishable with imprisonment **and** the defendant appears to the court to have the means to pay immediately; or
(b) the court is satisfied that the default is due to the offender's wilful refusal or culpable neglect and the court has considered or tried all other methods of enforcement and it appears to the court that they are inappropriate or unsuccessful.

The other methods referred to are distress warrants, application to the High Court or county court for enforcement, supervision, attachment of earnings and, if under 21, attendance centre.

5 Detention for one day or overnight at a police station. See p 214.

6 Suspended committal to prison. The court can order a suspended committal to prison for a period in accordance with the scale on p 213. This imprisonment can then be suspended for a definite period of time during which the defendant must pay the fine or alternatively the court may direct that the defendant shall pay at so much per week or month. Such a suspended committal can only be ordered if the offence for which the defendant was fined is punishable with imprisonment and the defendant appears to have sufficient means to pay; or the court is satisfied that the default is due to the offender's wilful refusal or culpable neglect and the court has considered all the other methods of enforcement and it appears that they are inappropriate or unsuccessful. See above.

The offender may apply to the court to vary the terms of the postponement and where a warrant falls to be issued, see p 214.

7 Supervision order. See p 212.

8 Deduction from benefit. After a means inquiry has been made the court may request the Department of Social Security to make payments towards a fine or compensation direct from the offender's benefit, subject to any right of review or appeal he may have.

9 Transfer to High Court or county court. If the defendant is a holder of shares or has certain kinds of assets, enforcement can sometimes be transferred to the High Court or county court. Consult the clerk.

Defendant already in prison. If a defendant, who has not paid part or the whole of a fine, is serving a sentence of imprisonment or is confined in a detention centre a committal warrant can be issued without any means enquiry taking place. The clerk will give notice to the debtor who may appear or make written representations.

Fines imposed by Central Criminal Court and crown courts

These fines are payable to, and enforceable by, magistrates' courts.

The whole fine or part of it can be remitted only with the consent of the higher court.

Defendants aged 18 to 21

The above provisions can also be employed in respect of defendants in this age group except that an order of detention in default of payment should only be ordered if a supervision order has already been tried or the court is satisfied that a supervision order is either undesirable or impracticable. These considerations must be noted on any committment warrant (*R v Oldham JJ, ex p Cawley* (1996) and *R v Stockport JJ, ex p Conlon* (1997)).

If the court has available to it an **attendance centre** for defaulters to the age of 25, the court can send the defendant for up to 36 hours in all in default of payment.

The clerk should be consulted as to the exact number of hours that the defendant should attend at the attendance centre.

Defendants aged 10 to 17

Maximum fine. Children under 14, £250; young persons, 14 or over, £1000, or, in either case the lesser sum applicable in the case of an adult.

Costs. The costs ordered must not exceed the amount of the fines unless a parent or guardian is ordered to pay.

Parental liability to pay. The child's parent or guardian must be ordered to pay the fine and costs unless he cannot be found or the court considers it would be unreasonable to order him to pay. In the case of a young person the court has a power to order the parent to pay. If the parent or guardian does not pay, enforcement takes place in the adult court as described on p 212.

Enforcement

The power to make a fines supervision order or an attachment of earnings order is available in the case of juveniles. In addition where the court is satisfied that the juvenile has had the money to pay but has refused or neglected to pay it may make an order requiring

(a) the parent to enter a recognizance to ensure that the defaulter pays the fine or balance; or
(b) the court may transfer the debt to the parent in which case further enforcement, if necessary, would be taken as if the fine has been imposed on that parent.

The parent must, according to the statute, consent before an order may be made for him to enter a recognizance. The parent's consent is not required for the responsibility for the fine to be transferred to him provided the court is satisfied in all the circumstances that it is reasonable to make the order.

If an attendance centre is available for persons of the debtor's class or description, he may be ordered to attend, up to the age of 25 years.

The powers mentioned under this heading must be exercised after a means enquiry. An order transferring the debt to the parent may be made in his absence provided he has been given adequate notice of the proceedings; if he is present, he must be given the opportunity of speaking to the court before such an order is made.

Deprivation of property and forfeiture

(Powers of Criminal Courts Act 1973, s 43, as amended)

Any court which has convicted a person of an offence and

(a) is satisfied
  - (i) that any property
  - (ii) which has been lawfully seized from him or was in his possession or under his control at the time when he was apprehended for the offence or when a summons in respect of it was issued
  - (iii) has been used for the purposes of committing, or facilitating the commission of any offence or was intended to be used for that purpose

or

(b) the offence (or an offence taken into consideration) consists of unlawful possession of property in the circumstances of (ii) above

may make an order to deprive him of that property.

Property. Does not include land.

Possession. Usually means physical possession but can include a legal right to possession. If there is any dispute the clerk should be consulted.

Facilitating. This includes the taking of any steps after the offence has been committed to dispose of property which is the subject of the crime or to avoid apprehension or detection. The property need not have been used personally by the defendant provided he intended it be used for criminal purposes, even by another.

The effect of an order. The accused is deprived of his rights in the property which passes into the possession of the police. The provisions of the Police Property Act 1897 (p 121) apply and a person may claim the property provided that he satisfies the court that either

(a) he had not consented to the offender having possession; or
(b) he did not know, and had no reason to suspect, that the property was likely to be used for the purpose of committing an offence.

If no successful claim is made the property will be sold and the proceeds disposed of in the same way as described at p 121.

Sentencing. The court may make an order under this section in respect of the property whether or not it also deals with the offender in respect of the offence in any other way, and may combine the making of the order with an absolute or conditional discharge.

Under previous legislation it was stated that an order depriving a defendant of property should not be made for the purpose of realising assets to pay fines or compensation (*R v Hull JJ, ex p Hartung* (1981)).

In considering whether to make a deprivation order the court shall have regard

(a) to the value of the property; and
(b) to the likely financial and other effects on the offender of the making of the order (together with any other order the court is contemplating).

But where the offence has resulted in a person suffering personal injury, loss or damage and the court has not been able to make a compensation order because of the defendant's lack of means, the proceeds of sale resulting from a deprivation order may be used for compensation.

This order only takes effect after a period of 6 months in order to allow a person to make a claim under the Police Property Act 1897.

Motor vehicles. Where a person has committed an offence under the Road Traffic Act 1988 which is imprisonable, eg driving with excess alcohol or whilst disqualified, the Road Traffic Act 1991 provides that the vehicle concerned is to be regarded as used for the purpose of committing the offence. Accordingly, the offender runs the risk of the court, after considering all relevant factors, depriving him of his vehicle.

Other provisions for forfeiture. Formerly the provisions described here were confined to offences punishable with at least 2 years imprisonment, but now they are available without regard to maximum penalty and so will overlap with some existing forfeiture powers, eg forfeiture of controlled drugs and firearms.

Guardianship order

(Mental Health Act 1983, s 37)

Limitations

Offence must be punishable in the case of an adult with imprisonment, even though the offender may be immune from imprisonment.

Two medical reports must be received indicating that the offender is suffering from one of four specified illnesses.

The minimum age for a guardianship order is 10.

Court must be of opinion (which it will usually form from the contents of the medical reports and a consideration of the circumstances of the offence) that a guardianship order is the most suitable method of dealing with the offender.

Court must also be satisfied that arrangements have been made for a guardian to take care of the patient.

Ancillary orders

Compensation, p 183
Costs, p 188
Disqualification, p 260
Endorsement, p 260
Deprivation of property and forfeiture, p 218
Legal aid contribution order, p 449
Restitution, p 239

Period of order. This is an indeterminate order but the patient's condition is reviewed periodically by the medical authorities.

General considerations

Medical evidence. The evidence can be two written reports by the doctors who made the examination, but the defendant has the right to insist that the doctors be present in court so that he can cross-examine them, and if the written reports only are before the court, then the defendant must be asked if he is agreeable to the court acting on those written reports.

Copies of the doctors' reports must be given to the defendant's advocate. If the defendant is not represented the substance of the reports should be explained to the defendant.

The defendant has the right to call his own medical evidence to rebut all or any part of the two reports.

The court can require the personal appearance of the doctors.

Effect of guardianship order. Once the guardianship order has been made the defendant is in effect handed over as a mental patient to the mental health authorities and the court has no more powers over the defendant and cannot stipulate what happens later. Thus, there can be no restriction order, and the court cannot stipulate the length of the guardianship order. The guardian will be a social worker or person approved by the local authority.

Normally it will lapse after 6 months, but the mental specialists can recommend an extension when it will be extended for a further 6 months. After that the order can be extended for one-year periods or until the mental health authorities consider it safe to grant the defendant a discharge.

As the defendant has now become a patient and not a prisoner his discharge from guardianship can be made on the advice of the mental specialist in charge of his case.

The defendant need not wait for the mental specialist to act, but can apply for his discharge at any time during the first 6 months of the guardianship order or on any occasion when the order is renewed.

The defendant's nearest relative can make application once a year to the Mental Health Review Tribunal for his release.

Hospital order

(Mental Health Act 1983, s 37)

Criteria

(a) defendant must have been convicted of an imprisonable offence, or (in certain circumstances) is proved to have committed an act which would amount to such an offence in the case of a normal person;

(b) court must be satisfied on written or oral evidence of two registered doctors that the defendant suffers from
   (i) mental illness;
   (ii) psychopathic disorder;
   (iii) severe mental impairment; or
   (iv) mental impairment;

(c) the mental disorder is of a nature or degree that makes it appropriate for him to be detained in a hospital;

(d) (pyschopathic disorder or mental impairment) such treatment is likely to alleviate or prevent a deterioration of his condition;

(e) the court is of the opinion having regard to all the circumstances including the nature of the offence and the character and antecedents of the offender and other available methods of dealing with him, that a hospital order is the most suitable means of dealing with him;

(f) justices have no jurisdiction to make a hospital order in respect of a defendant charged with an offence triable only on indictment (*R v Chippenham JJ, ex p Thompson* (1996)).

General considerations

Legal aid should be offered to the defendant if his means justify it, or he should be recommended to consult a solicitor if the court is considering a hospital order.

Medical reports. The court must obtain reports from two doctors, one of whom must be an approved mental specialist, certifying that the defendant is suffering from some form of mental disorder which warrants detention in hospital for mental treatment. The court can, with the consent of the defendant, act on the two written mental reports. The defendant has the right to insist that the doctors attend court so that they can be cross-examined, and he is also entitled to bring his own medical evidence to rebut the reports. The court can also require that the doctors attend in person.

If written reports are used copies must be given to the defendant's advocate.

If the defendant is not represented then the court should explain to the defendant the substance of the reports.

Before announcing that a hospital order is being made the court should ensure that a vacancy in a mental hospital has definitely been arranged; if it has not, consult the clerk. An adjournment may be necessary. Alternatively a hospital order may be possible with the defendant's date of admission deferred for up to 28 days.

Effect of a hospital order. The court does not fix the period that the defendant has to stay in hospital. The date of his release will be decided by the hospital authorities.

Normally the hospital order lapses after 6 months but it can be renewed for a further six months on the recommendation of the mental specialist in charge of the case, and thereafter the order can be renewed for one-yearly periods. The procedure is that the responsible mental specialist examines the patient and sends a report to the mental health authorities, which can be the hospital managers, who may then act on the recommendation to retain or discharge the patient. Thus the patient can be discharged at any time without reference back to the sentencing court.

The defendant, once a mental patient, can apply for his discharge at any time after the first 6 months of the order or whenever it is proposed to extend the order.

The defendant's nearest relative can apply for his discharge once a year to the Mental Health Review Tribunal.

Including a restriction clause in a hospital order (s 41). If the defendant is 14 or more and was convicted (as opposed to having 'done the act'), and the magistrates consider a court restriction should be imposed on his release, he can be committed to the crown court.

The crown court can make a hospital order, and include in it a restriction upon the date of release either for a specified period of time or indefinitely.

The magistrates can commit the defendant to prison pending his appearance at the crown court, or if satisfied that a vacancy is available at a mental hospital, can order him to be detained there pending his appearance at the crown court.

If the crown court includes a restriction clause the defendant cannot be discharged by the mental specialist or allowed out of the specified hospital without the consent of the Home Secretary.

The Home Secretary may at any time refer the case to a Mental Health Review Tribunal for their advice, but does not have to accept the advice if he considers that discharge of the patient is not in the public interest.

If the Home Secretary does decide to effect the release of the patient from the mental hospital, he has powers to impose conditions for the discharge such as the place of residence, a scheme of supervision and the liability to recall if a lapse occurs.

Remand for report on accused's mental condition (s 35). Where a doctor satisfies the court that there is reason to suspect that the accused suffers from one of several mental disorders and

(a) the accused has been convicted of an offence punishable on summary conviction with imprisonment or 'did the act' or has consented to this course of action; and
(b) it is otherwise impracticable to obtain medical reports; and
(c) arrangements have been made for his reception into a hospital,

the court may remand the accused in a hospital for up to 28 days. There may be further such remands for a total period of up to 12 weeks.

Interim hospital order (s 38). Where:

(a) an accused has been convicted of an offence punishable with imprisonment; and
(b) the court is satisfied on the evidence (written or oral) of two doctors that he is suffering from one of several mental disorders and it may be appropriate to make a hospital order; and
(c) arrangements have been made for his reception into a hospital,

the court may make an interim hospital order for up to 12 weeks initially before finally passing sentence. An interim hospital order may be further renewed for up to 28 days at a time subject to a total period of 6 months before sentence is imposed.

Imprisonment

Limitations

(a) Imprisonable offence.

(b) Presence of offender. Imprisonment may only be imposed in the presence of the defendant.

(c) Age limit. Defendant must be 21 or over. For offenders under 21 the appropriate custodial sentence would be detention in a young offender institution.

Criteria for imposing a custodial sentence. The court must be of the opinion:

(a) that the offence, or the combination of the offence and other offence(s) associated with it was so serious that only such a sentence can be justified for the offence; or
(b) where the offence is a violent or sexual offence, that only such a sentence would be adequate to protect the public from serious harm from the offender.

Other circumstances in which custody may be imposed. Nothing in paragraphs (a) and (b) above prevents the court imposing a custodial sentence on an offender who refuses to consent to a community sentence proposed by the court which requires his consent. A court may also impose custody for a wilful and persistent breach of a community order.

Serious offence means the kind of offence which when committed by a young person would make right-thinking members of the public knowing all the facts feel that justice had not been done by the passing of any sentence other than a custodial one (*R v Bradbourne* (1985)). The court must take account of all the information about the circumstances of the offence including any aggravating or mitigating factors as is available to it (Criminal Justice Act 1991, s 3).

Associated offence. An offence of which the offender has been convicted in the same proceedings or for which he is sentenced at the same time, or an offence taken into consideration.

Violent offence. An offence which leads, or is intended or likely to lead, to a person's death or to physical injury to a person, and includes an offence which is required to be charged as arson.

Sexual offence such as indecent assault, indecency with children and offences relating to the protection of children. Does not include offences relating to prostitution and brothels. Nor does it include offences such as indecent exposure.

Protection from serious harm. This refers to protecting members of the public from death or serious personal injury, whether physical or psychological, occasioned by further such offences committed by the offender.

Pre-sentence report. A magistrates' court, unless it considers it unnecessary to do so, must obtain and consider a pre-sentence report before forming an opinion on:

(a) whether the offence etc was so serious;
(b) (violent or sexual offence) only custody would be adequate to protect the public etc;
(c) the length of term commensurate with the offence;
(d) (violent or sexual offence) the length of term necessary to protect the public etc.

Failure to obtain pre-sentence report. Does not invalidate the sentence but the appeal court must obtain and consider such a report if the court below was not justified in forming the opinion that a report was not necessary.

Mentally disordered offender. Where an offender is or appears to be mentally disordered, ie suffering from a mental disorder within the meaning of the Mental Health Act 1983, the court must additionally obtain and consider a medical report before passing a custodial sentence unless the court considers it unnecessary to do so. The court must take any such information into account and consider the likely effect of any custodial sentence on his condition and any treatment for it. Failure to obtain a medical report does not invalidate any sentence but one must be obtained and considered by an appeal court.

Legal representation. The offender must first be given the opportunity to be legally represented unless he has been refused legal aid for financial reasons. Note the requirement is not that he should be represented but that he should have the opportunity to be.

Reasons for decisions

It is the duty of the court to state in open court:

1. that it is of the opinion that either or both of paragraphs (a) and (b) on p 223 apply;
2. that it is of the opinion that in the case of a violent or sexual offence it is necessary to pass a longer term than is commensurate with the seriousness of the offence to protect the public from serious harm from the offender;
3. why it is of that opinion and in all cases (including where a custodial sentence has been imposed following the offender's refusal to comply with a proposed requirement in a community sentence): explain to the offender in open court and in ordinary language why it is passing a custodial sentence on him or, if applicable, why imprisonment is for a longer term than would normally be commensurate with the seriousness of the offence.

Suspended sentences. All these limitations apply equally to suspended sentences.

General considerations

Consecutive sentences. If the defendant is sentenced to immediate or suspended imprisonment on each of two or more offences the terms will run concurrently unless the court orders they are to run consecutively. Consecutively means that one term of imprisonment follows another.

When a magistrates' court sentences an offender for two or more offences it may order that one sentence runs consecutively to the other. In addition (when sentencing for one or more offences) the court may order that a term of imprisonment shall be consecutive to a term already being served by the defendant. In such a case the term imposed should be stated to be consecutive to the total period to which the defendant is subject.

The total period of two or more consecutive sentences imposed on the same occasion by a magistrates' court must not exceed 6 months, unless either two or more of the offences are triable either way, when the total period may not exceed 12 months. If the defendant is convicted of two offences, one being an offence triable either way and one which is purely summary, the maximum total remains as 6 months. If the court orders a suspended prison sentence to take effect, it can order that sentence to take effect consecutively to a period of imprisonment for the later offence, even though the total period will exceed the above limits. When a previously suspended sentence is ordered to be served it should normally be made consecutive to a sentence imposed for the later offence.

Where several offences arise out of one incident consecutive sentences should not be imposed but the incident should be looked at as a whole and one appropriate period fixed. The same principle would apply to a series of offences committed against the same person over a relatively short period, eg an employee who falsifies a weekly claim for expenses.

Consecutive sentences are appropriate where although there is a single incident there is more than one offence but they do not arise as a matter of course from the principle offence. For example, the burglar who attacks a householder who discovers him, or an assault on a police officer effecting an arrest for another offence. Offences committed on bail should normally attract a consecutive sentence where imprisonment is appropriate as offending on bail is an aggravating factor.

When consecutive sentences are imposed the court should pay particular regard to the total period and reduce it if it is excessive; this is especially the rule to follow with young offenders and those receiving a first custodial sentence. One method of adjusting the total period in such cases is to consider concurrent rather than consecutive sentences.

Multiple offences. When sentencing a defendant for several offences it is best to refer to the nature of each offence and the sentence and to state the total time to be served. To say 'For the first offence you will go to prison for two months, for the second two months consecutive, for the third two months concurrent ...' can be quite meaningless. Some chairmen prefer to begin with what is perhaps the most important aspect of the sentence first: 'You will go to prison for a total of 6 months. That is made up of 2 months for stealing the watch, a further 2 months for stealing the camera . . . etc.'

When consecutive sentences are being considered the total period should be reviewed and reduced if it is excessive.

Period of imprisonment. Great care must be exercised in determining the period of imprisonment, especially if it is to be suspended. The length of a custodial sentence must not exceed a term justified by the seriousness of the offence(s) and where there is appropriate mitigation, may be shorter.

Magistrates' courts tend to consider sentences in units of months and the commonest terms are 3, 6 (and where appropriate) 9 and 12 months. It should be remembered that there is a complete discretion within the range available for a particular offence. It may be that for some offenders receiving a custodial sentence for the first time, a sentence of 7 or 14 days would be a salutary lesson.

Magistrates should reserve the maximum period available for an offence for those cases which are the worst type of case they would deal with.

Offences of attempt will not usually attract the same period as would the completed offence.

Time spent in custody on remand will be deducted from the sentence by the prison governor in fixing the date of release.

Suspended sentences. In any case where the court has power to impose imprisonment it has a discretion to suspend that sentence, that is, to postpone the time when the sentence must be served on condition that the defendant is not convicted of another offence which is punishable with imprisonment. This power must not be exercised unless the court would have imposed an immediate sentence of imprisonment if the power to suspend did not exist. The court must also be satisfied that the exercise of the power to suspend can be justified by the **exceptional circumstances** of the case. The court must also consider whether the additional imposition of a fine or compensation is warranted.

The Court of Appeal has stated that it is not possible to lay down a definition of 'exceptional circumstances'. It would depend on the facts of each individual case.

Although exceptional circumstances are not limited to the offence taken on their own or in combination, good character, youth and an early plea are not exceptional circumstances justifying a suspended sentence. They are common features of many cases (*R v Lowery* (1993)). They can amount to mitigation sufficient to persuade the court that a custodial sentence should not be passed or to reduce its length (*R v Okinikan* (1992)).

Nor in a case of breach of trust are treatment for depression and financial difficulties likely to be exceptional circumstances (*R v Bradley* (1994)).

The period (called the operational period) during which the liability to serve the sentence if reconvicted must be stated in court and cannot exceed 2 years. The court must explain the sentence clearly to the defendant.

In passing a suspended sentence the court must be careful to avoid the following dangers:

- imposing a suspended sentence where custody is not merited by the seriousness of the offence(s);

- imposing a term of imprisonment which, although suspended, is longer than is commensurate with the seriousness of the offence(s).

A suspended sentence should not be passed in respect of one offence on the occasion when either immediate imprisonment or a community service order is ordered in respect of another (*R v Starie* (1979)).

When determining a sentence for an offence committed during the operational period of a suspended sentence the sentence appropriate to that offence must be imposed.

Suspended sentence and fine. For many offences it is possible to impose a fine as well as suspended term of imprisonment. Courts must consider a fine but care should be taken in deciding such matters. If the defendant pays the monetary part of the penalty and then after a further offence is ordered to serve the prison sentence he may feel that he has been sentenced twice for his offence. On the other hand, if he is given a suspended sentence and avoids conviction during the operational period he may feel he has got away with it. Some would argue that the court ordering the suspended sentence to take effect would reduce the period because the monetary penalty had been paid, but this is neither a logically nor legally attractive argument. A careful explanation from the chairman emphasising the dual obligations of a single sentence is recommended. If the defendant defaults on the monetary part of his penalty he will be liable to imprisonment in accordance with the scale on p 212, not to the sentence which has been suspended.

Powers of court to deal with suspended sentence or conviction of further offence

A defendant is only in jeopardy if the further offence is punishable with imprisonment. If a defendant subject to a suspended sentence imposed by a magistrates' court is dealt with for a subsequent offence by the making of an absolute or conditional discharge, he is not in breach of the suspended sentence since these orders are not convictions for these purposes (*R v Moore* (1995)).

(1) If the suspended sentence was imposed **by the crown court** and during the operational period the defendant commits a further offence punishable by imprisonment for which he is convicted by a magistrates' court, the magistrates have two courses open to them.

(a) The defendant can be committed on bail or in custody back to the crown court. The higher court will then decide whether the suspended sentence shall take effect. The magistrates can also commit for sentence to the higher court in respect of the new offence at the same time. Or

(b) The magistrates' court can sentence the defendant for the further offence and their clerk will notify the crown court of their decision leaving it to the higher court to take what action it thinks fit. However if the magistrates' court deals with the subsequent offence by way of an absolute or conditional discharge these do not rank as a conviction for the purpose of proceedings in the crown court. It is wrong, however, to order discharge, when they are inappropriate, as a device to avoid the implementation of a suspended sentence and it is better to commit the defendant for sentence (*R v Tarry* (1970)).

(2) If the original suspended sentence was ordered by a magistrates' court any other magistrates' court before whom the defendant appears has four courses open to it.

(a) It can order that the suspended sentence takes effect unaltered. This **must** be ordered unless the magistrates are of the opinion that it would be unjust to do so in view of all the circumstances. One example where it could be unjust is when the subsequent offence is fairly trivial. But the Court of Appeal has stated that the fact that the subsequent offence was of a different character or committed in anger was not sufficient to permit the court not to activate the sentence in full (*R v Clitheroe* (1987)). This sentence should be ordered to be served consecutively to any other sentence for the new offence unless there are special circumstances.

 (If the magistrates do not order the suspended sentence to be carried out in full they **must** state their reason which should be inserted in the court register.) Or

(b) The magistrates can order that the suspended sentence be put into effect but for a specified shorter period than originally ordered and this sentence can be concurrent or consecutive to any other sentence passed by the same court or any other court. Or

(c) The magistrates can decide not to put the suspended sentence into effect but order that the operational period originally fixed with the suspended sentence shall be varied. The new operational period runs from the date of variation and can be for up to 2 years. Or

(d) The magistrates may make no order at all. In this event the offender may not be required to appear before the original sentencing court to be dealt with.

PARAGRAPH (a) MUST BE FOLLOWED UNLESS THE MAGISTRATES ARE OF THE OPINION IT WOULD BE UNJUST TO DO SO IN VIEW OF ALL THE CIRCUMSTANCES.

If the magistrates do not put the suspended sentence into effect in full they must state their reasons which should be inserted in the register.

The court should first consider the appropriate sentence for the current offence and should not consider it to be more serious only because it has been committed during the operational period (ie the period of suspension) of a suspended sentence. The court must then apply its mind to the suspended sentence as explained above. If the suspended sentence is to be brought into operation it should be ordered to be served after the expiry of any custodial sentence for the current offence unless there is some very good reason to the contrary. Likewise, it must be for the original period unless such an order would be unjust, as explained above.

How to announce

We have decided to pass a sentence of imprisonment on the defendant and we are of the opinion that:

((a) the offence (or the offence and other associated offences namely . . .) was so serious that only such a sentence can be justified for the offence; and/or

(b) this is a violent/sexual offence and only such a sentence would be adequate to protect the public from serious harm from him)

because (then explain why either or both of the paragraphs apply).(Violent/ sexual offence) **We are also passing a sentence of detention for a term longer than is commensurate with the seriousness of the offence as this is necessary to protect the public from serious harm from him because** (give reasons)

Accordingly (addressing the defendant) **you will be sent to prison for** (state period) **and this is because** (explain in ordinary language why he is receiving a custodial sentence and, where applicable, why he is receiving a term longer than is commensurate with the seriousness of the offence)

(Note – If there is more than one offence it should be clearly stated what the total period of imprisonment is to be.)

Ancillary orders

Compensation, p 183
Costs, p 188
Disqualification, p 260
Endorsement, p 260
Deprivation of property and forfeiture, p 218
Legal aid contribution order, p 449
Restitution order, p 238

Early release

A person subject to a term of imprisonment for less than 12 months will be automatically released after he has served one half of the term. In determining the period that has been served, time spent on remand in custody is to be taken into account. A person serving a term of 12 months and under 4 years is released on licence after serving one half of the original term and is unconditionally released after three quarters of the sentence.

Further offences. Where the offender commits an imprisonable offence before he would (but for his release) have served his sentence in full, the court which deals with him for the later offence may return him to custody for the whole or part of the period which begins with the making of the order of return, and is equal in length to the period between the date of commission of the new offence and the date of expiry of the original term.

Probation order

(Powers of Criminal Courts Act 1973, ss 2–3)

Limitations

Court must be of opinion that the supervision of the offender by a probation officer is desirable in the interests of securing the rehabilitation of the offender or protecting the public from harm from him or preventing the commission by him of further offences.

Court must first explain in ordinary language the effect of the order including any additional requirements therein, it must also explain that if he fails to comply with the order he may be dealt with in some other way for the offence for which the order is made and that the court may review the order on the application either of the offender or the supervising officer.

Offender, after having had the effect of the order explained as above, must express his willingness to comply with its requirements, if they include stipulations that the offender must undergo treatment for a mental condition or for drug or alcohol dependency.

Community sentence. The offence must be 'serious enough' to warrant the application of a community sentence. See p 151.

Age limits – Offender must be 16 or over.

Maximum period – 3 years.

Minimum period – 6 months.

Ancillary orders

Compensation, p 183
Costs, p 188
Disqualification, p 260
Endorsement, p 260
Deprivation of property and forfeiture, p 218
Legal aid contribution order p 449
Restitution, p 238

How to announce

The court is considering making a probation order in your case. That means you would be under the supervision of a probation officer for the

next (state the period of the order). **You must comply with the requirements of the probation order. They are:**

(1) that you will behave yourself;
(2) that you tell the probation officer if you change your address or your job;
(3) that you keep the appointments the probation officer will make for you to visit him at his office or for him to see you at home;
[(4) add any other requirements the court is considering.]

You must understand that if you fail to comply with these requirements you will be liable to be punished for the breach or dealt with in some other way for this offence we are dealing with today.

(Add in the case of mental, drug or alcohol treatment) .Because of these particular requirements we cannot make an order without your consent. Are you willing to keep those requirements? (If the defendant consents) **Then we make a probation order for years.**

General considerations

The purpose of probation is the ultimate re-establishment of the defendant in the community. It is intended to protect society and also to assist the defendant in becoming a more responsible person.

Provided the law has not fixed the sentence on conviction a probation order may be ordered for any defendant aged 16 or over and for any offence.

If a defendant appears before the court on two or more offences and a suspended prison sentence is imposed for one offence, a probation order cannot be made on any of the other offences.

The period of probation must be at least 6 months and not more than 3 years.

Before announcing a probation order, the court must explain the requirements of the probation order (see below) and ask the defendant if he is willing to comply with them if they include mental, drug or alcohol treatment. If he refuses an alternative sentence must be imposed.

Later the defendant will be served with a copy of a probation order specifying the requirements imposed on him. These requirements may vary from one court to another. The requirements which must be included in all orders are that the defendant shall notify any change of address to the probation officer and that he shall keep in touch with the probation officer in accordance with such directions as he may be given.

The court may decide to include a requirement relating to the offender's place of residence, after reviewing the circumstances of his home surroundings. Residence may be required at an approved probation hostel, or at some other place.

The name and address of the hostel or place of residence must be announced in court and entered in the register as well as recorded on the probation order.

Where residence is to be at an approved probation hostel or any other invitation, the period of residence shall be specified in the order.

The Secretary of State has made regulations concerning the regulation, management and inspection of approved probation hostels.

Where there are convictions for several offences, if probation is ordered in respect of one a custodial sentence, even if suspended, may not be ordered in respect of another.

Probation order requiring mental treatment

A requirement that the probationer receives mental treatment may be made after the court has received written or oral evidence from an approved mental specialist that the defendant would benefit from such mental treatment, but that his condition is not such as to warrant his detention under a hospital order.

If a written mental report is accepted in court a copy of it must be shown to the defendant's advocate. If the defendant is not represented the substance of the report must be explained to him.

Both the court and the defendant may insist on the personal appearance of the mental specialist who submitted the mental report, and the court has a duty to tell the defendant that he has this right to have the personal appearance of the doctor, and alternatively the defendant must be asked if he consents to the court acting on the written report.

The defendant or his advocate may call evidence to rebut the mental report. The following are the types of treatment that the court may order:

Treatment as a resident patient. Means admission by consent to a mental hospital within the meaning of the Mental Health Act 1983, or a mental nursing home, not being a 'special hospital' under the National Health Service Act 1977.

Treatment as a non-residential patient. Usually means attending a mental specialist at a psychiatric clinic.

Treatment by a medical practitioner named in the probation order. In effect this usually means one of the local consultant psychiatrists.

The court must announce the type of treatment ordered and record it in the register and insert it on the probation order.

Before announcing its decision the court should be satisfied that the necessary arrangements have been made with the hospital or psychiatrist. The defendant must consent to the arrangements.

Treatment for drug and alcohol dependency

Where the court is satisfied:

(a) the offender is dependent on drugs or alcohol;
(b) his dependency caused or contributed to the offence;
(c) his dependency requires and is susceptible to treatment,

it may include a condition of treatment by or under the direction of a person with the necessary qualifications or experience. Treatment may be as a resident or non resident, in an institution, or under the direction of a specified person. The nature of the treatment may not be specified.

Additional requirements

The court when making a probation order may include requirements specifying where or with whom the offender must reside. Any requirement may be included which the court considers to be necessary for securing the good conduct of the offender, protecting the public from harm from him or for preventing a repetition by him of a similar offence or other offences. Care should be taken in devising such requirements; they must be clear, enforceable and compatible with the nature of a probation order (a requirement to leave the country, for example, would not be compatible with a probation order).

Requirements may be included in the order that the offender shall

(a) present himself to a specified person; and/or
(b) present himself at a place (or places) specified in the order; and/or
(c) participate, or refrain from participating in activities which must be specified, and to do so either
  (i) on the specified day or days; or
  (ii) during the whole of the period of probation; or
  (iii) during a specified part of the probation period.

A probationer who is subject to any such requirement will be in breach of his order not only if he fails to present himself or participate etc but also if he fails to carry out the instructions of the officer or person in charge of the place or activity in which he must take part. He shall not be required to comply with such requirements for a longer total period than 60 days (or, in the case of sex offenders, such number of days as the court may specify).

No such requirement may be included in an order unless

(a) the offender consents in a case of mental, drug or alcohol treatment conditions (when he is asked whether he consents to the requirements of the order, all the requirements must be carefully explained);
(b) the consent has been obtained of any third person who will be involved (eg the person to whom the offender must present himself, if it is not the supervising probation officer);
(c) the court has consulted the probation officer (this consultation will generally be initiated by the probation officer in his pre-sentence report). The subject matter of this consultation is to be the offender's circumstances and the feasibility of securing compliance with the requirement.

Probation centres. The comments above apply *mutatis mutandis* to a requirement that the probationer shall attend a probation centre. A probation centre is a non-residential establishment provided by the probation service for use in connection with the rehabilitation of offenders. The effect of such a requirement includes an obligation on the part of the probationer not only to attend the probation centre, but to attend also any other place at which the activities, or any of them, of the centre are carried out.

Breach of probation order made by a magistrates' court (CJA 1991, Sch 2)

If a probationer is alleged to have failed to comply with a requirement of his probation order, the hearing must take place in the magistrates' court which made the probation order, or in the supervising magistrates' court.

If the failure is proved the court may deal with the probation as if he had just been convicted of the offence for which the probation order was made. This means that any other appropriate sentence may be imposed, but where compensation was ordered at the time the probation order was made that compensation order must stand. If the court decides to substitute another sentence for the probation order it should have information regarding the circumstances of the original offence.

If the court decides not to deal with the original offence and that the probation order should continue, it may order a fine of up to £1000, impose community service of up to 60 hours or an attendance centre order for the breach and allow the probation to continue.

Probation orders made by a crown court

When a higher court has made a probation order it is usually supervised by the magistrates' court of the area in which the probationer resides.

In the event of a breach of the order the magistrates' court has the power to commit the probationer in custody or on bail to the crown court for sentence, or alternatively it may punish the breach by a fine, a community service order or an attendance centre order in the case of an offender under the age of 21 and allow the probation order to continue. When the case is dealt with in the crown court it has the same powers to deal with the probationer as have been mentioned above in connection with the magistrates' court.

A magistrates' court may not revoke the order if it was made by the crown court, but may commit the defendant to custody or release him on bail until he is brought or appears before the crown court.

Revocation of probation order (CJA 1991, Sch 2)

Before the end of the probation period, the probation officer or the probationer can apply to a magistrates' court to revoke the probation order on the ground, for example, of good progress or to deal with the offender in some other way.

After hearing the application the magistrates' court can:

(a) refuse the application, thus leaving the probation order in force; or
(b) adjourn the application, eg to obtain further information or to see if the probationer maintains good progress; or
(c) terminate the probation order completely; or
(d) deal with the offender in some other way for the offence.

Substitute a conditional discharge for a probation order (s 11). If the probation officer or probationer can satisfy the court that a probation order has ceased to be appropriate, he can apply to the court to substitute a conditional discharge for the remainder of the probation period. A formal application must be laid and heard in open court.

Checklist for probation order

1 Offence – sentence not fixed by law.
2 Age – 16 years and over.
3 Supervision desirable to
   (a) secure rehabilitation;
   (b) protect public;
   (c) prevent further offences.
4 Offence(s) 'serious enough'.
5 Order suitable for offender.
6 Restriction on liberty commensurate with offence(s).
7 Explain
   (a) effect of order;
   (b) consequence of breach;
   (c) review.
8 Consent of offender where a treatment requirement for mental, drug or alcohol problems is imposed.

Restitution order

(Theft Act 1968, s 28)

Where goods have been stolen and a person is convicted of any offence with reference to the theft (whether or not the stealing is the gist of his offence) or such an offence is taken into consideration the court may make a restitution order.

Stolen includes obtaining by deception or blackmail.

Restitution. The court

(a) may simply order the defendant to restore the goods to the person entitled to them whether or not any application is made for restitution; or
(b) (where an application has been made) order the delivery over of any goods directly or indirectly representing the proceeds of the stolen goods; or
(c) where money was taken from the possession of the accused on his apprehension, order its payment to the aggrieved;

but the beneficiary of the restitution must not receive more than the value of the original goods, a matter particularly to note when a combination of orders under (b) and (c) is made.

Innocent purchasers. Sometimes the thief has sold the goods to an innocent purchaser. The goods will be restored to the owner but the court may also order the defendant to pay out of any monies in his possession when apprehended a sum to the innocent third party up to the amount he paid for the goods.

Making a restitution order. Can be made on conviction of the offender whether or not sentencing is otherwise deferred.

Evidence. In the opinion of the court the relevant facts must sufficiently appear from the evidence at the trial, or available documents (ie witness statements, depositions or other documents which were made for use and would have been admissible as evidence in the proceedings) together with any other admissions made.

Restriction order

(Football Supporters Act 1989, ss 15 and 22)

Where a person has been convicted of a relevant offence the court may make a restriction order which requires him to report at a police station at the time that a designated football match is being played outside England and Wales, ie the order prevents football hooligans from attending certain football matches played abroad. This should be contrasted with the complementary provisions of an exclusion order under the Public Order Act 1986 (p 205) which prohibits attendance at prescribed football matches *within* England and Wales.

Designated football match for the purpose of a restriction order means a match involving the national teams of England and Wales, Football League and Premier League clubs and any club playing in a UEFA competition played *outside* England and Wales.

Failure to comply with a restriction order is a criminal offence triable only by magistrates with a maximum penalty on level 3 and one month's imprisonment.

Relevant offence means:

(1) An offence in Sch 1 to the Football Spectators Act 1989 which includes:

(a) an offence under s 2 of the Sporting Events (Control of Alcohol etc) Act 1985;
(b) offences under the Public Order Act 1986, s 5 and Part III (racial hatred);
(c) an offence involving the threat or use of violence to a person or property;
(d) offences under the Football (Offences) Act 1991.

Offences (b)–(d) must be committed during a period relevant to a designated football match at any premises while the accused was at, or was entering or leaving or trying to enter or leave, the premises.

Relevant period. A period beginning two hours before the start of the match or, if earlier, two hours before the time it is advertised to start or the time at which spectators are first admitted to the premises, and ends one hour after the end of the match. Where a match is postponed or cancelled, the period includes the two hours before and one hour after the advertised start of the event. 'Designated football match' for the purposes of these offences and those described below (e)–(h) means any association football match played in England and Wales:

(i) in a competition organised by UEFA or which involves a team which represents a Football League or Premier League club, any national team or a club in a country outside England and Wales; and

(ii) that is played at a ground designated under the Safety of Sports Grounds Act 1975 or is occupied by a Football League or Premier League Club.

(2) The following offences committed on a journey to or from a designated football match where the court makes a declaration of relevance:

(e) offences under (b) and (c) above;
(f) drunkenness;
(g) an offence under s 1 of the Sporting Events (Control of Alcohol etc) Act 1985;
(h) driving whilst unfit or over the prescribed limit of alcohol, Road Traffic Act 1988, ss 4 and 5.

The prosecution must normally give five days notice of its intention to seek a declaration of relevance.

(3) Offences under paras (e) and (g) committed on journeys to designated matches played outside England and Wales.

(4) 'Corresponding offences' committed in countries designated from time to time by the Secretary of State.

Therefore an order can be made in respect of a relevant offence whether committed in England and Wales or abroad, but the restriction order will apply only to designated matches played abroad.

Offences committed abroad. Where the relevant offence was committed abroad the court may, on information being laid, issue a summons or warrant to bring the offender before the court to consider whether to make a restriction order.

Criterion. The court must be satisfied that making a restriction order in relation to the offender would help to prevent violence or disorder at or in connection with designated football matches.

Procedure. May only be made in addition to a sentence (which includes a probation order but not an order for conditional or absolute discharge) imposed in respect of the offence of which the accused was convicted. The court must:

(a) certify that the offence is a relevant offence where appropriate;
(b) specify the police station in England and Wales at which the person must report initially;
(c) explain to the person the effect of the order in ordinary language;
(d) give a copy of the order to the defendant, and send copies to the Football Spectators Restriction Orders Authority, the specified police station and, if appropriate, the relevant prison governor.

Duration. Where the person receives an immediate prison sentence but not other forms of detention a mandatory period of 5 years; any other case – 2 years.

Effect. The person is under a duty to report initially to the police station specified in the order within five days of the making of the order and thereafter to report to a police station of his choice when notified by the Restriction Orders Authority.

Exemption may be granted from reporting in respect of a particular match either an application to the Restriction Orders Authority or in cases of urgency to the police. Exemption might be granted, for example, to cover a stay in hospital or the funeral of a close relative.

Application to terminate. The person subject to the order may apply to the court to terminate the order after one year.

The court will have regard to the person's character, his conduct since the order was made, the nature of the offence which led to it and any other circumstances of the case.

Further application may not be made within six months of a refusal.

Appeal is to the crown court against the making of a restriction order.

Secure training orders

The Criminal Justice and Public Order Act 1994 introduces a new order to the youth court and the crown court, that of the secure training order. This order comprises half the period imposed being spent in detention in a secure training centre followed by the second half of the sentence in the form of supervision in the community.The sentence is therefore a determinate one and will be served in one of five proposed secure training centres, each of which is planned to accommodate 40 young offenders.

All the restrictions outlined under 'Restriction order' and contained in ss 1–4 of the Criminal Justice Act 1991 apply to secure training orders as they are defined as a custodial sentence.

Before making an order the court must be satisfied that the following circumstances pertain:

- *(a) that the offender stands convicted of an offence punishable with imprisonment in the case of an adult;*
- *(b) that the offender has been convicted of three or more imprisonable offences; and*
- *(c) that the offender, either on this or a previous occasion, has :*
  - *(i) been found by a court to be in breach of a supervision order under the Children and Young Persons Act 1969; or*
  - *(ii) been convicted of an imprisonable offence committed whilst he was subject to such a supervision order.*

Where a court makes a secure training order it shall state in open court that it is of the opinion that the above conditions are satisfied. Secure training orders will not be immediately available to courts and the Act itself allows for the power to make orders to be brought in progressively for offenders aged 14, 13 and 12 years. Where a secure training centre is not available (but the power to make an order exists) the court may commit to a place specified by the Secretary of State. This will normally be to a place run by a local authority but it could be run by a voluntary organisation or a person carrying on a registered children's home. Such a committal may last in the first instance for 28 days or until the offender is transferred to a secure training centre if that date is earlier. If a secure training centre does not become available at the end of the 28 day period the court on application may extend the period of committal and any subsequent period of detention in the secure trainng centre must be reduced by the period spent by the offender in the local authority or other accommodation specified by the Secretary of State.

Supervision requirements

As previously stated, the secure training order comprises half the time spent in detention and the other half subject to supervision. This supervision will be carried out by a probation officer or social worker for the petty sessional division or local authority area where the offender resides. The offender will be served with a notice of supervision (usually on his release) detailing the person responsible for supervision and any requirements with which he must comply.

Any failure to comply with the requirements of supervision may result in an information being laid before a justice of the peace who may issue a summons requiring the offender to appear before a youth court acting for that area. If the information is substantiated on oath and in writing then the justice of the peace may issue a warrant for the offender's arrest requiring him to be brought before such a court. The social worker or probation officer laying the information may do so in a petty sessional area:

(a) if the secure training centre is situated in it;
(b) if the order was made by a youth court acting for it;
(c) if the offender resides in it for the time being.

Such an information for breach of the supervision requirement will be heard by a youth court and if a failure to comply is proved to the satisfaction of that court it may order the offender to be detained in a secure training centre for a period not exceeding three months or the remainder of the period of the secure training order, whichever is the shorter. Alternatively the court may impose a fine not exceeding level 3 (Criminal Justice and Public Order Act 1994).

These provisions require a statutory instrument to bring them into force.

Supervision order (criminal proceedings)

(Children and Young Persons Act 1969, as amended)

Limitations

May be made only by a youth court.

Age limits – Person in respect of whom the order is made must be under 18.

Maximum period – 3 years.

Minimum period – None.

Consent – Consent of offender not required except for medical treatment or 'supervised activities'.

How to announce

This court makes a supervision order for year(s). You will be placed under the supervision of (an officer of the Council) (the probation officer).

Your supervisor will advise, help and befriend you. You must visit your supervisor and receive visits from him; you must also tell him if you change your address (or your work).

The court may discharge this order before it is completed upon application either by the supervisor or by you.

(If any requirements are to be added they should be explained in ordinary language and the offender should be asked whether he fully understands the obligations to be imposed upon him.)

If you do not comply with the provisions of the order you may be brought before the court again. The court will then reconsider the position and may make an alternative order.

Ancillary orders

Compensation, p 183
Costs, p 188
Disqualification, p 260
Endorsement, p 260
Deprivation of property and forfeiture, p 218
Legal aid contribution, p 449
Restitution, p 238

General considerations

A magistrates' court (as opposed to a youth court) cannot make a supervision order, but must remit the juvenile on bail or in local authority accommodation to a youth court which will usually be the youth court of the area in which the juvenile resides.

When a youth court makes a supervision order the effect is to place the juvenile under the supervision of a local authority or probation officer for up to 3 years. The youth court should announce as to whether the supervisor will be the local authority or the probation officer. The duty of the supervising officer is to advise, assist and befriend the juvenile.

The youth court should also announce the length of the order which can be made for up to 3 years.

Additional requirements

1 Residence. A supervision order may contain a requirement that the juvenile resides with a specified person who consents to such arrangement. Such a requirement shall be subject to any of the requirements detailed below and the effect of this order of priority is that, for example, a general requirement to reside with John Smith will not be broken by complying with a further requirement which involves residence elsewhere for a short period.

2 Intermediate treatment. A requirement may be included in a supervision order that the juvenile shall comply with directions given to him by his supervising officer. The initiative for giving directions then lies with that officer, not with the court, but the law describes the forms that those directions may take. Once the court includes the general requirement to comply with the supervising officer's directions then that officer may give directions requiring the juvenile to do any or all of the following things:

(a) To live at a place or at places specified by the officer for a period or periods so specified. This might be used, for example, in connection with a series of weekend residential courses and, as explained above, it would take precedence over a general requirement as to residence.
(b) To present himself to a specified person at specified times and places.
(c) To take part in specified activities on specified occasions. This and the preceding requirement might be used together to ensure the attendance of the juvenile, for example, on a day training course.

The total number of days upon which a juvenile may be required to comply with directions may not exceed 90 or such lower number as the court specifies. The inclusion of a requirement to comply with directions will almost always be the result of the supervisor's initiative, either at the time of making the order or later on an application to vary it by including such a requirement. Although in theory the court gives the supervisor a fairly blank cheque, in practice the supervisor will have set out for the court the kind of directions he intends to give. Having secured the inclusion of the requirement in the order, however, the supervisor is under no obligation to give any directions, or to give the same, or all of the directions which he may have previously indicated to the court. Some may see this as a derogation of the power of the youth court, but it is suggested that the better view is that it provides the supervisor with a useful element of flexibility in his handling of the case.

3 Mental treatment. Where the court is satisfied by the report of a medical practitioner specialising in mental health that a juvenile is suffering from mental ill health which may be susceptible to treatment, the court may include in a supervision order a requirement to undergo treatment for a specified period. That treatment must take one of the following forms and the requirement in the order will be framed accordingly:

(a) treatment by or under the direction of a registered medical practitioner specified in the order; or
(b) treatment as a non-resident patient in a place specified in the order; or
(c) treatment as a resident patient in a hospital or mental nursing home.

A juvenile aged 14 or more must consent before a requirement for mental treatment may be included and the court must be satisfied that arrangements have been made for the carrying out of the requirement.

4 Additional requirements in criminal proceedings. Requirements analogous to those discussed above may be included in a supervision order made in family proceedings (see Section 4, below). When dealing with a juvenile who has been found guilty of an offence there are further powers which the court can exercise. These requirements cannot be combined with an order for intermediate treatment under para 2 above.

(a) Supervised activities. The court may order the juvenile to do anything which a supervisor could require under para 2 above (intermediate treatment). On the face of it this looks like a duplication of para 2 but in fact there are two important differences. First, it is the court which spells out the requirements rather than leaving them to the discretion of the supervisor. Second, as these requirements are restricted to criminal proceedings, local authorities and the probation service have prepared schemes which are more rigorous than those for intermediate treatment. Although it is the court which specifies the requirements, in fact the reporting officer will set out his proposals in the social inquiry report for the court to incorporate in its order if it considers them to be suitable.

(b) Night restriction order. A requirement may be included which is called a night restriction and which is in the nature of a curfew. The period of restriction must not exceed 10 hours which must be between 6 p.m. and 6 a.m. The nature of the restriction is that the supervised person must during the specified hours remain at the place, or one of several places, specified in the order. The supervised person may not be required to suffer this restriction for more than 30 nights nor for any period beyond 3 months from the date of the order. Notwithstanding the restriction the supervised person may leave the specified place if when he does so he is accompanied by his parent, his supervising officer or any other person who is specified in the order. If only one place to which he is restricted is specified then that place must be the place where he lives; if more than one place is specified, the place where he lives must be one of those places.

(c) Non-participation. The court may also include a requirement that the juvenile shall refrain from participating in activities specified in the order either on specified days (eg every Saturday) or for the whole or part of the period of supervision.

The night restriction and the requirement to refrain from taking part in activities may not be included unless the court has consulted the supervisor as to the offender's circumstances and as to the feasibility of securing compliance with the requirement. The court must also be of opinion that the inclusion of such requirement is necessary to secure the good conduct of the juvenile or for the prevention of future offences by him. If the juvenile is under 16 the court must obtain and consider information about the family circumstances and the likely effect of the requirements on those circumstances before imposing the order.

(d) Residence in local authority accommodation. A juvenile who has been found guilty of a serious, imprisonable offence committed whilst he was the subject of a supervision order with a residence requirement or specified activities, may be made the subject of a requirement to live in local authority accommodation for a period of up to 6 months. The requirement may also stipulate that he is not to live with a named person.

The court must consult the authority concerned. The object of the requirement is not punitive but to remove the offender from undesirable surroundings so that the court must generally be satisfied that the offending behaviour was due to a significant extent to the circumstances in which he was living. The juvenile must be given an opportunity to be legally represented.

(e) Education. The Criminal Justice Act introduced a new power in criminal proceedings to add a requirement to a supervision order made in respect of a person of compulsory school age that he comply with arrangements made for his education. The court must:

(i) have consulted the supervisor as to the offender's circumstances; and
(ii) consider the requirement necessary to secure his good conduct or to prevent his further offending.

Alternative to custody. Where the court makes an order for supervised activities and would otherwise have imposed a custodial sentence it should state this in open court, record this on the supervision order itself and enter it in the register.

Variation and discharge

The powers to vary a supervision order are complex. They may be summarised as follows:

Supervised persons under 18 years

Applications to vary and discharge supervision orders. Are made to the youth court, which may discharge the order or vary it by cancelling any requirement or insert certain other requirements.

Breach of requirements. In addition to the powers described above, for breach of requirements, except those relating to mental treatment, the court may fine the offender or make an attendance centre order in respect of him. If the requirement breached was for supervised activities, the order may be discharged and the offender resentenced for the original offence only if the requirement was stated by the original court to be an alternative to custody.

Supervised person who has attained 18 years

The court may always resentence for the original offence where the order is discharged but may only impose custody where the requirement breached is for specified activities imposed as an alternative to custody.

Section three

Road traffic offences

Index and penalties for road traffic offences

Maximum fines and the standard scale

MCA 1980, s 32(9); Interpretation Act 1978, Sch 1	The **statutory maximum** fine on summary conviction of an offence triable either way, being the prescribed sum under MCA 1980, s 32	£5000
CJA 1982, s 37(2)	The **standard scale** giving maximum fines on an adult on conviction for a summary offence:	

level 1	£500
level 2	£1000
level 3	£1000
level 4	£2500
level 5	£5000

The following table contains an alphabetical list of the road traffic offences dealt with in this book, together with some others included to provide the maximum penalty. The column headed 'Normal fine' is for the reader's own notes: in it may be written the penalties recommended by the Magistrates' Association or agreed by the reader's own bench.

Offence and endorsement code	*Standard scale*	*Normal fine*	*Licence and penalty points*	*Page*
Abandoning a motor vehicle	level 4+ 3 months			
Accident, failing to				
give particulars AC 20	level 5 +6 months		E 5–10	305
report AC 20	level 5 +6 months		E 5–10	307
stop after AC 10	level 5 +6 months		E 5–10	305
Bicycle				
defective brakes	level 3			
riding				
careless	level 3			
dangerous	level 4			
inconsiderate	level 3			
two persons on	level 1			
when unfit through drink	level 3			
Brakes, defective				
on private vehicle CU 10 Δ	level 4		E*3	274
on goods vehicle CU 10 Δ	level 5		E*3	274
on bicycle	level 3			
Breath test, refusing DR 70	level 3		E 3–11	301
Car door, opening to cause injury or danger Δ	level 3 (25 units goods vehicles etc)			318
Car dumping	level 4 + 3 months			104
Careless driving CD 10	level 4		E 3–9	303
Common land, driving on Δ	level 3			
Dangerous condition				
using private vehicle in CU 20 Δ	level 4		E*3	277
using goods vehicle in CU 20 Δ	level 5		E*3	277
Dangerous load				
on private vehicle CU 50 Δ	level 4		E*3	
on goods vehicle CU 50 Δ	level 5		E*3	
Dangerous position, leaving motor vehicle in MS 10 Δ	level 3		E 3	
Date of birth, failing to give	level 3			
Defective tyre				
private vehicle CU 30 Δ	level 4		E*3	346
goods vehicle CU 30 Δ	level 5		E*3	346
Driver, failing to give particulars of date of birth	level 3			

Offence and endorsement code	*Standard scale*	*Normal fine*	*Licence and penalty points*	*Page*
Driving				
careless CD 10	level 4		E 3–9	303
dangerous† DD 30	level 5 + 6 months		D 3–11	279
disqualified BA 10	level 5 + 6 months		E 6	288
drink, under influence of DR 20	level 5 + 6 months		D 3–11	290
excess alcohol DR 10	level 5+ 6 months		D 3–11	293
excessive periods	level 4			
on footpath, common land, etc (RT Act) Δ	level 3			
without				
due care and attention CD 10	level 4		E 3–9	303
insurance IN 10	level 5		E 6–8	309
licence (excise)	£1000 or 5 times duty			329
reasonable consideration CD 20	level 4		E 3–9	327
test certificate				
(private)	level 3			342
(goods)	level 4			342
Drunk in charge DR 50	level 4 + 3 months		E 10	292
Excess alcohol				
driving DR 10	level 5 + 6 months		D 3–11	291
in charge DR 40	level 5 + 3 months		E 10	292
Excise licence				
failing to display Δ	level 1			
making false statement to obtain†	level 5			
using/keeping vehicle without	level 3 or 5 times duty			329
Eyesight, driving with defective MS 70	level 3		E 3	
Failing to				
comply with traffic sign Δ	level 3		+ 3	344
(constable or traffic warden on traffic duty) TS 40 Δ	level 3		E 3	
give				
name and address to police AC 20	level 5 +6 months		E 5–10	305
particulars after accident AC 20	level 5 +6 months		E 5–10	305

Offence and endorsement code	*Standard scale*	*Normal fine*	*Licence and penalty points*	*Page*
Failing to				
give				
specimen of				
breath DR 70	level 3		E 4	301
blood/urine/breath				
driving or attempting DR 30	level 5 + 6 months		D 3–11	299
in charge DR 60	level 4 + 3 months		E 10	299
statement by owner	level 3			
produce				
driving licence	level 3			282
insurance certificate	level 3			282
test certificate	level 3			282
wear seat belt (front Δ)	level 2			335
(rear Δ)	level 1			
report accident AC 20	level 5 +6 months		E 5–10	305
sign driving licence	level 3			
stop				
after accident AC 10	level 5 +6 months		E 5–10	305
at school crossing TS 60	level 3		E 3	
False declaration to obtain excise licence †	level 5			
False statement to obtain				
driving licence	level 4			
insurance	level 4			
Footpath, driving on (Highways Act 1835, s 72)	level 2			
Forging, etc				
driving licence, excise licence †	level 5			
insurance certificate †	level 5			
test certificate †	level 5			
Front seat, carrying child in Δ	level 3			335
Getting on to vehicle to be carried	level 1			
Heavy goods vehicle				
driving without LGV licence	level 3			287
overloading Δ	level 5			320
parking on verge, etc Δ	level 3			
using without plating certificate	level 3			
using without test certificate	level 4			
Holding on to vehicle to be towed or carried	level 1			

Offence and endorsement code	*Standard scale*	*Normal fine*	*Licence and penalty points*	*Page*
Hours, driving for excessive number	level 4			
Insecure load				
private vehicle CU 50 Δ	level 4		E*3	
goods vehicle CU 50 Δ	level 5		E*3	
Insurance				
using without, causing or permitting IN 10	level 5		E 6–8	309
failing to produce certificate	level 3			282
false statement to obtain	level 4			
Jay walking	level 3			
Licence				
driving otherwise than in accordance with LC 10 Δ	level 3		E 3–6	285
excise, keeping/using vehicle without	level 3 or 5 times duty			329
failing to produce for endorsement	level 3			
failing to produce to constable	level 3			282
LGV, driving otherwise than in accordance with	10 units			288
obtaining while disqualified	level 3			
Lights, driving or parking without Δ	level 4 (goods vehicle etc) level 3 (other)			312
Motor cyclists not wearing helmet Δ	level 2			315
Neglecting policeman's directions				
driver TS 40 Δ	level 3		E 3	
pedestrian	level 3			
Obstruction, causing unnecessary Δ	level 4 (goods vehicle etc) level 3 (other)			316
Opening door to cause danger or injury Δ	level 4 (goods vehicle) level 3 (other)			318
One way street, driving in wrong direction Δ	level 3		E 3	344
Overloading Δ	level 5			320
Owner failing to identify driver	level 3			
Parking				
heavy vehicle on footpath, verge Δ	level 3			
on offside at night Δ	level 4 (goods vehicle etc) 10 units (other)			

Offence and endorsement code	*Standard scale*	*Normal fine*	*Licence and penalty points*	*Page*
Parking				
on yellow lines Δ	level 3			
breach of regulations for on street parking places Δ	level 2			
(abuse of parking for the disabled) Δ	level 3			
off street parking places	level 2			
(abuse of parking for the disabled)	level 3			
failure to pay initial or excess charge	level 2 + amount unpaid			
interfering with meter with intent to defraud	level 3			
Pedal cycle, *see* Bicycle				
Pedestrian				
failing to comply with direction of constable on traffic duty	level 3			
Pedestrian crossing				
not giving precedence PC 20 Δ	level 3		E 3	323
overtaking within limits PC 20	level 3		E 3	324
stopping within limits PC 30 Δ	level 3		E 3	325
Provisional licence holder (See driving otherwise than in accordance with licence)				
Reasonable consideration, driving without CD 20	level 4		E 3–9	327
Record of hours, failing to keep	level 4			
Refusing blood/urine/breath specimen				
in charge DR 60	level 4 + 3 months		E 10	299
driving DR 30	level 5 + 6 months		D 3–11	299
Riding bicycle, *see* Bicycle				
Road fund licence				
keeping/using without	level 3 or 5 times duty			329
fail to display Δ	level 1			
false statement to obtain †	level 5			
Seat belt, failure to wear (front Δ)	level 2			333
(rear Δ)	level 1			
School crossing, fail to stop at TS 60	level 3		E 3	

Offence and endorsement code	*Standard scale*	*Normal fine*	*Licence and penalty points*	*Page*
Silencer, defective Δ	level 4 (goods vehicle etc) level 3 (other)			
Speeding SP 30 Δ	level 3		E 3–6(FP3)	336
motorway SP 50 Δ	level 4		E 3–6(FP3)	336
Stealing (or attempt) vehicle †				
UT 20	level 5 + 6 months		D (discretionary)	134
Steering, defective				
private vehicle CU 40 Δ	level 4		E*3	341
goods vehicle CU 40 Δ	level 5		E*3	
Taking motor vehicle without consent				
UT 40 (Criminal Attempts Act 1981)	level 5 6 months		D (discretionary)	130
Tampering with motor vehicle	level 3 + 3 months			140
Test certificate				
using etc vehicle without	level 3			342
using goods vehicle without	level 4			342
failing to produce	level 3			282
Traffic sign, non compliance with Δ	level 3		+3	344
Tyre, defective				
private vehicle CU 30 Δ	level 4		E*3	346
goods vehicle CU 30 Δ	level 5		E*3	346
Waiting on yellow lines Δ	level 3			

D means that the offence attracts an obligatory disqualification.
E means that the offence attracts an obligatory endorsement; in all such cases disqualification is discretionary.
* The defendant in cases thus marked is not liable to an endorsement if he satisfies the court that he did not know of the defect and had no reasonable cause to suspect that it was present.
+ Endorsable only if the sign is a traffic light (TS 10), double white lines (TS 20), Stop (TS 30), no entry sign or failure to comply with a green arrow traffic sign, abnormal load failing to observe procedure at railway crossing (TS 50), or vehicle contravening height restriction (TS 50).
† Triable either way.
Δ The prosecution may offer a fixed penalty instead of prosecuting in the normal way. See p 267.

Speed and distance chart

An approximate guide to the distance covered by a vehicle moving at a constant speed is that half the number of miles per hour is roughly the number of yards per second, eg 30 mph = 15 yds per second. The following table is more accurate than that and the distances are expressed in feet. But it must be borne in mind that the distance given will be covered only by a vehicle travelling at the speed given for the whole of the distance, ie at a constant speed. The table cannot therefore be used in the case of a vehicle slowing down or accelerating.

Miles per hour	*Feet per second*
20	29
30	44
40	59
50	73
60	88
70	103
80	117
90	132
100	146

Braking distances

(Taken, with permission, from the Highway Code)

The following braking table appears in the Highway Code. It must be taken as a guide only since no information is given with it as to whether a vehicle with disc or servo assisted brakes, or any particular tyres could improve upon these figures. The table cannot be used as evidence since it is clearly hearsay but it may be used to put to a witness in cross-examination. Moreover, the table, like any other part of the Highway Code, is embraced by s 38(7) of the Road Traffic Act 1988 which states:

> 'A failure on the part of a person to observe a provision of the Highway Code shall not of itself render that person liable to criminal proceedings of any kind, but any such failure may in any proceedings (whether civil or criminal and including proceedings under the Traffic Acts . . .) be relied upon by any party to the proceedings as tending to establish or negative any liability which is in question in those proceedings.'

Shortest stopping distances – in feet

> 'On a dry road, a good car with good brakes and tyres and an alert driver will stop in the distances shown. Remember these are shortest stopping distances. Stopping distances increase greatly with wet and slippery roads, poor brakes and tyres and tired drivers.'

Mph	*Thinking distance*		*Braking distance*		*Overall stopping distance*	
	m	ft	m	ft	m	ft
20	6	20	6	20	12	40
30	9	30	14	45	23	75
40	12	40	24	80	36	120
50	15	50	38	125	53	175
60	18	60	55	180	73	240
70	21	70	75	245	96	315

Endorsement and disqualification

The Traffic Acts impose on the courts an obligation to endorse the licence of any person convicted of certain offences. In the case of a convicted person who does not hold a driving licence this acts as an order to endorse any licence which he may obtain during the period when the endorsement is effective. An endorsement means that particulars of the offence and sentence will be recorded in code (as to which see p 268) on the defendant's licence, unless it is a foreign licence. In the case of a foreign licence, the order for endorsement should be made (subject to there being special reasons for not making it, see below) and the clerk will notify the DVLA. The court must order endorsement unless it decides after hearing sworn evidence (which may be no more than the evidence given during the trial of the offence) that there are special reasons for not doing so.

Special reasons. This has become a term of art; it has a significance which is determined by law rather than by the ordinary meaning of the words. In order to avoid endorsement or compulsory disqualification the defendant must give to the court at least one specific reason why he should not be penalised by endorsement (or disqualification in cases where that is mandatory) and that reason must meet all of the following criteria:

(a) it must be a mitigating or extenuating circumstance;
(b) it must not amount to a legal defence to the charge;
(c) it must be directly connected with the circumstances in which the offence was committed, and not relate solely to the circumstances of the offender;
(d) it should be a factor which the court ought properly to take into consideration when deciding the sentence (*R v Wickens* (1958)).

Case law has provided very many examples of circumstances under (c) above which may, and other circumstances which may not, be accepted as special reasons and some circumstances (eg the distance driven by the defendant) may be accepted or rejected according to the offence with which he is charged. For this reason examples are not set out here since they may confuse rather than clarify the position. Magistrates are recommended always to consult the clerk before reaching any final decision on this question.

Disqualification. Disqualification is mandatory for certain offences. In every case where the court can order an endorsement it has the discretion also to disqualify. Thus it can be seen how important it may be for a defendant to persuade the court that there are special reasons for not endorsing, because if he is successful and the court does not order endorsement, it may not disqualify. In cases where disqualification is mandatory, eg causing death by dangerous driving and drinking and driving offences, the defendant may submit special reasons for not disqualifying while conceding the endorsement.

For offences of theft of vehicles, going equipped to steal vehicles and taking vehicles without consent, the court may disqualify even though there is no power to endorse the licence. Disqualification may also be imposed for offences of assault involving a motor vehicle and, indeed, where following a motoring incident one driver follows another and assaults him the power to disqualify will arise (*R v Ragesh Patel* (1994)). A discretionary disqualification may not be imposed where the defendant is also liable to be disqualified under the penalty points provisions (see below).

Length of disqualification. A minimum period of disqualification must, in the absence of special reasons, be imposed in the following cases:

driving with excess alcohol/whilst unfit	one year; three years where second offence
refusing to supply a specimen	within ten years
dangerous driving	one year

Dangerous driving also carries a mandatory disqualification until a test is passed.

There is a tendency for magistrates to think of disqualification in units of 6, 12, 18 and 24 months. Research has shown that the longer the period of disqualification the more it is likely to be disobeyed. Moreover, the driver who is disqualified, say for 2 years, will probably decide within a few weeks that he will ignore the ban. There is, therefore, a strong case for short-term disqualifications especially, for example, bad cases of careless driving and young men charged with driving licence offences (see below for disqualification under the penalty points system).

Disqualification starts on the day on which the order is made and that day counts as one full day of the disqualification.

Disqualification for life. Such a disqualification will be rare. Only where there are exceptional circumstances should a disqualification for life be imposed (*R v Rivano* (1993)), for example, where there is psychiatric evidence that the driver would indefinitely be a danger to the public if allowed to drive (*R v King* (1993)) or evidence of many previous convictions which indicated the same possibility (*R v Buckley* (1994)).

The penalty points system

Persons convicted of certain offences must be disqualified from driving, eg for driving with excess alcohol. A court has a discretion to disqualify any person who has been convicted of an endorsable offence and will do so where the particular offence with which it is dealing is serious. The person who persistently commits minor endorsable offences may therefore escape these mandatory or discretionary disqualifications but will be caught by the disqualification imposed under the penalty points system. This provides in essence that where a person accumulates 12 or more penalty points over a 3 year period, he must generally be disqualified for a minimum period.

Penalty points. Every endorsable offence attracts a number of penalty points varying from 2 to 11. Some offences (including careless driving, uninsured use of a vehicle and failing to stop or report after an accident) give the court a discretion to attach a number of penalty points within a range, so indicating the court's view of the relative gravity of the offence. The choice of the number of penalty points in these cases will on occasion determine whether a disqualification must be imposed. For example, Brian A Driver has already accumulated 8 penalty points and is convicted of careless driving for which anything from 3–9 penalty points may be awarded. If the court imposes 3 points, Driver escapes disqualification because he does not reach a total of 12; but if the court imposes more than 3 then he must be disqualified, subject to his proving mitigating circumstances amounting to exceptional hardship.

When a driver is convicted of a single endorsable offence his licence will be endorsed with the number of penalty points appropriate to that offence, or with a number within the appropriate range. However, where he is convicted of a number of offences committed on the same occasion (which is not the same as saying on the same day) the number of points to be endorsed will usually be the number for the offence attracting the highest number. For example, if in addition to his careless driving conviction (3–9 penalty points) Brian A Driver is also convicted of driving whilst disqualified (6 penalty points) and driving in a play street (2 penalty points) then his endorsement will show at least 6 penalty points, that being the highest figure. If the court decides to endorse 8 penalty points for the careless driving (that being a number within the range for that offence) then the endorsement would show 8 penalty points. It is these 8 penalty points which count towards disqualification, not the total number for the three offences.

Two things will be evident from this in the normal situation:

(a) although every endorsable offence has a penalty points value, the endorsement relating to that offence may show a higher number; and
(b) when a conviction relates to a number of offences committed on the same occasion the number of penalty points which count towards disqualification is the number relating to the offence with the highest number of penalty points.

However, the court may if it thinks fit decide to accumulate the points for offences committed on the same occasion. If it does so it must state its reasons in open court and enter them in the register.

Penalty points to be taken into account

Subject to there being grounds for mitigation, disqualification is incurred when the number of penalty points to be taken into account reaches or exceeds 12. The following penalty points are to be taken into account at the time of conviction:

(a) those endorsed at the time of that conviction. Where a person is made subject of a mandatory or discretionary disqualification no penalty points for the offence for which he was disqualified will be taken into account, for the purpose of imposing an additional disqualification under the penalty points provisions;

(b) those endorsed previously in respect of any offence committed within three years of the present offence, except where a disqualification under the penalty points provisions has been ordered, in which case the court is only concerned with the penalty points incurred since that disqualification.

Therefore, only a disqualification under the penalty points provisions will have the effect of 'wiping clean' any points previously incurred.

Period of disqualification

Once a defendant becomes liable for disqualification under this scheme he may be disqualified for any period at the court's discretion, but this discretion is limited by the fixing of minimum periods. These minimum periods are as follows:

(a) 6 months if no previous disqualification is to be taken into account;
(b) one year if one previous disqualification is to be taken into account; and
(c) 2 years if there is more than one such disqualification.

For a prior disqualification to be taken into account it must have been imposed within three years of the latest offence which has brought the offender's total of penalty points up to 12. Such disqualification may have been imposed

(a) for an offence for which it was obligatory (eg driving with excess alcohol); or
(b) for an offence for which it was optional (eg a bad case of careless driving); or
(c) for 12 or more penalty points

and must have been for a period of 56 days or more and was not imposed for stealing a motor vehicle, taking without consent or going equipped for theft.

Mitigating grounds

When a defendant becomes liable to disqualification under this procedure he may claim that there are grounds for mitigating the normal consequences of conviction and if the court finds such grounds it may reduce the minimum period to which the offender is liable or it may decide not to disqualify. In either event it must state its reasons which will be recorded. The court's discretion, however, is limited. It may not take into account:

(a) any circumstances which are alleged to make the offence (or any of them) not a serious offence;
(b) the fact that disqualification would cause hardship (but it may take account of exceptional hardship);
(c) any circumstances which have been taken into account during the previous three years so as to avoid or reduce disqualification.

So, for example, Ivor Zimmer is liable to disqualification but successfully avoids it by pleading that being disabled a disqualification would cause exceptional hardship because his specially adapted vehicle is his only means of getting to work. If he is convicted and attracts a disqualification again within 3 years he is unable to put forward that ground for avoiding disqualification but once 3 years have passed, that ground is resurrected and may be used again.

Under the penalty points scheme only one disqualification is imposed irrespective of the number of offences. In the event of an appeal against any one or more of the offences, the disqualification will be treated as having been imposed on each offence and in any event the crown court has the power to alter sentences imposed by the magistrates' court for several offences even if there is only an appeal against the sentence on one offence.

Summary. Upon conviction of certain offences the court must order endorsement unless either there are special reasons (although the Road Traffic Offenders Act uses the plural it has always been treated as the singular) for not doing so, or in the case of some offences under the Construction and Use Regulations, the defendant did not know of and had no reason to suspect the condition of the vehicle. These offences are noted in the table on p 257.

No disqualification may be ordered unless it is for an endorseable offence (except for offences of theft, going equipped and taking vehicles without consent). Some few offences carry a compulsory order for disqualification and this must be imposed by the court unless there are special reasons for not doing so.

The term 'special reasons' has a very narrow meaning, in particular, hardship to the defendant is excluded from consideration.

A period of disqualification takes effect immediately. This includes disqualification for 12 or more penalty points. Only one period of disqualification is ordered under the penalty points scheme irrespective of the number of offences. The 3-year period during which penalty points are to be counted runs between dates of offence, not conviction. The 3-year period during which the circumstances once used as mitigating grounds for not disqualifying under the penalty points system may not be used again is measured between dates of their original use and the present conviction.

Where appeal against sentence is lodged, the court may suspend the effect of disqualification until the appeal is *heard*. This should not be done automatically but only after careful consideration.

Disqualification until passes a test

The court *must* disqualify an offender until he passes an extended driving test where:

(a) he is convicted of an offence of dangerous driving; or
(b) in circumstances as may (in the future) be prescribed by the Secretary of State a conviction for any endorsable or disqualifiable offence.

The court has a *discretion* to disqualify until an ordinary test of competence is passed where the offender has been convicted of any offence involving obligatory endorsement. The defendant is entitled to drive but must display L plates and be supervised. In cases where the court is exercising its discretion it must have regard to the safety of road users and an order is inappropriate as a punishment, but is suitable for the following cases:

(a) for people who are growing aged or infirm, or show some incompetence in the offence which needs looking into;
(b) where the defendant is disqualified for a long period for the offence and there is doubt about his ability to drive at the expiry of the disqualification period;
(c) where the manner of the defendant's driving suggests a threat to the safety of other road users (*R v Miller* (1993)). See the Road Traffic Offenders Act 1988, s 36.

Interim disqualification

A magistrates' court may impose an interim disqualification on a person where:

(a) it commits him to the crown court for sentence or remits his case to another magistrates' court; or
(b) it defers or adjourns his case before passing sentence. An interim order of disqualification may continue until the defendant is finally dealt with subject to a limit of 6 months and any subsequent order of disqualification will be reduced by the period of the interim order.

Disqualification by crown court

Where the crown court either convicts or sentences a person who was convicted by a magistrates' court of an offence punishable with at least 2 years imprisonment it may disqualify the defendant for an unlimited period if it is satisfied that a motor vehicle was used (whether by him or by an accomplice) to commit or to facilitate the commission of the offence.

The effect of endorsement on new drivers

Drivers within the first two years of first passing a driving test are in a probationary period. If, during that period, they accumulate six or more penalty points on their licence DVLA will automatically revoke their driving licence when it is sent to them or they are notified by the court.

This is not a disqualification but the new driver will only be entitled to hold a provisional licence until they pass a retest, which will restore their previous entitlements. Revocation will occur whether the penalty points are added following a conviction by a court or following a fixed penalty.

Points accumulated before the test was taken will count, unless they were committed more than three years before the current offence. Points accumulated after the test is passed will count if the *offence* is within two years of the date on which the test was passed.

Driving licence codes

Offences and the sentences imposed therefor are recorded on driving licences in code. The codes are reproduced below by permission of the Department of the Environment.

Endorsement code

Causing or permitting

Offences as coded below, but with zero changed to 4, eg IN 10 becomes IN 14.

Inciting

Offences as coded below, but with zero changed to 6,eg DD 30 becomes DD 36.

Periods of time

Periods of time are signified as follows: D = days; M = months; Y = years.

Code	Accident offences
AC 10	Failing to stop after an accident.
AC 20	Failing to give particulars or to report an accident within 24 hours.
AC 30	Undefined accident offence.
	Disqualified driver
BA 10	Driving whilst disqualified by order of court.
BA 20	Driving whilst disqualified by reason of age (obsolete).
BA 30	Attempting to drive whilst disqualified by order of court.
	Careless driving
CD 10	Driving without due care and attention.
CD 20	Driving without reasonable consideration for other road users.
CD 30	Driving without due care and attention or without reasonable consideration for other road users (primarily for use by Scottish courts).
CD 40	Causing death by careless driving when unfit through drink.
CD 50	Causing death by careless driving when unfit through drugs.
CD 60	Causing death by careless driving with alcohol level above the limit.
CD 70	Causing death by careless driving, then failing to supply specimen for analysis.
	Construction and use offences
CU 10	Using a vehicle with defective brakes.
CU 20	Causing or likely to cause danger by reason of use of unsuitable vehicle or using a vehicle with parts or accessories (excluding brakes, steering or tyres) in a dangerous condition.

CU 30 Using a vehicle with defective tyres.
CU 40 Using a vehicle with defective steering.
CU 50 Causing or likely to cause danger by reason of load or passengers.
CU 60 Undefined failure to comply with Construction and Use Regulations.

Reckless driving

DD 30 Reckless driving (obsolete).
DD 40 Dangerous driving.
DD 60 Manslaughter or culpable homicide while driving a vehicle.
DD 70 Causing death by reckless driving (obsolete).
DD 80 Causing death by dangerous driving.

Drink or drugs

DR 10 Driving or attempting to drive with alcohol concentration above limit.
DR 20 Driving or attempting to drive while unfit through drink.
DR 30 Driving or attempting to drive then refusing to supply a specimen for laboratory testing.
DR 40 In charge of a vehicle with alcohol concentration above limit.
DR 50 In charge of a vehicle when unfit through drink.
DR 60 In charge of a vehicle then refusing to supply a specimen for laboratory testing.
DR 70 Failing to provide specimen for breath test (roadside).
DR 80 Driving or attempting to drive when unfit through drugs.
DR 90 In charge of a vehicle when unfit through drugs.

Insurance offences

IN 10 Using a vehicle uninsured against third party risks.

Licence offences

LC 10 Driving without a licence (obsolete).
LC 20 Driving otherwise than in accordance with a licence.
LC 30 Driving after making a false declaration about fitness when applying for a licence.
LC 40 Driving a vehicle having failed to notify a disability.
LC 50 Driving after a licence has been revoked or refused on medical grounds.

Miscellaneous offences

MS 10 Leaving a vehicle in a dangerous position.
MS 20 Unlawful pillion riding.
MS 30 Playstreet offences.
MS 40 Driving with uncorrected defective eyesight or refusing to submit to a test. (Obsolete code, see now MS 70 and MS 80.)
MS 50 Motor racing on the highway.
MS 60 Offences not covered by other codes.
MS 70 Driving with uncorrected defective eyesight.
MS 80 Refusing to submit to eyesight test.

MS 90 Failure to give information as to identity of driver in certain cases.

Motorway offences

MW 10 Contravention of Special Road Regulations (excluding speed limits).

Non-endorsable offences

NE 99 Disqualification under CJA 1972, s 24 and PCCA 1973, s 44 (and for offences of unauthorised taking see p 270).

Pedestrian crossings

PC 10 Undefined contravention of Pedestrian Crossing Regulations (primarily for use by Scottish courts).
PC 20 Contravention of Pedestrian Crossing Regulations with moving vehicle.
PC 30 Contravention of Pedestrian Crossing Regulations with stationary vehicle.

Provisional licence offences (*obsolete, see now LC 20*)

PL 10 Driving without 'L' plates.
PL 20 Not accompanied by a qualified person.
PL 30 Carrying a person not qualified.
PL 40 Drawing an unauthorised trailer.
PL 50 Undefined failure to comply with conditions of a provisional licence.

Speed limits

SP 10 Exceeding goods vehicle speed limit.
SP 20 Exceeding speed limit for type of vehicle (excluding goods or passenger vehicles).
SP 30 Exceeding statutory speed limit on a public road.
SP 40 Exceeding passenger vehicle speed limit.
SP 50 Exceeding speed limit on a motorway.
SP 60 Undefined speed limit offence.

Traffic directions and signs

TS 10 Failing to comply with traffic light signals.
TS 20 Failing to comply with double white lines.
TS 30 Failing to comply with a 'Stop' sign.
TS 40 Failing to comply with directions of a constable or traffic warden.
TS 50 Failing to comply with a traffic sign (excluding 'Stop' signs, traffic lights or double white lines).
TS 60 Failing to comply with a school crossing patrol sign.
TS 70 Undefined failure to comply with a traffic direction or sign.

Theft or unauthorised taking (*obsolete (except UT 50), see now NE 99*)

UT 10 Taking and driving away a vehicle without consent or an attempt thereat (primarily for use by Scottish courts).

UT 20 Stealing or attempting to steal a vehicle.
UT 30 Going equipped for stealing or taking a vehicle.
UT 40 Taking or attempting to take a vehicle without consent; driving or attempting to drive a vehicle knowing it to have been taken without consent, allowing oneself to be carried in or on a vehicle knowing it to have been taken without consent.
UT 50 Aggravated taking of a vehicle.

Special codes

TT 99 Disqualification for accumulating 12 or more penalty points.
NSP (No separate penalty.) Where court does not impose penalty points for minor offences committed at the same time as a more serious one.

Sentence code

The sentence is represented by four characters, eg G 02 Y (probation order 2 years). The first letter indicates the nature of the sentence, the middle two numbers (0 always precedes what would otherwise be a single figure) and the final letter indicate the period of the sentence, if any, as hours (H), days (D), months (M), or years (Y). Apart from the special code TT 99 which indicates a disqualification under the penalty points procedure there is no code to represent disqualification because this appears in a special column on the licence. In the case of an absolute discharge there is no period so the code J 000 is used.

The first letter of the code indicates the sentence as follows:

A imprisonment
B detention in a place approved by the Secretary of State
C suspended sentence of imprisonment
E conditional discharge
F bound over
G probation
H supervision order (youth court)
I no separate penalty
J absolute discharge
K attendance centre
M community service order
P young offender institution
S compensation
T hospital or guardianship order
W care order

Fixed penalties

For some time it has been possible to avoid the expense of court proceedings for some motoring offences by the expedient of the prosecution offering the defendant a 'fixed penalty ticket'. If he accepts the offer he pays the required sum and the matter is settled, otherwise he is summoned to court and the matter proceeds in the usual way.

In the interests of relieving the burden on the courts of having to deal with many minor motoring cases, the fixed penalty system (formerly almost exclusively confined to parking offences) has been greatly extended to cover a wide range of offences. These are noted in the index on p 250 and include a number of offences which carry an endorsement.

A summary of the procedure is as follows:

1 Offering the fixed penalty

When a constable observes that a 'fixed penalty' offence has been committed, he must decide whether it is endorsable or not.

Non-endorsable offences. He may give the fixed penalty ticket to the driver or affix it to the vehicle if the driver is not present.

Endorsable offences. The driver must be present and the officer will require him to produce his driving licence for examination. If the driver is not liable to disqualification because he will not have accumulated 12 or more penalty points, the officer may offer him the option of a fixed penalty and invite him to surrender his licence in exchange for a receipt which he may use as evidence that he is a licence holder. It is then for the driver to decide whether to accept the offer of a fixed penalty.

If the driver does not have his driving licence with him, the procedure is modified in that he may be required to produce his driving licence within 7 days at a chosen police station where it will be inspected and, if appropriate, a fixed penalty offered.

Note: There are no fixed penalties for endorsable offences when the driver is not present (but see 'Conditional offer of fixed penalty', below), nor where he is present but declines the offer. Also the police have a discretion whether to offer a fixed penalty so that, for example, a constable might decline to offer it for an isolated offence which is serious in nature.

2 Paying the fixed penalty

The defendant has to pay the fixed penalty within 21 days (or such longer period as is allowed by the ticket) to the clerk to the court responsible for fixed penalties.

Fixed penalty	*Offences*
£40	Those involving obligatory endorsement.
£40	Illegal parking on a 'Red Route'.
£30	Illegal parking in London (except illegal parking on a 'Red Route').
£20	Other non-endorsable offences, and illegal parking outside London.

For the purpose of the higher parking penalties, London is regarded as the

Metropolitan Police District.The licence that was surrendered to the police is sent to the clerk who places the endorsement on it and returns it to the defendant when the penalty has been paid.

3 Instituting proceedings

In any case where a fixed penalty has been offered the defendant can at any time before the time for payment has expired, request a hearing before the magistrates and plead guilty or not guilty as he thinks fit.

4 Where the fixed penalty is not paid

In the case of an endorsable offence, the defendant's licence will already be in the possession of the police who will have forwarded it to the clerk responsible for fixed penalties. If the penalty is unpaid at the end of the required period, the police will register the penalty at the court for the area in which the defendant lives and the clerk who already holds the licence will endorse it and return it to the defendant. Unfortunately for him the penalty is registered as a fine 50 per cent above the fixed penalty. Similar provisions apply to non-endorsable offences where the ticket is given to the driver.

Where the offence is non-endorsable and the ticket was affixed to the vehicle, the police send a notice to the person they believe to be the owner requesting him either to pay the penalty or to inform them who is the actual owner. If he fails to co-operate by not replying at all, he will have the enhanced penalty registered against him. He is similarly liable if he replies and admits he was the owner unless either (a) he pays the penalty, or (b) persuades the actual driver to pay it for him, or (c) he returns a form signed by the person who was actually driving and who requests a court hearing.

5 Enforcement of payment

Once a penalty has been registered, it is regarded as a fine. Non-payment of the registered penalty will result in enforcement proceedings being taken in the manner described at p 212.

6 Penalty points

If the accused has committed several endorsable offences on the *same occasion*, and one is dealt with under the fixed penalty procedure and his licence is to be endorsed, the penalty points for those offences dealt with at a court hearing are to be treated as being reduced by those points to be endorsed under the fixed penalty procedure.

Conditional offer of fixed penalty

The Road Traffic Act 1991 provides for the police to issue a notice to the keeper of the vehicle requiring information as to the identity of the driver. If the keeper fails to give the information he will be guilty of an endorsable offence. Where the driver is identified, a conditional offer of a fixed penalty is sent to him and if he wishes to accept the offer he will send his driving licence and payment to the fixed penalty office within 28 days of the issue of the offer. The fixed penalty will be accepted unless the details of the licence disclose that the offender is liable to be disqualified under the penalty points provisions. In this case the police will be notified and a summons issued in the normal way.

This procedure will be phased in and initially confined to offences detected by automatic detection devices.

Brakes

Charge

Using, causing or permitting to be used on a road a motor vehicle or trailer with defective brakes

Road Vehicles (Construction and Use) Regulations 1986, reg 18;
Road Traffic Act 1988, s 41A(b)

Maximum penalty – For goods vehicle fine level 5. Other motor vehicles or trailers fine level 4 (for fines see p 209). For endorsement and disqualification see below, and also under 'Sentencing'.

'Goods vehicles' for this purpose include vehicles adapted to carry more than 8 passengers; as to whether this includes the driver, consult the clerk.

If the defendant can satisfy the court that he did not know and had no reasonable cause to suspect the deficiency of the brakes then disqualification and endorsement cannot be ordered. The defendant does not have to establish this point beyond reasonable doubt but merely that it is true on the balance of probabilities.

Penalty points – 3.

Fixed penalty – £40.

Legal notes and definitions

Goods vehicle. Means a motor vehicle or trailer constructed or adapted for the carrying or hauling of goods or burden.

The law requires that every part of every braking system and of the means of operating the braking system must be maintained in good and efficient working order and must be properly adjusted. The offence is an absolute one and the vehicle must have proper brakes at all times. If the charge is using the prosecution need not prove that the defendant knew of the defect. If the vehicle had no brakes at all then he will be charged under a different regulation.

Using. This does not mean only driving along a road; mere presence on a road, even in a useless condition, may constitute using (*Pumbien v Vines* (1996)). The term means 'to have the use of the vehicle on the road'. The test to be applied is whether or not such steps had been taken as would make it impossible for anyone to use the car. 'Use' involves an element of control, management or operation as a vehicle. Therefore an accused who was in the driving seat of a 'vehicle' where the steering was locked, there was no ignition key, the brakes were seized on and the engine could not be started was not 'using' it when it was being towed along the road. It was an inanimate hunk of metal. It would be different if there was a possibility of control, ie its steering could be operated and its brakes were working, even if its engine were not working. In doubtful cases the clerk should be consulted. A person, limited company or corporate body which owns a vehicle that is being driven in the course of the owner's business is using the vehicle (*West Yorkshire Trading Standards v Lex Vehicle Leasing* (1996)). Knowledge of the facts which constitute the offence is not necessary. A passenger in a car knowing the driver to be uninsured and allowing himself to be carried in it in pursuance of a joint enterprise is a person using the vehicle for insurance purposes (*Stinton v Stinton* (1994)).

Causing. This implies some express or positive mandate from the person causing the vehicle to be used or some authority from him and knowledge of the *fact* which constitutes the offence (but there need be no *intention* to commit an offence). Acquiescence could amount to permission (see below) but falls short of a positive mandate (*Redhead Freight Ltd v Shulman* (1988)).

Permitting. This includes express permission and also circumstances in which permission may be inferred. If the defendant is a limited company or corporate body it must be proved that some person for whose criminal act the company is responsible permitted the offence. A defendant charged with permitting must be shown to have known that the vehicle was being used or it must be shown that he shut his eyes to something that made it obvious to him that the vehicle was being used on a road.

Motor vehicle. Means a mechanically propelled vehicle intended or adapted for use on roads. 'Intended' does not mean intended by the user of the vehicle either at the moment of the alleged offence or for the future nor the intention of the manufacturer or the wholesaler or the retailer. The test is whether a reasonable person looking at the vehicle would say that one of its users would be a road user. If a reasonable man applying the test would say 'Yes, this vehicle might well be used on a road' then the vehicle was intended or adapted for such use. If that were the case then it is nothing to the point if the individual defendant says that he normally used the vehicle for scrambling and was only pushing it home on this occasion because there was no other means of taking it home, or something of that sort (*Chief Constable of Avon and Somerset v Fleming* (1986)).

For 'mechanically propelled' see the note on p 329.

A trailer. Means any vehicle being drawn by a motor vehicle.

A road. Means any highway (including footpaths and bridleways) and any other road to which the public has access and includes bridges and public car parks (*Cutter v Eagle Star* (1997)).

Sentencing

If the defendant proves that he did not know, and had no reasonable cause to suspect, that the brakes were deficient, endorsement and disqualification cannot be ordered. The defendant only has to prove that it is more probable than not that this was the case. Otherwise he can be disqualified and the licence **must** be endorsed unless there are 'special reasons'; see p 260.

It may sometimes be appropriate to grant a conditional or absolute discharge but if this course is adopted then disqualification can be imposed. Endorsement must still be ordered unless 'special reasons' exist.

If it appears to the court that the accused suffers from some disease or physical disability likely to cause his driving to be a source of danger to the public then the court shall notify the licensing authority.

When the vehicle concerned is a goods vehicle the fine will reflect the potential danger to the public and to the driver of the vehicle, and the gross weight and nature of the load may well be relevant.

For fines see p 209.

Dangerous condition

Charge

Using, causing or permitting to be used a motor vehicle or trailer on a road when

[the condition of the motor vehicle or trailer, or of its accessories or equipment]
[the purpose for which it is used]
[the number of passengers carried by it, or the manner in which they are carried]
[the weight, position or distribution of its load, or the manner in which it is secured]

is such that the use of the motor vehicle or trailer involves a danger of injury to another person

Road Traffic Act 1988, s 40A

Maximum penalty – For goods vehicle or vehicle adapted to carry more than 8 passengers fine level 5. For other vehicles or trailers fine level 4 (for fines see p 209).

Licence must be endorsed unless special reasons exist. May be disqualified for any period and/or until he passes a driving test. Endorsement and disqualification cannot be ordered if defendant can satisfy the court that he did not know of, and he had no reasonable cause to suspect, the dangerous condition.

The defendant does not have to prove this beyond reasonable doubt. He need only prove that on the balance of probabilities it is true.

Penalty points – 3.

Fixed penalty – £40.

Legal notes and definitions

Goods vehicle. Means a motor vehicle or trailer constructed or adapted for the carriage of goods or burden. The clerk should be consulted if there is a question whether a vehicle is a goods vehicle.

Using, causing, permitting. See the notes under these headings for the offence of defective brakes on p 274.

Road. Means any highway (including footpaths and bridleways) and any other road to which the public has access and includes bridges.

Motor vehicle. See p 275.

The offence is an absolute one. It is no defence that the defect was latent, and only became apparent during the journey. The section requires that the vehicle (or trailer) and all its parts and accessories are both in good repair and efficient working order.

The wording of the summons or charge should specify the exact part or accessory which is said to be dangerous. The court can allow the prosecution to amend the wording to remedy such an omission and to offer the defence an adjournment if it needs further time to prepare its case.

Sentencing

If the defendant can establish that he did not know and he had no reason to suspect the dangerous condition, in this case endorsement and disqualification cannot be ordered. The defendant does not have to prove this beyond reasonable doubt. He need only prove that on the balance of probabilities it is true.

If it appears to the court that the accused suffers from some disease or physical disability likely to cause his driving to be a source of danger to the public then the court shall notify the licensing authority.

For fines see p 207.

Dangerous driving

Charge

Driving a mechanically propelled vehicle dangerously on a road or other public place

Road Traffic Act 1988, s 2 (as substituted by Road Traffic Act 1991)

Maximum penalty – Fine level 5 and 6 months (for fines see p 209). Must disqualify for at least one year unless special reasons. The disqualification may be for any period exceeding a year. If disqualified he *must* also be ordered to pass an extended driving test. Must endorse licence unless special reasons exist.

Crown court – 2 years imprisonment and unlimited fine.

Penalty points – 3–11.

Mode of trial

Consider first the general guidance on p 446. In general, offences of dangerous driving should be tried summarily except for the presence of one or more of the aggravating factors (a)–(e), outlined under 'Sentencing' on p 280.

Legal notes and definitions

Driving. See the note under the offence of no driving licence on p 286.

Mechanically propelled vehicle. See p 329.

Dangerously. Means that the defendant's driving falls far below what would be expected of a competent and careful driver *and* it would be obvious to a competent and careful driver that driving in that way would be dangerous.

A person is also to be regarded as driving dangerously if it would be obvious to a competent and careful driver that driving the vehicle in its current state would be dangerous.

Dangerous refers to danger either of injury to any person or of serious damage to property.

In determining what would be expected of, or obvious to, a competent and careful driver in a particular case, regard shall be had not only to the circumstances of which he could be expected to be aware but also to any circumstances shown to have been within the knowledge of the accused.

In determining the state of the vehicle regard may be had to anything attached to or carried on or in it and to the manner in which it is attached or carried.

Road. See p 275.

Public place. See p 288.

Warning of proceedings. If the defence claim that notice should have been given within 14 days of intention to prosecute, consult the clerk.

Sentencing

(See Table A on p 154 for available sentences.)

If the prosecution have not brought an alternative charge of careless driving and the court finds the defendant not guilty of dangerous driving but the allegations amount to an offence of careless driving or inconsiderate driving, he may be convicted of one of these offences.

If convicted of dangerous driving the defendant's licence must be endorsed and he must be disqualified from holding a licence for at least one year. If special reasons are found (p 260) he may avoid endorsement or a disqualification. If he is not disqualified the court must determine the number of penalty points to be recorded on any endorsement.

In June 1984 the Lord Chief Justice expressed his concern at the leniency of sentences for reckless driving (now dangerous driving) imposed by the crown court. His remarks have to be treated with care by magistrates for two reasons. First, the Court of Appeal was mainly concerned, though not exclusively, with offences of causing death by reckless driving – a matter which cannot be tried by magistrates. Second, the crown court would normally be dealing with cases of reckless (dangerous) driving where magistrates had themselves decided that the offence was too serious to be tried summarily. In *R v Morris* (1995) the Court of Appeal upheld a sentence of 18 months' imprisonment for a man driving dangerously, disqualified and drunk with previous convictions for dangerous driving, despite his guilty plea.

It is clear that magistrates should treat offences of reckless (dangerous) driving as serious.

The Lord Chief Justice gave guidelines for considering the gravity of these cases (with modifications to make them appropriate for magistrates' courts). Aggravating features include:

(a) consumption of alcohol or drugs;
(b) racing at a grossly excessive speed, showing off;
(c) disregarding warnings from passengers;
(d) prolonged, persistent and deliberate course of very bad driving;
(e) previous convictions, particularly for bad driving or driving with excess alcohol.

Mitigating factors include:

(a) a 'one off' piece of reckless driving, a momentary reckless error of judgment, briefly dozing at the wheel or failing to notice a pedestrian at a crossing;

(b) good driving record;

(c) good character generally;

(d) a plea of guilty would always be taken into account in favour of the defendant;

(e) sometimes the effect on the defendant, if he was genuinely remorseful or shocked (*R v Boswell*).

Forfeiture of vehicle. See p 218.

Failing to produce driving licence, insurance certificate or test certificate

Charge

1 Being the driver of a motor vehicle on a road,

OR

2 Being a person whom a police constable reasonably believed to have driven a motor vehicle when an accident occurred owing to its presence on a road,

OR

3 Being a person whom a police constable reasonably believed had committed an offence in relation to the use on a road of a motor vehicle, failed on being so required by a police constable to produce (his driving licence) (the relevant certificate of insurance) (the relevant test certificate) for examination.

Road Traffic Act 1988, s 164 (driving licence); s 165 (insurance and test certificates)

Maximum penalty – Fine (for fines see p 209). No power to disqualify or endorse.

Legal notes and definitions

Right to demand production. Before the police officer is entitled to require the defendant to produce his driving licence or certificate of insurance the defendant must:

(a) be driving a motor vehicle on a road; or
(b) have been reasonably believed by the police to be the driver of a motor vehicle which was on a road and involved in an accident; or
(c) have been reasonably believed by the police to have committed a motor vehicle offence on a road;

in addition, where a requirement is made to produce a test certificate, the vehicle must require a test certificate.

Purpose of production. In the case of a driving licence, to enable the constable to ascertain inter alia the holder's name and address; in the case of test and insurance certificates the person must give his name and address and those of the owner where required.

Driver. See the notes under the heading 'driving' for the offence of driving without a licence on p 286.

Person supervising a learner driver. In the circumstances (a)–(c) outlined above the supervisor may be required to produce his driving licence.

Motor vehicle. See p 275.

Road. Means any highway (including footpaths and bridleways) and any other road to which the public has access and includes bridges.

Constable. Includes a police constable of any rank. Traffic wardens also have power to require production of a driving licence and the giving of a name and address in certain, very limited, circumstances. Certain vehicle examiners may also require production of documents.

Insurance certificate. The law requires that the insurance certificate be produced and not the policy or a premium receipt, unless the vehicle is covered by a certificate of security instead of a conventional insurance policy. Instead of an insurance policy the compulsory insurance of a motor vehicle can be covered by depositing £500,000 with the Accountant-General of the Supreme Court and a duplicate copy of this certificate will suffice instead of an insurance certificate. It will also be acceptable to produce a certificate in the prescribed form signed by the vehicle's owner (or by an agent on his behalf) stating that he has £500,000 on deposit with the Accountant-General of the Supreme Court.

If the vehicle is subject to a hire-purchase agreement either party to that agreement can be the 'owner'.

If the motor vehicle is owned by a local authority or a police authority then that authority may issue a 'Certificate of Ownership' in a prescribed form which makes an insurance certificate unnecessary.

Defences

(a) If the defendant is unable to produce his documents at the time, he can elect to produce them at some police station of his own choosing within 7 days. Although it is not compulsory, the constable will issue the defendant with a special form (HORT1) requiring him to produce the documents.

A driving licence has to be produced in *person*; insurance and test certificates merely have to be *produced*.

(b) If the documents were not produced within the 7 days it is a defence if they were produced (in person for a driving licence) at the specified police station as soon as was reasonably practical. Or

(c) It is also a defence if it was not reasonably practicable for the documents to be produced in the required manner before the day on which the proceedings for non-production were commenced by the laying of an information. A defendant may instead produce a *current* receipt for a licence surrendered for a fixed penalty.

The burden of proof to establish any of these defences rests with the defendant, however he does not have to prove his point beyond reasonable doubt but only on the balance of probabilities.

Sentencing

The generosity of the available defences leaves the defendant with little excuse. Failure to produce involves the police in a good deal of work, usually including visiting the defendant to interview him.

For fines see p 209.

Driving licence offences

Charges

Driving on a road a motor vehicle otherwise than in accordance with a licence to drive a vehicle of that class

Road Traffic Act 1988, s 87

Maximum penalty – Fine level 3. May disqualify for any period and must endorse, unless special reasons exist (except where the driving of the accused was in accordance with any licence that could have been granted to him).

Penalty points – 3–6 (fixed penalty 3).

Fixed penalty – £40.

Legal notes and definitions

On an appropriate application the Secretary of State may grant a provisional licence with a view to the applicant passing a test of competence to drive. A provisional licence is subject to conditions and restrictions such as to class of vehicle which may be driven, or, in the case of motor cycles, the power of the engine. Breach of any of these conditions or restrictions is an offence (s 87 of the Road Traffic Act and the Motor Vehicles (Driving Licence) Regulations 1987).

For driving a motor car a provisional licence holder must comply with the following conditions:

(a) *Learner plates.* He must clearly display front and rear in a conspicuous position a red letter 'L' of regulation size (102mm x 89mm x 38mm) on a white background (178mm x 178mm; the corners may be rounded off).
(b) *Supervision.* He must be supervised by a qualified driver. This offence applies to three-wheeled cars.

Supervised. Means that the supervisor must have been in a suitable part of the vehicle for supervising. For example, if the supervisor was in a rear seat from which it was difficult to supervise, the court may decide the defendant was not supervised. If a supervised driver is convicted of an offence, eg driving without due care, the supervisor can be convicted of aiding and abetting.

Qualified driver. Means that the supervisor must have held a full licence to drive the same type of vehicle for at least 3 years and be at least 21 years of age (exemption is provided for the military).

Motor cyclists who are learners must not drive or ride a motorcycle to which a sidecar is not attached and carry a passenger. A motor cycle which has a bare chassis or framework attached to its side does not have a side car.

Driving. A person steering a car whilst another person pushes the vehicle is driving. A person who walks alongside his car, pushing it and steering it with one hand is not driving it. A motor cyclist sitting on his machine and propelling it along with his feet is driving but he is not driving it if he walks beside it pushing it (*Gunnel v DPP* (1993)).

A person pushed a motor cycle along a road, its lights were on and he had used the brakes. At some point he had turned the ignition on for long enough to warm up the exhaust pipe. When apprehended he was astride the machine and was wearing a crash helmet. It was held to be within the magistrates' discretion to find that he was driving (*McKeon v Ellis* (1987)). A person is driving who steers and brakes a vehicle being towed by a rope or chain. The position with regard to a vehicle drawn by a rigid tow bar has not been authoritatively decided but a case decided in 1985 implies that a person in the driving seat of the towed vehicle in such a case is not driving. The nature of the force used to put or keep a vehicle in motion is irrelevant in determining whether a person is driving. The essence of driving is the use of the driver's controls in order to direct the movement, however that movement is produced. An important test in deciding whether a person is driving is whether he was in a substantial sense controlling the movement and direction of the vehicle. If he is, then the question has to be answered whether his actions fall within the ordinary meaning of the word 'driving'. It is also helpful to consider whether the defendant himself deliberately set the vehicle in motion and also the length of time that he was handling the controls. A person who knelt on the driving seat of a vehicle, released the handbrake and thereafter attempted to reapply the handbrake to stop the movement of the vehicle was held to be driving the vehicle. However a momentary seizing of the steering wheel causing the vehicle to swerve cannot properly be said to be driving (*DPP v Hastings* (1993)).

Motor vehicle. See p 275.

A road. Is any highway (including footpaths and bridleways) and any other road to which the public has access and includes bridges.

Burden of proof. Proof that the driver held the appropriate driving licence rests with the defendant. The prosecution does not have to prove that the defendant did not hold a licence.

The driver does not have to prove this beyond reasonable doubt. He need only prove that on the balance of probabilities he did hold a licence.

Employers. No employer shall let an employee drive unless the employee holds the appropriate driving licence, and it is his responsibility to make the necessary check that the employee has such a licence. Thus the employer is liable for permitting unless he can prove that his employee was licensed. Being misled by the employee is probably not a defence though the court might consider it a mitigating circumstance.

A partner is not the employee nor employer of another partner in the same firm.

Sentencing

If it appears to the court that the accused suffers from some disease or physical disability likely to cause his driving to be a source of danger to the public, then the court shall notify the licensing authority. Even if the accused has never obtained a licence, the court may consider it appropriate to bring the disease or disability to the attention of the licensing authority in case the accused should apply for a licence at some future date.

A defendant will generally not have a licence because he has not passed a test. Therefore, the case is serious and may attract a high fine and compulsory endorsement.

For fines see p 209.

Large goods vehicles

It is an offence to drive a large goods vehicle (or to employ a person to do so) unless the driver holds a large goods vehicle driving licence authorising him to drive large goods vehicles of that class. The LGV licence is an additional entitlement to the ordinary licence.

Penalty. Same as for an ordinary licence. For definition of large goods vehicle consult the clerk.

Under the provisions of the Road Traffic (Driver Licensing and Information Systems) Act 1989 existing Heavy Goods Vehicle Licences will be phased out. Instead a driver who passes an appropriate test of competency and who satisfies the Secretary of State that he is a fit person may be granted a 'large goods vehicle licence' which is in effect an ordinary driving licence which authorises the holder to drive vehicles of the classes formerly covered by a Heavy Goods Vehicle Licence. The penalty for driving without a licence is the same as for an ordinary licence.

The new style licences were issued from 1 October 1990 for licences commencing on or after 1 January 1991 and as existing HGV licences become due for renewal.

Driving whilst disqualified

Charge

Driving a motor vehicle on a road when disqualified for holding or obtaining a driving licence

Road Traffic Act 1988, s 103

Maximum penalty – Fine level 5 and 6 months imprisonment (for fines see p 209). May disqualify for any period and/or until a driving test has been passed. Must endorse unless special reasons. Triable only by magistrates.

Penalty points – 6.

Legal notes and definitions

Time limit. Subject to overall maximum of 3 years, proceedings may be brought within 6 months from when, in the prosecutor's opinion, he had sufficient evidence to warrant proceedings. A certificate signed by or on behalf of the prosecutor, as to when that date was, is conclusive evidence on that point.

Driving. See the notes under the offence of driving without a licence on p 286. Once it is established that a person was driving, he may continue to be the driver of a vehicle although his conduct has changed and he no longer fulfils the test mentioned on that page.

Motor vehicle. See p 275.

Road. Means any highway (including footpaths and bridleways) and any other road to which the public has access and includes bridges.

Disqualified. The prosecution must prove the defendant was driving and that the record of disqualification relates to that defendant (*R v Derwentside JJ, ex p Heaviside* (1995)).

Knowledge. It is not necessary to prove that the defendant knew he was disqualified, nor that he knew he was on a road.

Sentencing

(See Table B on p 155 for available sentences.)

If it appears to the magistrates that the accused suffers from a disease or physical disability likely to cause his driving to be a source of danger to the public, they must notify the licensing authority in case the accused applies for a licence at some future date.

The gravity of this offence lies largely in the flouting of a penalty imposed by the court – often for the protection of the public. The offence often attracts a custodial sentence.

Recent (1990) research sponsored by the Home Office indicated that there are approximately 257,000 drivers in Britain who have been disqualified of whom 17% have been caught driving whilst disqualified and 36% of disqualified drivers who responded to a survey admitted having driven whilst disqualified.

The offence does not apply to offenders who are driving under age. They are guilty of driving otherwise than in accordance with a licence, see p 285.

'Drunken' driving

Charge

Driving or attempting to drive a mechanically propelled vehicle on a road (or public place) when unfit through drink or drugs

Road Traffic Act 1988, s 4(1), as amended

Maximum penalty – Fine level 5 and 6 months imprisonment (for fines see p 207). Must disqualify for at least one year unless special reasons. The disqualification may be for any period exceeding a year. He may also be ordered to pass a driving test. Must endorse licence unless special reasons exist.

Previous convictions – Where there is a previous conviction during the 10 years preceding the current offence, the compulsory disqualification must be for at least 3 years unless special reasons exist.

A previous conviction for driving (or attempting to drive) a motor vehicle with alcohol over the prescribed limit or a previous conviction for refusing a blood etc specimen in such circumstances counts as a previous conviction for this offence.

Penalty points – 3–11.

Legal notes and definitions

The charge may allege either driving or attempting to drive. It must not allege both.

The court must be satisfied that the defendant drove (or attempted to drive) a mechanically propelled vehicle on a road or public place when his ability to drive properly was impaired by drink or drugs. The offence is one of strict liability and therefore the defence of insanity is not available (*DPP v H* (1997)).

Driving. See the notes under this heading for the offence of driving without a licence, p 286.

Mechanically propelled vehicle. See p 329.

Road. Means any highway (including footpaths and bridleways) and any other road to which the public has access and includes bridges.

Public place. Need not be a road. A field or enclosure at the rear of licensed premises for parking cars has been held to be a public place.

Whether the scene of the charge is a road or public place is a question of fact for the court to decide.

Unfit. A person is taken to be unfit to drive if his ability to drive properly is for the time being impaired. It need not be proved that the defendant was *incapable* of driving.

The court may take note of such evidence as, for example, where there is evidence of drink or drugs:

(a) driving erratically;
(b) colliding with a stationary object for no apparent reason;
(c) the defendant's condition – slurred speech, staggering, mental confusion. Also account may be taken of evidence of an analyst's certificate where the accused has given a sample of blood/breath/urine.

Even where the defendant has taken a drink subsequent to the incident the certificate may be evidence of the amount of alcohol consumed at the time of the incident unless the accused proves on the balance of probabilities that had he not consumed the subsequent drink his ability to drive would not have been impaired.

A witness who is not an expert can give his impressions as to whether an accused had taken drink but he may not give evidence whether the accused was fit to drive.

Drink or drugs. Drink means an alcoholic drink. Drugs can refer to medicine, ie something given to cure, alleviate or assist an ailing body, or it can be something which, when consumed, affected the control of the body. Accordingly, 'glue sniffing' would come within the ambit of this offence.

Alternative verdict. If the allegation is 'driving' the court may convict on the basis of attempting to drive. Where the defendant is found not guilty of an offence under s 4(1) but the allegations amount to or include an offence under s 4(2) (being in charge when unfit to drive through drink or drugs) the court may convict him of that offence (s 24 of the Road Traffic Offenders Act 1988 as substituted by s 24 of the Road Traffic Act 1991).

Sentencing

See Table B on p 155 for available sentences and the notes to the offence of 'Alcohol over the prescribed limit' on p 293.

Drunk in charge

Charge

Being in charge of a mechanically propelled vehicle on a road (or public place) when unfit through drink or drugs

Road Traffic Act 1988, s 4(2), as amended

Maximum penalty – Fine level 4 and 3 months imprisonment (for fines see p 207). May disqualify for any period and/or until a driving test has been passed. Must endorse unless there are special reasons.

Penalty points – 10.

Legal notes and definitions

See the notes for the offence of 'drunken driving' on p 290.

In charge. This is a potentially wide concept. There must be proof of some connection, which can be less than attempting to drive, between the defendant and a motor vehicle on a road or public place. The owner or a person who had recently driven the vehicle would be 'in charge' unless he put the vehicle in someone else's charge or unless there was no realistic possibility of his resuming actual control, eg where he was at home in bed or a great distance from the car (*DPP v Watkins* (1989) where there is further guidance in respect of defendants who are not the owner or have not recently driven the vehicle). A qualified driver supervising a provisional licence holder is 'in charge'.

A person is deemed not to be in charge if he proves (on the balance of probabilities) that at the material time the circumstances were such that there was no likelihood of his driving the vehicle so long as he remained unfit to drive through drink or drugs but in determining whether there was such a likelihood the court may disregard any injury to him and any damage to the vehicle.

Sentencing

See Table B on p 155 for available sentences and the notes to the offence of 'Alcohol over the prescribed limit' on p 293.

Alcohol over prescribed limit offences

Charge 1

Driving (or attempting to drive) a motor vehicle on a road (or public place) with alcohol above the prescribed limit

Road Traffic Act 1988, s 5(1)(a)

Maximum penalty – Fine level 5 and 6 months imprisonment (for fines see p 209). Must disqualify for at least one year unless special reasons. The disqualification may be for any period exceeding a year. The defendant may also be ordered to take a test again. Must endorse licence unless special reasons.

It is not a special reason that the defendant's driving was not impaired.

Previous convictions – Where there is a previous conviction during the 10 years preceding the current offence, the compulsory disqualification must be for at least 3 years unless special reasons.

A previous conviction for driving (or attempting to drive) a motor vehicle when unfit through drink or a previous conviction for refusing a blood or urine specimen in such circumstances count as a previous conviction for this offence.

Penalty points – 3–11.

Legal notes and definitions

The charge may allege either driving or attempting to drive. It is important to note that it must not allege both. The prosecution need not prove that the defendant's ability to drive was impaired.

Driving. See the notes under the offence of no driving licence on p 286.

Motor vehicle. See p 275.

Road. Means any highway (including footpaths and bridleways) and any other road to which the public has access and includes bridges.

Public place. Need not be a road. A field or enclosure at the rear of licensed premises for parking cars has been held to be a public place.

Whether the scene of the charge is a road or public place is a question of fact for the court to decide. It is basically a question of whether at the relevant time the public enjoyed access to the place where the offence was committed.

Prescribed limit. If a blood specimen was provided by the defendant the prescribed limit is 80 mg of alcohol in 100 ml of blood; if a urine specimen, 107 mg of alcohol in 100 ml of urine; if breath, 35 μg of alcohol in 100 ml of breath. Comparison of these levels is achieved by multiplying a breath/alcohol level by 2.3 and rounding up to convert to blood alcohol. The following conversion table relates blood, urine and breath levels.

Blood	*Urine*	*Breath*	*Blood*	*Urine*	*Breath*
80	107	35	133	177	58
83	110	36	136	181	59
85	113	37	138	184	60
87	116	38	140	187	61
90	119	39	143	190	62
92	122	40	145	193	63
94	125	41	147	196	64
97	129	42	149	199	65
99	132	43	152	202	66
101	135	44	154	205	67
103	138	45	156	208	68
106	141	46	159	211	69
108	144	47	161	214	70
110	147	48	163	217	71
113	150	49	166	220	72
115	153	50	168	223	73
117	156	51	170	226	74
120	159	52	172	230	75
122	162	53	175	233	76
124	165	54	178	236	77
126	168	55	180	239	78
129	171	56	182	242	79
131	174	57	184	245	80

Breath tests. (See p 301 for more detail.) A constable in uniform may require a person to submit to a breath test if the constable reasonably suspects him to have alcohol in his body or to have committed a traffic offence while the vehicle was in motion. The test may also be required in these circumstances after a person has ceased to be a driver. If the test indicates the presence of alcohol the driver need not, but may be, arrested and taken to a police station where he will be required to offer a specimen of blood, urine or breath at the choice of the police. The roadside breath test may be taken by blowing into a bag or into a machine, but these devices are a preliminary test and the sample of breath used in these tests is not the one which is analysed to determine its alcohol content.

If the police require a breath sample for analysis it will be analysed in a machine called either a Lion Intoximeter 3000 or a Camic Breath Analyser. They both work in a similar way, analysing the level of alcohol in the breath by the absorption of infra red radiation and giving a printed record of the result of two samples of breath given within a short time. The lower reading is the one which will be used to determine whether a prosecution will follow. Each machine works with a simulator, a device enabling the machine to check itself for accuracy. If for any reason the police decide not to use the machine they may ask for a sample of blood or urine.

The form of print-out from the machine will vary slightly according to which machine is used, both will give the subject's name and the time and date of the test. They will show the results of each of two samples given by the subject and the results of each of two checks which the machine carries out to prove its accuracy. These calibration checks must show a reading within a range of 32–38 μg; figures outside this range on either check will render the test void.

The print-out will be signed by the operator and by the subject and a machine-produced copy will be handed to the driver, the other copy being retained by the police. It is unlikely that a prosecution will follow if the lowest reading is less than 40, but if it is 50 or less the driver is entitled to ask for an analysis of a sample of blood or urine. In the absence of any suggestion that the machine was not used properly and providing the calibration checks show readings within the parameters mentioned above, the print-out from the machine is evidence of the level of alcohol in the breath without further proof provided that a print-out was handed to the accused at the time it was produced, or served on him more than 7 days before the hearing, either personally or by registered or recorded post.

Evidence by certificate. A certificate signed by an authorised analyst stating the proportion of alcohol in the specimen is admissible without the analyst being called as a witness: the same applies to a certificate signed by a doctor who took a blood specimen from the defendant.

The defendant is entitled to insist on the attendance at court of the analyst or doctor. As the police were bound to provide the defendant with specimens of blood or urine taken at the same time, it is possible that sometimes a defendant may call his own analyst to give evidence as to the proportion of alcohol.

If difficulty arises about the provision of a specimen to a defendant, or about the admissibility of a certificate, the clerk should be consulted. The police are entitled to divide the specimen into three parts and not two.

The High Court has quashed a conviction because a pathologist declared the blood specimen handed to the defendant to be inadequate for examination.

The defendant is entitled to be acquitted if he can raise a reasonable doubt about the accuracy of the machine. However the prosecution do not have to prove a specific alcohol content, but that the alcohol content exceeded the prescribed limit so that where an accused called expert evidence to show that the variation in readings on the breath machine was unacceptable but where it was conceded that the readings must have been 5 microgrammes above the limit, he was convicted.

Special reasons. It is not a defence to the charge that unknown to him the defendant's drink had been laced. If this is put forward as a reason for not disqualifying the question must be answered whether the extra drink by itself is what took the level of alcohol in the blood over the limit and the defendant, if there is any doubt, should be invited to call expert evidence. Note that even if special reasons are proved this only gives the justices a discretion not to disqualify. They may still do so depending on the circumstances of the case (*Donahue v DPP* (1993)).

Driving in an emergency may amount to a special reason not to disqualify, but only where a sober, reasonable and responsible friend of the defendant present at the time, but unable to drive, would have advised the defendant to drive (*DPP v Bristow* (1996)).

Drinking after driving. If the accused claims that the alcohol level was increased because he had taken drink after ceasing to drive then he must prove on the balance of probabilities that the post-driving drink took him over the limit and that he was not over the limit while he was driving. This is because the law requires the court to assume that the alcohol level at the time of the driving was not less than that at the time of the test. If an accused wishes to raise this defence he will almost certainly have to call medical or scientific evidence.

Alternative verdict. If the allegation is 'driving' the court may convict him on the basis of attempting to drive. Where the defendant is found not guilty of an offence under s 5(1)(a) but the allegations amount to or include an offence under s 5(1)(b) (being in charge of a vehicle with excess alcohol in breath, blood or urine) the court may convict him of that offence.

Sentencing

Structure of the sentencing decision. See p 157.

Available sentences. See Table B on p 155.

Custodial sentence. See p 151.

Community sentence. See p 153.

Fine. See p 209.

Forfeiture of vehicle. See p 218.

Disqualification. See p 260.

High risk offenders. Drivers who are convicted of the following offences are regarded as high risk offenders (for endorsement codes see p 267):

(a) one disqualification for drinking and driving with alcohol $2^1/_2$ or more times the legal limit (DR 10 and DR 50);
(b) two disqualifications for drinking and driving within 10 years (DR 10, DR 20, DR 40 and DR 50);
(c) one disqualification for refusal to provide a specimen for analysis (DR 30 and DR 60).

The DVLA will write to a high risk offender and explain that the disqualification is considered to be an indication of a drink problem. Shortly before the expiry of the disqualification, a further letter will be sent explaining what must be done to apply for the return of the licence. The applicant will have to submit to a medical examination and pay an administration fee and medical fees to the examining doctor.

If it appears to the court that the accused suffers from a disease or physical disability likely to cause his driving to be a source of danger to the public, it must notify the licensing authority.

The fact that the amount of alcohol is only slightly over the statutory limit is NOT a special reason for avoiding imposing disqualification and endorsement.

The 12 months mandatory disqualification is to be regarded as a minimum and not as a tariff and should be increased in appropriate cases. The Divisional Court has said that 69 µg is an appropriate case.

If the defendant submits as a special reason for not disqualifying him that he was obliged to drive by some sudden crisis or emergency he must show that he acted responsibly and that the crisis or emergency was not one which arose through his own irresponsibility or lack of reasonable foresight. The driving must have been only to the extent occasioned by the emergency.

Reduced disqualification for attendance on course (Road Traffic Offenders Act 1988, s 34A). This section is currently only in force on an experimental basis in a number of designated areas. *Where the relevant section is in force the court may reduce the period of disqualification where a person has completed an approved course by a date specified in the order.*

This power applies where there is a conviction for driving (or being in charge) under the influence of drink or drugs; driving etc with excess alcohol (pp 293 and 290); or failing to provide a specimen (p 299).

The court must have made an order for disqualification for not less than 12 months.

The reduction specified must be not less than three months and not more than one quarter of the original period (ie 9 months disqualification must remain where the original unreduced period was 12 months).

Criteria. *The court must be satisfied:*

(a) a place on the course is available;
(b) the offender is of or over 17 years;
(c) the court has explained the effect of the order in ordinary language, the amount of fees payable and that they must be paid before beginning the course;
(d) the offender consents.

On completion, the organiser of the course will give the offender a certificate for presentation to the court.

Charge 2

Being in charge of a motor vehicle on a road (or public place) having consumed alcohol over the prescribed limit

Road Traffic Act 1988, s 5(1)(b)

Maximum penalty – Fine on level 4 and 3 months imprisonment (for fines see p 209). May disqualify for any period and/or until a driving test has been passed. Must endorse unless there are special reasons.

Penalty points – 10.

Legal notes and definitions

In charge. See notes on p 292.

The defendant is entitled to be acquitted if he can establish that there was no likelihood of his driving whilst he probably had an excessive proportion of alcohol in his blood. He only has to prove that this is true on the balance of probabilities. He does not have to prove it 'beyond reasonable doubt'.

See also the legal and sentencing notes for the previous offence, on p 292.

Sentencing

See Table B on p 155 for available sentences and the notes for the previous offence. See *R v Shoult* (1996) on the use of imprisonment.

Refusing specimen of blood, urine or breath

Charge

Failing, without reasonable excuse, to provide a specimen of blood, urine or breath for analysis

Road Traffic Act 1988, s 7(6)

Maximum penalty – This varies according to whether it is alleged the defendant was driving or in charge. Accordingly the summons should make clear which of the alternative offences on pp 292 and 293, is alleged.

(a) If the defendant drove or attempted to drive a motor vehicle on a road or public place fine on level 5 and 6 months imprisonment. Must disqualify for at least one year unless special reasons. The disqualification may be for any period exceeding a year. The defendant may also be ordered to take a test again. Must endorse licence unless special reasons.

For a subsequent offence committed within 10 years of a previous conviction must disqualify for at least 3 years and must endorse unless special reasons.

A previous conviction for driving (or attempting to drive) a motor vehicle when unfit through drink (see p 290) or a previous conviction for driving (or attempting to drive) with alcohol over prescribed limit (see p 293) count as a previous conviction for this offence.

Penalty points – 3–11.

(b) If the defendant was in charge of a motor vehicle on a road or a public place fine level 4 and 3 months imprisonment. May disqualify for any period and/ or until a driving test has been passed. Must endorse unless there are special reasons.

Penalty points – 10.

Legal notes and definitions

A constable, in the course of an investigation into whether a person has committed an offence under s 3A (causing death by careless driving where under the influence of drink or drugs) or s 4 or 5 of the Road Traffic Act may require him to provide two specimens of breath or a specimen of blood or urine for analysis.

If the case concerns a refusal to provide a blood specimen, an offence is committed if the defendant would only allow blood to be taken from an inappropriate part of the body (toe, penis, etc). In one case a woman refused to provide a blood or urine specimen and claimed embarrassment, there being no doctor or policewoman present. The High Court ruled this amounted to refusal. An agreement to provide a specimen which is conditional will generally be treated as a refusal. In the case of a sample of breath being required for analysis it must be provided in such a way as to make that analysis possible, that is, the required quantity at the required pressure.

Reasonable excuse. The Court of Appeal has said: 'In our judgment no excuse can be adjudged a reasonable one unless the person from whom the specimen is required is physically or mentally unable to provide it, or the provision of the specimen would entail a substantial risk to health.' The fact that a driver has not consumed alcohol at all, or that he has consumed alcohol since being involved in an accident, does not amount to a reasonable excuse for not providing a specimen.

Defendant must have been warned of consequences of refusing a specimen

The Act expressly directs a policeman requesting a specimen to warn the defendant that a failure to provide such a specimen may make the defendant liable to prosecution. If this warning has not been given, the magistrates can dismiss the charge. If the driver is incapable of understanding the warning (for example, because he does not understand English sufficiently) he may not be convicted if he refuses to provide a sample.

There are three possible ways of providing a specimen: breath, blood or urine. The current law places the choice entirely in the hands of the police who will use the breath-analysis machine, only offering the defendant blood or urine if the machine is broken or unavailable, or where there are medical reasons for not requiring a sample of breath. Where the police require a specimen of blood for analysis they are not required to offer the motorist a preference but must ask whether there are any reasons why a specimen cannot or should not be taken by a medical practitioner (*DPP v Warren* (1993)).

Sentencing

Where either the defendant was driving or attempting to drive or where he was in charge see Table B on p 155 and see the notes to the offence of 'Alcohol over the prescribed limit' on p 293.

Refusing to take breathalyser test

Charge

Failing, without reasonable excuse, to provide a specimen of breath for a breath test when required to do so by a policeman in uniform

Road Traffic Act 1988, s 6(4)

Maximum penalty – Fine of level 3. Must endorse unless special reasons. Disqualification discretionary.

Penalty points – 4.

Legal notes and definitions

The policeman must have been in uniform at the time he requested the defendant to take a breath test and used a Home Office approved breathalyser.

A defendant can only be required to take this test by a constable in uniform who has reasonable cause for suspecting:

(a) the defendant *is* driving or attempting to drive a motor vehicle on a road or other public place and has alcohol in his body or has committed a traffic offence whilst the vehicle was in motion; or
(b) he *has been* driving or attempting to drive on a road or other public place with alcohol in his body and he still has alcohol in his body; or
(c) he *has been* driving or attempting to drive a motor vehicle on a road or other public place and has committed a traffic offence whilst the vehicle was in motion.

For these purposes 'driving' includes being 'in charge'.

In addition, where there has been an accident, a constable (whether in uniform or not) may require any person who he has reasonable cause to believe was driving or attempting to drive or in charge of the vehicle at the time of the accident to provide a breath test.

The instructions on the breath test device need not be strictly observed. If the constable had no reason to suspect that the motorist had drunk alcohol in the previous 20 minutes he can be required to take the test immediately.

Motorist in hospital. If a motorist is in a hospital as a patient, he can still be required to take a breath test, provided that the doctor in immediate charge of him is notified and does not object.

Reasonable excuse. If the defendant satisfies the magistrates that he had a reasonable excuse for failing to take a breath test he is entitled to be acquitted. Such a defendant will probably be rare. One example may be that the defendant was hurrying to get a doctor to deal with an emergency. The degree of proof required of the defendant is to prove that this point is probably true. He does not have to establish it beyond reasonable doubt.

The clerk should be consulted if the defence raise this point.

Sentencing

Since 'reasonable excuse' is a defence (see above) conviction implies that the defendant had no excuse and therefore this is not a trivial offence and carries an endorsement.

Due care

Charge

Driving a mechanically propelled vehicle on a road or other public place without due care and attention

Road Traffic Act 1988, s 3, as amended

Maximum penalty – Fine level 4 (for fines see p 209). May disqualify for any period and/or until a driving test has been passed. Must endorse unless special reasons.

Penalty points – 3–9.

Legal notes and definitions

Mechanically propelled vehicle. See p 329.

Road. See p 275.

Public place. See p 290.

Due care and attention. The standard of driving expected by the law is that of the degree of care and attention to be exercised by a reasonable and prudent driver in the circumstances. The standard of careful driving expected in law from a motorist is the same for all, even the holder of a provisional licence.

A skid may or may not be due to lack of care, but being overcome by sleep is not a defence.

Where a motorist is confronted by an emergency during the course of driving, he should be judged by the test of whether it was reasonable for him to have acted as he did and not according to the standard of perfection yielded by hindsight.

If the driving complained of was due to a mechanical defect in the vehicle, that is a defence unless the defendant knew of the defect, or he could have discovered it by exercising prudence; but the burden of proof remains on the prosecution to establish beyond reasonable doubt a lack of due care and attention.

Observance or non-observance of the Highway Code can be used to establish or disprove guilt.

Warning of proceedings. If the defence claim that notice should have been given within 14 days of intention to prosecute, consult the clerk.

Careless or inconsiderate driving (s 3) and dangerous driving (s 2). Where the magistrates see fit, they may allow informations for an offence under s 3 and s 2 to be heard together. In this event, if the defendant is convicted of one offence, the second information should be adjourned *sine die*. Should the driver successfully appeal against conviction, he can later be tried on the second information.

Alternatively, where there is a single information alleging dangerous driving and the magistrates do not find this proved, they may convict of careless driving in the alternative.

Emergency vehicles. The same standard of care and attention is required of the drivers of fire engines, ambulances, coastguard and police vehicles as of any other driver. That standard is that the driver takes 'due' care and pays 'due' attention.

Driving. See the note under the offence of no driving licence on p 286.

Sentencing

Endorsement must be ordered unless special reasons exist.

If it appears to the court that the offender suffers from a disease or physical disability likely to cause his driving to be a source of danger to the public, then the court shall notify the licensing authority who may take steps to withdraw the driving licence.

It is the actual carelessness or inattention of the driver which is punishable, not the consequences thereof. An example of this is provided by a case decided in 1984. A motor cyclist went through a red traffic light at a junction and knocked down and killed a pedestrian. The defendant was concentrating on the vehicle in front of him which was turning right. He had an unblemished driving record.

The Lord Chief Justice said that the unforeseen and unexpected results were not in themselves relevant to the penalty. The primary consideration was the quality of the driving, the extent to which the motorist on the particular occasion fell below the standard of the reasonably competent driver, in other words, the degree of carelessness and culpability. The death of the victim was not relevant. Where death results from careless driving and the driver was unfit through drink or drugs or had consumed alcohol in excess of the prescribed limit, he may commit an offence under s 3A of the Act which is triable only at the crown court, and is punishable with up to 5 years imprisonment and an unlimited fine.

However, the unforeseen consequences might be relevant to culpability, eg that the defendant had not seen the pedestrian until it was too late; it was clearly not a case of momentary inattention as the defendant was not keeping a proper lookout throughout the sequence of the traffic lights.

Disqualification is optional but should be seriously considered for a second offence. The court may disqualify until a test is passed; a useful provision for the very elderly driver.

Failing to stop and give details after accident

Charge

As a driver of a mechanically propelled vehicle, owing to the presence of which on a road, an accident occurred whereby injury was caused to another person (or damage caused to another vehicle or to roadside property or injury to an animal)
[failed to stop]
[upon being reasonably required to give his name and address, the name and address of the owner of the vehicle and the number of the vehicle, failing to do so]

Road Traffic Act 1988, s 170(4), as amended

Maximum penalty – Fine level 5 and 6 months imprisonment. May disqualify for any period and/or until a driving test has been passed. Must endorse unless there are special reasons.

Penalty points – 5–10.

Legal notes and definitions

Charge. The one charge may include both factual situations without offending the rule against duplicity (*DPP v Bennett* (1992)).

Relationship between the offences of failing to stop and give details and failing to report an accident. Where an accident has occurred in the circumstances described above, there is an obligation on the driver to stop at the scene of the accident. If he does not, he commits the offence described here. Having stopped at the scene of the accident, he has a duty to give his name and address, the name and address of the owner of the vehicle and the identification marks of the vehicle to any person having reasonable grounds for such a request. If he fails to do so, he has also committed the offence described here. Unless he has actually given his particulars to such other person, he must report the accident at a police station or to a police constable *as soon as reasonably practicable*, and in any case within 24 hours of the accident, otherwise he commits the offence at p 307.

Mechanically propelled vehicle. See p 329.

A road. See p 275.

An animal. Means any horse, cattle, ass, mule, sheep, pig, goat or dog.

Roadside property. Means any property constructed on, fixed to, growing in or otherwise forming part of the land on which the road in question is situated, or land adjacent thereto.

The law requires the driver to give the appropriate particulars upon being reasonably required to do so. It is not sufficient to report the incident to the police within 24 hours. Where the defendant was the driver of the vehicle involved in the accident, there is a rebuttable presumption that the defendant knew that he had been involved in the accident. If the defendant can satisfy the court that he was unaware of any accident he must be acquitted (*Selby v Chief Constable of Avon and Somerset* (1987)).

The degree of proof required of the defendant is to satisfy the court that this was probably true; he does not have to prove this beyond reasonable doubt.

Driver. The notes under the heading 'driving' for the offence of driving without a licence on p 286 may be of assistance. A person may continue to be the driver of a motor vehicle if having fulfilled the requirements mentioned on that page he ceases to do so by reason of a change of activity.

Accidents involving personal injury (to a person other than the driver). The driver must at the time produce his certificate of insurance to a constable or other person having reasonable cause to require it. If he does not do so, he must report the accident as described above and produce his insurance certificate. Otherwise he commits an offence under s 170(7) of the Road Traffic Act 1988 – maximum penalty a fine of up to level 3. There is a defence if the certificate is produced within 7 days of the accident at a police station specified by him at the time when the accident was reported. This provision does not apply to the driver of an invalid carriage.

Sentencing

If it appears to the court that the accused suffers from a disease or physical disability likely to cause his driving to be a source of danger to the public, then the court shall notify the licensing authority who may take steps to withdraw the driving licence.

The gravity of this offence is lessened if the defendant subsequently reports the accident.

The number of penalty points must be fixed to reflect the gravity of the circumstances of the offence.

For fines see p 209.

Failing to report after accident

Charge

As a driver of a mechanically propelled vehicle, owing to the presence of which on a road an accident occurred whereby injury was caused to another person (or damage caused to another vehicle or to roadside property or to an animal), not giving his name and address to any person having reasonable grounds for requiring this information, failing to report to the police as soon as reasonably practicable and in any case within 24 hours

Road Traffic Act 1988, s 170(4), as amended

Maximum penalty – Fine level 5 and 6 months imprisonment. May disqualify for any period and/or until a driving test has been passed. Must endorse unless there are special reasons.

Penalty points – 5–10.

Legal notes and definitions

Relationship between the offences of failing to stop and give details and failing to report an accident. See p 305.

Mechanically propelled vehicle. See p 329.

A road. See p 275.

An animal. Means any horse, cattle, ass, mule, sheep, pig, goat or dog.

Report. Means approaching the police oneself as soon as reasonably practicable, even if no one else was present at the scene of the accident and therefore there was nobody present to ask for the driver's particulars.

If the defendant were approached by a police officer within 24 hours of the accident, that would not constitute reporting the accident.

If the defendant can satisfy the court that he was unaware that an accident had occurred, he must be acquitted of this charge.

The degree of proof is to satisfy the court that this was probably true. The defendant need not prove this beyond reasonable doubt.

If the defendant gave his name and address to the other party he need not report the accident to the police.

Roadside property. Means any property constructed on, fixed to, growing in or otherwise forming part of the land on which the road in question is situated or land adjacent thereto.

Driver. See note under no driving licence on p 286. A person does not necessarily cease to be a driver if having met the requirements mentioned on that page, he ceased to do so by reason of a change of activity.

Reasonably practicable. A driver is not saved from conviction because he reported the accident within 24 hours if he could reasonably have reported it sooner. If, for example, he continued his journey after the accident and drove past a police station he would need a very strong reason for not reporting at that station. It appears that he is not obliged to go in search of a public telephone in order to telephone the police. It is for the court to decide what is 'reasonably practicable' in the particular circumstances of each case and the test is not 'Is it reasonable for the defendant to have reported the accident earlier?' but 'Did he report it as soon as practicable?'.

Sentencing

See sentencing notes to previous offence on p 306.

No insurance (using, causing, or permitting)

Charge

Using (or causing or permitting to be used) a motor vehicle on a road when there is not in force a policy of insurance or security against third party risks

Road Traffic Act 1988, s 143

Maximum penalty – Fine level 5. May disqualify for any period and/or until defendant has passed a driving test. Must endorse unless special reasons.

Penalty points – 6–8.

Legal notes and definitions

Motor vehicle. See p 275.

A road. Means any highway (including footpaths and bridleways) and any other road to which the public has access and includes bridges.

Security in respect of third party risks. The requirement to have insurance or a security does not apply to a vehicle owned by a person who has deposited with the Accountant General of the Supreme Court the sum of £500,000, at a time when the vehicle is being driven under the owner's control. Nor does it apply to vehicles owned by bodies such as local authorities or the police. Certain other undertakings may have instead of insurance a security given by an insurer that the undertaking will meet any liability it may incur.

Time limit. Subject to overall maximum of 3 years, proceedings may be brought within 6 months from when, in the prosecutor's opinion, he had sufficient evidence to warrant proceedings. A certificate signed by or on behalf of the prosecutor as to when that date was is conclusive evidence on that point.

Burden of proof. If the prosecution prove that the defendant used a motor vehicle on a road, the burden of proof shifts to the defendant to establish that he was insured. The defendant does not have to prove beyond reasonable doubt; he need only prove that he was probably insured.

Insurance certificate. This is in law the main item of proof of insurance and until it has been delivered to the insured he is held not to be insured. Mere proof that he has paid the premium or holds an actual policy is not sufficient.

Using on a road. This expression does not in law only mean driving the vehicle along the road; its mere presence on a road, jacked up and without a battery, may constitute using on a road (*Pumbien v Vines* (1996)). A vehicle which is being towed is being used. In any given case where doubt exists consult the clerk. See also p 274 (Brakes).

A person, limited company or body corporate which owns a vehicle that is being driven in the course of the owner's business is using the vehicle.

Causing involves an express or positive mandate from the defendant to the driver.

Permitting. Permission must be given by someone able to permit or withhold permissions but may be express or inferred. See further the note under this heading on p 274 (Brakes).

Defence open to employed drivers. An employed driver cannot be convicted if he can prove that:

(a) the vehicle did not belong to him; and
(b) it was not in his possession under a hiring contract or on loan to him; and
(c) he was using it in the course of his employment; and
(d) he did not know and had no reason to believe he was not insured.The degree of proof required from the defendant is to prove that this defence is probably true; he does not have to prove beyond reasonable doubt.

The Motor Insurers' Bureau is a company funded by insurers transacting compulsory motor insurance. Under an agreement with the Secretary of State for Transport the Bureau, subject to certain limitations and exceptions, will compensate the victims of uninsured motorists. A brief outline of the scheme is given here (for the full details see the text of the agreement which is published by HMSO).

To obtain compensation the victim must obtain judgment in a civil court against the uninsured driver, having given the MIB notice within 7 days of starting the proceedings. If the judgment is not met within 7 days the victim will be entitled to be compensated by the MIB.

Compensation is payable for personal injury or for damage to property (except for the first £175 of the claim in respect of property damage and this figure will be the relevant limit of a compensation order made against an uninsured driver in the magistrates' court).

There are exceptions to claims against the MIB such as claims in relation to crown vehicles but more particularly where damage is to the claimant's own vehicle which he himself has failed to insure as required by the Road Traffic Act or where the claimant is the passenger in a vehicle which he knew had been stolen or unlawfully taken or was being used without insurance.

A separate agreement covers the case of victims of untraced drivers.

Sentencing

Endorsement must be ordered unless special reasons exist.

If it appears to the court that the accused suffers from some disease or physical disability likely to cause his driving to be a source of danger to the public, then the court shall notify the licensing authority who may take steps to withdraw the driving licence.

Clearly a lower level of fine may be appropriate for the vehicle sitting unused outside the owner's house, whereas deliberate driving around without insurance cover aggravates the seriousness considerably.

Although using a vehicle without insurance is a serious offence which merits a stiff fine, there may be occasions when it is inappropriate to impose the usual penalty, for example, where the defendant is charged with driving whilst disqualified, a matter which is invariably accompanied by a summons for using the vehicle without insurance. It is submitted that the defendant is being punished twice over if the sentence for each offence is the same as it would be for the individual offences, as one of the attributes of a driving whilst disqualified offence is that there is generally no insurance in force.

For fines see p 209.

Lights

Charge

1 Using or causing or permitting to be used on a road a vehicle without every front position lamp, rear position lamp, headlamp, rear registration plate lamp, side marker lamp, end-outline marker lamp, rear fog lamp, retro reflector and rear marking with which it is required to be fitted by the Regulations, and every stop lamp and direction indicator, running lamp, dim-dip device, headlamp levelling device and hazard warning signal device with which it is fitted in good working order and, in the case of a lamp, clean.

2 Using, causing or permitting to be used on a road any vehicle with a headlamp, front fog lamp, or rear fog lamp so as to cause undue dazzle or discomfort to other persons using the road

3 Using or causing or permitting to be used on a road a vehicle which is in motion between sunset and sunrise (or between sunrise and sunset in seriously reduced visibility), (or allowing to remain at rest, or causing or permitting to be allowed to remain at rest, on a road any vehicle between sunset and sunrise) unless every front position lamp, rear position lamp, rear registration plate lamp, side marker lamp and end-outline marker lamp with which the vehicle is required by the Regulations to be fitted is kept lit and unobscured.

4 Using, or causing or permitting to be used on a road a vehicle which is fitted with obligatory dipped beam headlamps without such lamps being lit during the hours of darkness (or in seriously reduced visibility)

Road Vehicles Lighting Regulations 1989, reg 23(1) (charge 1); reg 27 (charge 2); reg 24(1) (charge 3); reg 25(1) (charge 4);

Road Traffic Act 1988, s 42

Maximum penalty – Fine level 4 (goods vehicles etc), level 3 (private vehicles) (for fines see p 209). No power to disqualify or endorse.

Fixed penalty – £20.

Legal note and definitions

Using, causing or permitting. The charge should allege only one of these. For 'using', 'causing' and 'permitting' see p 274.

The obligatory minimum requirements for an ordinary motor car are two front position lights, two headlights (with a dipped beam facility), direction indicators, hazard warning lights, two rear position lamps, one rear fog lamp (vehicles first used after 1 April 1980), two stop lamps, a rear registration plate lamp and two rear reflex reflectors.

These requirements vary according to the category of vehicle concerned. If the matter is in dispute the clerk will be able to provide a list of the requirements.

Vehicle. Means a vehicle of any description and includes a machine or implement of any kind drawn or propelled along roads whether by animal or mechanical power.

Road. Means any road or highway to which the public has access and includes bridges and footways.

Front position lamp. Means a lamp used to indicate the presence and width of a vehicle when viewed from the front.

Hours of darkness. Means the time between half an hour after sunset and half an hour before sunrise. An almanac can be produced to establish this period if it is in dispute.

Exempted vehicles include

(a) Pedal cycle and hand drawn vehicles are not required to be fitted with lamps between sunrise and sunset.
(b) Vehicles temporarily imported or proceeding to port for export provided they comply with international Conventions.
(c) Military vehicles which comply with certain requirements.
(d) Vehicles drawn or propelled by hand which have an overall width (including load) not exceeding 800 millimetres are not required to be fitted with lamps and reflectors except when they are used on a carriageway between sunset and sunrise (unless they are close to the near side or are crossing the road).

Possible defences include

Offence 1 where a defective lamp or reflector is fitted to the vehicle which is in use between sunrise and sunset if the lamp etc becomes defective during the journey or if arrangements have been made to remedy the defect with all reasonable expedition.

Offence 3 where the vehicle is a car or does not exceed 1525 kilograms and is parked on a road with a speed limit of 30 miles per hour or less in force and the vehicle is parked in a designated parking place or lay-by or is parked parallel to the kerb, close to it and facing the direction of traffic and is not less than 10 metres from a junction.

Offence 4 Except where there is seriously reduced visibility, the car is on a road restricted to 30 miles per hour by virtue of a system of street lighting which is lit at the time of the alleged offence.

Sentence

If it appears to the court that the defendant suffers from any disease or disability likely to cause his driving to be a source of danger to the public, the court shall notify the licensing authority.

Although this offence lends itself to a fairly fixed rate, that rate should vary according to

(a) whether the vehicle was moving or stationary; and
(b) whether the road was lit or unlit.

For fines see p 209.

Motor cyclist not wearing helmet

Charge

Being a person driving (or riding on) a motor cycle on a road, did not wear protective headgear

Motor Cycles (Protective Helmets) Regulations 1980, reg 4;
Road Traffic Act 1988, s 16(4)

Maximum penalty – Fine level 3 (for fines see p 209). There is no power to endorse or disqualify.

Fixed penalty – £20.

Legal notes and definitions

Where the person actually in breach of the regulations by not wearing a helmet is over 16, there can be no prosecution of another person for aiding and abetting. However, aiders and abettors of defendants under 16 can be prosecuted.

Riding on. This includes a pillion rider but not a passenger in a side-car.

Protective headgear is defined in the regulations as being that which complies with a certain British Standard. Headgear manufactured for use by persons on motorcycles which appears to afford the same or a greater degree of protection than laid down by the Standard is also included. But before any helmet satisfies the definition it must also be securely fastened to the head of the wearer by the straps or fastenings provided on the helmet. An unfastened helmet, therefore, would not suffice.

Driving. See the notes under this heading for the offence of driving without a licence on p 286 but bear in mind the exemption mentioned at (b) below.

Exemptions. There is no requirement to wear a helmet:

(a) if the motor cycle is a mowing machine;
(b) if the motor cycle is being propelled by a person on foot;
(c) if the driver is a Sikh and is wearing a turban.

Sentencing

The wearing of a helmet contributes greatly to the rider's safety. A small fine will meet most cases.

For fines see p 209.

Obstruction

Charge

Causing unnecessary obstruction of a road by a person in charge of a motor vehicle or trailer

Road Vehicles (Construction and Use) Regulations 1986, reg 103;
Road Traffic Act 1988, s 42

Maximum penalty – Fine level 4 (goods vehicle etc), level 3 (otherwise) (for fines see p 207). No power to disqualify or endorse.

Fixed penalty – £20.

Legal notes and definitions

Unnecessary obstruction. There need be no notice or sign displayed as is the case where a driver is charged in parking offences. This offence can be committed on a road to which local parking regulations are applicable.

If the vehicle is parked in a lawfully designated parking place then there can be no charge of obstruction.

The High Court has ruled that a motorist who left his car on a road 24 ft wide for 75 minutes did not commit this offence.

A taxi-driver was held by the High Court to have committed this offence in waiting in the road to turn right, thereby holding up heavy traffic.

The question is one for the justices to decide on the facts of each case. An obstruction caused by a doctor answering an emergency call may, for example, be unnecessary.

A road. Means any highway (including footpaths and bridleways) and any other road to which the public has access and includes bridges. A road is provided as a means of transit from one place to another and not as a place to park motor vehicles.

Trailer. Means any vehicle drawn by a motor vehicle.

A motor vehicle. See p 275. If left on a road for an unreasonable time may constitute an unnecessary obstruction.

Sentencing

An average case will not usually attract more than a small fine; where there is a complete disregard for the convenience or safety of others (eg access of fire appliances or ambulances) a heavier fine is called for.

For fines see p 209.

Opening door

Charge

Opening a door of a motor vehicle or trailer on a road so as to cause injury or danger

Road Vehicles (Construction and Use) Regulations 1986, reg 105;
Road Traffic Act 1988, s 42

Maximum penalty – Fine level 4 (goods vehicle etc), level 3 (otherwise) (for fines see p 207). No power to disqualify or endorse.

Fixed penalty – £20.

Legal notes and definitions

Motor vehicle. See p 275.

Trailer. Means any vehicle drawn by a motor vehicle.

Road. Means any highway (including footpaths and bridleways) and any other road to which the public has access and includes bridges.

The offence. Consists of opening or causing or permitting a door to be opened so as to cause injury or danger to any person. The offence can be committed by a passenger as well as the driver. If a child opened the door and his parent was present and knew the child was about to open the door, then the parent could be charged with permitting. If the child opened the door on the instructions of a parent then the latter could be guilty of causing the offence. Door opening, permitting or causing are all identical offences for the purpose of the penalties that may be inflicted. Only one of the offences should be alleged.

The prosecution does not have to prove carelessness; nor that someone was actually struck or injured. It is enough if the act caused danger.

Sentencing

If it appears to the court that a driver suffers from some disease or physical disability likely to cause his driving to be a source of danger to the public, then the court shall notify the licensing authority who may take steps to withdraw his driving licence.

The amount of the fine will vary according to the circumstances. It will rarely be appropriate to impose a fine less than the fixed penalty. When the offence is very dangerous, eg where it causes a motor cyclist to swerve to the offside of a busy main road, this will aggravate the seriousness. Where actual injury is caused a similar level of penalty should apply.

For fines see p 209.

Overloading

Charge

Using, causing or permitting to be used on a road a vehicle which exceeds the maximum (gross weight) (train weight) (weight for specified axle) shown on the (plating certificate) (manufacturer's plate fitted to the vehicle)

Road Vehicles (Construction and Use) Regulations 1986, reg 80;
Road Traffic Act 1988, s 41B

Maximum penalty – Fine level 5 (for fines see p 209). Not endorsable.

Fixed penalty – £40.

Legal notes and definitions

Certain vehicles specified in reg 66 must be fitted with a plate which contains information prescribed in Sch 8 or the relevant EC Directives. In particular the plate must show the maximum gross weight, train weight and weight for each axle. The weights may be specified by the manufacturer and are the limits at or below which the vehicle is considered fit for use, having regard to its design, construction and equipment and the stresses to which it is likely to be subjected in use. Further the weights must also be specified at which the use of the vehicle will be legal in Great Britain having regard, inter alia, to the maximum weights set out in regs 75–79. This is a 'manufacturer's plate'.

In addition, goods vehicles are now covered by the compulsory 'type approval' system whereby the Secretary of State issues a certificate that a type of vehicle conforms with the appropriate requirements and the manufacturer issues a Certificate of Conformity that the vehicle conforms with the approved type. This certificate is *treated* as a 'plating certificate' and a plate (which is in fact a piece of paper) is affixed to the vehicle, which is *deemed* to be a 'ministry plate' (for this and 'plating certificate' see below).

After one year and annually thereafter goods vehicles must be submitted for a goods vehicle test and at the *first* test the vehicle will also be examined for the purpose of issuing a 'plating certificate'. The examiner will issue a certificate containing information similar to that on the plate previously affixed to the vehicle. If the vehicle passes its goods vehicle test the ministry plate will remain affixed in a conspicuous and readily accessible position on the vehicle and in the cab. Only one plating certificate is issued, but it will be amended where there has been a 'notifiable alteration' to the vehicle.

Using; causing; permitting. See p 274.

Road. See p 275.

Vehicle. The provisions concerning manufacturers' plates cover such vehicles as non-agricultural tractors of various weights which do not carry loads, buses and various trailers. This article is concerned with offences committed by goods vehicles, being the most commonly encountered in the magistrates' court.

Maximum gross weight. The sum of the weights to be transmitted to the road surface by all the wheels of the motor vehicle (including any load imposed by a trailer on the vehicle).

Maximum train weight. The maximum gross weight and the weight transmitted to the road surface by any trailer drawn.

Maximum axle weight. The sum of the weights to be transmitted to the road surface by all the wheels of that axle.

Multiple charges. Under the former regulations 'gross', 'train' or 'axle' weight were the subject of separate charges and not combined into one. It was not oppressive for there to be a charge in respect of each axle that was overweight and for exceeding the gross weight. The new regulations are worded slightly differently but it is still permissible to prefer several charges where appropriate (*Travel-Gas v Reynolds* (1988)).

Evidence. Unless proved to the contrary the weight indicated on a ministry plate is presumed to be the weight recorded on the relevant plating certificate.

Defences. In the case of a goods vehicle it is a defence for the accused to prove:

(a) that at the time when the vehicle was being used on the road it was proceeding to a weighbridge which was the nearest available one to the place where the loading of the vehicle was completed for the purpose of being weighed, or was proceeding from a weighbridge after being weighed to the nearest point at which it was reasonably practicable to reduce the weight to the relevant limit without causing an obstruction on any road; or
(b) in a case where the limit of that weight was not exceeded by more than 5%, that limit was not exceeded at the time the loading of the vehicle was originally completed and that since that time no person has made any addition to the load (eg a load which becomes wet owing to falling rain).

The degree of proof required from the defendant is to prove that the defence is probably true; he does not have to prove beyond reasonable doubt.

Sentencing

Overloading a goods vehicle is potentially a very serious offence. The steering and braking capabilities of the vehicle may be adversely affected. Excess axle weights are particularly liable to damage road surfaces and the drains beneath.

In addition there may be substantial commercial advantages to an operator. The fines imposed should reflect this. HGV drivers are often treated more seriously than non-HGV drivers and separate penalties are often appropriate for each offence summoned. Penalties may be doubled in the case of the owner of an HGV. In deciding the culpability it may be useful to consider the percentage of the overload rather than simply the number of kilograms in excess.

For fines see p 209.

Pedestrian crossing (failing to accord precedence)

Charge

Failure of a driver of any vehicle to accord precedence to a pedestrian within the limits of an uncontrolled pedestrian crossing

'Zebra' Pedestrian Crossings Regulations 1971, reg 8 (or 'Pelican' Pedestrian Crossings Regulations and General Directions 1987, reg 17);
Road Traffic Regulation Act 1984, s 25(5)

Maximum penalty – Fine of level 3 (for fines see p 209). If the offence was committed in a motor vehicle, the court may disqualify for any period and/or until a driving test has been passed. Must endorse unless special reasons exist.

Penalty points – 3.

Fixed penalty – £40.

Legal notes and definitions

Vehicle. A bicycle is a vehicle (but not in the case of offences of stopping in an area *adjacent* to a zebra crossing, see p 325).

Zebra crossing. A driver should approach such a crossing in a manner that enables him to stop before reaching it, unless he can see there is no pedestrian on the crossing.

The law imposes a very strict duty on the driver and the prosecution has the advantage of not having to prove any negligence or want of care. It would, however, be a sufficient defence to satisfy the magistrates that the failure to accord precedence was due to circumstances over which the defendant had no control (eg being attacked by a swarm of bees, or a sudden brake failure).

The High Court in Scotland has held that where a woman was pushing her child in a pram and the pram was on the crossing but she herself had not actually stepped onto the crossing, the mother had the right of way.

The limits of the crossing are marked by studs bordering the striped lines. The broken white line along the striped crossing is to indicate where vehicles should give way.

The sections of pedestrian crossings on each side of a dual carriageway, central street refuge or reservation are considered to be two separate crossings.

A crossing may still legally remain a crossing even if one or more of its stripes are missing, discoloured or imperfect, or if a globe or one of its lights is missing, or even if some of the studs have disappeared. The magistrates should consult the clerk if a submission is made on any of these matters.

The regulations require pedestrians to cross 'with reasonable despatch'.

On each side of crossings are zigzag lines parallel to the carriageway. These indicate the 'area controlled by the crossing'. On the approach side of the crossing it is an offence for a vehicle to overtake another vehicle in that area if that vehicle is either the only other vehicle in the area or is the nearest vehicle of several to the crossing. 'Overtaking' includes allowing part of the rearmost vehicle to pass the front of the overtaken vehicle, a complete passing is not necessary. The prohibition on overtaking does not apply if the overtaken vehicle is stationary otherwise than to allow pedestrians to cross (eg if it is waiting to turn left or right) or if the crossing is for the time being controlled by a policeman or traffic warden, but it applies where a vehicle has stopped to wait for pedestrians to step onto the crossing, for example as a courtesy. It also applies when the pedestrians have passed the stationary vehicle which is overtaken.

Pelican crossings. Similar provisions apply. A vehicle approaching such a crossing shall proceed with due regard to the safety of other users of the road. When a red light shows the vehicle must stop, similarly where a constant amber light shows, a vehicle must stop except where the vehicle cannot safely be stopped in line with the signal. Where there is a flashing amber light, a vehicle must accord precedence to pedestrians already on the crossing. Failure to comply with any of the regulations is an offence with a maximum penalty of a fine on level 3.

Pedestrian. A person walking and pushing a bicycle is a pedestrian. He ceases to be a pedestrian if he uses the bicycle to carry him, for example, by placing one foot on a pedal and pushing himself along with the other.

Precedence means allowing the pedestrian to go before the vehicle. Once the pedestrian has safely passed the vehicle's line of travel the vehicle may proceed even though the pedestrian is still on the crossing.

Sentencing

If it appears to the court that the defendant driver of a motor vehicle suffers from some disease or physical disability likely to cause his driving to be a source of danger to the public, then the court shall notify the licensing authority who may take steps to withdraw the driving licence. A fine will generally be considered.

For fines see p 209.

Stopping on pedestrian crossing

Charge

That a driver of a vehicle caused it or any part of it to stop within the limits of zebra crossing

'Zebra' Pedestrian Crossings Regulations 1971, reg 9;
Road Traffic Regulation Act 1984, s 25(5)

Maximum penalty – Fine level 3 (for fines see p 209). If the offence was committed in a motor vehicle, the court may disqualify for any period and/or until the defendant has passed a driving test. Must endorse unless special reasons exist.

Penalty points – 3.

Fixed penalty – £40.

Legal notes and definitions

The defendant must be acquitted if he establishes any of the following:

(a) that circumstances beyond his control compelled him to stop;
(b) that he had to stop to avoid an accident.

The degree of proof required from the defendant is to prove that one of these is probably true; he does not have to prove one of them beyond reasonable doubt.

The term 'vehicle' includes a pedal cycle.

This charge does not apply to a push-button controlled crossing which is subject to special regulations.

A crossing may still legally remain a crossing even if one or more stripes are missing, discoloured or imperfect, or if a globe or its light is missing or even if some of the studs have disappeared. Consult the clerk.

Stopping in area adjacent to zebra crossing. It is also an offence to stop in a zebra-controlled area, ie the part of a road indicated by zig-zag lines at either side of the crossing (reg 12).

For the purposes of this regulation 'vehicle' does *not* include a pedal cycle.

Defences are:

(a) that circumstances beyond his control compelled him to stop;
(b) that he had to stop to avoid an accident;

(c) that the stopping was for the purpose of allowing free passage to pedestrians on the crossing;
(d) that he had to stop for fire brigade, ambulance or police purposes, because of demolitions, repairs to road, gas, water, electricity services etc;
(e) that he stopped for the purpose of making a left or right turn;
(f) a stage carriage or express carriage vehicle (not on a trip or excursion) in the controlled area beyond the zebra crossing for the purposes of picking up or setting down passengers.

Sentencing

If it appears to the court that the defendant driver of a motor vehicle suffers from some disease or physical disability likely to cause his driving to be a source of danger to the public, then the court shall notify the licensing authority who may take steps to withdraw the driving licence.

A fine is usually appropriate in most cases.

For fines see p 209.

Reasonable consideration

Charge

Driving a mechanically propelled vehicle on a road or other public place without reasonable consideration for other persons using the road or place

Road Traffic Act 1988, s 3, as amended

Maximum penalty – Fine level 4 (for fines see p 209). May disqualify for any period and/or until a driving test has been passed. Must endorse unless special reasons exist.

Penalty points – 3–9.

Legal notes and definitions

At the time of the offence there must have been other people also using the road. They could be passengers in the defendant's vehicle. Another example of this offence is driving the vehicle through a muddy puddle and splashing pedestrians.

If no other person but the driver is using the road then this charge fails.

Observance or non-observance of the Highway Code can be used to establish or disprove liability.

The driver alleged to have committed this offence must give his name and address on request to any person having reasonable grounds for requiring it, otherwise he commits an offence under s 168 of the Act, maximum penalty fine on level 3.

Mechanically propelled vehicle. See p 329.

Road. See p 275.

Public place. See p 290.

Warning of prosecution. If the defence claim that notice should have been given within 14 days of intention to prosecute, consult the clerk.

Other persons using the road. May include passengers in the defendant's vehicle. There must be evidence that another road user was inconvenienced by the manner of driving adopted by the accused.

Careless or inconsiderate driving (s 3) and dangerous driving (s 2). Where the magistrates see fit, they may allow informations for an offence under s 3 and s 2 to be heard together. In this event, if the defendant is convicted of one offence, the second information should be adjourned *sine die*. Should the driver successfully appeal against conviction for reckless driving, he can later be tried on the second information.

Alternativcly, where there is a single information alleging dangerous driving and the magistrates do not find this proved, they may convict of driving without reasonable consideration in the alternative.

Driving. See the note under the offence of no driving licence on p 286.

Sentencing

In rare cases it may be appropriate to grant an absolute discharge; if this course is adopted disqualification can be imposed. Endorsement must be ordered unless special reasons exist.

If it appears to the court that the accused suffers from some disease or physical disability likely to cause his driving to be a source of danger to the public then the court shall notify the licensing authority who may take steps to withdraw the driving licence.

It is the lack of consideration rather than the consequences of it which determines the punishment.

Most cases would attract a fine in the mid-region of the range.

For fines see p 209.

Road fund or excise licence

Charge 1

Using or keeping on a public road a mechanically propelled vehicle when no excise licence is in force

Vehicle Exercise and Registration Act 1994, s 29

Maximum penalty – A fine of level 3 or 5 times the value of the licence, whichever is the greater. No power to disqualify or endorse.

In addition to a fine the court is compelled, in certain cases, to order the defendant to pay loss of duty. See below under 'Sentencing'.

Legal notes and definitions

The charge must stipulate whether the defendant is being charged with using or keeping. One charge cannot allege both.

Prosecutor and time limit. Only the Secretary of State, the police acting with his approval, or a person or authority authorised by that Secretary of State can conduct the prosecution. Proceedings must start within 6 months of their receiving sufficient evidence to warrant proceedings; subject to an overall limit of 3 years from the offence.

Using. In law means not only driving the vehicle but can also include the vehicle's mere presence on the road. The owner is not liable to be charged with using the vehicle if he allowed some other person to have the vehicle and who used it outside the scope of the authority given by the owner.

Keeping. Means causing the vehicle to be on a public road for any period, however short, when the vehicle is not in use.

Public road. Refers to a road repairable at the public expense. This is different from the more usual definition of a road which means any highway (including footpaths and bridleways) and any other road to which the public has access and includes bridges.

Mechanically propelled vehicle. Means a vehicle with some form of engine; thus even a motor assisted pedal cycle comes within the legal definition even if the rider is just pedalling the machine without the use of the engine. A car does not cease to be a mechanically propelled vehicle after removal of its engine, nor if there is some temporary defect which prevents the engine working. If the condition of the vehicle is such that there is no reasonable prospect of it ever being made mobile again, then it ceases to be a mechanically propelled vehicle.

Employees, drivers, chauffeurs. It has been decided that it is oppressive to prosecute an employee who was not responsible for licensing the vehicle.

A dishonoured cheque. If offered in payment of the licensing fee renders the licence void. The licensing authority will send a notice requiring the excise licence to be delivered up within 7 days of the posting of the notice. Failure to comply is an offence punishable with a maximum fine of level 3 or 5 times the annual rate of duty applicable (Customs and Excise Management Act 1979, s 102). For liability for back duty see below.

Exempted vehicles. Certain vehicles are exempt from duty and the clerk can supply a list: ambulances, fire engines, military vehicles, some agricultural vehicles; vehicles going for a *pre-arranged* test and some vehicles acquired by overseas residents, vehicles more than 25 years old, calculated from the 31 December of the year of first registration. This latter class of vehicles must still be licenced annually and display a VED disc. See Sch 2 of the 1994 Act.

Sentencing

The fine and the arrears of duty should be announced as separate items; we do not commend the practice of some courts of announcing a single sum and stipulating that it includes the back duty.

Liability for back duty

If the defendant was the person who *kept* the vehicle at the time of the offence the court must order him to pay an amount to cover the loss of duty. Such order is in addition to a fine and the chairman of the court must announce two amounts, viz the amount of the fine and the amount of the lost duty.

If the court decides not to impose a fine but to grant an absolute or conditional discharge the court must still order the payment of the lost duty as well and this must be announced. It must be stressed that this provision applies only if the defendant is the person who *kept* the vehicle at the time of the offence. Thus this provision would not apply to an employed lorry driver but would apply to a private motorist who kept and used his own vehicle. It would also apply to a company which kept and used its own vehicles.

Dishonoured cheques. In relation to licences taken out on or after 27 July 1989 the court must, in addition to any penalty it may impose under s 102 of the Customs and Excise Management Act 1979, order the defendant to pay an amount to cover the loss of duty incurred for the period for which he had the benefit of the licence.

Calculating back duty. This period will usually commence with the date of the expiry of the expired licence, or when the defendant notified his acquisition of the vehicle to the appropriate authority. It will terminate with the date of offence. If there is doubt about the length of the 'relevant period' consult the clerk. Back duty is calculated for each month or part thereof. Use on one day in a month will render him liable for back duty for the whole month.

Previous convictions. If the defendant has a previous conviction in respect of the same vehicle for a similar offence for which the court made an order for lost revenue then in the present proceedings the relevant period will commence with the day after the date of the previous offence.

Costs can be ordered as well as a fine and back duty.

Defence against back duty. If the defendant can prove any one of the following in respect of any part of the relevant period back duty cannot be ordered against him for that part of the relevant period:

(a) the vehicle was not kept by him; or
(b) he paid duty in respect of the vehicle for any month or part of a month (where relevant) whether or not on a licence. The defendant does not have to establish this beyond reasonable doubt but only that his contention is probably true.

A person is liable for all the periods when he kept a vehicle without a current tax whether it was on a public road or not. It is not obligatory for a person to tax a car that is kept off the road, but if he ventures onto the road without tax he may find himself with a liability extending back over the time when it was not taxed or to the date when he notified his acquisition of the vehicle.

Charge 2

Fraudulently using a vehicle excise licence

Vehicle Exercise and Registration Act 1994, s 44

Maximum penalty – Fine level 5 (for fines see p 209). No power to disqualify or endorse.

Crown court – Unlimited fine and 2 years imprisonment. Triable either way.

Legal notes and definitions

Other offences. The offence can also be committed by forging or fraudulently altering, lending or allowing to be used by another a licence or registration document under the Act. It is also an offence fraudulently to use etc a numberplate. Exhibiting an altered vehicle excise licence on a car parked on private land does not amount to fraudulent use within the meaning of the Act (*R v Johnson* (1994)).

Fraudulently. Does not merely cover economic loss by the evasion of excise duty but also includes the case where the defendant intends by deceit to cause a public official such as a police officer to act, or refrain from acting, in a way in which he otherwise would not have done. See *Terry* (1984) and *R v Macrae* (1994) on forgery of a licence.

Sentencing

The majority of cases are dealt with in the magistrates' court where a fine in the lower range may often be appropriate. It should be noted that unlike most either way offences this offence is not punishable with imprisonment by a magistrates' court, accordingly sentences such as community service are not available.

For fines see p 209.

Seat belts

Charge

Unlawfully did drive or ride in a motor vehicle of a class specified in the Motor Vehicles (Wearing of Seat Belts) Regulations 1993 otherwise than in accordance with the provisions of those Regulations

Road Traffic Act 1988, s 14

Maximum penalty – Fine level 2 (for fines see p 209). No power to endorse or disqualify.

Unlawfully did drive a motor vehicle with a child in the front seat not wearing a seat belt

OR

Unlawfully did drive a motor vehicle with a child in the rear seat not wearing a seat belt

Motor Vehicles (Wearing of Seat Belts by Children in Front Seats) Regulations 1993
Road Traffic Act, s 15

Maximum penalty — (Front seat) level 2
(Rear seat) level 1

No endorsement or disqualification.

Fixed penalty – £20.

Legal notes and definitions

Criminal liability. Only the person actually committing the contravention can be prosecuted. There are no provisions for another person to be prosecuted for aiding and abetting etc and causing or permitting.

Specified passenger's seat is the front seat alongside the driver's seat, or, if there is more than one such seat, the one furthest from the driver's seat. If there is no seat alongside the driver's seat, then the specified passenger's seat is the foremost forward facing seat furthest from the driver's seat, unless there is a fixed partition separating it from the space in front of it and alongside the driver's seat as, for example, in a London type taxi cab.

Class of vehicle. Every motor car registered on or after 1 January 1965, every 3-wheeled vehicle not weighing more than 225 kg manufactured on or after 1

March 1970 and first used on or after 1 September 1970 and heavy motor cars first used on or after 1 October 1988, eg goods vehicles and minibuses.

Seat belt. The seat belt must comply with the requirements of the relevant regulations, about which the clerk will advise.

Exemptions. Every driver and every person occupying the specified passenger's seat, as defined above, must wear a seat belt when in the vehicle, even when the vehicle is stationary, except a person who is

(a) using a vehicle constructed or adapted for the delivery or collection of goods or mail to consumers or addressees, as the case may be, whilst engaged in making local rounds of deliveries or collections;
(b) driving the vehicle while performing a manoeuvre which includes reversing;
(c) a qualified driver, and is supervising a provisional licence holder while that person is performing a manoeuvre which includes reversing;
(d) the holder of a valid certificate in a form supplied by the Secretary of State, containing the information required by it, and signed by a registered medical practitioner to the effect that it is inadvisable on medical grounds for him to wear a seat belt;
(e) a constable protecting or escorting another person;
(f) not a constable, but is protecting or escorting another person by virtue of powers the same as or similar to those of a constable for that person;
(g) in the service of a fire brigade and is donning operational clothing or equipment;
(h) the driver of
    (i) a taxi which is being used for seeking hire, or answering a call for hire, or carrying a passenger for hire, or
    (ii) a private hire vehicle which is being so used to carry a passenger for hire;
(i) a person by whom a test of competence to drive is being conducted and his wearing a seat belt would endanger himself or any other person;
(j) occupying a seat for which the seat belt either
    (i) does not comply with the relevant standards or
    (ii) has an inertia reel mechanism which is locked as a result of the vehicle being, or having been, on a steep incline;
(k) riding in a vehicle being used under a trade licence, for the purpose of investigating or remedying a mechanical fault in the vehicle.

Children under 14 years. The above regulations do not apply but it is an offence under s 15(2) of the Road Traffic Act 1988 punishable with a maximum fine on level 2 for a person without reasonable excuse to drive on a road with a child under 14 years in the front of a motor vehicle who is not wearing a seat belt.

The seat belt must conform with the Motor Vehicles (Wearing of Seat Belts by Children) Regulations which provide for the use of special child restraining devices, or, according to age, adult seat belts for use in the front passenger seat.

Exemptions similar to those at (d) and (j) apply. Generally it is now unlawful to drive a vehicle with a small child in the front unless he is wearing a suitable restraint.

Rear seat belts. It is also compulsory for both adults and children in the rear seats of a vehicle fitted with seat belts to wear them. If a child (ie a person under 14 years) on the rear seat is not wearing a seat belt (with a booster cushion where necessary, or a child restraint), the driver of the vehicle will incur liability (maximum penalty a fine on level 1). In the case of a passenger aged 14 years or more, only he will be liable (maximum penalty a fine on level 2), there are no provisions for the driver to be guilty of aiding and abetting the offence. There is no liability where all available seat belts are in use.

The following table[1] summarises the main legal requirements for wearing seat belts.

	Front seat	*Rear seat*	*Whose responsibility*
Driver	Must be worn if fitted	—	Driver
CHILD under 3 YEARS OF AGE	Appropriate child restraint must be worn	Appropriate child restraint must be worn	Driver
CHILD AGED 3–11 and under 1.5 metres (about 5 feet) in height	Appropriate child restraint must be worn if available. If not, an adult seat belt must be worn	Appropriate child restraint must be worn if available. If not, an adult seat belt must be worn	Driver
CHILD AGED 12 or 13 or younger 1.5 metres or more in height	Adult seat belt must be worn if available	Adult seat belt must be worn if available	Driver
ADULT PASSENGERS	Must be worn if available	Must be worn if available	Passenger

Speeding

Charge

Driving a motor vehicle on a road at a speed exceeding a statutory limit

Road Traffic Regulation Act 1984, ss 81 (84 or 86) and 89

Maximum penalty – Fine level 3 (for fines see p 209). May disqualify for any period and/or until a driving test has been passed. Must endorse unless there are special reasons.

Note – Speeding on a motorway may be charged under s 17 of the Road Traffic Regulation Act 1984 in which case the maximum penalty is a fine on level 4.

Penalty points – 3–6. (Fixed penalty – 3.)

Fixed penalty – £40.

Legal notes and definitions

Speeding can be considered under five main headings:

(A) Speeding on restricted roads (s 81).
(B) Speeding on motorways (s 17).
(C) Breaking the speed limit imposed by the Secretary of State for the Environment or highway authorities on roads other than restricted roads (s 84).
(D) Driving a vehicle at a speed in excess of that permitted for that class of vehicle (s 86).
(E) Breaking a temporary or experimental speed limit imposed by the Secretary of State for the Environment on certain specified roads (s 88). These classes of speeding are dealt with in the above order on the following pages.

Warning of prosecution must have been given to the defendant except in circumstances prescribed in s 2 of the Road Traffic Offenders Act 1988, as amended (eg following an accident).

Evidence. The Road Traffic Offenders Act 1988, s 20 (as substituted by the Road Traffic Act 1991) provides that it will be sufficient for evidence of an offence of speeding or contravening a red traffic light to be obtained by approved devices, such as a Gatso camera, which also records speeds and times as appropriate. The record must be signed by the police and the defendant given 7 days notice of its intended use. The accused may require the attendance of the person who signed the document not less than 3 days before the trial. See

'Conditional offer of fixed penalty' on p 272.

If the evidence merely consists of one witness's opinion that the defendant was exceeding the speed limit there cannot be a conviction. If the single witness is supported by a speedometer, stop watch, radar meter or Vascar, then there can be a conviction.

The evidence of two witnesses estimating the speed at the same time can result in a conviction, but if their estimates refer to speeds at different parts of the road then that will not suffice.

If a vehicle was being used for the purpose of the fire brigade, the police, or the ambulance services, and the driver can establish that observing the speed limit would have hindered him in the execution of his official duties, then that could be accepted as a successful line of defence by the court. It is for the court to decide this issue as there is no inherent right for all such vehicles to exceed the speed limit, for instance an empty ambulance merely returning to its garage or a fire engine out on routine test carry no exemption from a speed limit.

The defendant merely has to prove that this defence is probably true; he need not prove it beyond reasonable doubt.

Although the driver must be identified, the fact that he was driving when stopped is prima facie evidence that he drove over the whole distance for which he was timed.

Speed limit signs. If the defendant submits that the speed sign was unlawful because of its size, composition, character or colour, etc, the clerk should be consulted.

Category A – speeding on restricted roads (s 81)

Legal notes and definitions

Restricted road. A road becomes a restricted road in one of two ways:

(a) it has a system of street lamps placed not more than two hundred yards apart, in which case the speed limit is 30 miles per hour; or
(b) it is directed by the relevant authority that it becomes a restricted road, in which case the speed limit is again 30 miles per hour.

A road restricted by (a) above need not display 'repeater' signs but a road in category (b) does have to display the repeater '30' signs.

The relevant authority may direct that an (a) category road may be derestricted. 'Restricted road' is a term of art referring to a road having a 30 miles per hour limit because of the above provisions. Confusingly, restricted road is commonly, but erroneously, used to refer to any road having a speed limit less than the overall maxima of 70 miles per hour for motorways and dual carriageways and 60 miles per hour for single carriageways.

The limit on a restricted road of 30 mph can be altered by the Secretary of State for the Environment and the Home Secretary acting jointly.

A vehicle which is limited to a lower speed than the limit for the road must always conform to its own scheduled speed limit, for example, a lorry drawing more than one trailer is limited to 20 mph and must keep to that limit even on a restricted road where a 30 mph limit is in force.

Category B – speeding on motorways (s 17)

Motorway. The clerk can provide a detailed definition if it should be necessary. The motorway includes the hard shoulder and access and exit roads.

The general speed limit on a motorway is 70 miles per hour although there are lower speed limits on certain stretches of motorway.

Contraventions of certain temporary restrictions on motorways (eg for roadworks) are offences under s 16 and also carry an endorsement.

Category C – driving a motor vehicle at a speed in excess of a limit imposed on a road, other than a restricted road, by the highway authority (s 84)

Legal notes and definitions

For the purposes of this offence the appropriate highway authority for trunk roads is the Secretary of State for the Environment. For non-trunk roads the appropriate authority is either the Secretary of State for the Environment or the local authority (for instance a county council or, in London, the relevant London borough) but the local authority has to have his consent.

These speed limits can be ordered to be in general use or merely during specified periods.

This is the provision which enables a 40 or 50 (or whatever) miles per hour limit to be imposed on a specified road. If the road would otherwise be a 'restricted' (ie having a limit of 30 miles per hour) road, eg because of having lamp posts not more than 200 yards apart, it ceases to be a 'restricted' road when an order is made imposing a limit under this provision.

Category D – driving a motor vehicle at a speed exceeding the limit prescribed for that class of vehicle (s 86)

Legal notes and definitions

Permitted speed limits for restricted classes of vehicles include:

	Motor-way	*Dual carriageway*	*Other road*
Coach or motor caravan having an unladen weight exceeding 3.05 tonnes or adapted to carry more than 8 passengers			
(a) if not exceeding 12 metres in overall length	70	60	50
(b) if exceeding 12 metres in overall length	60	60	50
Car, motor caravan, car-derived van drawing one trailer, eg a caravan	60	60	50
Goods vehicle maximum laden weight not exceeding 7.5 tonnes (except car-derived van and articulated vehicles)	70	60	50
Goods vehicle maximum laden weight exceeding 7.5 tonnes	60	50	40
Articulated goods vehicles			
(a) maximum laden weight not exceeding 7.5 tonnes	60	50	50
(b) maximum laden weight exceeding 7.5 tonnes	60	50	40

Category E – where temporary or experimental speed limits have been imposed by the Ministry of Transport (s 88)

Legal notes and definitions

The Secretary of State for the Environment may, for a period of up to 18 months, impose a speed limit on all roads or on certain specified roads in the interests of safety or traffic flow. The limit may be general or apply only at specified times.

Unless such an order directs otherwise, it will not interfere with existing speed limits on restricted roads or roads which are already the subject of an order. It is an order under this provision which has imposed a general speed limit of 70 miles per hour on dual carriageways and 60 miles per hour on single carriageways. Originally of a temporary nature, the order has now been made indefinite.

A speed limit may be imposed on a stretch of road for a temporary period to prevent danger from works on or near the highway.

These provisions do not apply to motorways.

Sentencing

If it appears to the court that the accused suffers from some disease or physical disability likely to cause his driving to be a source of danger to the public, then the court shall notify the licensing authority who may take steps to withdraw the driving licence.

Most courts have their own tariff or method of determining the exact fine. The following factors should be considered in assessing seriousness:

(a) the type of vehicle;
(b) the nature of the road;
(c) whether the offence was committed during the hours of darkness and if so whether on lit or unlit road;
(d) weather conditions;
(e) time of day and use of road at the time.

Defective steering

Charge

Using, causing or permitting to be used on a road a motor vehicle with defective steering

Road Vehicles (Construction and Use) Regulations 1986, reg 29;
Road Traffic Act 1988, s 41A(b)

Maximum penalty – For a goods vehicle, fine on level 5, otherwise level 4 (for fines see p 207).

Penalty points – 3.

Fixed penalty – £40.

Legal notes and definitions

All the details as to maximum penalty, legal notes, exemption from endorsement and disqualification, and definitions and sentencing set out on pp 274–276 for defective brakes apply to this charge of defective steering.

As with brakes, the law demands that the steering fitted to a motor vehicle on a road shall at all times be maintained in good and efficient working order and properly adjusted.

No test certificate

Charge

Using, causing or permitting a motor vehicle to be on the road first registered 3 or more years previously without having a test certificate in force

Road Traffic Act 1988, s 47(1)

Maximum penalty – Fine level 3. Vehicles adapted to carry more than 8 passengers, level 4 (for fines see p 209). No power to endorse or disqualify.

Legal notes and definitions

Passenger vehicles carrying more than 8 passengers. These vehicles and some taxis and ambulances must be tested after one year.

Motor vehicle. See p 275.

Road. Means any highway (including footpaths and bridleways) and any other road to which the public has access and includes bridges.

Using. This does not in law only mean driving a vehicle along a road; its mere presence on a road, even in a useless condition may constitute using (*Pumbien v Vines* (1996)). The test is whether steps had been taken to make it impossible for a driver to drive the vehicle. Where doubt exists consult the clerk. A person, limited company, a corporate body which owns a vehicle that is driven in the course of the owner's business is using the vehicle. See p 274.

Causing. This implies some express or positive mandate from the person causing the vehicle to be used; or some authority from him and knowledge of the facts which constitute the offence.

Permitting. This includes express permission and also circumstances in which permission may be inferred.

If the defendant is a limited company, it must be proved that some person for whose criminal act the company is responsible permitted the offence. A defendant charged with permitting must be shown to have known the vehicle was being used or that he shut his eyes to something that would have made the use obvious to him.

Examples of exempted vehicles include:

Goods vehicles the design gross weight of which exceeds 3500 kg.

Motor tractors.
Articulated vehicles, and their several parts.
Works trucks.
Pedestrian-controlled vehicles.
Invalid vehicles.
Some taxis.
Certain vehicles from abroad and Northern Ireland only here temporarily.
Vehicles en route for export.
Agricultural motor vehicles.

Examples of exempted uses include:

(a) that by a previous arrangement the vehicle was being used for the purpose of taking it for a test or for bringing it back from a test;
(b) that the examiner or a person under his personal direction was using the vehicle in the course of or in connection with a test;
(c) that following an unsuccessful test the vehicle was being used by being towed to a place where it could be broken up.
(d) that by a previous arrangement the vehicle was being taken to or from a place where it was to be or had been taken to remedy defects on the ground of which a test certificate had been refused.

The defendant need not prove either kind of exemption (ie exempted vehicle or exempted use) beyond reasonable doubt; he need only prove this defence is probably true.

Renewal of certificate. A certificate lasts for one year. Within one month from the expiry of the certificate, the vehicle may be retested and a further certificate issued to commence on the expiry of the existing certificate.

Sentencing

This offence is more serious if it is committed with a vehicle that would not pass the test, or would pass only if money is spent bringing it up to standard. In such cases, other offences are usually associated with it. In other cases a small fine is usual. The fine might be increased according to the length of time the vehicle has been untested.

Traffic signs

Charge

Failing to comply with the indication given by a traffic sign

Road Traffic Act 1988, s 36

Maximum penalty – Fine level 3 (for fines see p 209). Endorsement and disqualification can only be ordered if the vehicle was a motor vehicle and the traffic sign was one of the following: **Stop, Traffic Lights** (including portable traffic lights and green filter arrows), **No Entry Sign** or **Double White Lines.** For these signs disqualification can be for any period or until the accused has passed a driving test. Must endorse for these signs unless there are special reasons.

Endorsement and disqualification also apply to drivers of 'abnormal loads' at railway level crossings who fail to phone the signalman before crossing and to drivers of vehicles which contravene relevant height restrictions.

Penalty points – 3 (only for endorsable offences).

Fixed penalty – £40 (endorsable offences); £20 (otherwise).

Legal notes and definitions

It is not a defence that the sign was not seen.

The defendant can only be convicted if at the time of the offence he was warned of possible prosecution, or a summons or a notice of intended prosecution was served within 14 days upon the registered owner of the vehicle. It will be presumed that this requirement was complied with unless the contrary is proved.

The offence applies to all vehicles including pedal cycles and is not limited to mechanically propelled vehicles.

Even wheeling a pedal cycle in contravention of the sign is an offence.

A traffic sign. This is presumed to be of correct size, colour and type unless proved to the contrary by the defence.

Automatic traffic lights are presumed to be in proper working order unless the contrary is proved by the defence.

Traffic lights. It is an offence if any part of the vehicle crosses the 'stop' line when the light is red, for example, if the front part of the vehicle is already over the line and the light turns red an offence is committed if the rear part of the vehicle then crosses the line with the light still at red.

Double white lines. It is an offence to overtake or park in contravention of double white lines in the middle of the road.There are certain exceptions, however, such as passing a slow moving road sweeper or a taxi stopping to allow a passenger to alight or board. Ask the clerk for details.

A road. Means any highway (including footpaths and bridleways) and any other road to which the public has access and includes bridges.

Signs to which the offence applies. These include:

Emergency traffic signs placed by a constable on the instructions of a chief officer of police.
[1] Stop at major road ahead.
Give way at major road ahead.
Stop one way working.
[1] No entry.
Arrow indicating direction to be followed.
Arrow indicating keep left or right.
[1] Red light including portable light signals and at automatic level crossings.
[1] Double white lines.
Keep left dual carriageway.
Turn left at dual carriageway.
[1] Drivers of 'abnormal loads' at railway level crossings.
[1] Prohibition on vehicles exceeding specified height.
[1] Green arrow traffic signals.
No 'U' turn.
Mini roundabout sign.

1 Only these offences qualify for endorsement and disqualification.

Sentencing

Endorsement and disqualification can only be ordered if the vehicle was a motor vehicle and the traffic sign was one of those mentioned under 'Maximum penalty'.

If it appears to the court that the accused suffers from some disease or physical disability likely to cause his driving to be a source of danger to the public, then the court shall notify the licensing authority who may take steps to withdraw the driving licence.

The fine will depend to some extent on the sign ignored.

For the endorsable offences a moderate fine may be considered.

Defective tyres

Charge

Using, causing or permitting to be used on a road a motor vehicle or trailer with defective tyres

Road Vehicles (Construction and Use) Regulations 1986, reg 27;
Road Traffic Act 1988, s 41A(b)

Maximum penalty – For a goods vehicle, fine level 5, otherwise level 4 (for fines see p 209). May disqualify for any period and/or until a driving test has been passed. Must endorse unless special reasons exist.

For 'special reasons', see p 260.

Penalty points – 3.

Fixed penalty – £40.

Legal notes and definitions

All the details as to legal notes, exemption from endorsement and disqualification, definitions and sentencing set out on p 274 for defective brakes also apply to these charges.

It is an offence for a tyre on a car or light van (gross weight not exceeding 3500 kg) and their trailers to be in any of the following conditions:

(a) tyre being unsuitable having regard to the use to which the vehicle is put;
(b) tyre being unsuitable having regard to types of tyres on other wheels;
(c) tyre not so inflated as to make it fit for use to which vehicle is being put;
(d) break in fabric of tyre;
(e) ply or cord structure exposed;
(f) the grooves of the tread pattern of the tyre do not have a depth of at least 1 millimetre throughout a continuous band comprising the central three-quarters of the breadth of the tread and round the entire outer circumference of the tyre;
(g) tyre must be free from any defect which might damage the road surface or cause danger to persons in the vehicle or on the road.

Consult clerk for complete list.

The law requires all tyres of a motor vehicle or trailer on a road to be free from any defect which might in any way cause damage to the road surface or cause danger to persons in or on a vehicle or to other persons using the road.

If no tyre is fitted at all the offence will be brought under a different regulation.

Two or more defective tyres. If a vehicle has two or more defective tyres, a separate charge should be alleged for each.

Sentencing

As for 'brakes' on p 274. A vehicle with two defective tyres is much more dangerous than a vehicle with only one defective tyre. The penalty should usually ensure that it is cheaper to keep the vehicle in good condition than to risk a fine.

The penalty should also reflect the potential danger not only to the driver and passengers in the offending vehicle, but to other road users.

Section four

Family proceedings

Contents

Family proceedings

Magistrates' courts have an extensive jurisdiction in family proceedings which for this purpose are defined to include proceedings under the Children Act 1989, applications for maintenance of a spouse under the Domestic Proceedings and Magistrates' Courts Act 1978, applications for consent to marry (Marriage Act 1949, s 3) adoption (Magistrates' Courts Act 1980, s 65) and domestic violence applications (Family Law Act 1996).

The Children Act 1989 has created a largely concurrent jurisdiction between the three courts which deal with the welfare of children – the High Court, county court and magistrates' court – and as far as practicable the procedures in the three courts have been assimilated. All these courts also have jurisdiction in adoption proceedings and this coming together of the separate jurisdictions will lay the foundations for one unified family court.

In using the term 'family proceedings' it should be noted that the term is also used in a different and more restricted sense when referring to the power of the courts to make orders in family proceedings under the Children Act, see p 358.

The family proceedings court

Jurisdiction in the magistrates' court resides in the 'Family Proceedings Court'. Parties to a private dispute (ie one not involving a local authority) are able, subject to practical and financial limitations, to choose whether the High Court, county court or magistrates' court is to hear their case, whereas all care proceedings (which include most matters formerly heard in wardship) will commence in the family proceedings court. In the case of care proceedings the justices' clerk will allocate such cases to the more appropriate court, eg more lengthy or complex matters to the county court where they will be heard there or transferred on to the High Court.

Family proceedings panel

Only those justices who have been appointed to the Family Proceedings Panel may adjudicate in the family proceedings court. Justices were appointed by the bench at its meeting in October 1991 and serve until 31 December 1993 and for periods of three years at a time thereafter.

Each court, except in unforeseen circumstances, will be presided over by a panel member specially trained as a chairman and must so far as is practicable comprise both a man and woman.

Privacy

The courtroom. So far as is consistent with the due dispatch of business, family proceedings should be heard separately from the hearing of other business (MCA 1980, s 69).

Persons present during the hearing. Only the following are allowed to be present:

(a) officers of the court;

(b) parties to the case before the court, their solicitors and counsel, and witnesses and other persons directly concerned with that case;
(c) representatives of newspapers or news agencies;
(d) persons permitted by the court to be present, but permission shall not be withheld from a person who appears to the court to have adequate grounds for attendance (MCA 1980, s 69).

More stringent requirements apply to adoption proceedings, when persons included in paragraphs (a) and (b) only may be in court.

Restrictions on reporting. The press may not report particulars of the proceedings other than:

(a) the names, addresses and occupations of the parties and witnesses;
(b) the grounds of the application and a concise statement of the charges, defences and counter-charges in support of which evidence has been given;
(c) submissions on points of law and the court's decision on them;
(d) the decision of the court and any observations of the court on making it.

In adoption proceedings the press may also not report matters at (a) and (b) and must not identify the child in any way (MCA 1980, s 71).

Evidence

In any family proceedings in a magistrates' court, hearsay evidence given in connection with the upbringing, maintenance or welfare of a child is admissible.

Reasons for decision

The reasons for decisions of the family proceedings court must be announced and recorded at the time the decision is made and a copy of that record will be available on demand from the clerk to any person who is considering an appeal. The reasons must be drawn up in consultation with the court clerk but they will be the justices' reasons (or the reasons of a majority of them) and not those of the clerk. It is advised that the justices retire with the clerk and after making their decision they formulate their reasons and ask the clerk to write them down before returning to court to announce the decisions.

(a) Guidance to the courts on the giving of reasons is contained in *Re B (Procedure in Family Proceedings Courts)*(1993).
(b) Reasons may not be amplified later when an appeal is lodged (*Hillingdon London BC v H* (1992)).
(c) Reasons must be formulated before making an order (*Hertfordshire CC v W* (1993)).
(d) Reasons must be given for all decisions including interim orders, granting or refusing leave or on the refusal of an application to adjourn (*T v W* (1997)).
(e) If the recommendations of a guardian ad litem or welfare officer are not followed reasons for that should be given (*S v Oxfordshire CC* (1993)).

The welfare of the child (Children Act 1989)

The welfare principle

> 'When a court determines any question with respect to:
>
> (a) the upbringing of a child; or
> (b) the administration of a child's property or the application of any income arising from it,
>
> the child's welfare shall be the court's paramount consideration' (s 1(1)).

The test is amplified by two more provisions:

Delay

> 'the court shall have regard to the general principle that any delay in determining the question is likely to prejudice the welfare of the child' (s 1(2)).

Welfare checklist

Where a court is considering an *opposed* application to make, vary or discharge a 'section 8' order (see p 358), or is considering making, varying or discharging a care or supervision order it must have regard in particular to a 'checklist' of factors:

(a) the ascertainable wishes and feelings of the child concerned (considered in the light of his age and understanding);
(b) his physical, emotional and educational needs;
(c) the likely effect on him of any change in his circumstances;
(d) his age, sex, background and any characteristics of his which the court considers relevant;
(e) any harm which he has suffered or is at risk of suffering;
(f) how capable each of his parents, and any other person in relation to whom the court considers the question to be relevant, is of meeting his needs;
(g) the range of powers available to the court under this Act in the proceedings in question (s 1(3)).

It should be noted that the wishes and feelings of the child will normally be communicated to the court through the guardian ad litem or welfare officer. Only in rare or exceptional cases should justices see children in private for this purpose (*Re M (A Minor)* (1993)).

Presumption of no order. The court should only make an order if it is in the child's best interests.

Parental responsibility

The primary responsibility for the upbringing and care of children resides with their parents. Accordingly the Act refers to parental 'responsibilities' rather than parental 'rights'. Under the former law the obligations of parents to their children were not articulated as clearly as they might have been. In practice most disputes between parents concern residence and contact. The law now seeks consciously to emphasise that in reality both parents have an enduring responsibility for their children which continues whether or not the child is living with them unless and until the child reaches 18 years of age or is adopted.

Accordingly it is necessary to determine who has parental responsibility for a child.

Persons having parental responsibility for a child

(a) (where they were married to each other at the time of the child's birth) the mother and the father (s 2(1)) ('married etc' includes where the parents married subsequent to the birth);
(b) (where the parents were not so married) the mother alone, unless
    (i) the parents make an agreement to share parental responsibility; or
    (ii) the father makes a successful application to the court for an order granting him parental responsibility which is then shared equally with the mother (s 4).

Once parental responsibility is acquired under para (a) above it can never be lost unless the child is adopted or reaches 18 years of age. Parental responsibility acquired under para (b) may be brought to an end by an order of the court.

The court may also make orders in **family proceedings** which grant parental responsibility to other persons *in addition* to the parents, in which case parental responsibility is shared.

Definition. Parental responsibility means 'all the rights, duties, powers, responsibilities and authority which by law a parent has in relation to the child and his property' (s 3(1)).

A desire to exercise parental responsibility is something the courts should encourage (*Re S a Minor* (1995)) and an order may be made in favour of a father if the court is satisfied of:

(a) the degree of commitment he has shown to the child;
(b) the degree of attachment which exists betweem him and the child;
(c) the reasons for his applying for the order.

(*Re G (A Minor)* (1994).)

Acquisition of parental responsibility by father (s 4)

The Family Law Reform Act 1987 provides that as a general principle in legislation passed after the Act came into force and in certain other statutes in the relationship between two people no regard is to be paid to whether any of their parents or forebears have been married. The legislation refers to a child whose parents have not been married. Where a child is born to such parents the father does not at that stage have parental responsibility. However, he may apply to the court under s 4 of the 1989 Act for an order that he shall have parental responsibility for the child and if given this he will share it equally with the mother. Such an order may subsequently be discharged on a further application made by the father or mother.

Proof of parentage. There is a rebuttable presumption that a child born to parents who are married is the child of both of them. Where parentage is in dispute various methods of proof are available.

1 Evidence of the father. As these are civil proceedings, he may be compelled to give evidence on behalf of the mother. His evidence on oath may provide the corroboration for her testimony.

2 Blood tests. Part III of the Family Law Reform Act 1969 empowers the court to give a direction for the use of blood tests (on application of either party) to be made on the mother, child and defendant. The rules are complicated so that when a court has blood tests in mind, it should first consult the clerk.

No person can be compelled to submit to a blood test, even though a direction has been given. However, if there is a failure to do so, the court may draw such inferences, if any, from that fact as appear proper in the circumstances.

While blood tests cannot determine who is the actual father of a child, in about 80 per cent of cases these tests can establish that a man cannot possibly be the father of a child and thus he can only be excluded from paternity.

Even if not excluded it should be recognised that the man may still **not** be the father. Magistrates may direct blood tests on an application for a declaration of parentage under s 27 of the Child Support Act (*Re E (Child Support: Blood Tests)* (1995)).

However, it is now possible to employ DNA genetic fingerprinting which is not merely an 'exclusionary' test but can prove parentage with almost complete certainty. It will also be possible to order DNA tests of bodily samples other than blood.

3 Evidence of a conviction or a finding of adultery in previous matrimonial proceedings. If the complainant wishes to use s 11 or s 12 of the Civil Evidence Act 1968 by proving that the defendant was convicted of an offence of having unlawful sexual intercourse with the complainant at the material time or if she wishes to rely on a finding of adultery in previous matrimonial proceedings, she may do so but the clerk should be consulted.

4 Evidence of gestation. It is only common sense that the magistrates are going to consider the credibility of the complainant's evidence having regard to the normal period of gestation. The law has definitely concluded that two weeks is too short a period of human gestation. The normal period for gestation is 280 days, but pregnancies can be shorter or longer. Children have survived pregnancies of 26 or 27 weeks. The High Court has held that the period of gestation may be as long as 307 days.

However, in accordance with the general principle that a court should decide a case on the evidence before it and not its own personal knowledge or prejudices, where the period of gestation is an issue in dispute, the court should require the calling of expert evidence for its guidance.

Appointment of guardian (s 5)

Where a child has no parent with parental responsibility for him or a parent or guardian in whose favour a residence order has been made has died while the order was in force, any person may apply to the court to be appointed as the child's guardian and thereby acquire parental responsibility.

Orders with respect to the upbringing of children

Orders with respect to children

Although parents have parental responsibility for their children, it will be necessary on occasion for the court to intervene either, for example, to resolve a dispute between parents as to how their responsibility should be exercised, or where individuals such as foster parents wish to acquire parental responsibility. It may also be appropriate to provide specifically for the upbringing of children involved in other family proceedings such as adoption, domestic violence and for maintenance of a spouse and in family proceedings under the Children Act itself: applications to acquire parental responsibility by unmarried fathers (s 4); appointment of guardians (s 5); applications for financial relief (Sch 1); care proceedings (see p 361) and applications for an education supervision order (see p 379). Where the state wishes to intervene compulsorily to protect the welfare of a child it must satisfy the 'threshold' criteria described under 'Care proceedings' below. In all these **family proceedings** the court may make one or more of the following orders. (References are to the Children Act 1989.)

Welfare reports (s 7)

A court considering any question with respect to a child under this Act may ask a probation officer or local authority social worker to report to the court on matters relating to the welfare of that child (s 7(1)). Information contained in such reports will be supplied to the parties in the proceedings. The welfare officer may not give assurances of confidentiality and the court will only withhold information contained in reports in the most exceptional circumstances where real harm would be caused to the child by disclosure (*Re G (Minors)* (1993)).

Section 8 orders

The court may make one or more of the following orders under s 8 of the Act.

Contact order requiring the person with whom the child lives to allow the child to visit or stay with or otherwise have contact with the person named in the order. The court should regard contact with both parents to be a right of the child which should not be denied due to earlier difficulties suffered after the parent separation (*Re H (Minors)* (1992)).

Prohibited steps order that no step which a person with parental responsibility might take, shall be taken without the consent of the court.

Residence order settling the arrangements to be made as to with whom a child is to live.

Specific issue order giving directions to determine a specific question in connection with any aspect of parental responsibility for a child.

Availability. A s 8 order may be made

(a) in the course of any family proceedings
  (i) on the application of a person entitled to apply or who has obtained the leave of the court to apply;
  (ii) where the court considers that the order should be made even though no application has been made;
  (iii) at any time during proceedings even though the court is not in a position finally to dispose of these proceedings; and

A court will not normally hold a detailed hearing of a case to determine an application for leave to apply but may in a disputed case hear the main parties to form a broad view of the merits of the application (s 10(a) Children Act and *Re F and R (s8 Order Grandparents application)* (1995)).

Persons who may apply for a s 8 order

	Contact	*Prohibited steps*	*Residence*	*Specific issue*
Parent/Guardian	√	√	√	√
Person with residence order	√	√	√	√
Party to marriage re child of family	√	*	√	*
Person with whom child has lived for 3 years	√	*	√	*
Persons with consent of				
(1) persons with residence order	√	*	√	*
(2) (child in care) local authority	√	*	√	*
(3) those with PR	√	*	√	*
Other applicants	*	*	*	*
Local authority	–	*	–	*

Notes

* Leave of the court required.

- A residence order grants parental responsibility to the person in whose favour it is made.
- A specific issue or prohibited steps order shall not be made with a view to achieving a result which could be achieved by making a residence or contact order.
- No court may make a s 8 order other than a residence order in respect of a child in the care of a local authority.
- Local authority foster parents need consent of the authority unless they are relatives or child has lived with them for three years.

The making of a residence order will give the person in whose favour the order is made parental responsibility for the child (subject to some limitations – eg there is no power to consent to adoption) whilst the order is in force (s 12). Certain persons who do not have parental responsibility may not apply for prohibited steps or specific issue orders as these would be an unwarranted interference in the exercise of the parental responsibility of others.

Children in care and applications by local authorities (ss 9 and 10). No s 8 order, except a residence order (which has the effect of discharging a care order), may be made with respect to a child in the care of a local authority. Conversely a local authority may not apply for a residence or contact order in respect of a child not in their care; those matters are more appropriately dealt with in care proceedings where 'threshold' criteria have to be fulfilled. Specific limitations are placed on applications by local authority foster parents.

Welfare criterion and welfare checklist. See p 355.

Welfare reports. See p 358.

Delay and court timetable. In order to avoid delay (see p 355) rules of court provide for the court to draw up a timetable with a view to determining the issue without delay (s 11(1)).

Is a court order necessary? A court shall not make an order under the Act unless it considers that doing so would be better for the child than making no order at all (s 1(5)).

Duration of orders. A s 8 order cannot be made in respect of a child who has attained 16 years, or extend beyond that age unless there are exceptional circumstances (s 9).

Transfer of proceedings. Provision is made for a case under the Children Act 1989 to be transferred from one court to another either horizontally to another family proceedings court or vertically to the county court.

The overall test is whether the interests of the child demand that the proceedings be transferred. The clerk will advise on factors likely to affect this finding.

Supplementary provisions. A s 8 order may contain directions about how it is to be carried into effect, impose conditions which must be complied with by any person named in the order and make such incidental, supplemental or consequential provision as the court thinks fit (s 11(8)).

Investigation by the local authority (s 37). Where it appears to the court that it may be appropriate to make a care or supervision order it may direct the local authority to undertake an investigation of the child's circumstances. If the court is considering making an interim care order then the proceedings become specified and a guardian ad litem may be appointed: see p 362.Where the authority decides not to apply for such an order it must report to the court generally within 8 weeks giving its reasons, details of any services or assistance the authority will provide and any other action it proposes to take, and the proceedings cease to be specified proceedings.

Family assistance orders (s 16)

Whether or not the court makes a s 8 order, it may make a family assistance order requiring a probation officer or social worker to advise, assist or befriend a parent, the child or a person with whom the child is living or who has a contact order.

Care proceedings

A local authority may provide accommodation for any child within their area if they consider that to do so would safeguard or promote his welfare and in certain cases, such as where children have been abandoned or are in need, are under a duty to do so. However, such accommodation may not be provided where any person with parental responsibility who can arrange for his accommodation objects. The only means whereby a local authority may compulsorily obtain the care of a child is as a result of an order made by a court in care proceedings.

Directions appointments

On receipt of an application in care proceedings the clerk must fix a date for a court hearing or directions appointment. The purpose of a directions appointment at which the parties, their legal advisers and a guardian ad litem may be present is to ensure that those facts which are and are not in dispute are clearly identified, that a guardian is appointed where appropriate if this has not already been done and that a timetable is set. The parties will be under a duty to disclose to each other and the court in written form the evidence on which they intend to rely. The magistrates may then read the evidence in advance of the hearing so that the oral evidence may be directed to matters in dispute. There may be more than one directions appointment during the course of the proceedings. The President of the Family Division of the High Court has intimated that care proceedings should where practicable be concluded within three months.

Applications

Applicant. The local authority or an 'authorised person' (at present only the NSPCC).

Grounds for application (s 31). The court must be satisfied (on the balance of probabilities):

(a) that the child concerned is suffering, or is likely to suffer, significant harm; and
(b) that the harm, or likelihood of harm, is attributable to
   (i) the care given to the child, or likely to be given to him if the order were not made, not being what it would be reasonable to expect a parent to give him; or
   (ii) the child's being beyond parental control.

The use of the terms 'is suffering or is likely to suffer' means that if, after a local authority had initiated protective arrangements, the need for these ceases because the child's welfare is satisfactorily provided for otherwise, it will not be possible to found jurisdiction on the situation at the time of initiation of these arrangements. It is only permissible to look back from the date of disposal to the date of initiation of protection where local authority arrangements had been continuously in place (*Re M* (1994), HL).

In order to establish that a child was likely to suffer significant harm in the future within the meaning of s 31 of the Children Act 1989 so as to enable the court to make a care or supervision order, there has to be a real possibility of the risk, based on actual facts rather that mere suspicions (*Re H* (1996) HL).

Harm means ill-treatment or the impairment of health or development.

Development means physical, intellectual, emotional, social or behavioural development.

Health means physical or mental health;

Ill-treatment includes sexual abuse and forms of ill-treatment which are not physical.

Significant. Where the question whether harm suffered by a child is significant turns on the child's health or development, his health or development shall be compared with that which could reasonably be expected of a similar child.

Appointment of guardian ad litem (s 41). The court must appoint a guardian ad litem unless it is satisfied that it is not necessary to do so in order to safeguard the interests of the child.

The guardian will be appointed from the panel of guardians referred to on p 381.

The duties of the guardian include instructing a solicitor on behalf of the child and also preparing a report for the assistance of the court. The guardian's paramount consideration is to have regard to the need to safeguard and promote the best interests of the child.

Welfare paramount and checklist. See p 355.

Delay. The court must draw up a timetable to dispose of the application (see p 351).

Necessity for a court order. The court should ask itself whether an order would be better for the welfare of the child than making no order.

Orders of the court

Care order. The local authority designated in the care order has parental responsibility for the child. Parents will retain their parental responsibility but the local authority may determine the extent to which the parents may meet their parental responsibility for him. The authority may only do this if it is necessary to safeguard or promote the child's welfare (s 33(4)).

Before making a care order the court must consider the arrangements made or proposed for contact with the child by his parents and other specified persons (s 34). There is a presumption (which is rebuttable) that there will be reasonable contact. The court may make an order regulating contact on application or of its own motion and may also make an order that there be no contact. In a matter of urgency and for no more than 7 days a local authority may terminate contact without a court order. There is no power given to the court to impose conditions when making a care order (*Re T (A Minor)* (1994)).

Age limit. No care or supervision order may be made in respect of a child who has attained 17 years (16 if married).

Duration. A care order, unless it is brought to an end earlier, will continue in force until the child reaches 18 years (s 91(12)).

Supervision order. Places a child under the supervision of a probation officer or social worker for an initial period of one year. The order may be renewed for an aggregate maximum period of 3 years. The supervisor is to advise, assist and befriend the child and the order may require him to notify any change of address and to allow the supervisor to visit him.

The order may include a requirement to comply with directions for intermediate treatment (see p 245), and psychiatric and medical treatment (see p 246).

Obligations may be imposed on a person with parental responsibility or with whom the child is living to take reasonable steps to ensure the child complies with the requirements made of him. The making of a supervision order brings to an end any earlier care or supervision order.

Interim orders (s 38)

On an application for a care or supervision order or where in other family proceedings the court has directed the local authority to investigate the child's circumstances, the court may make an interim care or supervision order.

The court must be satisfied that there are reasonable grounds for believing that the circumstances are as mentioned in the grounds for a care or supervision order set out on p 362. Interim orders (which are renewable) may not extend for more than 4 weeks at a time except to extend for up to 8 weeks from the making of the initial order.

In deciding the period of an interim order, the court shall consider whether any party opposed to the making of the order was in a position to argue his case against the order in full.

Exclusion requirement

An exclusion order may be part of an interim care order and specify that:

(a) someone leave a dwellinghouse in which he is living with the child concerned;
(b) someone be prohibited from entering a dwellinghouse in which the child lives;
(c) someone be excluded from a defined area in which a dwelling is located (the dwelling must be where the child lives).

The following criteria must be satisfied:

(1) there are reasonable grounds for believing that the child is suffering or is likely to suffer significant harm; and
(2) that the harm or likelihood of harm is attributable to the care given to the child, or likely to be given to him if the order were not made, not being what it would be reasonable to expect a parent to give him; and
(3) the court decides to make an interim care order on the basis of (1) and (2) being satisfied; and
(4) there is reasonable cause to believe that if someone is excluded from a dwellinghouse in which the child concerned lives, the child will cease to suffer, significant harm;and
(5) that someone else living in the dwelling(who need not be a parent or a relation) is both:
    (a) able and willing to give the child the care which it would be reasonable to expect a parent to give him; and
    (b) consents to the exclusion requirements.

Duration. The exclusion requirement will usually be of the same length as the interim care order but will cease to have effect if the local authority remove the child from the dwelling in question for a continious period of 24 hours.

Undertaking. The court may instead of making an exclusion requirement accept an undertaking to the same effect.

Discharge and variation of care and supervision orders (s 39)

A care order may be discharged or a supervision order varied or discharged on the application of:

(a) a person with parental responsibility for the child;
(b) the child himself;
(c) the local authority designated in the order.

On discharging a care order a supervision order may be substituted. Further application may not be made within 6 months except by leave of the court (s 91(15)).

Appeals (s 94)

Appeals lie to the High Court. Where the family proceedings court makes a decision which dismisses an application for a care or supervision order and the child was subject to an interim order, the court may make a care or supervision order respectively which will continue until the end of the period during which an appeal may be made or determined. Similar provisions apply where a care or supervision order has been discharged (s 40).

Financial provision

The family proceedings court may order a person to pay maintenance for a child and, where appropriate, to his spouse. Maintenance for a spouse may be ordered in proceedings under ss 2, 6 or 7 of the Domestic Proceedings and Magistrates' Courts Act 1978. Maintenance for a child may be ordered either in proceedings under the 1978 Act or in a free-standing application under the Children Act 1989, Sch 1 which will, of course, cover applications both where the parties are married and otherwise.

Applications under DPMCA 1978, s 2

Application under s 2 may be made for an order for financial provision on the ground that the respondent

(a) has failed to provide reasonable maintenance for the applicant or for a child of the family; or
(b) has behaved in such a way that the applicant cannot reasonably be expected to live with the respondent; or
(c) has deserted the applicant.

On any one of those grounds the court may make an order

(i) that the respondent makes periodical payments for the maintenance of the applicant and/or any child of the family; and/or
(ii) that the respondent pays a lump sum in respect of the applicant and/or any child of the family.

Periodical payments for maintenance may be ordered to be paid weekly, monthly, or at any other convenient interval and they may be backdated to the date of the application. The court may also fix a term for which they should be paid. For example, after William and Mary separated William paid £5 weekly in respect of their son. Ten weeks later the court decided in Mary's favour and ordered William to pay £10 weekly from the date of application until the date of hearing (the amount the court thinks he should have paid) thence £15 weekly, being £10 for Mary and £5 for the child. Moreover in a case, for example, where the husband is expecting an improvement in his financial position on a future date, the original order may provide for an increase in the payments on or after that date.

Method of payment. Payment is normally to be made through the clerk of the court but exceptionally, at the wish of the payee, may be made direct to her. The court may instead direct that payment be made by standing order or direct debit or make an attachment of earnings order.

No single lump sum may exceed £1000, but an order may provide for lump sums, say for a wife and two children (£3000) totalling more than that. A lump sum provision might be used, for example, to apportion savings or to purchase school uniforms etc. A lump sum may be ordered to be paid by instalments.

When deciding what financial provision (if any) to make **for an applicant** it is the duty of the court to have regard to all the circumstances of the case, first consideration being given to the welfare while a minor of any child of the family who has not attained the age of 18 and in particular:

(a) the income, earning capacity, property and any other financial resources which each of the parties has, or is likely to have in the foreseeable future, including in the case of earning capacity which it would in the opinion of the court be reasonable to expect a party to the marriage to take steps to acquire;
(b) the financial needs, obligations and responsibilities which each of the parties has or is likely to have in the foreseeable future;
(c) the standard of living they enjoyed before the occurrence of the conduct which is the ground for making the order (this may be different from the standard of living at the time of parting);
(d) the parties' ages and the duration of the marriage;
(e) any physical or mental disability of either party;
(f) the contributions made, or which are likely in the foreseeable future to be made, by each party to the welfare of the family including that made by looking after the home or caring for the family;
(g) anything else which the court considers to be relevant to take into account; this may include the conduct of each of the parties if that conduct is such that it would be inequitable to disregard it.

'First consideration being given to the welfare . . . of any child', means that the child's welfare is not paramount but of first importance in deciding maintenance payments (*Suter v Suter and Jones* (1987)).

When considering what financial provision to make in respect of **a child of the family** the court must have regard to the following matters:

(a) the financial needs of the child;
(b) the child's income, property, resources and earning capacity, if any;
(c) any physical or mental disability of the child;
(d) the standard of living enjoyed by the family before the occurrence of the conduct which is the ground for making the order (see (c) above);

(e) the manner in which the child was being and in which the parties expected him to be educated or trained;
(f) those considerations mentioned at (a) and (b) above in respect of the applicant.

Additionally, in the case of a child of the family who is not a child of both parties to the marriage:

(g) whether, and if so, the extent to which and the basis on which the respondent assumed responsibility for the child's maintenance and the period of time during which he discharged such responsibility;
(h) whether in assuming and discharging such responsibility the respondent knew that the child in question was not his own child; and
(i) the liability of any other person to maintain the child.

An order in respect of the wife will cease if she remarries and orders for children will cease normally when the child attains 17, or 18 years if the court specifies this. This may be extended if the child is being educated, or trained, even though the child may be in gainful employment at the same time. It may also be extended if there are special circumstances justifying it, for example, a disabled person unable to work.

Agreed orders (DPMCA 1978)

Section 6. Either party to a marriage may ask the court for an order making financial provisions simply on the ground that the other party has agreed to make those provisions. In such a case there is no limit to the amount of any lump sum. The court before making such an order must be satisfied:

(a) that the respondent (or the applicant) has agreed to make the financial provisions detailed in the application for the order; and
(b) that there is no reason to think that it would be contrary to the interests of justice to make the order; and
(c) where there is financial provision for children, that the order would either provide or make a proper contribution towards the financial needs of the child.

If the court is not satisfied with the adequacy of any financial provision it may suggest some other provision and, if the parties consent, it may make an order accordingly. If the parties do not consent the application is to be treated as an application for an order in the ordinary way.

Section 7. Where parties to a marriage have lived apart for a continuous period of 3 months without either one having deserted the other, the court may make an order for financial provision even though the grounds stated earlier do not exist and neither is there agreement about financial provisions. In applying for an order under these circumstances the applicant must specify in the application the aggregate amount of voluntary payments made by the respondent for the maintenance of the applicant and/or the children during the 3 months immediately preceding the application. This aggregate figure then sets the limit on the amount which the court may order. The court may make an order for periodical payments provided that the amount payable during any 3 month period under the order will not exceed the aggregate sum referred to in the application. There is no power to include lump sums in this kind of order. If the court thinks that the best it can do in these circumstances would be inadequate it may treat the application as an application for an order in the ordinary way.

Reconciliation

When an application for an order under s 2 of the Act is made, the court must consider whether there is any prospect of reconciliation before dealing with the application.

Orders under the Children Act 1989

If there are children involved, the court must not dismiss or make any of the above applications without considering whether to make an order under s 8 of the Children Act 1989: contact, prohibited steps, residence or specific issue (but note the court must consider that making an order would be better for the child than making no order at all).

Fixing the amount

In a case decided in 1984 (*Vasey v Vasey*), the Court of Appeal gave guidance to justices considering the amount of maintenance to award. The judges said that the court should carefully examine each of the guidelines on p 366 and make a finding on each point. Then the magistrates should conduct a balancing exercise, weighing one with another so that the needs and responsibilities could be set against the resources available. If in an exceptional case the justices decided that conduct was relevant, that must be put into the balance. It was an 'exceptional case' because experience showed that it was dangerous to make judgments about the cause of the breakdown of a marriage without a full inquiry, since the conduct of one spouse could only be measured against the conduct of the other, and marriages seldom broke down without faults on both sides.

Nevertheless courts often wish to arrive at a starting point for discussion and *sometimes*, except in the case of a short marriage, where the wife is able to work and there are no children, a starting point for determining the amount of the maintenance for the wife may be obtained by adding together the joint gross incomes and dividing by three. This is known as the one-third guideline; it must never be thought of as a rule, for it is not. Neither must it be applied inflexibly or to all marriages. The one-third figure is a starting point, an indicator of the amount the wife may expect to receive. The amount of maintenance properly due to her might be very different as, for example, where the husband undertakes to make certain payments for mortgage, rates, school fees, etc thus relieving the wife of her share of those responsibilities. The one-third guideline would be inappropriate for persons living on social security, a pension or a very small income. In grossing the wife's income it is advised that child benefit and single parent allowances and any benefit payable in respect of a chronically ill or disabled child should be ignored. The figure arrived at by applying this guideline is the maintenance for the wife; a contribution to the maintenance of the children will be payable in addition out of the husband's income.

When the husband has a second family to support it may be better to allow him to do so, if he is working, at the expense of his first family. This is because the first wife, having no husband, is better placed to receive supplementary benefit than would be the second (or common law) wife whose entitlement to state aid would be limited by her husband's earnings.

So much guidance has been given by the Family Division in recent years on the question of maintenance that a court would be unwise to consider this aspect of the order without the help which the clerk can provide. The current rates of benefit should also be available to the court in appropriate cases and these can be obtained in the form of a leaflet from the local office of the DSS or in the form of the Statutory Instrument which from time to time varies the amounts.

Tax. Periodical payments are paid gross (without deduction of tax) and are not taxable in the hands of the recipient. The payer will not receive tax relief on his payment except on those to a divorced or separated wife up to the married couple's allowance (£1790 for 1997-98) until the recipient remarries when payments will cease. There is accordingly no tax relief on payments direct to children. 'Old' orders will continue to receive tax relief but this relief will be progressively phased out since the relief will be pegged at the level obtained in 1988–89.

Financial provision for children (DPMCA 1978, s 3 and Children Act 1989, Sch 1)

The court may order a party to proceedings under the Domestic Proceedings and Magistrates' Courts Act 1976 or a parent in proceedings under Sch 1 to the Children Act 1989 to make the following financial provision:

(a) periodical payments for the maintenance and education of the child;
(b) payment of a specified lump sum.

The making of an order for financial provision is not dependent on the making of any other order with respect to the child.

Periodical payments. These may be ordered to be made at weekly, monthly or any other intervals. At the discretion of the court, the payments may be ordered to commence at any time not earlier than the date of the application. The order usually ends when the child reaches his birthday following the date he attains school leaving age (ie 17 years), unless the court thinks it right in the circumstances to order a later date.

If the court is asked to make an order extending beyond 17 years old then the limit is the child's eighteenth birthday unless:

(a) the child is, or will be, receiving instruction at an educational establishment; or is undergoing training for a trade, profession or vocation (in either case whether or not he is in gainful employment); or

(b) there are special circumstances justifying the court in making an order extending beyond the child's eighteenth birthday (such a circumstance, for example, might be a handicap or disability rendering the child totally dependent on a parent).

Persons over 18 years may apply for financial provision from their parents in circumstances where the court may extend periodical payments beyond a child's eighteenth birthday.

Method of payment. See p 366.

Lump sum. The court may order a lump sum of up to £1000 (which can be paid by instalments).

Amount of the order. When deciding what financial provision to make for the child, including whether or not to make a lump sum order, the court must have regard to the following matters, among other circumstances of the case:

(a) the income, earning capacity, property and other financial resources which each parent of the child has or is likely to have in the foreseeable future;
(b) the financial needs, obligations and responsibilities which each parent of the child has or is likely to have in the foreseeable future;
(c) the financial needs of the child;
(d) the income, earning capacity (if any), property and other financial resources of the child;
(e) any physical or mental disability of the child.

Variation of maintenance orders

The court may vary the provisions of any maintenance order it has made. In respect of maintenance for a spouse, the commonest applications are to vary the financial provisions of the order where the husband's income has been reduced or increased or where the husband pleads that a child whom he is having to support is wage earning.

When dealing with an application to vary the amount of maintenance the court is generally concerned with considering a change of circumstances since the previous order was made. This is not an inflexible rule and the court has to look at the reality of the situation. The court may have to look afresh at the means of the parties and fix the amount of maintenance as they would do so when making a new order. It is not necessary to establish a change of circumstances since an order made in divorce proceedings was registered in the magistrates' court where the payer clearly cannot afford the order and there was clearly some mistake in the fixing of the original amount.

Enforcement of an order

If a payer falls behind in his maintenance payments the magistrates can grant a summons or a warrant to secure his appearance before the court for an inquiry into his means.

If the court is satisfied that the payer has a good reason for failing to pay the instalments (such as ill health), and is satisfied that he has no resources with which to meet the arrears then it has the power to remit part or all of the arrears; but the recipient must be given an opportunity to make written or oral representations against such a remission, unless the court considers it unnecessary or impracticable to give her such an opportunity. The starting point for courts is that arrears over a year old should not be enforced unless there are special circumstances (*B v C* (1995)). Courts can adjourn these cases to give the payer another chance to clear the arrears but if the court is not inclined to an adjournment it may make the following orders:

(a) Direct that payment be made by standing order or direct debit.
(b) Order the issuing of a **distress warrant** for the seizure and sale of his property.
(c) Make an **attachment of earnings order.** Such an order requires the employer to make weekly (or other periodical) payment into court of a fixed amount from the payer's wages.

An attachment of earnings order will be able to follow him to his next job. If the court decides upon an attachment of earnings order it should inform the clerk before announcing this decision as the clerk has to obtain certain information as to the precise details of the job and works number (if any).

The court must announce two figures. First, the **protected earnings rate**, which is the amount reasonable for the payer to retain having regard to his resources and needs.

The second figure is the **normal deduction rate** which is the amount the court thinks reasonable to cover his liability under the order.

(d) If the court is satisfied that the defendant either has wilfully refused to pay or culpably neglected to pay and an attachment of earnings order is inappropriate (because, for example, the defendant is likely to change his job to thwart an attachment of earnings order) the court can send the defendant to prison unless he pays the arrears immediately. The actual period of imprisonment is limited by the amount of arrears in accordance with this table (adapted from that used in criminal proceedings):

Arrears	*Imprisonment*
not exceeding £200	7 days
exceeding £200 but not exceeding £500	14 days
exceeding £500 but not exceeding £1000	28 days
exceeding £1000	6 weeks

Imprisonment may not be ordered in the absence of the debtor.

If the defendant goes to prison and serves part of the sentence then the amount to secure his release is reduced proportionately.

If the defendant serves the full sentence or part of it the arrears are not automatically wiped out.

A person cannot be committed to prison twice for the same period of arrears but such arrears remain due from him and could still be enforced against him by, for example, a distress warrant (see (b) above) or by an attachment of earnings order (see (c) above).

(e) **Make a suspended committal to prison** for the same reasons as applied in (d) above. The length of imprisonment will be determined in accordance with the table above.

The sentence of imprisonment can be suspended for a fixed time to give the payer time to pay the whole amount or suspended whilst he pays a fixed sum regularly each week off the arrears (in addition to a sum as maintenance as laid down in the order).

If the defendant fails to comply the clerk sends him a notice inviting the defendant to provide within 8 days written reasons why the suspended committal order should not be put into effect. If no written answer is received within 8 days the committal warrant is released.

If the defendant submits his reasons they are put before a single magistrate who can either direct that the matter be considered in open court or direct the clerk to release the committal warrant.

If the defendant goes to prison and serves part of the sentence the amount to secure his release is reduced proportionately.

The serving of all or even part of the prison sentence does not automatically wipe out the arrears as a debt.

A defendant serving a sentence under (d) or (e) is entitled to apply for review of his committal to prison. It is first considered by a single magistrate who may either refuse a further review or direct that the application be considered in open court.

Magistrates reviewing a committal order have wide powers. They can remit all or part of the arrears (see 'remission' on p 371), put the committal into effect, or allow it to continue on the same terms as before, or further suspend the committal on new terms.

Domestic violence

Non molestation orders

Non molestation orders provide a remedy to any asssociated person from molestation. Molestation includes, but is much wider than, violence and will cover any serious pestering or harassment which is of such a degree as to merit the intervention of the family proceedings court.

Who can apply?

(1) Associated persons. This includes husbansd and wives, divorced couples and cohabitants and former cohabitants. Other applicants may include a wide range of relatives, those who live or have lived in the same household

(other than lodgers, tenants and employees) and those who have agreed to marry one another. In relation to a child the definition includes parents, natural parents and adoptive and those with paternal responsibilities.

(2) Authorised third parties.
(3) Children under 16 with leave of the High Court.
(4) The court of its own motion when dealing with an application in family proceedings.

Criteria for grant

When considering whether or not to grant an application for a non molestatioon order the court shall have regard to all the circumstances including the need to secure the health, safety and well being of:

(i) the applicant;
(ii) the person for whose benefit the order is made;
(iii) any relevant child. A relevant child, includes any child whose interests the court considers relevant, any child who is living with or ought reasonably be expected to live with either party and a child who is the subject of adoption or Children Act proceedings.

Duration. The order may be for a specified duration or until further order but if made in the course of other family proceedings, it will expire if these proceedings are dismissed or withdrawn.

Content of the order. The order may probibit the respondent from molesting a named associated person(s) and relevant child. The court should endevour to be specific as to what acts are prohibited so that the order is both understandable and enforcable.

Variation. A non molestation order may be varied by:

(i) the person who applied for it;
(ii) the respondent;
(iii) the court itself where the order was made of its own motion.

Ex parte applications. An application may be made in the absence of the respondent and if necessary to a single justice in exceptional circumstances. In addition to looking at all the circumstances the court must consider whether there is any risk of significant harm to the applicant or a relevant child and whether it is likely that the applicant would be deterred or prevented from pursuing the application. The court also has power to make an ex parte order where it has reason to believe that the respondent knows of the proceedings but is deliberately evading service.

If an ex parte order is made then a hearing should be listed as soon as is just and convenient to allow for representations to be made.

Power of arrest. A power of arrest must be attached where both parties have had notice of the hearing and the respondent used or threatened violence against the applicant or a relevant child, unless the court is satisfied that they would be adequately proteced without such a power.

Where an ex parte order is made a power of arrest may be attached to the order where the respondent used or threatened violence against the applicant or a relevant child and they are at risk of significant harm from the respondent if the power is not attached immediately.

Enforcement

A power of arrest is attached to ensure compliance with the order and to protect the applicant or relevant child.The power allows a constable to arrest without warrant a person whom he has reasonable cause to suspect has breached the non-molestation order. The duration of the power will be the same length as the order it attaches to.

If no power of arrest is attached the applicant may give evidence on oath of a breach and, if satisfied there are reasonable grounds, the court may issue a warrant for the arrest of the respondents.

If arrested for a breach the respondent must be produced to the court within 24 hours (excluding Christmas day Good Friday and Sunday).

Sanction for breach

Upon hearing a breach application the court may adjourn the case and may remand the respondent to a later date on civil bail, with or without conditions. If the breach is proved on the balance of probabilities the court may order the respondent:

(a) to pay a sum not exceeding £50 for every day he is in breach up to £1000, or a sum not exceeding £5000;or
(b) to be committed to custody for a period not exceeding two months or until he has remedied his default in such shorter period.

Any committal to custody may be suspended upon condition of obedience to the order.

Undertakings

Where the court has the ability to make a non molestation order, and there have been no threats of violence or violence used, they may accept an undertaking from the parties. An undertaking is a promise by a party to the court that they will do or refrain from doing some defined act.

Sanctions. The sanctions for breach of an undertaking are the same as those outlined above for breach of an order.

Occupation orders

The family proceedings court share a jurisdiction with the county court and the High Court to make declaratory and regulatory occupation orders. These orders deal with rights of occupation or exclude a person from all or part of the dwelling.

These applications will be unusual in the family proceedings court and should be the subject of detailed consultations with the court clerk.

Protection of children (Children Act 1989)

Police powers (s 46)

Where the police have reasonable cause to believe that a child would otherwise suffer significant harm, they may remove the child to suitable accommodation and keep him in police protection for up to 72 hours. They must also inform the local authority, persons having parental responsibility for the child and anyone with whom he was living before he was taken into police protection.

Duties of the local authority (s 47)

Where a local authority are

(a) informed that a child is
  (i) the subject of an emergency protection order (see p 376), or
  (ii) in police protection, or
(b) have reasonable cause to suspect that a child is suffering or is likely to suffer, significant harm

they must make such enquiries as they consider necessary to enable them to decide whether they should take any action to safeguard or promote the child's welfare.

The action which the local authority may take may include applying for one of the following orders.

Child assessment order (s 43)

Only a local authority or the NSPCC may apply for this order. Where the court is satisfied that:

(a) the *applicant* has reasonable cause to suspect that the child is suffering, or is likely to suffer, significant harm;
(b) an assessment of the state of the child's health or development or of the way in which he has been treated is required to enable the applicant to determine whether or not the child is suffering or is likely to suffer significant harm; and
(c) it is unlikely that such an assessment will be made, or be satisfactory, in the absence of an order under this section

it may make a child assessment order.

Welfare of child and necessity for order. See pp 355 and 360.

Guardian ad litem. See p 381.

Notice must be given where reasonably practicable to the child's parents and others specified in s 43(11) of the Act.

The order must specify the date by which the assessment is to begin and will have effect for up to 7 days from that date. It is then the duty of any person who is in a position to produce the child to do so to such person as is named in the order and to comply with court directions concerning the assessment.

A child may be kept away from home only in accordance with directions in the order and only if it is necessary for the purposes of the assessment. Where the child is away from home, the order must contain such directions as the court thinks fit with regard to contact with other persons.

Assessment and emergency protection. A court cannot make a child assessment order where there are grounds for making an emergency protection order and it considers it ought to make such an order.

Emergency protection order (s 44)

An emergency protection order authorises the removal of a child to accommodation provided by the applicant for the period specified in the order.

Grounds. Any person may apply for an emergency protection order. The court may make the order where it is satisfied:

(a) (all applicants) there is reasonable cause to believe that the child is likely to suffer significant harm if he is not removed to accommodation provided by the applicant; or
(b) (local authority applicant) enquiries are being made because of the local authority's suspicion that the child is suffering or is likely to suffer significant harm (see p 361) which are being frustrated by an unreasonable refusal of access and access is required as a matter of urgency; or
(c) (NSPCC) the applicant has reasonable cause to suspect that a child is suffering or is likely to suffer significant harm and enquiries into the child's welfare are being frustrated as in (b) above.

The court may consider any evidence (including hearsay) which it considers relevant to the application.

Welfare of child and necessity for order. See pp 355 and 360.

Guardian ad litem. See p 381.

Effect of the order

(a) Directs any person in a position to do so to produce the child on request to the applicant.
(b) Authorises removal of the child to the applicant's accommodation and his retention there.
(c) Gives parental responsibility to the applicant which he may only exercise to the extent reasonably required to safeguard or promote the child's welfare.
(d) May contain directions as to any medical or psychiatric examination of the child.
(e) Presumes contact with parents and other persons specified in s 44(13) of the Act subject to any more restrictive direction in the order.

(f) May require a person who has information relating to the child's whereabouts to disclose that information (s 48).
(g) May authorise the applicant to enter premises specified in the order and search for the child (s 48(3)).

Where the court is satisfied that there is reasonable cause to believe that there may be another child on the premises who should be subject to an emergency protection order, it may authorise the applicant to search for that child and if the applicant is satisfied that the grounds for an order are satisfied the order has effect as if it were an emergency protection order (s 48).

Exclusion requirement

As with interim care orders if the court is able and decides to make an emergency protection order but is satisfied that the reasons and grounds for making the order would be removed if someone is excluded from the dwelling in which the child lives and that someone else living there is both:

(a) able and willing to give to the child the care which it would be reasonable to expect a parent to give him; and
(b) consents to the exclusion requirement,

the court may make the requirement.

The requirement may:

(a) specify that someone leave the dwellinghouse in which he is living with the child concerned;
(b) specify that someone be prohibited from entering a dwellinghouse in which the child lives;
(c) exclude someone from a defined area in which a dwellinghouse is located (the dwellinghouse must be where the child lives).

This allows the child to remain in its dwelling despite the making of the order.

Undertaking. The court may, instead of making an exclusion requirement, accept an undertaking to the same effect.

Warrant of entry. The intentional obstruction of a person exercising powers of search and removal of a child subject to an emergency protection order is a criminal offence. Where it appears to the court that a person has been or is likely to be prevented from exercising these powers by being refused entry to premises or access to the child, it may issue a warrant authorising the police to assist using reasonable force if necessary.

Duration. An emergency protection order shall have effect for such period not exceeding 8 days as may be specified in the order with special provision for public holidays. This period normally includes any period already in police detention. The order may be extended once for a further period of up to 7 days.

Discharge. The child, his parents, or anyone having parental responsibility or with whom the child was living prior to the making of the emergency protection order may apply to the court after 72 hours to have the order discharged unless they were present at the making of the order. There is no right of appeal in respect of the making of an emergency protection order.

Child abduction

Child Abduction Act 1984. It is a criminal offence triable either way for a person 'connected' with a child under 16 to take or send the child out of the United Kingdom without the appropriate consent.

'Connected' persons include a parent or a person having custody, or in whose favour a residence order is in force, or a person reasonably believed to be the father of an illegitimate child.

'Appropriate consent' is that of persons who are parents, guardians, or who have custody of the child, or in whose favour a residence order is in force or that of a court.

Provision is also made for the protection of children subject to various court proceedings such as care, and adoption. It is also an offence for other persons to take children from the lawful control of any person having lawful control of the child.

The Act provides certain defences for the person who has taken the child out of the jurisdiction.

School attendance and truancy proceedings

(Education Act 1944)

A magistrate who is a member of the local authority which is also the education authority should not adjudicate in this type of case.

The educational duty of every parent or guardian of a child or young person of compulsory school age is 'to cause him to receive efficient fulltime education suitable to his age, ability and aptitude and to any special educational needs he may have, either by regular attendance at school or otherwise'.

Compulsory school age is normally from 5 to 16. The actual date when a pupil reaches school-leaving age may be after his sixteenth birthday, for example, the date the term ends. Education legislation prescribes the exact dates and if there is any doubt in a particular case as to whether a 16-year-old has passed the date or not, consult the clerk. In this type of proceedings the pupil must be presumed to be of compulsory school age unless his parents prove the contrary.

As against a parent there are two types of proceedings, which can only be brought by a local education authority:

(1) The local education authority can serve a school attendance order requiring the parent to register the child at the school named in the order. Before doing this the local education authority must have served on the parent a notice giving the parent at least 14 days in which to satisfy it that the child is already

receiving efficient full-time education suitable to his age, ability and aptitude and to any special educational needs he may have. If the education authority wishes to continue proceedings it must serve a notice stating the school it intends to specify in the order (or, if it thinks fit, several schools from which the parent can choose one). Thus the first set of proceedings is in effect for **failure to comply with a school attendance order.**

(2) The second type of proceedings is where the child or young person is a registered pupil at a school but has failed to attend regularly. This is an absolute offence; but a child shall not be deemed to have failed to attend school regularly if:

(a) he was absent with leave; or
(b) he was absent through sickness or any unavoidable cause; or
(c) he was absent on a day of religious observance kept by the religious body to which his parent belongs; or
(d) his parents prove that the school is not within walking distance and the local authority have not arranged transport. If one of these defences is raised, consult the clerk.

If convicted in either set of proceedings the parent can be fined on level 3. The court may direct the local education authority to bring proceedings before the family proceedings court for an education supervision order.

Education supervision orders

The power to bring care proceedings on the ground of failure to attend school was abolished by the Children Act 1989. Care proceedings were felt to be inappropriate where the child is suffering from a schooling problem rather than poor parenting. However the statutory grounds have to be satisfied on evidence of non-school attendance alone (*Re O (A Minor)* (1992)). The local education authority may bring proceedings for an education supervision order on the ground that a child is not being educated properly (where, for example, he is not complying with a school attendance order or is not attending regularly at a school at which he is a registered pupil, see above p 378). Unless previously discharged, an education supervision order will last for one year initially but may be extended for periods of up to 3 years at a time until the child reaches school leaving age. The supervisor is under a duty to advise, assist and befriend and give directions to the child and his parents to secure that the child is properly educated. A parent who persistently fails to comply with a direction may be guilty of an offence (maximum a fine on level 3).

Adoption proceedings

(Adoption Act 1976)

An adoption order is an order giving parental responsibility for a child to the adopters. As a result, the original parents disappear from the scene in the sense that there is no continuing contact with the child (but the court can make a contact order; this is only done in the most unusual and exceptional circumstances). This is the fundamental distinction between adoption and other family proceedings, which usually provide for contact to the child by the non-resident parent. Another consequence of an adoption order is that any pre-existing orders for maintenance or orders under the Children Act 1989 are extinguished.

An adoption order can be made in respect of any child under the age of 18 years who is not, or has not been, married and can be made even if the child has previously been adopted.

Applications for an adoption order

The applicants. An application can be made either by a married couple where one spouse is the father or mother of the child and aged at least 18 and the other spouse is at least 21, or by an individual over the age of 21. Apart from this, an application cannot be made by more than one person. Where an applicant is married but his partner is not a party to the application, the applicant cannot proceed unless the court is satisfied that his spouse cannot be found, they are separated on a permanent basis or the spouse is incapable, on medical grounds, of joining in the application. Where the application is by the natural mother or father alone, the court must be satisfied that the other parent is dead or cannot be found, or there is some other reason for excluding him.

Identity of the applicants. Where the applicants wish their identity to be confidential, they may apply for a serial number to be assigned to them. This number will be used instead of their names.

Residence of the child with the applicants. Where the applicant is a parent, step-parent or relative of the child, or the child was placed with the applicants by an adoption agency, the child must be at least 19 weeks old at the date of the making of the adoption order and at all times during the preceding 13 weeks must have had his home with one or both of them.

In any other case the child must be at least 12 months old and have lived with the applicants continuously for the 12 months preceding the making of the order.

Application to the court

An adoption application is made in a lengthy prescribed form which is comprehensive and, if completed correctly and truthfully, should ensure that the applicants are qualified to make the application.

The court. An application can be made to the High Court, county court or magistrates' court except that an application involving the *applicants* or *child* living abroad cannot be made to the magistrates' court. (The natural parents may live abroad, however, and that is no bar to the proceedings being heard in the magistrates' court.) The magistrates' court will be that acting for the area within which the child is at the date of the application.

Notice to local authority. Unless the child was placed with the applicant by an adoption agency, the applicant must give the local authority three months notice to enable the authority to investigate the suitability of the applicant and the circumstances of the placing for adoption.

Parental consent. An adoption order cannot be made unless either the legitimate parents have agreed or the court has dispensed with consent. The application should indicate whether or not the parents will consent to the adoption.

The consent of each parent can only be dispensed with on one of the following grounds, that he:

(a) cannot be found or is incapable of giving agreement;
(b) is withholding his agreement unreasonably;
(c) has persistently failed without reasonable cause to discharge the parental duties in relation to the child;
(d) has persistently ill-treated the child;
(e) has seriously ill-treated the child (but only where, because of this conduct or other reasons, the rehabilitation of the child within the household of the parent or guardian is unlikely). (See *Re L* (1962).)

Where the applicant wishes parental consent to be dispensed with, the application should contain a statement of facts on which he intends to rely.

Statement by medical practitioner. Where the child was not placed for adoption by an adoption agency or is not a child of one of the applicants, there should be a medical report made not more than three months earlier than the application, on the health of the child and each applicant.

Preliminary proceedings

When he has received the application the clerk will check to see it is all in order and the clerk will fix a date for the hearing (bearing in mind, where appropriate, the necessity of three months notice to the local authority) and send notice to all the interested parties including the parents, the local authority, the adoption society and any person liable to make payments for the child.

Reporting officers and guardians ad litem. It is the duty of every local authority to maintain a panel of social workers and probation officers who are qualified in adoption work. These panel members must be independent of the local authority involved in a case and therefore the social workers retained on the panel may be employed by other local authorities in a different area, or may have retired from full-time social work.

When an application for adoption is received, the court will consider whether the parents are willing to agree to the adoption. If they are, a reporting officer will be appointed from this panel. The reporting officer's duties are to enquire of the parents to ensure that their consent is given freely and unconditionally and with full understanding of what is involved and to obtain this consent in writing.

On the other hand, where the parents appear to be unwilling, the court shall appoint a guardian ad litem from the panel to investigate the case. Even where the parents are willing, a guardian ad litem may be appointed where it appears to the court that the welfare of the child requires it. (Note: reporting officer and guardian ad litem describe the role of the officer in a particular case. The same person may be appointed to cover both duties.) The guardian will consider any report submitted by a local authority or adoption agency and any statement of facts relating to the dispensing with parental consent and any other matters which appear to be relevant. He will advise the court whether the child should be present at the hearing and submit a report for the assistance of the court in deciding whether to make an order. The contents of the report are confidential.

The parties are not entitled as of right to see this report but if it contains adverse comments on some point they should be told and invited to address the court on them. If the magistrates feel that something in the report should be disclosed they should consult the clerk. The child may be asked to leave the court room if any disclosure is to be made.

The hearing

Welfare of the child. In reaching any decision relating to the adoption of a child, a court shall have regard to all the circumstances, first consideration being given to the need to safeguard and promote the welfare of the child throughout his childhood, and shall as far as practicable ascertain the wishes and feelings of the child regarding the decision and give due consideration to them, having regard to his age and understanding.

Sitting of the court. The court sits in private. The *only* persons permitted to be present are officers of the court, parties to the case, their solicitors and counsel, witnesses and other persons concerned in the case (ie the press cannot be present nor 'any other person whom the court may permit to be present').

Presence of the parties. The child must be present unless it appears to the court there are special circumstances rendering such attendance unnecessary. The applicants must be present except that, in the case of a married couple, one of the spouses may not attend provided his application has been verified by a declaration before a justice of the peace or other specified person. Any other person on whom notice has been served may attend and be heard on the question of the making of an adoption order.

Confidentiality. Where the applicants wish their identity to be kept confidential, it will be necessary, where the application is opposed, to conduct the hearing in two parts, hearing each side in the absence of the other.

Points to be considered by the court

Before granting the adoption order the court must be satisfied on the following points:

(a) That all the preliminary matters have been satisfied, ie are the applicants qualified to make the application? Has the child resided with them long enough? If they are married, have they proved this by producing a certificate to the court?

(b) That all the requisite notices have been sent, and all the necessary consents have been obtained.
(c) That the court has given first consideration to the need to safeguard and promote the child's welfare.
(d) That no payment or other reward has been made or given or agreed in consideration of the adoption except any such payment or reward that is sanctioned by the court.
(e) Since adoption proceedings are 'family proceedings' within s 8 of the Children Act 1989, the court has the power to make a s 8 order (p 359). In particular, the court may bear in mind the power to make a residence order in favour of a step parent or relative instead of, or in addition to, an adoption order. This may be relevant where one of the applicants is a step parent following remarriage after divorce (not death).

Powers of the court. The court has power to:

(a) Refuse or grant an adoption order.
(b) Impose terms or conditions in the adoption order, eg the child's education and religious upbringing or even access. Great care should be taken before making conditions and the clerk should be consulted about the advisability and drafting of any condition.
(c) Make an interim order for up to 2 years by way of a probationary period and this order can contain terms as to the maintenance, education and supervision of the welfare of the infant.
(d) Where an order is refused, in exceptional circumstances, the child may be placed under the supervision of a local authority or probation officer, or placed in the care of a local authority.

Costs. Where the court considers an application it has the power to order the applicant to pay all or part of the costs of the guardian ad litem or reporting officer or any respondent attending the hearing.

Appeal. Any appeal from the making of or refusal to make an adoption order lies to the High Court as in other family proceedings.

Freeing for adoption

This is a procedure very similar to that for an adoption order but does not replace it. The applicant can only be an adoption agency and, like an adoption, the order freeing the child for adoption can be made only with the consent of the parents or after their consent has been dispensed with. The essential difference from adoption is that parental responsibility is transferred to the agency and not to the prospective adoptive parents.

The advantages of such a procedure are these:

(a) The issue of parental consent is resolved at an early stage. Where the child has been placed with an agency, the period of time before an adoption order is made can be lengthy. Accordingly the natural parent is in a state of uncertainty and can change his mind at any stage before the hearing.
(b) When a freeing order has been made, the adoption agency can plan the

future of the child with more certainty.

(c) The prospective adopters can enter wholeheartedly into the application knowing that there will be no contested hearing with the natural parents.

There is one exception to the rule that the natural parents disappear from the scene after a freeing order has been made. A parent may make a declaration that he does not wish to be involved in any further questions regarding the child's adoption. If he does *not* make such a declaration, the adoption agency must inform him after 12 months if the child has not yet been adopted or placed for adoption. In this event, he may apply for the freeing order to be revoked.

When adopters make an application for adoption in respect of a child who has been freed for adoption, there is no need for a reporting officer to be appointed as the question of parental consent has already been resolved.

General matters

Disclosure of records. Although all the arrangements for the adoption will have been handled confidentially, when the child is 18 he may apply to the Registrar General for access to the court records and this may reveal to him the identity of his natural parents.

Confidentiality. Under no circumstances should a magistrate ever reveal anything he learns in connection with adoption proceedings. To do so would almost certainly result in his dismissal as a magistrate.

Conditions. These should rarely be attached to an adoption order under s12(6) of the Adoption Act 1976 against the wishes of the adopters. Such conditions are likely to cause resentment and could affect the stability which the child should enjoy after adoption (*Re S (a minor)* (1995)).

Section five

The youth court

Juveniles

(Children and Young Persons Acts 1933, 1963 and 1969)

Children (those aged under 14) and young persons (those aged 14 or under 18) are juveniles. Cases involving juveniles are heard in the youth court apart from exceptional cases in criminal proceedings where the juvenile appears before the adult magistrates' court charged with an adult defendant. The adult court may also remand a juvenile.

(References are, unless specifically stated otherwise, to the Children and Young Persons Act 1933.)

Determining the age of the defendant

If the exact age of a child (under 14) or young person (14 or under 18) is not known, his age will be the age that he appears to be to the court after it has considered all the available evidence.

The youth court

The magistrates are members of the youth court panel selected from the whole bench because it is felt they are specially qualified to deal with juvenile offenders.

Each youth court should (except in unforeseen circumstances) consist of three such magistrates, at least one of whom should be male and one female and the court should be presided over by the chairman or a deputy chairman of the panel.

The courtroom. Juveniles should be kept separate from adult offenders and the youth court shall not sit in a room which is used for normal criminal proceedings within one hour before or after those proceedings.

Persons present during the hearing. Only the following are allowed to be present:

(a) members and officers of the court;
(b) parties to the case before the court, their solicitors and counsel, and witnesses and other persons directly concerned with that case;
(c) bona fide representatives of newspapers or news agencies;
(d) such other persons as the court may specially authorise to be present.

Restrictions on reporting. The press may not report details of the name, address or school of a juvenile who is a defendant or witness in any proceedings before the youth court or any other details including the printing of a photograph which would identify him.

These restrictions may be lifted:

(1) in order to avoid an injustice to a juvenile or in certain circumstances where a juvenile is unlawfully at large on application of the Director of Public Prosecutions; or

(2) the juvenile is convicted and the court , having listened to representations of the parties, believes it is in the public interest to do so.

Criminal proceedings

A child under the age of 10 cannot be guilty of any offence (s 50). There is a presumption of innocence in the case of children aged 10 or under 14 which the prosecutor must rebut by showing not only that the child committed the offence, but also that he knew that what he was doing was seriously wrong. See *L v DPP* (1996) for examples. The presumption grows weaker as the child grows older. This presumption has been attacked but remains valid until changed by statute (*C v DPP* (1995), a House of Lords case).

Attendance of parent

Unless the court considers it unreasonable to do so, it must insist on the attendance of the parent or guardian of a child or young person under 16 years. In respect of those who are 16 and 17 years old, the court has a discretion. 'Parent' will include a local authority where the juvenile is in their care. At all stages of the proceedings, if a parent refuses to attend a warrant can be issued against him or her.

Remands (1969 Act, s 23)

A juvenile may be remanded in the way described in Section nine (Court procedure). Defendants who have attained 17 years are remanded in the same manner as an adult. Where bail is refused in respect of a defendant under 17 years, he will generally be remanded into local authority accommodation. Where the juvenile is remanded into local authority accommodation the local authority may apply to the court to use secure accommodation in certain circumstances.

Secure accommodation. Where a juvenile is remanded into local authority accommodation he may not be kept in accommodation provided for the purpose of restricting liberty unless the youth court (or magistrates' court) which remands him is satisfied:

(a) that
  (i) the juvenile has a history of absconding and is likely to abscond from any other description of accommodation; and
  (ii) if he absconds he is likely to suffer significant harm; or
(b) that if he is kept in any other description of accommodation he is likely to injure himself or other persons.

Where the juvenile is charged with an offence carrying 14 years imprisonment or more or with an offence of violence or he has previously been found guilty of an offence of violence the criteria that must be established are that non-secure

REMANDS IN THE YOUTH COURT

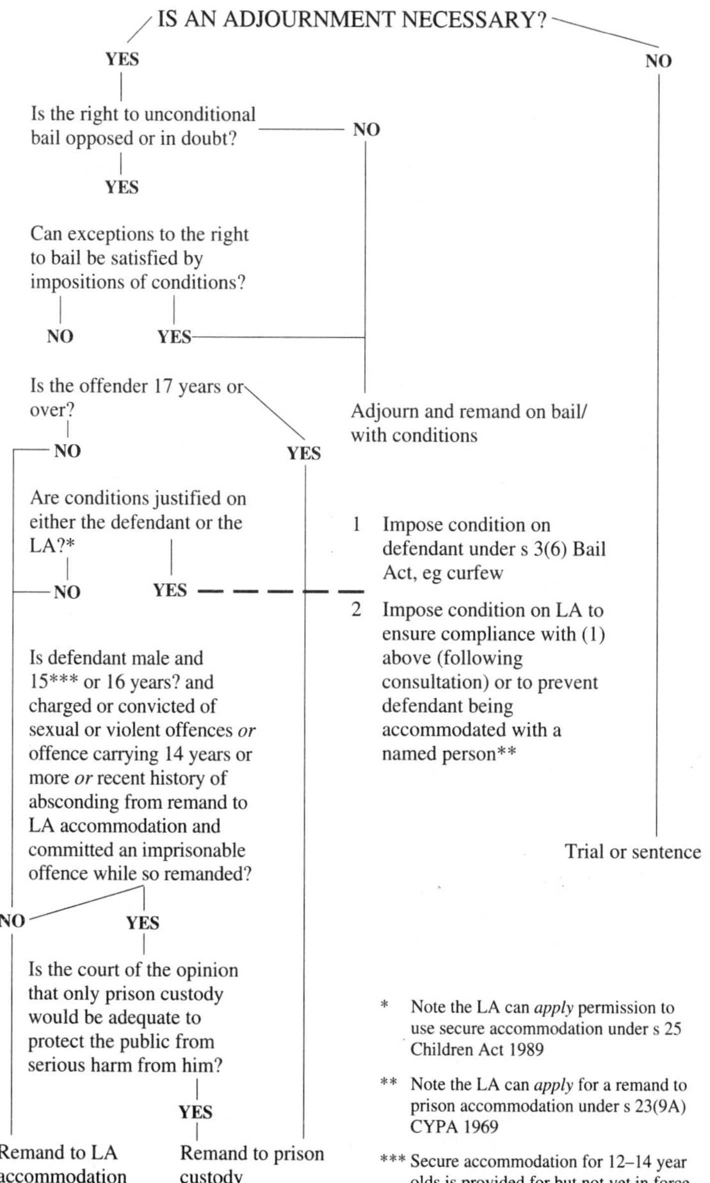
IS AN ADJOURNMENT NECESSARY?
YES
NO
Is the right to unconditional bail opposed or in doubt?
NO
YES
Can exceptions to the right to bail be satisfied by impositions of conditions?
NO
YES
Is the offender 17 years or over?
Adjourn and remand on bail/ with conditions
NO
YES
Are conditions justified on either the defendant or the LA?*
1 Impose condition on defendant under s 3(6) Bail Act, eg curfew
NO
YES
2 Impose condition on LA to ensure compliance with (1) above (following consultation) or to prevent defendant being accommodated with a named person**
Is defendant male and 15*** or 16 years? and charged or convicted of sexual or violent offences *or* offence carrying 14 years or more *or* recent history of absconding from remand to LA accommodation and committed an imprisonable offence while so remanded?
Trial or sentence
NO
YES
Is the court of the opinion that only prison custody would be adequate to protect the public from serious harm from him?
YES
Remand to LA accommodation
Remand to prison custody

* Note the LA can *apply* permission to use secure accommodation under s 25 Children Act 1989

** Note the LA can *apply* for a remand to prison accommodation under s 23(9A) CYPA 1969

*** Secure accommodation for 12–14 year olds is provided for but not yet in force.

accommodation is inappropriate because:

(a) the juvenile is likely to abscond from such accommodation; or
(b) the juvenile is likely to injure himself or other people if he is kept in any such accommodation.

This application is under s 25 of the Children Act 1989. However, the welfare of the child is relevant, not paramount, in a remand situation (*Re M (a minor) (secure accommodation)* (1995)).

The maximum period of authorisation is the length of the remand or, in the case of committal to the crown court, 28 days.

Conditions. After consultation with the local authority, the court may require a juvenile remanded to their accommodation to comply with conditions analogous to those for conditional bail (see p 459). The court may also impose requirements on the authority to ensure the juvenile's compliance with those conditions and may stipulate that he be not placed with a named person.

Remand to remand centre or prison. In two situations the remand will be to prison accommodation:

(1) where the juvenile is committed for sentence under the provisions of s 37 of the Magistrates' Courts Act 1980 (committal with a view to a sentence of detention being imposed in excess of the magistrates' powers, see p 175); or
(2) where the juvenile is male, has attained the age of 15 (extension to cover 12–14 year olds is not yet in force) is legally represented or has had legal aid refused on financial grounds, and the court has consulted with a probation officer or social worker where the following conditions are satisfied:
    (a) he is charged with or has been convicted of a violent or sexual offence, or an offence punishable in the case of an adult with imprisonment for a term of 14 years or more; or
    (b) he has a recent history of absconding while remanded to local authority accommodation and is charged with or has been convicted of an imprisonable offence alleged or found to have been committed while he was so remanded;

and (in either case) the court is of opinion that only remanding him to a remand centre or prison would be adequate to protect the public from serious harm from him. This means serious offences and not just the risk of further offences (*R v Croydon Youth Court, ex p G* (1995)).

Juveniles and committal for trial

(a) If the charge is homicide the juvenile must be committed for trial (Magistrates' Courts Act 1980, s 24).
(b) If the offence is punishable by 14 years imprisonment or more (or indecent assault or causing death under the Road Traffic Act 1988) and the juvenile is aged at least 10 and not more than 17 he must be committed for trial if

the magistrates consider that in the event of his being found guilty he should be detained for a long period. If the magistrates are not of that opinion he must be tried summarily (s 53).

(c) If a juvenile is jointly tried with someone aged 18 or older, the juvenile must be tried summarily unless the magistrates consider it necessary in the interests of justice to commit both for trial (Magistrates' Courts Act 1980, s 24).

The clerk should be consulted when this point arises.

It is suggested that the chairman announces the decision as to whether the juvenile shall be committed for trial or tried summarily so as to make it clear that this point has been considered. This will prevent any suggestion being made that the juvenile was committed for trial and a summary trial not considered.

Procedure

The general principle is that the court should have regard to the welfare of the child or young person (s 44). Because of the youth of the defendant the court must take care to ensure that he understands the proceedings and the charge should be explained in simple terms appropriate to his age and understanding. If not represented, his parents should be allowed to assist him in his defence.

Oath. In the youth court, the evidence of children under 14 years must be given unsworn, otherwise the defendant and all the witnesses use a modified form of oath which commences 'I promise before Almighty God to tell the truth' etc. This oath is also used by a juvenile who gives evidence in the adult court (1963 Act, s 28).

Remission to a local court. Where the court before which a juvenile appears is not the youth court for the area in which he resides it may (and if it is an adult magistrates' court, it must unless it exercises its limited powers of sentence) remit him to be dealt with by his local youth court. This would normally be done, for example, where reports are required and the case has to be adjourned in order to obtain them. The court may give directions as to whether the defendant should be bailed or kept in custody until he appears before the local court.

Possible orders for juveniles

See the Outline of sentencing on p 149, and also the notes on each type of sentence in the 'Sentencing' section on pp 145–244.

Payment of fines, costs and compensation. See p 216.

If a juvenile is found guilty of an offence in a magistrates' court (as opposed to a youth court) because he has been jointly tried in the magistrates' court with a defendant aged 18 or older, the magistrates' court can only impose one of the following:

(a) absolute discharge;
(b) conditional discharge;
(c) fine.

Costs, compensation, endorsement and disqualification can also be imposed. If the magistrates' court considers some other sentence appropriate the juvenile must be remitted on bail or in care to a youth court which will usually be the youth court of the area where he resides.

Binding over parents. The court is required to bind over the parents of an offender aged under 16 years who has been convicted of an offence to take proper care of him and exercise proper control over him; in the case of 16 and 17 year olds there is a discretion to do so. Although the consent of the parents is required, an unreasonable refusal will attract a fine of up to £1000.

Fines. In relation to fines, it should be noted that in the case of 16 and 17 year olds there is now a power for the court to order a parent to pay any fine instead of the former duty to do so. Also, where a local authority has parental responsibility for a juvenile who is in their care or is provided with accommodation by them, they are to be treated as the person's parent for the purpose of a parent's responsibility to pay a fine etc. Where a parent etc is responsible for payment it will be his means that are taken into account, not those of the juvenile: see also p 209.

Section six

Liquor licensing

Licensing committee

(References are, unless specifically stated otherwise, to the Licensing Act 1964 as amended by the Licensing Act 1988.)

Magistrates who are not debarred (see disqualifications below) may be appointed to serve on the licensing committee which may be composed of up to twenty members (the Secretary of State may direct that a committee may have more) and not less than five. The appointment usually takes place at the Meeting of Magistrates in October but may take place in November or December (Sch 1).

If a magistrate sits on a licensing committee when he knows that he is disqualified he can be fined up to £100 in the High Court (s 193).

Disqualifications (s 193)

1 Any magistrate is disqualified if in private life, either alone or in partnership, he is a brewer, distiller, manufacturer of malt for sale, retailer of malt or intoxicating liquor within the county for which he is a magistrate.

2 A magistrate is disqualified if he is a shareholder or stockholder in a company which is a brewer, distiller, manufacturer of malt for sale, retailer of malt or intoxicating liquor within the county for which he is a magistrate, unless before his appointment, he discloses to the other magistrates the nature of his interests. If he does not hold the stock in beneficial ownership he will not then be disqualified. If he does have beneficial ownership, but the brewing etc side of the business is so small in relation to the whole of the business that it does not afford a reasonable ground for suggesting he is not a proper person to be a member of the committee, the justices may appoint him to the committee.

In all cases where a justice may possibly be disqualified, the clerk should be consulted.

If a magistrate is on the licensing committee and during his term of office acquires an interest in the liquor trade as set out above then he automatically disqualifies himself but at the next appointment of members of the licensing committee he can be reappointed if the appointing magistrates consider his interests do not debar his further appointment.

3 If a magistrate serving on the licensing committee has a beneficial interest in the premises which are the subject of an application then he must not adjudicate on the application. If he has a legal interest only in the premises as opposed to a 'beneficial' interest (eg he is a trustee owner), he is not disqualified. If a company or other body of which a magistrate is a beneficial shareholder and stockholder has an interest in the profits of the premises, the magistrate is not disqualified if the nominal value of his shares is £25 or less, or if his holding is one hundredth or less of the issued or stock holding.

Licensing sessions procedure

Evidence

If an application to renew a justices' licence is opposed or the application is for revocation of a justices' licence (s 20A), the evidence must be on oath; in other cases it is a matter for the committee's discretion though most committees require the evidence to be on oath.

Majority decision (s 192)

In every case before the committee the decision is based on a majority decision and the chairman has no casting vote or second vote if the committee is equally divided. If the committee is equally divided the clerk should be consulted since decisions of the committee are expressed by a majority of those present, whether voting or not. The result of an equality of votes will vary according to the nature of the application.

To make this point about majority decision clearer, examples are given. If twelve justices are hearing an application for a new licence and three abstain from voting with five voting in favour and four against, the application must be refused because the five voting in favour do not represent a majority of the twelve magistrates who are sitting. On the other hand if twelve magistrates are sitting with seven voting in favour, four against and one abstention then the application would be successful as the seven voting in favour represent a majority of the twelve sitting.

A majority of the licensing justices present at a licensing sessions may resolve to sit in more than one division. The voting procedures described above apply to each division (s 192A).

Quorum

Three magistrates form a quorum.

Statutory notices

An applicant must serve notices of the application on various persons, such as the police, clerk of the committee, local authority and fire authority. The notice (except for transfer and renewals) must also be published in a newspaper circulating in the locality where the premises are situated, and displayed at the premises. It is suggested that when the applicant has completed the presentation of his case the clerk should be asked if all the relevant notices for the case have been properly served and proved. The clerk will know which notices are compulsory in any given application.

If through inadvertence or misadventure an applicant has not complied with these requirements the licensing committee can either refuse the application or postpone the hearing to enable the applicant to remedy the omission.

Costs (s 193B)

The licensing justices have discretion on the hearing of any application relating to licensed premises to award such costs as they consider just and reasonable to the applicant by any person opposing the application or by the applicant to any such person. The Home Office has indicated that the power is not intended to deter the genuine objector, or applicant, but rather to deter those who make persistent unreasonable objections or applications. Costs should generally not be ordered against the police acting fairly in the performance of their duty (*R v Totnes JJ* (1990)).

'On-licence' application (Sch 2)

An on-licence authorises the licensee to sell by retail any intoxicating liquor, for consumption on the proposed premises or to take away.

Occasionally the application may be limited to certain types of intoxicating liquors.

When granting the licence the licensing committee can impose conditions. If the applicant so requests the licence may authorise the sale of liquor on weekdays and not on Sunday or the licence granted in a holiday resort may be only operative during certain months covering, say, the holiday season.

Objections

A person or company objecting to the grant of a new licence need not give prior notice but can make their objection known at the hearing. After details of the application have been read out the clerk should ask if there are any objectors present. If a number are present and unrepresented they may elect one or two of their number to act as spokesmen.

Written petitions

Sometimes an applicant or an objector may submit a list of signatures to support their case and these are admissible but it is entirely up to the licensing committee how much value they place on such a petition.

Points for the committee to consider

1 The committee must be satisfied that the premises are structurally adapted to the class of licence required and although the committee will have before it plans of the area and premises it is desirable for the committee to inspect the premises before the hearing.

The committee should pay particular attention to any representations made by the fire authority and give close attention to the proposed toilet arrangements, ability of the publican and his staff to supervise the public part of the premises, car parking arrangements, and washing up of glasses and crockery.

2 The committee must also be satisfied that the proposed licensee is a suitable person having regard to his character and experience in the licensing trade. Certain persons are disqualified persons from being licensees, eg a person convicted of forging a justices' licence, or making use of one, or a person who has been convicted of permitting licensed premises, of which he was licensee, to be used as a brothel. A complete list of those disqualified can be provided by the clerk (s 9).

3 Although the Licensing Act does not expressly require that the applicant must prove local need it is now widely accepted that need should be proved. The closing of existing licensed premises may establish local need or the existence of a new housing estate or other development may do this. Alternatively the applicant may bring witnesses to prove the inadequacy of the existing numbers of licensed premises.

The licensing committee has a discretion as to whether it will grant an application. An unsuccessful applicant or objector has the right of appeal to the crown court.

If the premises are suitable and the on-licence is refused the applicant can without further notice apply for a restaurant licence, a residential licence or a combined restaurant and residential licence. See p 399.

'Off-licence' application (Sch 2)

An off-licence authorises the licensee to sell by retail for consumption off the premises either:

(a) any intoxicating liquor, or
(b) beer, cider and wine only.

In a licensing planning area the consent of the licensing planning committee is no longer required for an off-licence application.

The application should specify either category (a) or (b) above.

When granting an off-licence the licensing committee cannot attach conditions. As to the justices' power to require the applicant to give undertakings (preferably in writing) to the committee which he must observe or run the risk of not having the licence renewed, consult the clerk.

The licensing committee should be satisfied that the provisions made at the premises for the storage of the intoxicating liquor and supervision of sales are satisfactory. The holder of the off-licence must ensure that sales are not made *by* a person under 18 unless the sale is specifically approved by the licensee or an adult acting on his behalf. Failure to comply is an offence punishable with a fine of up to £200 (s 171A).

The notes made under on-licence covering 'objections', 'written petitions' and 'points for the committee to consider' (except structural adaptation) also apply to off-licence applications.

An unsuccessful applicant cannot apply for a restaurant or residential licence as in the case of an unsuccessful application for an on-licence.

The unsuccessful applicant or objector has the right of appeal to the crown court.

Provisional on- or off-licence application (s 6)

If the proposed premises are not yet in existence or not completed an application may be made for a provisional grant of an on- or off-licence.

Plans of the proposed premises must be placed before the licensing committee and if the committee grants the application the premises must be built in accordance with the plan. Any deviation from the plan must receive the consent of the licensing committee.

When the premises have been completed according to the plans approved by the licensing committee the provisional licensee may apply for the provisional licence to be made final. It is suggested that members of the committee should inspect the finished premises before granting the final order.

Where licensing justices are satisfied that the premises though not yet complete are likely to be so before the following licensing sessions they may direct that the final declaration may be made by a single licensing justice before the next sessions.

In a case where the notice of application mentioned a full licence when in fact the applicant wanted a provisional licence, the High Court ruled that the application was valid for a provisional licence.

Alternatively the applicant may submit a plan sufficient to identify the site of the premises and a sufficient description of the premises as will give a general indication of their proposed size and character. The committee shall deal with the application as if it were deposited plans, assume the premises will be fit and convenient for the purpose but any provisional grant must be affirmed by the committee within 12 months of the grant (s 6(5)). The applicant must deposit plans and the justices must affirm the provisional grant if satisfied that if completed in accordance with the plans the premises would be fit and convenient for their purpose (s 6(6)).

Restaurant licence application (Part IV)

This can only be granted if the premises are structurally adapted and bona fide used or intended to be used for habitually providing the customary main meal at midday or in the evening or both.

Refusal

The licensing committee can only refuse the application on one or more of the following grounds:

(a) the applicant is under 18;
(b) the applicant is not a fit and proper person;
(c) the premises are not structurally adapted or bona fide used or intended to be used for providing regular midday or evening meals;
(d) that during the previous 12 months whilst a licence was in force the premises had been badly conducted;
(e) that during the previous 12 months the condition that other beverages other than intoxicating liquor should be equally as available for sale has been broken;
(f) that a large proportion of the customers were young persons under 18 unaccompanied by and paid for by someone over the age of 18;
(g) that intoxicating liquor is to be sold by self-service methods;
(h) that after taking reasonable steps the police and fire authority have not been able to inspect the premises;
(i) that during the previous 12 months a justices' on-licence for the premises has been forfeited;
(j) that the premises are not suitable and convenient having regard to their character, condition, and the nature and extent of their proposed use and that intoxicating liquor can only be supplied as an ancillary to a table meal;
(k) that the trade done in the premises does not habitually consist to a substantial extent in providing the type of table meals to which intoxicating liquor would be ancillary.

If the application is refused the licensing committee must give the applicant written reasons for refusal.

Conditions of a restaurant licence

A restaurant licence must contain the following two conditions and the committee can add certain others:

(a) that suitable beverages (including drinking water) other than intoxicating liquors will be as readily available as intoxicating liquor;
(b) that intoxicating liquor will only be sold or supplied to persons taking table meals at the premises and for consumption with their meals.

Where a restaurant serves meals continuously on Christmas Day it may sell liquor without a break in the afternoon (s 95).

Residential licence application (Part IV)

This can only be granted if the premises are bona fide used, or intended to be used, for habitually providing for reward board and lodging (including breakfast) and provide at least one other customary main meal.

The committee can only refuse a residential licence on one or more of the grounds which are listed as (a) to (j) above (grounds for refusing a restaurant licence) except that condition (2) below (relating to the need to provide a sitting-room) should be added to (e) on p 400 (relating to non-intoxicating liquor being as available in a licensed restaurant as intoxicating drink). Ground (j) is modified in that justices will have regard to the provision of a sitting room (instead of, in the case of a restaurant licence, intoxicating liquor being supplied as ancillary to a meal). Also the adaptation or use referred to in (c) should be for the purpose of habitually providing for reward board and lodging including breakfast and one other at least of the customary main meals.

If the committee decide to refuse a residential licence, they must supply the applicant with written reasons for the refusal.

Conditions of a residential licence

(a) The committee must include a condition that intoxicating liquor shall only be sold or supplied at the premises to residents or their private friends being bona fide entertained by them at their expense, and shall be consumed by such residents or friends either at the premises or off the premises with a meal which was supplied at the premises.

(b) Unless the committee considers there is good reason for not doing so, they must also include a condition that paying guests will have available to them at the premises a sitting-room (known as a dry-room) which is not also used as a bedroom and where intoxicating liquor or substantial refreshment is not served.

The committee can also add certain other conditions.

Residential and restaurant licence application (Part IV)

Application can be made for a **combined residential** and **restaurant licence** if the premises are suitable.

The conditions and rules governing such a licence are the same as those laid down for a separate residential or restaurant licence. See above.

Renewal of licences (s 7)

Licences granted after 4 January 1989 remained in force until the end of a 'licensing period' which ended on 4 April 1992. Thereafter licences will remain in force for a three year period ending on a triennial of that date, ie the current licensing period will end on 4 April 1998. If a licence is granted in the last 3 months of a licensing period it will last until the end of the following licensing period (s 26).

All licences to which there is no objection are usually renewed *en bloc* at the appropriate Annual Licensing Meeting (or as it is often called, the Brewster Sessions) which is held in the first fourteen days of each February.

The clerk to the justices may grant applications to renew licences made to the Annual Licensing Meeting where no objections have been made unless with regard to a particular application the justices have otherwise directed or in other specified circumstances (s 193A).

If there is no objection to renewal the licensing committee cannot refuse a renewal. There is a right of appeal to the crown court if a renewal is refused.

The licensing committee can itself object to a renewal. In that event it is customary for the licensing committee to arrange for the police or the clerk of the court to serve a written notice of objection on the licensee.

If a renewal is refused and the applicant lodges an appeal to the crown court, although not essential, the licensing committee can be legally represented at the crown court.

Any person intending to object to a renewal should serve a written notice on the licensee and the clerk to the licensing justices at least 7 clear days before the Annual General Licensing Meeting specifying his reasons.

If no such notice has been served the objector cannot object.

Evidence concerning a renewal must be on oath.

The clerk or chairman of the licensing committee should check whether there have been any objections before the general renewal of licences is announced.

Structural alterations (s 19)

If the licensing committee considers that an on-licence should only be renewed if certain structural alterations are made to the premises they may require to be deposited with the clerk a plan of the premises and order that within the time specified by the order the alterations should be carried out in the part of the premises where intoxicating liquor is sold or consumed. These alterations are those which the licensing committee deems reasonably necessary to secure the proper conduct of the liquor business.

There is a right of appeal to the crown court against such an order.

Old on-licences (prior to 1904) (s 12)

An old on-licence, that is, one that held a justices' licence prior to the Licensing Act 1904, has certain privileges and renewal can only be refused on certain limited grounds which the clerk can supply to the committee. These privileges may have been forfeited if the type of intoxicating liquor that may be sold or supplied has subsequently been extended.

Old beerhouse licences (prior to 1869) (s 12)

Old licences for selling beer and cider in force prior to the Wine and Beerhouse Act 1869 also have certain privileges and can only be refused a renewal on certain grounds which the clerk can supply to the committee. These privileges may have been forfeited if the type of intoxicating liquor that may be sold has been extended.

Restaurant and residential licences

Renewal of restaurant and residential licences can only be refused on the same grounds that are listed for refusing a new licence of this type. The list will be found on p 393.

Revocation of licences (s 20A)

The licensing justices may revoke a justices' licence at a sessions other than at the sessions when the renewal of the licence falls to be considered, either of their own motion or on the application of any person. The power to revoke may be exercised on any ground on which the licensing justices might refuse to renew the licence.

An incorporated association is a 'person' within the meaning of s 20A and can bring proceedings to revoke a justices' licence (*R v Maidstone Crown Court, ex p Harris* (1994)).

Twenty-one days notice must be given of the application or of the justices' proposal to exercise the power to the licence holder and the justices' clerk where appropriate.

Evidence must be given on oath.

The decision to revoke has no effect until the time for appealing against the decision has expired, or the appeal has been disposed of.

Transfer of licence (s 8)

A transfer of licence refers to the transfer of the licence from one *person* to another and must not be confused with removal of a licence.

Removal of a licence is the authorised transferring of a licence from one set of *premises* to another.

A transfer of licence can only be granted by the licensing committee at a licensing session and the committee must be satisfied that the new licensee taking over is a fit and proper person. The committee will probably rely heavily on the police enquiries and whether the police have any objections.

The committee should bear in mind that the clerk can supply them with a list of persons who are automatically disqualified from holding a justices' licence.

If the committee is satisfied that the person applying for the transfer to himself is a fit and proper person to hold a justices' licence then the transfer can only be made in the following cases:

(a) if the licensee has died it can be transferred to his representative or to the new tenant or to the occupier of the premises;
(b) if the licensee has become incapable through illness or other infirmity then the licence can be transferred to his assigns, the new tenant or the occupier of the premises;
(c) if the licensee has become bankrupt then the licence can be transferred to the trustee, the new tenant or the occupier of the premises;

(d) if the licensee or his representatives have given up or are about to give up occupation then the licence can be transferred to the new tenant or occupier;
(e) if the occupant of the premises, being about to quit them, has wilfully omitted or neglected to apply for a renewal then the licence can be transferred to the tenant or occupier of the premises;
(f) if the owner of the premises or his agent has been granted a protection order and application is made at the first or second licensing sessions occurring after the date of the protection order the licence can be transferred to the owner or his agent.

Provisional justices' licence

Applications can also be made for the transfer of provisional grants.

Objections

An objector is not obliged to give prior written notice of his objection to the transfer of a licence.

Right of appeal

There is a right of appeal to the crown court against a refusal to transfer.

Protection orders (ss 10–11)

A protection order is granted by magistrates in a petty sessional court and not by the licensing committee.

A protection order temporarily authorises someone other than the licensee to exercise the licensee's rights of selling at the premises and is effective until the second licensing session which takes place after the date of the protection order. It is designed to fill the gap in such cases as where licensed premises are passing from one person to another before an application can be made to the licensing sessions.

Normally the applicant for a protection order must give the police 7 days notice of the application but if the matter is urgent such notice as the magistrates consider reasonable will be enough.

A protection order can only be granted if the magistrates are satisfied that the applicant is a person entitled to be granted a transfer at a licensing session. If a licence is forfeited or if in certain cases a licensee has become disqualified then a protection order can be granted to the owner of the premises or his agent.

A second protection order can be granted if the magistrates are satisfied that the first applicant consents, or no longer proposes to apply for a transfer, or is not qualified for a transfer or is unable to carry on the business.

When considering whether to grant a protection order, magistrates do not have a general discretion under s 7(3) of the Rehabilitation of Offenders Act 1974 to consider 'spent' previous convictions of the applicant, and should do so only when those seeking the admission of such evidence can show that there was no other way of doing justice (*R v Hastings Justices, ex p Mc Spirit* (1994)).

Removal of a licence

A removal is the authorised transferring of a licence from one set of premises to another. There are two kinds of removal, **special removals** and **ordinary removals.**

Special removals (s 15)

Only old on-licences (in force prior to 1904) can be the subject of special removals. They can only be removed to premises that are in the same licensing division as the existing premises so long as the committee considers the proposed premises are suitable and convenient, and that the existing premises are to be pulled down for some public purpose, or the premises have been rendered unfit by fire, tempest or other unforeseen and unavoidable calamity.

Any person may oppose the application and if the removal is refused by the committee there is a right of appeal to the crown court.

If the new premises are fit and convenient the application can only be turned down on certain limited grounds, a list of which the clerk can supply to the committee.

Note – A **special removal** must not be confused with a **planning removal** in a licensing planning area, in which case the licensing planning committee will have proposed a removal of a licence to other premises and, after the proposal has been confirmed, the local licensing committee in whose division the licence will be after removal can only refuse the removal on certain limited grounds. In this kind of case the clerk should be consulted.

Ordinary removals (s 5)

An on-licence or an off-licence can be the subject of an **ordinary removal**. If the proposed premises are in a different area the application will have to be made to the licensing committee of the area in which the proposed premises are situated.

Residential and restaurant licences cannot be transferred by ordinary removal procedure. Fresh application has to be made for a licence for the new premises.

The applicant for an ordinary removal need not be the present licensee, in which case the latter must be served with a notice of the application. If the removal is granted it will then also act as a transfer of the licence to the applicant.

The committee must be satisfied that there is no objection to the removal such as an objection from the present licensee (if different from the applicant) or the owner of the present premises or any other person whom the magistrates consider has a right to object.

The proposed premises must, in the opinion of the committee, be fit and convenient and they should have inspected the premises prior to the hearing and should hold a plan of the area and the premises. The licensing planning committee must have no objection if the proposed new premises are in a licensing planning area.

Provisional order of ordinary removal (s 6)

When premises are about to be constructed or are in the course of construction a person interested in the premises can apply for a provisional removal and the procedure is similar to that set out on p 399 for a provisional on-licence.

If the application is granted then the premises must be built in accordance with the officially approved plan and officially approved modifications.

When the licensing committee is satisfied that the finished building accords with the deposited plan the applicant can apply for the order to be made final and the committee must make the order.

Alterations to on-licensed premises (s 20)

If the alterations have been ordered by a lawful authority, eg a public health authority, there is no need to obtain the consent of the licensing committee. Subject to that the following is a list of alterations to on-licensed premises which may not be made without the prior permission of the licensing committee:

(a) Alterations which give increased facilities for drinking in a public part of the premises or in a part of the premises which is open to all residents or some residents.
(b) Alterations which conceal from observation a public part of the premises used for drinking or a part of the premises used for drinking by all or some residents.
(c) Alterations which affect the communication between the public part of the premises where intoxicating liquor is sold and the rest of the premises or affect the communication with the street or public way.

It is not possible for consent to be given retrospectively (*R v Croydon Crown Court, ex p Bromley Licensing JJ* (1988)).

If any such alteration is made without the licensing committee's consent proceedings may be taken in the ordinary magistrates' court to order the forfeiture of the licence or to order that the premises be restored to their original approved condition. There is a right of appeal to the crown court against such an order.

Before hearing an application to alter licensed premises members of the licensing committee may inspect the premises and may require plans showing the proposed alterations to be deposited. It is a common practice where alterations are approved for two copies of plans showing the alterations to be so endorsed and signed by a member of the committee, one copy being handed to the applicant and one being retained by the clerk.

If the application to alter the premises is refused the applicant has a right of appeal to the crown court.

If the licensed premises have been demolished and only a cleared site remains, this type of application cannot be used to obtain authority for the proposed new premises.

If the licensed premises are still in existence sometimes proposed alterations appear to be so extensive that in fact they constitute the destruction of one building and the erection of another. It might appear that it would be more appropriate for the applicant to apply for a new licence or a provisional order of removal than a mere approval for alterations.

The test is whether or not the proposed premises will be within the ambit of the existing licence. If they are not application should be made for a provisional new licence or an order of removal (see pp 399 and 405).

Alterations to off-licensed premises

The consent of the licensing committee is not required for alterations to an off-licence but if the licensee makes drastic alterations he may run the risk of having his renewal of licence refused or his licence revoked.

Surrender of justices' licence

In *Drury and Samuel Smith Old Brewery (Tadcaster) Ltd v Scunthorpe Licensing Justices* (1992), it was held that in the absence of specific statutory authority in respect of licences, a licensing committee could accept the surrender of a justices' licence only where either

(a) the existing licence was subject to a condition which the licensee wished to have removed; or
(b) the licensee wished to open premises elsewhere and offered to surrender one or more existing licences for other premises in the same licensing area.

Clubs (Part II)

Clubs which supply intoxicating liquor fall into the two categories of licensed clubs and registered clubs.

Licensed clubs (s 55)

The licence (which can only be granted by a licensing committee at its licensing sessions) is in effect an on-licence to which certain conditions are attached.

A licensed club may be one where one or more proprietors own the premises and contents and will be entitled to any profits personally. Members may make payments to the proprietor. Or a licensed club may be a members' club which, for one reason or another, is not legally qualified to become a registered club.

Application is made in the same way as for an on-licence (see p 391). The licensing committee may insert conditions to restrict the supply of intoxicating liquor. The sort of conditions that may be ordered by the licensing committee are as follows:

(a) that intoxicating liquor may only be supplied to a member who has been a member for 2 days, or whose nomination or application for membership was made at least 2 days previously or is being entertained as a non-paying guest of a full member who is paying for the drink;
(b) intoxicating liquor shall not be supplied for consumption off the premises except to a member in person;
(c) there shall be rules for the election of members and a copy of such rules shall be deposited with the clerk of the licensing committee who shall be notified of any alteration within a stipulated period;
(d) an up-to-date list of all members with their names and addresses shall be kept on the premises and shall be produced on demand for inspection by a constable in uniform.

Registered clubs (s 40)

A retail *sale* of alcohol must be authorised by a justices' licence, eg an on-licence, off-licence or a licence for a club under s 55. However, in a registered club the premises and contents belong to the members and also any profits. What would appear to be a *sale* of liquor to a member is in fact a distribution of the club's assets and no justices' licence is required. However for a supply of liquor by a club to a member on club premises, the law requires a club to have either a justices' licence as above or a registration certificate granted by a *magistrates' court* (ie not a licensing committee) (s 39).

The magistrates should verify with the clerk that the prescribed application procedure has been followed and whether the application form or club rules lodged with that form contain anything which debars the club from being granted a registration certificate. The clerk will advise whether the club rules comply with Sch 7 of the Licensing Act 1964 because if they do the court may assume that the club has met the main qualifications for registration.

Objections. Any objection to the application must be in writing stating the grounds of objection and served on the clerk of court in duplicate. He serves one copy on the applicant.

Grounds of objection are:

(a) defects in the application;
(b) unsuitability of the premises;
(c) non-compliance with requirements for qualification for a registration certificate (see below);
(d) unfitness of the applicant;
(e) premises are disqualified for being granted a registration certificate;
(f) disorderly conduct or habitual breach of certain rules;
(g) habitual use of the premises for unlawful purposes, indecent displays and certain other abuses.

If any of the above objections are proved the court may refuse a registration certificate.

When an objection has been made the magistrates' court has power to award costs.

Qualifications. The club must satisfy the court on the following points before a club registration certificate can be granted.

(a) An interval of at least 2 days between a member's nomination (or application for membership) and his admission.
(b) The club must be established and conducted in good faith as a club. The court must have regard to any arrangement which ties the club to obtaining its liquor from any special source and to any arrangement which diverts the club's money, profit or property elsewhere than to the club's own benefit, charitable, benevolent or political purposes. There must be arrangements for providing information about the club's finances and premises. The nature of the premises and rules about sales to non-members must also be considered.
(c) There must be at least 25 members.
(d) Intoxicating liquor must only be supplied to members or guests or sold in accordance with the club rules (which in turn must be suitable within the meaning of para (2) above).
(e) An *elective* committee must control the intoxicating liquor.
(f) No person can receive commission or a percentage or similar payment on purchases of intoxicating liquor or receive a pecuniary benefit from the supply of intoxicating liquor to members except for the general gain.

Duration of club registration certificate (s 40). The certificate remains in force for one year after the date it is granted. All the points listed above which relate to grounds for objection and the qualifications needed for the granting of a certificate also apply to an application for renewal.

When a club has held a certificate for two consecutive years at the second application for renewal the court has power to renew for any period up to 10 years.

Cancellation of club registration certificate (s 44). Application can be made by the police or local authority for the cancellation of the certificate at any time on the grounds numbered (c) to (g) on p 402. This is in addition to the court's power to refuse a renewal of the certificate, if objection is made to renewal.

Permitted hours in registered clubs (s 62)

The permitted hours for drinking shall be:

(a) on days other than Christmas Day the general licensing hours;
(b) on Christmas Day, the hours determined by the rules of the club being not more than $6^1/_2$ hours in aggregate beginning not earlier than noon and ending not later than 10.30 p.m. There must be a break of not less than 2 hours in the afternoon which must include the hours from 3 to 5 p.m. and

there shall not be a drinking period after 5 p.m. of more than three-and-a-half hours.

Registered societies

Special provisions apply to a club which is also a society registered under the Industrial and Provident Societies Act 1965 or the Friendly Societies Act 1974, or is a miners' welfare institute. Consult the clerk.

Occasional licences (s 180)

Only the holder of an on-licence can apply for an **occasional licence** (ie not a registered or proprietary club, or an off- or residential licence. A holder of a restaurant licence can apply in certain circumstances.) It entitles him to sell at premises other than those for which he holds a licence.

An occasional licence cannot be granted for Christmas Day, Good Friday or any day appointed for public fast or thanksgiving.

He applies to the magistrates' court in whose area the proposed premises are situated giving at least 24 hours notice to the police. The magistrates have complete discretion to grant or refuse such an application.

The licensee can make written application by post to the court provided it is in duplicate and arrives at the court one month before the date of the proposed function. One copy is served on the police by the clerk.

The magistrates may at their discretion insist upon a personal application even if the postal procedure has been followed.

An occasional licence may range from just a few hours on one day or up to a period of 3 weeks.

If the occasion for which a licence is applied is likely to last for longer than 3 weeks, such as an exhibition, then the magistrates can grant more than one occasional licence to cover the longer period.

The usual rules concerning permitted hours do not apply, although courts of course do impose restrictions in line with permitted hours or, where appropriate, special orders of exemption (see p 413).

Occasional permission

(Licensing (Occasional Permissions) Act 1983)

Although an occasional licence (described above) authorises the sale of liquor at a place which would not otherwise be licensed, it may be granted only to a person holding a current justices' licence; furthermore, an occasional licence is granted by the magistrates' court, not by the licensing committee. In these two particular respects it may be contrasted with an occasional permission, which may be granted by the licensing committee to an applicant who is not a licence holder. The effect of an occasional permission is to authorise the sale of liquor at a function arranged by an 'eligible organisation'. This expression means an organisation not carried on for private gain. But the fact that a private individual may be the ultimate beneficiary of monies, eg money raised to enable a sick person to travel abroad for treatment, would not by itself render the organisation ineligible. Furthermore, the organisation need not be a permanent one, any association of persons will be eligible if it is not carried on for private gain, even if it is brought into being solely to arrange the function which is the reason for the application.

Application is made in writing to the justices' clerk not less than three weeks before the date of the function whereupon the clerk will give the applicant written notice of the licensing sessions at which the application will be heard. There must be at least 15 days between the receipt of the application and the hearing.

Licensing justices are obliged to give reasons in writing for requiring an applicant to attend a hearing in person where that applicant had made a successful application in their licesing district within the previous 12 months.

At the hearing, the licensing justices must satisfy themselves of the following matters:

(a) that the applicant is a member of an eligible organisation provided that the application is countersigned by an authorised officer if the member is not himself an officer;
(b) that the applicant s a fit and proper person to sell intoxicating liquor;
(c) that the place where the function is to be held is situated in the committee's licensing district and that it is a suitable place for the sale of intoxicating liquor;
(d) that the sale of liquor at the function is not likely to result in disturbance or annoyance to residents in the neighbourhood or to any disorderly conduct.

When granting an occasional permission, the licensing committee will specify the kinds of liquor which may be sold (these will have been mentioned in the application, but the committee need not grant all that the applicant seeks) and the hours during which it may be sold. These hours need not correspond with the local permitted hours. The occasional permission must be limited to one continuous period not exceeding 24 hours (*R v Bromley JJ, ex p Bromley LVA* (1984)). The committee may attach any conditions it sees fit to the permission and it is an offence if anyone fails to comply with such conditions. Not more than 12 occasional permissions may be granted in respect of functions held by the same organisation or branch in any period of 12 months.

The holder of an occasional permission is at risk of committing a number of offences created by the Act, for example, selling liquor to persons under 18, failing to comply with conditions of the permission or to produce it to a constable within a reasonable time. Most courts are issuing an explanatory note with the written occasional permission.

Permitted hours

It is an offence for a person, except during permitted hours

(a) to sell or supply to any person in licensed premises or a registered club any intoxicating liquor for consumption on or off the premises;
(b) to consume in or take from such premises any intoxicating liquor.

The maximum penalty is a fine of £1000 (s 59). These provisions do not apply to occasional licences (p 404).

Permitted hours in licensed premises (s 60). These are, on weekdays (for the purposes of permitted hours Christmas Day and Good Friday are treated as Sundays) 11.00 a.m. to 11.00 p.m., and Sundays 12 noon to 10.30 p.m. without a break. On Christmas day there is a break of four hours beginning at 3.00 p.m.

If satisfied that the requirements of the district make it desirable the licensing justices may order that the permitted hours on a weekday begin not earlier than 10.00 a.m.

Permitted hours for off-licences begin at 8.00 a.m. on a weekday, and on Sundays (except where Christmas day falls on a Sunday) at 10.00 a.m. The permitted hours for off-licensed premises on Sundays are therefore from 10.00 a.m. through to 10.30 p.m. without a break. (For permitted hours in registered clubs see p 403.)

At the end of permitted hours 20 minutes is allowed for 'drinking up' time extended to half an hour where liquor is supplied as an ancillary to a meal (s 63).

Various exemptions are provided by s 63 to cover persons residing on licensed premises and other special situations.

The provisions described above are known as the 'general licensing hours' and may be curtailed in certain circumstances by a 'restriction order'.

Restriction order (s 67A). With respect to any on-licensed premises the licensing justices (or in the case of any registered club, the magistrates) may make a restriction order which specifies any time between 2.30 p.m. and 5.30 p.m. on weekdays, and between 3.00 p.m. and 7.00 p.m. on Sundays and Good Friday, when permitted hours are not to apply, ie imposes a break on all-day drinking. A restriction order lasts for as long as the justices direct up to 12 months. An application for a restriction order may be made by:

(a) the police;
(b) any person living in the neighbourhood, or any body representing people who do;
(c) any person carrying on, or managing or otherwise in charge of a business in the neighbourhood;
(d) the head teacher or other person in charge of any educational establishment in the neighbourhood.

The grounds for making a restriction order are that it is desirable

(a) to avoid or reduce any disturbance of or annoyance to persons living or working in the neighbourhood or customers or school pupils due to the use of the premises; or
(b) to avoid or reduce the occurrence of disorderly conduct in the premises or

> the occurrence in the vicinity of the premises of disorderly conduct on the part of persons resorting to the premises.

The holder of the licence or any club may appeal to the crown court against the justices' decision and the operation of the restriction order will be suspended pending the appeal unless the justices or the crown court otherwise order.

A restriction order may be varied or revoked by the licensing justices or magistrates' court on an application by the licensee or a club. If a restriction order is in force, a licensee must display conspicuously a notice of the effect of the order on the premises.

Special order of exemption (s 74)

This is in effect an extension of the permitted hours for some special occasion. Twice weekly dances at a hotel are not special occasions. The application is made to the police in the Metropolitan Police District or the City of London. Elsewhere such an application is made to the magistrates' court (not the licensing committee).

The applications are made either by the holder of an on-licence or by the secretary of a registered club.

The magistrates determine whether they will consider it a special occasion, and if so, whether they will grant the application.

Instead of a personal application before the court a written application is possible. It must be in duplicate and arrive at the court one month before the date of the function. The clerk serves one of the copies on the police. The magistrates may at their discretion insist upon a personal application even if the postal procedure has been followed.

When dealing with these applications the court should ask itself the following questions: (1) Is the event capable of being in law a 'special occasion'? (2) On the material before the court is it in fact a special occasion? (3) Should the court in its discretion grant the application?

1 Is the occasion capable of being a special occasion? In other words, as a matter of law could anybody contend that this is a special occasion?

(a) It may be a special occasion from a national point of view, eg a public festival, or from a local standpoint (which can include a 'personal' occasion such as a wedding). The more local the occasion the more carefully it will have to be scrutinised. Weddings are certainly special occasions. A Saturday before a bank holiday is *capable* of being a special occasion but whether it actually is must be decided according to local circumstances in 2 below.

(b) The more frequently the occasion is held, the less likely it is to be special, eg a dance held twice weekly is not special. Football matches every Saturday are probably over the borderline, and are therefore not special.

(c) If the occasion is created by the licensee *for the purposes of his licensed business* that is unlikely to be capable of being a special occasion. But note, for example, that a registered sports club applying for extensions for special competitions and events will probably not be creating occasions *for the purposes of its licensed business*.

2 Is it a special occasion in the locality in which the premises are situated? If the occasion is in law capable of being special, the justices must decide whether in their locality the occasion is special. Each locality may have its own meaning to the words 'special occasion' and it is up to the justices in each district to say whether a certain time and place come within that description.

3 In their discretion should the justices grant the application? The magistrates may decide that an occasion is special but refuse to grant the application in their discretion because, for example, they feel there is a risk to public order or of inconvenience to local residents.

All three questions must be answered in the affirmative before the application can be granted.

General order of exemption (s 74)

Application sometimes can be made for a general order of exemption which permanently alters the drinking hours at a registered club or on-licensed premises.

The premises whether a registered club or licensed premises must be situated in the immediate neighbourhood of a public market or place where people follow a lawful trade or calling. The intention is to provide drinking facilities for those attending a public market or those working inconvenient hours such as shift work at docks or those working at early morning markets.

Although this order is granted by a magistrates' court, in view of the fact that granting the order is going to alter the drinking facilities for the area on a permanent basis it may be thought to be desirable that the magistrates hearing the application should include members of the licensing committee.

Before granting such an order extending the drinking hours the magistrates should satisfy themselves that there is such a need for a considerable number of persons. The magistrates have a discretion as to the times they are willing to add to permitted hours and they can revoke or vary any such order.

Supper hour certificate (s 68)

The holder of an on-licence can apply to the licensing committee for a supper hour certificate the effect of which is that the licensed premises or club can sell or supply liquor continuously from the end of the first part of the general licensing hours (ie the morning session) to the beginning of the second part (ie when the evening session begins) (applicable only to Christmas Day) and for an extra hour at the end of the permitted hours in the evening.

The licensing committee has to satisfy itself that the premises are suitable and there is a bona fide intention to supply substantial table meals at which drink is to be available as an ancillary to the meal.

The High Court has ruled that this certificate is intended for persons who serve meals as an ordinary part of their trade in an area set aside for that purpose and which was available at the normal times of the day when meals were served.

A registered club can make a similar application to a magistrates' court.

It is suggested that the magistrates ask the clerk to confirm that the correct application procedure has been followed.

Special hours certificate (ss 76–83)

Licensed premises or a registered club can apply, the former to the licensing committee and the latter to a magistrates' court, for a special hours certificate if they are also licensed (or certified in the case of a club) for music and dancing and can establish that the premises are suitable and that they are or will be in fact used to provide music, dancing and substantial refreshment to which the sale of intoxicating liquor is ancillary.

If satisfied on these points the justices *may* grant a special hours certificate with or without limitations.

Unless limitations are imposed, the special hours certificate extends the permitted hours for the supplying or selling of liquor on weekdays until 2.00 a.m. the following morning. In the Inner London area (but not in the City of London) the extension is to 3.00 a.m. and not 2.00 a.m.

Permitted hours automatically end at midnight on a day when music and dancing is not provided after midnight, or when the music and dancing ends if that is between midnight and 2.00 a.m. Also the permitted hours will end in accordance with any limitation imposed on the certificate by the justices.

The justices may grant a certificate limited as to particular times of the day (and differing provisions may be made for different days of the week), particular days of the week and periods of the year (s 78A). The certificate must be limited to those days on which the premises are or are intended to be used for the purposes of music and dancing (s 80).

Provisional certificates (ss 77A and 78ZA). The power to grant provisional special hours certificates parallels arrangements for the grant of provisional liquor licences. For premises with an on-licence or a provisional on-licence, the grant of a provisional special hours certificate will be conditional on the licensing justices' being satisfied that there is a provisional or full entertainments licence in force; and that premises will be structurally adapted for and used for music and dancing and the provision of substantial refreshment, to which the sale of alcohol will be ancillary. In the case of registered clubs, the magistrates' court will need to be satisfied that there is in force a certificate of suitability of club premises for music and dancing issued under s 79 of the 1964 Act .

It is possible to apply to these certificates the same types of limitations (ie on times of day, days of the week and periods of the year) as can be applied to full special hours certificates under ss 79A and 80 of the 1964 Act. If they refuse an application, impose limitations or refuse to consent to modifications of plans or to declare a provisional grant final, the licensing justices or the magistrates' court must give their reasons in writing to the applicant.

Revocation (s 81). A special hours certificate is revoked if no music and dancing licence or certificate is in force for the premises. The police may apply to revoke the certificate on several grounds:

(a) the premises have not been used for music, dancing and substantial refreshment to which the sale of intoxicating liquor is ancillary;
(b) there has been a conviction for an offence of selling liquor outside permitted hours;
(c) that during the extra period granted by the certificate persons have been resorting to the premises for intoxicating liquor rather than for dancing or for obtaining refreshments other than alcoholic liquor;
(d) that it is expedient to revoke the certificate on the grounds of disorderly or indecent conduct on the premises or on that part of the premises to which the certificate relates.

On an application to revoke under grounds (a)–(c) the justices may instead attach to the certificate limitations as to the particular times of day. Such limitations may also be attached to a certificate on the express application of the police (s 81A).

Extended hours order (s 70)

If licensed premises have a supper hour certificate and are adapted and bona fide used (or bona fide intended to be used) to provide music and other entertainments in addition to substantial meals at which liquor is ancillary then the **licensing committee** can extend the permitted hours up to any time not later than 1 a.m.

The extension may be limited to certain weeks, days or months. The committee must have regard to the comfort and convenience of other nearby premises and can insert in the certificate conditions for the neighbours' benefit.

'Entertainment' must be live entertainment by live performers. Thus, films, recordings, radio, television etc would not qualify as 'entertainment'; but a band playing dance music would.

A registered club can also apply for such a certificate to a **magistrates' court.**

An extended hours order remains in force unless otherwise varied or revoked as long as there is a justices' licence in force for the premises.

It is suggested that the magistrates ask the clerk to confirm that the correct application procedure has been followed.

Children's certificates (s 168A and Sch 12A)

Children under 14 who are accompanied by an adult are allowed to be admitted to certificated bar premises in certain circumstances.

Before granting a children's certificate, licensing justices must be satisfied that the bar area to which the application relates constitutes an environment in which it is suitable for children under 14 to be present, and that meals and beverages other than intoxicating liquor will be available for consumption in that area (which must be a condition of the grant). Other conditions may be imposed, including a restriction on the days and/or hours during which the certificate is operational.

A children's certificate will normally be operational until 9.00 p.m., although the licensing justices may approve a later finishing time, where appropriate, on application by the licensee.

A certificate remains in force until revoked. The licensee can take steps himself effectively to surrender his certificate.

A licensee has a right of appeal to the crown court against the refusal of a children's certificate, in relation to any conditions attached to the grant of a certificate, in relation to an application for an extension of the finishing time, and against a decision to revoke a certificate.

Employment of persons under 18 in bars (ss 170,170A)

There is a prohibition on the employment of persons under the age of 18 in the bars of licensed premises, but 16-17 year olds are allowed to work in a bar under certain conditions provided they are on a training scheme approved for the purposes by the secretary of state.

Exemption orders at designated sports grounds

(Sporting Events (Control of Alcohol etc) Act 1985)

Where licensed premises or a registered club are situated in a designated sports ground, the permitted hours shall not include any part of the period of any designated event (for 'designated sports ground' and 'designated sporting event' see p 127). Therefore, for example, no alcohol could be sold at a football league match.

Exemption order

A complaint can be made to the magistrates' court (ie not the licensing committee) for the area in which the premises are situated, for an order exempting the premises from this prohibition by including in the permitted hours such period as the magistrates order. Twenty-eight days notice must be given and a plan of the sports ground showing the premises within that ground where it is proposed to sell or supply intoxicating liquor must be sent to the court.

Scope of order. An order may extend the permitted hours to include such period of the designated sporting event as the court considers appropriate, but the order *cannot* extend to any part of the premises from which the sporting event may be directly viewed. Thus, for example, alcohol could not be sold in a directors' or sponsors' box overlooking the pitch (but see the special provision for 'designated period', p 127).

These restrictions cannot be evaded by the granting of an occasional licence or by a registered club using the provisions of the Licensing Act 1964, s 39, or by any sales being made wholesale as opposed to retail.

Criterion for making an order. The court must be satisfied that having regard in particular to the arrangements made for the admission of spectators and for regulating their conduct, an order in the terms proposed is not likely to be detrimental to the orderly conduct or safety of spectators.

Conditions. It must be a condition of the order that the holder of the justices' licence or a person designated by him, or a person designated by a registered club must be in attendance during the designated sporting event and must have given his name and address in writing to the police. Other conditions may also be attached to the order.

Duration of the order. Lasts for 5 months and may be renewed but ceases on the transfer of the licence or the club ceasing to be registered.

Variation and revocation. The police (or, in certain circumstances, the local authority) may apply to revoke or vary the order.

Appeal. An aggrieved party to the proceedings may appeal to the crown court (with certain exceptions relating to individual sporting events).

Emergency police powers. A senior police officer may, in advance of the event but where it is not practical to apply to a magistrates' court, suspend or vary an exemption order for a particular event. During the course of an event any constable in uniform may order the closure of bars at the ground where the supply of intoxicating liquor would be detrimental to the orderly conduct or safety of spectators at that event.

Gaming Act 1968

Amusement with prizes (AWP) machines in public houses or other premises having a justices' on-licence (s 34)

A permit under the Gaming Act 1968 is necessary if some types of amusement machines are used in public houses or other premises which have a justices' on-licence; this also applies to other premises, such as restaurants and coffee bars, which do not have a justices' on-licence.

A permit is necessary for these premises if the amusement machine is a slot machine which is constructed or adapted for playing a game of chance and in which the element of chance is provided by the machine itself. If the slot machine has the element of chance and offers an unlimited jackpot or prizes in excess of £5 or goods valued at over £8.00 it will not be an amusement machine and therefore it could not be authorised by a permit.

The Act requires applications for permits for an amusement with prizes machine to be made to the local authority, except where the machine will be used in a public house or in other premises which have a justices' on-licence (not being a restaurant or residential licence). These applications must be heard by the licensing committee (not betting and gaming licensing committee). Under previous similar legislation a permit was refused because it was considered that 'drinking and gambling did not mix'. The High Court ruled this was not a valid reason for refusing a permit.

All-cash machines. A new type of amusement-with-prizes (AWP) machine – the 'all-cash-machine' – was introduced with effect from 20 June 1996.

The all-cash machine does away with the need to pay out in the form of tokens and non cash prizes above a certain limit. The maximum cash prize has been set at £10. The maximum stake is the same as for AWP machines at 30p and the limit on stakes and prizes will be subject to similar preiodic reviews.

(a) Age restrictions for all-cash machine. Statutory controls have been introduced with the intention of minimising the playing of all cash machines by under 18s. For all-cash machines in liquor licensed premises, the 1968 Act requires licencees to place all-cash machines in a bar. This has the same meaning as in the Licensing Act 1964. These machines cannot therefore be located in children's rooms or family rooms away from the bar area. Contravention of the condition is an offence under s 38(6B) of the 1968 Act. However ,the machines may be put in bar areas covered by children's certificates, where under 14s must be accompanied by adults. The justices' power to impose such conditions as they think fit on the grant of a children's certificate is unchanged (Sch 12A to the Licensing Act 1964).

(b) Ages. There is no legal duty on licensees to prevent under 18s playing all-cash machines in the bar area.

(c) Safeguards. These changes do not otherwise affect justices' existing statutory powers on grant and renewal of s 34 permits for AWP machines:

Paragraph 10 of Sch 9 to the 1968 Act gives justices an explicit power to grant or renew a section 34 permit subject to a condition limiting the number of machines.

Paragraph 8(2) of that Schedule gives justices a general discretion to grant or renew permits. The justices decide how to exercise this discretion.

As an additional voluntary protection, machine suppliers have built into the all-cash machines a notice stating that they are not intended for use by under 18s. These notices do not have the force of law.

(d) Permits. The all-cash machine is covered by the same 3-year permit under s 34 as AWP machines in current use. The fee remains at £32. Permit holders do not have to apply for variations before they can have the all-cash machine. They can operate the all cash machines instead of or as well as their existing AWP machines, subject to the limit on numbers specified in the permit. Justices have the opportunity to review the siting and use of all-cash machines when permits next come up for renewal.

Method of application. There is no set timetable and no formal procedure as to the service of notices has been prescribed.

Procedure at the hearing. If no objection is made to the application a permit can be granted without hearing evidence. Before an application is refused (or a condition inserted), the applicant must be given an opportunity to be heard and the committee must notify its reasons to the applicant.

On granting a permit, the committee can impose a condition limiting the number of amusement machines which can be in use at the premises.

Discretion of the committee. The committee has a discretion whether or not to grant the application. It can, for example, refuse on the grounds that installing the machine would be undesirable by reason of the purpose for which the premises are used or the persons by whom the premises are used. The committee's discretion is unfettered, and therefore it is lawful for it to consider demand if appropriate (*R v Chichester Crown Court, ex p Forte* (1995)).

Duration of permit. Once granted or renewed the permit lasts for such period as the licensing justices decide, but not less than three years from the date it is granted. If the licensee leaves, the permit will lapse and the incoming licensee will have to apply for a new permit if he wishes to continue with the amusement with prizes machines.

Appeal. An unsuccessful licensee can appeal to the crown court. So can a licensee who has been granted a permit and who wishes to appeal against a condition imposed by the committee.

Conditions automatically imposed by the Gaming Act 1968. These include:

(a) Not more than 30p or 30 penceworth of tokens can be inserted at any one time.
(b) No prize may exceed £5 in cash, or £8.00 in kind, or a combined value cash (not exceeding £5 and kind up to a total value of £8.00. In the case of all-cash machines, the maximum cash prize is £10.
(c) Where, instead of a prize, tokens are given for use to play a further game, no money can be given. Tokens can only be exchanged for non-monetary prizes at the appropriate rate.
(d) The machine can offer a money prize and a free turn or turns where the aggregate prize must not exceed £5 £in cash.

Except for the above prizes, no articles, benefit or advantage can be given. Thus no advantage such as improved odds can be carried over into a later game.

If the machine delivers tokens they cannot be accumulated with a view to changing them for a single prize worth more than £8.00.

Authorising equal chance games at public houses and other premises holding a justices' on-licence (s 6)

The Gaming Act 1968 prohibits gaming in public places which include licensed premises; but dominoes and cribbage in public houses are exempt. Although permission for dominoes and cribbage need not be obtained, the licensing committee can impose requirements or restrictions to forbid high stakes, and also to ensure that dominoes and cribbage are not the primary inducement for customers to resort to the premises.

As far as other games are concerned, under s 6 of the Act publicans and holders of a justices' on-licence (but NOT the holders of a restaurant or residential licence) can apply to the licensing committee for an order permitting the playing of such games; but the game must be one in which each player has an equal chance of winning. Similar requirements or restrictions (to forbid high stakes etc) can be imposed.

Method of application. It appears that no formal procedure has been prescribed. It is deemed prudent to give notice of the application to the police.

Discretion of the committee. The committee has a general discretion whether or not to grant the application.

Imposing requirements or restrictions. The committee can impose requirements or restrictions to ensure that such games:

(a) are not played for high stakes; and
(b) do not amount to the primary inducement for customers to resort to the premises.

Revocation and variation. The committee can revoke or vary any order that is granted.

Duration of order. It will continue until it is revoked or varied; or until the premises cease to hold a justices' on-licence.

Notification to the police. The clerk must serve a copy of the order on the holder of the licence and send a copy to the police.

Section seven

Betting and gaming licensing

Betting licensing committee

(Betting Gaming and Lotteries Act 1963)

A betting licensing committee is a committee of magistrates appointed by the local magistrates at the meeting of magistrates in each October.

It comprises at least 5 and not more than 15 magistrates.

Three constitute a quorum.

The committee hears applications to grant, renew or cancel bookmakers' permits, betting office licences and betting agency permits. The last named are rare and are not dealt with in this book. If such an application does come before the committee the clerk should be consulted.

Applications for a bookmaker's permit or betting office licence

The applicant has to serve certain statutory notices and it is suggested that when the applicant has completed his presentation of the case the clerk should be asked if all the necessary notices have been served, including one upon HM Customs and Excise.

Betting licensing sessions – court procedure (Sch 1)

Evidence

If no objection is made to an application to grant or renew a bookmaker's permit or betting office licence the committee can proceed without hearing the applicant.

If the committee considers it appropriate they can require any evidence to be given on oath.

Objections

The committee can only refuse to grant a bookmaker's permit or betting office licence on certain grounds which are set out on the following pages.

An objector must serve the clerk with two written copies of the grounds for his objection, and the clerk is responsible for serving one copy on the applicant.

Normally the objector must carry out this procedure within 14 days of the appearance of an advertisement in a newspaper advertising notice of the application.

A similar procedure must be taken by an objector to a renewal of a betting licence. Normally the objector must do this before the closing date for receiving objections, which date will be specified by the clerk in his newspaper advertisement in February giving public notice of the day in April when annual renewals are due to take place.

If a late objection is made the committee has a discretion whether or not to hear it. If it is decided to hear the objection the applicant must be given sufficient time to consider the written grounds for objection. An adjournment may be necessary.

Court fees

For granting a bookmaker's permit	£160
For renewing a bookmaker's permit	£20
For granting a betting office licence	£125
For renewing a betting office licence	£25

Costs

The committee can order an unsuccessful objector to pay costs to the applicant and vice versa.

Duration of permits and licences

Prior to 1 September 1997 the bookmaker's permit and the betting office licence remained in force until 31 May which falls not less than 3 months nor more than 15 months after the permit or licence was granted, and they required annual renewal. However from that date, the duration of licences and permits was extended to three years.. All licences and permits issued 1 September 1997 should be in the first three-yearly cycle, running to 31 May 2000.

Renewal applications for permits and licences can be dealt with by clerks to the appropriate authority unless there are objections.

Not transferable

A bookmaker's permit cannot be transferred to another person or limited company. The second person or company must apply for a new permit.

A betting office licence cannot be transferred from one set of premises to another; a fresh application must be made for each set of premises. Nor can the licence be transferred from one person or company to another at the same premises; a new application must be made.

Death of holder. The legal personal representatives of the deceased holder of the licence or permit can continue business under the licence for 6 months after his death. If they can satisfy the committee that further time is necessary to wind up the deceased's estate and there are no circumstances that make it undesirable, the committee can grant a further extension of 6 months and repeat this extension for a further 6 months when the extension runs out.

Change of address. The holder of a bookmaker's permit is required to notify the horserace betting levy board of a change of his office address.

Refusal of bookmaker's permit

The committee must refuse to grant a new permit or renew an existing one if any one or more of the following grounds exist:

(a) The applicant (not being a body corporate) is under 21.
(b) The applicant is disqualified from holding a bookmaker's permit following a conviction for certain betting offences or a conviction of other offences involving fraud or dishonesty. A full list can be supplied by the clerk.
(c) The applicant (not being a body corporate) is not resident in Great Britain or was not resident during the 6 months prior to the application.
(d) The applicant is a 'body corporate' which is not incorporated in Great Britain.
(e) The applicant, during the previous 12 months, has been refused the grant or renewal of a bookmaker's permit or betting agency permit because the committee was not satisfied that he was a fit and proper person or the Horse Racing Levy Board do not approve of his application.
(f) The applicant has had his bookmaker's permit cancelled during the previous 12 months.

The committee **may** refuse to grant or renew a bookmaker's permit on either of the following grounds:

(i) That the committee is not and has not been satisfied that the applicant is a fit and proper person, despite the fact that with his application the applicant has to enclose two character references.

If the applicant is a limited company the application has to include two character references in respect of two persons upon whose instructions or directions the company's employees are accustomed to act.

The committee will usually rely on the police so far as the references are concerned.

In deciding whether a person is a fit and proper person to hold a bookmaker's permit the committee must have regard to whether or not he has paid in full his bookmaker's levy to the Levy Board and to the circumstances in which any failure to pay arose; and also whether or not he has paid the general betting duty due from him to HM Customs and Excise.

In assessing the applicant's character the committee must disregard any convictions under the Betting Act 1853 or any corresponding offences under local Acts of Parliament, or offences under the Street Betting Act 1906 committed on or before 1 December 1961, and certain convictions under the Betting and Gaming Act 1960 committed before 1 December 1961.

(ii) The committee can refuse to grant or renew a bookmaker's permit if it is satisfied that being granted or renewed it would be managed by or carried on for the benefit of a person who would be refused the grant or renewal of a permit for any of the reasons mentioned above.

Grounds for refusing a betting office licence

The committee **must** refuse to grant or renew a betting office licence if it is not satisfied on the following points:

(a) that the applicant will hold either a bookmaker's permit or betting agency permit when the licence comes into force or continues in force. This does not apply if the applicant is the Totalisator Board;
(b) that the premises are or will be enclosed;
(c) that the betting office will have its own means of access to the street without passing through premises where some other business is carried on.

The committee **may** refuse to grant or renew a betting office licence on any or more of the following grounds:

(a) that the committee think that having regard to the layout, character, condition or location of the premises they are not suitable for a betting office;
(b) that the grant or renewal of a betting office licence is inexpedient having regard to the demand for the time being in the locality for the facilities etc and the existing number of betting offices already available in the locality;
(c) that the premises have not been conducted properly under the licence.

If the committee refuses to grant or renew a bookmaker's permit or a betting office licence it must notify the applicant of the refusal forthwith.

The applicant has a right of appeal to the crown court and the committee can be legally represented at such an appeal. The clerk should be consulted as the committee will wish to ensure that the use of public funds for their legal representation has been authorised.

Cancellation of bookmaker's permit

Any person can apply for forfeiture and cancellation of a bookmaker's permit, eg a dissatisfied punter.

The application for forfeiture and cancellation must be made in the prescribed form and accompanied by two copies of the grounds on which the application is based. Upon receiving the documents the clerk must submit them to any one member of the betting licensing committee, who may resolve the matter in one of two ways:

(a) If he considers that further consideration of the application is unnecessary or inexpedient before the next April meeting of the committee when the licence would come up for renewal he may direct that the application be refused but the applicant will be entitled to rely on the same grounds for presenting an objection at the annual meeting at which permits are renewed.

Again, if the member of the committee considers that the matters raised in the application have been or ought to have been raised by way of objection when the permit was orginally granted or last renewed, or if the matters raised are or have been the subject of proceedings for certain offences under the Betting, Gaming and Lotteries Act 1963 or offences involving fraud or dishonesty, then again the member of the committee may refuse the application for cancellation of the bookmaker's permit. (This is because the court that dealt with the offences would have cancelled the permit if they thought it appropriate.)

As before, the applicant may use the same grounds to object to the renewal of the permit when it comes up for consideration at the next April meeting.

(b) The alternative action the member of the committee can take is to direct that the application to cancel the bookmaker's permit be referred to the betting licensing committee. The clerk must then give the applicant, the bookmaker and the police 21 days notice of the date when the betting licensing committee will meet to decide the issue. The clerk must also serve on the bookmaker a copy of the applicant's grounds for seeking cancellation of the bookmaker's permit.

It may be that the police themselves are seeking the cancellation and are themselves the applicant; if they are not the applicant they are entitled to make representations at the hearing.

The hearing before the betting licensing committee

The committee must refuse the application to cancel a bookmaker's permit if it is satisfied that the matters raised have been or ought to have been raised by way of objection when the permit was originally granted or renewed, or if the committee is satisfied that the matters raised are or have been the subject matter of proceedings for certain offences under the Betting, Gaming and Lotteries Act 1963 or offences involving fraud or dishonesty then the committee must refuse the application for cancellation as that aspect will have been already judicially considered by a court.

The committee must not cancel a bookmaker's permit except for the following reasons:

(a) that the bookmaker is no longer a fit and proper person. A failure to pay bookmaker's levy to the Levy Board, or to pay general betting duty to HM Customs and Excise entitles the betting licensing committee to rule that the bookmaker is no longer a fit and proper person; or
(b) that the business is being managed by or carried on for the benefit of someone who would be refused a permit if he himself applied either because he would be held to be disqualified from holding a permit or because he was not a fit and proper person to hold a permit.

In coming to their decision as to whether to cancel a bookmaker's permit the committee must disregard any conviction for offences under the Betting Act 1853 or corresponding offences under local Acts of Parliament or offences under the Street Betting Act 1906 committed on or before 1 December 1961, or certain offences under the Betting and Gaming Act 1960 committed before 1 December 1961.

If the committee decides not to cancel the permit it must give written notice to the applicant for cancellation, stating that his application for cancellation of the permit is refused without prejudice to his right to raise the matter again when the permit next comes up for annual renewal.

If the committee decides to forfeit and cancel the permit there is a right of appeal to the crown court and the cancellation will not take effect until the appeal has been decided or abandoned.

The committee has power to order an unsuccessful applicant for cancellation of a bookmaker's permit to pay costs to the bookmaker and vice versa.

Cancellation and forfeiture of betting office licences

With effect from 1 September 1997:

(i) a court is enabled to order the cancellation and forfeiture of a betting office licence held by a person convicted of managing a betting office in contravention of the rules set out in Sch 4 to the 1963 Act;

(ii) new provision is made for the cancellation of betting office licences. The three new discretionary grounds upon which a licence can be cancelled are:
- having regard to their layout, character and condition, they are not suitable for use as a licensed betting office, or
- they have not been properly conducted under the licence,or
- they have not been used as a licensed betting office in the period of 12 months ending with the date on which the applicationis made and the licence has been in force for at least 12 months.

Opening hours of licensed betting offices

Licensed betting offices may remain open until 10 p.m., **only** during the months April to August inclusive. They have to remain closed:

(a) between 10 p.m. and midnight during April, May, June, July and August;and
(b) between 6.30 p.m. and midnight at any other time of the year.

Betting offices are allowed to open on Sundays at the same times as on other days of the week.

Bingo club licence

(Gaming Act 1968)

A bingo club licence is a gaming licence (see below) which contains a restriction pursuant to para 25 of Sch 2 of the Act limiting the type of gaming to bingo. As it is a gaming licence the procedures and notes mentioned below also apply here except for grounds of refusal numbered (6) and (7) on p 426, and for the compulsory restrictions mentioned on p 427. The applicant must first obtain a Certificate of Consent from the Gaming Board which will be limited to bingo and then the applicant must apply to the betting and gaming licensing committee for the area in which the premises are situated. Reference should therefore be made to gaming club ('casino') licences below.

The court fee for a bingo club licence is £2640 (compared with £32,030 for a full gaming licence) and £1835 for Gaming Board Consent.

A gaming licensing committee is entitled to hear an application for a bingo hall licence under Sch 2 to the Act even though the premises to which the application relates have not yet been built *(R v Hitchin Gaming Licensing Commmittee, ex p Gala Leisure Ltd* (1996)).

Gaming licence

(Gaming Act 1968)

The Act is aimed at strictly controlling the issue of such licences. An applicant must first obtain a certificate of consent from the Gaming Board of Great Britain. Without this no applicant can proceed with the second step of his application which is to obtain a gaming licence from the betting licensing committee for the area in which the proposed premises are situated.

Method of application to gaming licensing committee (Sch 2)

Application to a betting and gaming licensing committee may be made at any time.

It is suggested that the betting licensing committee ask their clerk to confirm that the correct application procedure has been followed.

The newspaper advertisement must be strictly limited to mentioning only prescribed matters; but an inadvertent misprint does not invalidate the advertisement (*R v Brighton Gaming Licensing Committee, ex p Cotedale Ltd* (1978)).

Procedure at the hearing. If no objection is made, or if objections have been withdrawn, the licence can be granted without hearing evidence.

The committee can impose restrictions on such matters as the times when and the parts of the premises where gaming can take place; also on the types of gaming that can take place.

If a licence is granted the court fee is £32,030 (and £6120 for Gaming Board Consent).

Grounds for refusing a licence. The committee can require evidence tendered by the applicant or an objector to be upon oath. The Act requires the committee to take into consideration advice tendered to it by the Gaming Board, and the advice may be based on a local, or a regional or even national viewpoint. If the Gaming Board's advice is in writing, the applicant is entitled to obtain a copy of it by writing to the clerk of the betting licensing committee.

An application can be refused on any of the following grounds:

(a) The committee is not satisfied that a substantial demand *already* exists for the type of gaming proposed. The committee is expected to take into consideration gaming facilities existing in reasonably accessible areas, as well as inside their own area.
(b) The layout, character, condition, or location of the premises are unsuitable.
(c) The applicant is not a fit or proper person; or would merely be a front for others who are not fit and proper persons.

(d) Reasonable facilities to inspect the premises have been refused to the committee (or its representatives), the officials of the Gaming Board, police, local authority or fire authority.
(e) Gaming duties under the Finance Acts have not been paid.
(f) The premises are not in a prescribed licensed club area.
(g) There is direct access to the premises from other private premises not in the licence.

It is a mandatory ground for refusal where a disqualification order under s 24 of the Act has been made prohibiting the holding of a licence for the premises.

Compulsory restrictions. The committee must include restrictions banning bingo, dancing, music, or entertainments by live performers.

The committee can award costs to be paid to an applicant by an objector, and vice versa.

Duration of gaming licence. The licence will expire 12 months after it is granted. Application for renewal must be lodged not later than two months nor earlier than five months prior to the expiry date.

Appeal. An unsuccessful applicant, or one who is dissatisfied with a restriction that the committee has imposed on his licence, can appeal to the crown court.

The Gaming Board can also appeal to the crown court against the grant of a licence, or because, in the Board's opinion, a restriction imposed on a licence is inadequate. No other objector has a right of appeal to the crown court.

Gaming machine registration certificates

(Gaming Act 1968, Part III)

A bona fide members' club or a proprietary club can apply to its local gaming licensing committee for a registration certificate under Part III of the Act which will entitle the club to use a maximum number of three gaming machines (jackpot machines) at the club premises. There is no need for the club to obtain the prior consent of the Gaming Board.

A gaming machine is a slot machine for playing a game of chance in which the element of chance is provided by the machine itself. It offers a large or unlimited jackpot to winners. It should not be confused with an amusement with prizes machine which can also be a slot machine for playing a game of chance; an amusement machine must comply with the requirements of s 34 of the Act. For the procedure for applying for an amusement with prizes machine permit for licensed premises see p 419.

Method of application for gaming machine registration certificate (Sch 7). It is suggested that the gaming licensing committee ask the clerk if the correct procedure has been followed.

Procedure at the hearing. The Act envisages the police being the only objector. If no objection is made by them, a registration certificate can be granted without hearing evidence. The committee can require evidence to be given on oath particularly in a contested application.

Grounds for refusing. The committee **must** refuse a registration certificate if it appears that the machine or machines will be installed on premises which are frequented wholly or mainly by persons under 18 years.

The committee **may** refuse on any of the following grounds:

(a) The club is not a bona fide members' club. A proprietary club can be granted a certificate. It is a matter for the committee's discretion in each application. The clerk should be consulted.
(b) The club has less than 25 members.
(c) The club is of a merely temporary character.

The committee can order the applicant to pay costs to the police, or vice versa.

Duration of registration certificate. Five years from date of issue.

Appeal. An unsuccessful club can appeal to the crown court, but the police have no right of appeal to the crown court against a certificate being granted.

Registration certificate for members' club for gaming

(Gaming Act 1968, Part II)

A miners' welfare institute or a bona fide members' club which has 25 or more members and is not of a temporary character can apply for a registration certificate under Part II of the Act. Gaming must not be the principal purpose of the club, but bridge and whist clubs are expressly authorised to apply for such registration certificates. There is no need to obtain a certificate of consent before making the application to the gaming licensing committee. The gaming can include bingo.

Effect of registration. The gaming licensing committee will not decide what types of gaming can take place under the registration certificate. That point is dealt with by the Act and regulations made under the Act. As already mentioned bingo is authorised. Generally speaking a banker's game will be illegal and so will any gaming in which each player does not have an equal chance of winning; but pontoon and chemin de fer will be legal.

Only members of 48 hours standing and their bona fide guests will be allowed to participate in the gaming. Anyone participating must be present in the gaming room. If a charge is imposed it must not exceed £2 per person per day, 'day' meaning 24 hours starting from noon. (No charge can be imposed on a guest.) In addition a club or institute, whether registered under the Act or not, may generally charge £6 per day for gaming consisting of whist and/or bridge where no other gaming (except by means of gaming machines) takes place on that day, or 50p for other gaming where the chances are equal (guests may be subject to these charges). A club registered under the Act may make both charges, ie £2 and £6 or 50p, as the case may be. A non-registered club may only make the charge for bridge and whist, or the 50p for equal chance games; pontoon and chemin de fer will be prohibited.

Method of application to gaming licensing committee. It is suggested that the committee ask the clerk to confirm that the correct application procedure has been followed.

Procedure at the hearing. If no objection is made or objections have been withdrawn, the committee can grant a registration certificate without hearing evidence. In a contested case the committee can require the evidence to be given on oath. The committee can order an objector to pay costs to the applicant and vice versa.

The committee can impose restrictions limiting the gaming to a particular room or rooms.

Grounds for refusing. The committee **must** refuse the application if any of the following apply:

(a) the club is not a bona fide members' club (eg it is in fact a proprietary club in which one or more individuals own the club and take the profits);
(b) the club has less than 25 members;
(c) the club is of a merely temporary character;
(d) the principal purpose of the club is gaming, but this does not apply to bridge and whist clubs.

Duration of registration certificate. It will expire 12 months after it was granted. Application for renewal (which may be for a period of up to 10 years) must be lodged not later than two months nor earlier than five months prior to the expiry of the certificate.

Appeal. An unsuccessful club, or one dissatisfied with a restriction included in its certificate, can appeal to the crown court. If a certificate is granted the Gaming Board can appeal to the crown court against the grant.

Section eight

Council tax

Background

The administration and enforcement of the council tax is regulated by the Council Tax (Administration and Enforcement) Regulations 1992. An estimatied 21 million council tax bills will be sent out in 1996.

Recovery and enforcement

In most respects council tax recovery mirrors community charge recovery. The first action the courts are involved in is the issue of a summons by a single justice or a justice's clerk against the alleged debtor following a complaint by a local authority of non-payment. Prior to this the local authority will have served a demand notice on the liable person and when payment has not been forthcoming the authority must serve a reminder notice. If payment is not made within 7 days of the issue of the reminder notice the whole amount outstanding becomes due after a further 7 day period. The final step the local authority takes before making a complaint for a liability order is the issue of a final notice. Such notice will state the sum outstanding and the amount of any costs reasonably incurred in obtaining the liability order. The court will fix a date when the applications for the liability order will be heard.

A summons may be served on a person by delivering it to him; leaving it in his usual or last known place of abode; sending it to him by post to that address or leaving it or sending it by post to an address given by the person as an address at which the service of the summons will be accepted (eg a solicitor's office). In the case of a company service can be effected at the company's registered office.

The court hearing

The court hearing is conducted as a complaint and the complainant council may make out their case for a liability order on the balance of probabilities, whether or not the non-payer appears in court. In order to be successful the council must satisfy the court that:

(a) council tax has been set by resolution of the authority;
(b) a sum due has been demanded in accordance with the regulations as set out above; and
(c) summons has been served.

It follows that if the amount has not been demanded in accordance with the regulations or has been duly paid then this will amount to a defence. Further, any complaint for a liability order made more than 6 years after the amount became due will not be valid.

Evidential requirements

Much of the evidence may be produced by way of certificate, for example, a certified copy signed by the appropriate officer showing the council's resolution setting the amount of the council tax for the given local authority area. In addition:

(a) computer generated documents are admissible so long as the document constitutes or forms part of a record compiled by the authority;
(b) direct oral evidence of any facts stated would have been admissible; and
(c) where the document has been produced by a computer it is accompanied by a certificate which:
    (i) must identify the document and the computer by which it was produced;
    (ii) include a statement that at all times the computer was operating properly and, if not, whether this would have an effect on the accuracy of the contents of the document;
    (iii) give appropriate explanations to the contents of the document;and
    (iv) be signed by a person occupying a responsible position in relation to the operation of the computer.

The only legitimate defences against the making of the liability order are outlined above and such matters as pending appeals at the valuation tribunal as to the correct banding, or disputes as to the amount owed, will not amount to a reason for the court to decline to issue a liability order.

The liability order

Where magistrates are satisfied that the local authority have made out their case then they must issue a liability order, they have no further discretion. This order will include an order for reasonable costs. A liability order gives the local authority the power to take their own enforcement action such as attachment of earnings orders, distress warrants, deductions from income support, etc. Matters which may be raised at a valuation tribunal are not relevant in enforcement proceedings.

Committal proceedings

Following the failure of these or other enforcement methods the local authority may apply to the court for a means enquiry to be held with a view to a committal to prison in default of payment of the outstanding council tax. A warrant of commitment may only be applied for if the local authority have first attempted to levy distress and have received a report that the bailiffs were unable to find sufficient goods on which to levy the amount outstanding. In order to secure the debtor's attendance the court may issue a summons or a warrant for his arrest. At the committal hearing the court will enquire into the defaulter's means and may impose a period of 3 months maximum to be served in imprisonment where they are satisfied that failure to pay is due to the person's wilful refusal or culpable neglect. Justices using this power should be satisfied of the criteria on a criminal standard of proof or a high civil standard (*R v South Tyneside JJ, ex p Martin* (1995)) The defaulter must be present before court and although local authorities are not under a statutory obligation to exhaust all other remedies before making an application for committal, it may well be advisable for them to do so. Courts will therefore be keen to see such action being tried as clearer evidence that the defendant is culpable in his neglect to pay and not just unable to pay through impecuniosity or mismanagement.

When dealing with a committal application then the magistrates may:

(a) issue a warrant for commitment;
(b) fix a term of imprisonment and postpone the issue of the warrant until such time and on such conditions as the court thinks fit. Note that where a warrant is issued after postponement and, since the term of imprisonment was fixed, part-payments have been made, these payments will reduce the imprisonment in a proportion to the full amount outstanding;
(c) adjourn the application;
(d) dismiss the application;
(e) remit all or part of the sum owing. Previous case law points to the fact that, as with rates enforcement, this may only be appropriate if the debtor cannot afford to pay; remission remains an option only up to the point at which a term of imprisonment has been fixed (*Harrogate Council v Barker* (1995)).
(f) theoretically the court might find wilful refusal or culpable neglect but not issue a commitment warrant as the matter does rest within its discretion. Once a warrant of commitment has been issued or a term of imprisonment fixed, a charging authority may not take further steps to recover the debt under the liability order (reg 52).

The Council Tax (Administration and Enforcement) Regulations 1992, reg 47(2) make it clear that on an appplication for commitment to prison being made the court shall, in the debtor's presence, enquire into his means and enquire whether the failure to pay which has led to *the application* is due to his wilful refusal or culpable neglect. In other words, the court's enquiries concern the period of time after the issue of the liability order but before the application for a commitment to prison. This in fact makes it even more important that local authorities pursue all available options to them under the authority's liability order before coming into court to ask for a commitment warrrant to be issued.

Although the council may only deduct 5% of debtors' benefit payments direct from income support a magistrates' court may order a payment in excess of this figure in appropriate circumstances (*R v Felixstowe etc Magistrates' Court, ex p Herridge* (1994)).

Suspended commitments

Where a commitment to prison is issued but postponed on terms it appears that the court must hold a further enquiry before the commitment warrant is issued to take the defaulter to prison. This was considered in *R v Faversham and Sittingbourne Justices, ex p Ursell* (1992). The court considered that a futher enquiry into a commitment warrant postponed on terms was necessary before that warrant could be issued. This was a further opportunity to enable the court to be satisfied that the conditions had not been met by the debtor as well as giving the debtor a further opportunity to explain his default.

The role of a defaulter was considered in *R v Wolverhampton Stipendiary Magistrate, ex p Mould*. This was a case under the community charge legislation. The role of the defaulter was defined as going beyond the mere giving of evidence. He could also:

(a) challenge the evidence given by the charging authority as to indebtedness and any steps to levy distress;
(b) challenge the information given about his means;
(c) submit that failure to pay was not due to wilful refusal or culpable neglect; and
(d) even if it was, that a warrant of commitment postponed on suitable conditions was to be preferred to immediate custody.

Where the defaulter fails to attend, however, there appears to be no reason why the court should not issue a warrant committing them to prison for breach of the condition so long as they have been given notice of the hearing.

A number of cases have emphasised that before committing a debtor to prison the court must have considered all available alternatives to attempt recovery of the sum due (*R v Newcastle-under-Lyme Justices, ex p Massey* (1993)).

Section nine

Court procedure

Court room procedure

Proceedings to be in open court

Magistrates conducting a summary trial must generally sit in open court (MCA 1980, s 121)

There are various exceptions to the rule of 'open justice': special statutory provisions govern the conduct of proceedings in a youth court (p 387) and a family proceedings court (p 353) including particular restrictions in adoption proceedings (p 380). Also, statute provides for a court to sit in camera when considering evidence in proceedings under the Official Secrets Act 1920.

Power to clear court while child or young person is giving evidence in certain cases. Where, in any proceedings in relation to an offence against or any conduct contrary to decency or morality, a juvenile is called as a witness, the court may be cleared of persons other than members or officers of the court, parties to the case, their counsel or solicitors, and persons otherwise directly concerned with the case, but *bona fide* representatives of the press may not be excluded (CYPA 1933, s 37).

Apart from the statutory exceptions evidence must be given in open court except where it may be necessary to depart from this principle where the nature or circumstances of the particular proceedings are such that the application of the general rule in its entirety would frustrate or render impracticable the administration of justice (*A-G v Leveller Magazines Ltd* (1979)).

The High Court has commented on the magistrates' decision to hear mitigation in camera because embarrassing and intimate details of the defendant's personal life would have to be given by her and she had an overwhelming fear of revealing them publicly. The judges felt the magistrates' exercise of their discretion was unsustainable and out of accord with principle (*R v Malvern JJ, ex p Evans* (1987)).

Non-disclosure of evidence given in open court. Sometimes where the court decides not to sit in camera there is a request that a witness may write down his name on a piece of paper or use a pseudonym. In criminal cases at least this should only be done where the criteria for sitting in camera are met and such a device is normally only encountered in blackmail cases. Such a power is not designed for the benefit of the comfort and feelings of defendants such as where publication of a defendant's address might cause him to be harassed by his former wife (*R v Evesham JJ, ex p McDonagh* (1987)).

Reporting of court proceedings

Apart from the special provisions governing the youth and family proceedings courts referred to above, the press may report all legal proceedings held in public (Contempt of Court Act 1981, s 4(1)). There are certain exceptions to the general rule:

(a) *Children and young persons:* The court may direct that no newspaper may reveal the name and address or other specified particulars calculated to lead to the identification of any juvenile concerned in the proceedings either as a witness or a defendant, nor that any picture shall be published, except as permitted by the court (CYPA 1933, s 39).
(b) After an allegation of rape and other sexual offences (see p 98) has been made the general rule is that no material likely to lead to the identification by the public of the complainant may be published or broadcast.
(c) *Publication of matters exempted from disclosure in court:* Where a court has allowed a name or other matter to be withheld from the public in proceedings before the court, the court may give such directions prohibiting the publication of that name or matter in connection with the proceedings as appear to the court to be necessary for the purpose for which it was so withheld (Contempt of Court Act 1981, s 11). The order must be in writing and must state with precision its exact terms, extent and purpose.
(d) *Power to postpone publication of reports of court proceedings:* Where it appears to be necessary for avoiding a substantial risk of prejudice to the administration of justice in those proceedings or in any other proceedings pending or imminent the court may order that the publication of any report of the proceedings or any part of the proceedings be postponed for such period as the court thinks necessary for that purpose (Contempt of Court Act 1981, s 4(2)). The order should be no wider than is necessary for the prevention of prejudice to the administration of justice (*R v Horsham JJ, ex p Farquharson* (1982)) and must be in writing and must state with precision its exact terms, extent and purpose.

Photographs and sketches in court. No person shall take or attempt to take a photograph, or make or attempt to make any portrait or sketch of a justice or party or witness to proceedings, in a court room or in a court building or precincts or entering or leaving them (Criminal Justice Act 1925, s 41).

Tape recorders. It is a contempt of court to use a tape recorder (other than for the purpose of making an official transcript) in a court without the leave of the court (Contempt of Court Act 1981, s 9). Guidelines for the decision whether to grant leave were given in a practice direction by the Lord Chief Justice in 1982 which may be summarised thus:

(a) Has the applicant a reasonable need to use the tape recorder?
(b) Is there a risk of a recording being used to brief witnesses?
(c) What is the possibility of distracting proceedings or distracting or worrying witnesses?

Misbehaviour in court

Misbehaviour by members of the public

(a) Where persons misbehave in court the first approach should be to attempt to calm down offenders by an appeal to reason and good manners. A court can also consider putting the case back for a 'cooling off' period and the chairman may also make mention in very general terms of the court's powers to maintain order.

(b) If this is not successful a court has power to order persons disrupting the court to leave the court room. If they refuse, and their removal is necessary to enable justice to be administered properly, the court may order a court security officer or the police to remove such persons using force if necessary.

(c) Where persons are misbehaving in court it is possible for the magistrates to exercise their power to **bind over** miscreants (see p 173). However, the ancient power of binding over has to some extent been replaced by a new power for magistrates to deal with contempt of court.

Contempt of court

Charges

(a) Wilfully did insult AB being a justice of the peace (or a witness before the court, or an officer of the court, or a solicitor or counsel having business before the court) during his sitting or attendance in court or when he was going to or returning from the court; or

(b) wilfully interrupted the proceedings of a magistrates' court; or

(c) wilfully misbehaved in a magistrates' court.

(Contempt of Court Act 1981, s 12.)

Maximum penalty – Fine of level 4 and one month. Proceedings under s 12: offender may be ordered to be taken into custody by an officer of the court or a constable and detained until the rising of the court in addition to or instead of the penalty mentioned above. A person under 18 years may not be committed for contempt.

Legal notes

Wilfully insult. The word 'insult' has to be given its ordinary English meaning. In a case decide in 1985, it was held that a person who had *threatened* a defendant had not 'insulted' him and was not in breach of s 12.

Officer of the court. This term is not defined in the Act. It will apply to the justices' clerk and his staff, presumably whether or not they are concerned in the particular proceedings in which the insult occurs. If there is any doubt, the matter could certainly be resolved by simply alleging misbehaviour in court.

Procedure. By the nature of such proceedings, feelings may be running high and it is a grave matter to punish someone for contempt of court. Accordingly magistrates should be careful not to act in haste. The court should allow time for reflection. If necessary the case can be put back to the end of the court list. If the offender is removed to the cells, he should have the opportunity of speaking to his solicitor or receiving other legal advice (legal aid is available for contempt proceedings). The offender should always be given the opportunity to apologise to the court and it may be that a genuine apology together with the brief period spent in the cells may suffice. If it is necessary to punish the offender imprisonment should be the last resort. Where a person has been in prison, for example, because he refuses to apologise he may apply subsequently to the magistrates to purge his contempt by apologising and the magistrates may then order his release from custody.

Where the disorder in court is so overwhelming magistrates should retire immediately and allow the police to restore order. Where the offenders are subsequently dealt with, they should be dealt with individually.

Witnesses. In addition to the powers outlined above, where a witness refuses to take the oath or to answer a question, he may be committed to prison for a period of up to 1 month (and ordered to pay a fine on level 4). He may be released immediately he changes his mind and decides to co-operate with the court. This advice may ensure his compliance.

Defendants. Disorderly defendants may be dealt with as outlined above. However, a court is naturally reluctant to deal with the case in the absence of a defendant. Accordingly, if the defendant has to be ejected the court should carefully consider adjourning the case for a 'cooling off' period. The more serious the case the less appropriate it will be to proceed in the defendant's absence. The defendant should be informed that he will be readmitted to the court any time he is prepared to conduct himself properly.

Mode of trial proceedings

Where a person is accused of an offence triable either way, the magistrates cannot conduct committal proceedings or try the offence themselves until 'mode of trial' proceedings have taken place. However, before determining mode of trial the court will invite the defendant to indicate his plea, having explained to him that he may be committed to the Crown Court for sentence if the court considers its powers are insufficient. If the defendant indicates a plea of guilty he will be treated as convicted and the court will proceed to sentence, or committal to Crown Court for sentence, If the defendant fails to intimate a plea or intimates a plea of not guilty the court will hear representations on the seriousness of the case, both from the prosecutor and the defendant. The court at this stage is only concerned with the gravity of the offence and not with the character of the defendant, and previous convictions of the accused are, therefore, irrelevant and should not be mentioned. The prosecutor should therefore give the court an outline of the prosecution case so that the gravity of the offence can be ascertained, eg in an assault case: the description of the injuries caused and whether a weapon was used. The defence may then make representations if it wishes before the magistrates make their decision.

Matters to which the court is to have regard

(a) the nature of the case;
(b) whether the circumstances make the offence one of a serious character;
(c) whether the punishment which a magistrates' court would have power to inflict for it would be adequate; (*R v Flax Bourton Magistrates* (1996));
(d) any other circumstances which appear to the court to make it more suitable for the offence to be tried in one way rather than the other (Magistrates' Courts Act 1980, s 19(3)).

If the magistrates feel able to deal with the case the defendant is given a choice of which court he wishes to try the offence. Before he makes his choice he *must* be warned that if he elects summary trial and pleads guilty or is convicted after a trial he may still be committed for sentence if the court is of the opinion that the offence (or the combination of the offence and other associated offences) is so serious that the magistrates' powers of punishment are insufficient, or, in the case of a violent or sexual offence, a longer sentence is necessary for protection of the public.

In order to promote greater consistency of approach to the making of mode of trial decisions, the Lord Chief Justice has now issued the guidelines the essence of which is as follows, with the emphasis on more cases being dealt with by magistrates.

General guidelines

(a) The court should never make a decision just for convenience or expedition.
(b) Where there is a dispute on the facts at this stage, the court should rely on the prosecution version.
(c) The defendant's antecedent and personal circumstances are irrelevant.
(d) The fact that the offences before the court are specimen offences is relevant.
(e) Offences to be taken into consideration are irrelevant.
(f) Complicated issues of fact and/or law will tend to make the case more suitable for the crown court.

Except for the presence of one or more 'qualifying factors' either way offences should be tried summarily. Qualifying factors are features which indicate that trial at the crown court is more appropriate. These qualifying factors are set out in the articles of the relevant offences in Section one.

Criminal damage offences. Where the value of the damage is under £5000 the offence is tried summarily. If over this amount the offence is triable as an ordinary either way offence. The court must therefore first decide whether the value of the alleged damage is above or below £5000. If the value is not clear the defendant can elect summary trial and will only be liable for the reduced penalty for the summary only offence with no possibility of a committal for sentence. Otherwise he can elect to have the matter tried as an ordinary either way offence. If the offence is part of a series of offences of criminal damage, it is the aggregate value of all the offences which determines whether the offences are triable either way.

Commital for trial at crown court

Magistrates have no power to try the guilt or innocence of an accused charged with an offence triable only at the crown court or with an offence triable either way where either the magistrates themselves have declined jurisdiction in mode of trial proceedings or the accused has elected to be tried at the crown court.

The function of the magistrates is to hold committal proceedings in order to inquire into the evidence of the prosecution. Magistrates dealing with committal proceedings are referred to examining justices. They examine the prosecution case to decide whether there is sufficient evidence to put the defendant on trial by jury. The sole test for the justices to apply is whether the prosecution has adduced sufficient evidence to satisfy them that there is a triable issue to be put before a jury.

A magistrates' court will consider only documentary evidence and exhibits tendered by the prosecution, together with representations by both parties, when determining whether there is a case to answer. No witness will be called to give evidence or be cross examined. The defence may accept that there is a prima facia case in which case the charge will be committed to Crown Court for trial.

General provisions concerning committal proceedings

The hearing. The committal proceedings may take place before only one magistrate but any hearing must take place in open court unless for any part, or the whole, of the proceedings, the ends of justice would not be served by having a sitting in open court. The evidence shall be tendered in the presence of the accused unless his disorderly conduct has made it impracticable for him to remain in court or he is ill and is represented by an advocate and has consented to the evidence being tendered in his absence(Magistrates' Courts act 1980, s4)

Publicity. Only the following matters may be contained in any report of committal proceedings:

(a) the identity of the court and the names of the examining justices;
(b) the names, addresses and occupations of the parties and witnesses and ages of the accused and witnesses;
(c) the offence or offences, or a summary of them, of which the accused is or are charged;
(d) the names of counsel and solicitors engaged in the proceedings;
(e) any decision of the court to commit the accused or any of the accused for trial, and any decision of the court on the disposal of the case of any accused not committed;
(f) where the court commits the accused or any of the accused for trial, the charge or charges, or a summary of them, on which he is committed and the

court to which he is committed;

(g) where the committal proceeding are adjourned, the date and place to which they are adjourned;

(h) any arrangement as to bail on committal or adjournment;

(i) whether legal aid was granted to the accused or any of the accused.

These restrictions automatically apply unless an accused chooses to have reporting restriction lifted. Where there are several accused, and they are not unanimous in wanting restriction to be lifted, the magistrates must decide whether it is in the interests of justice to do so. Further, the restriction do not apply where the accused are all discharged in the proceedings or after the conclusion of the trial in the crown court.

Summary offences
(Criminal Justice Act 1988, s 41)

Where an accused is sent for trial for an offence triable either way, the magistrates may also send him for trial for any connected summary offences provided they are either imprisonable or endorsable. At the crown court, if the accused is convicted of the indictable offence, he may also plead guilty to the summary offences and be dealt with, the crown court having the same powers as the magistrates with respect to the summary offences. If he denies the summary offences he may not be tried for them in the crown court, but proceedings may then continue in the magistrates' court.

Certain summary offences including common assault, damage and taking without consent may be heard at the Crown Court if they arise from the same facts or evidence as an indictable charge being committed to the Crown Court or they part of a series of offences of the same or similar character as the indictable charge (Criminal Justice Act 1988, s 40).

Legal aid

(Legal Aid Act 1988, Parts V and VI)

Circumstances in which legal aid is available in a magistrates' court include:

(a) any person who is to appear before a magistrates' court or a youth court in respect of an offence; this includes an application for the removal of a disqualification from driving (*R v Recorder of Liverpool, ex p McCann* (1994));

(b) a person who is to appear before a magistrates' court to answer a complaint for a binding over order;

(c) a person who is committed for trial or for sentence to the crown court, or who is committed to the crown court to be dealt with (eg for breach of a probation order);

(d) a person who proposes to appeal to the crown court;

(e) a person at risk of a further remand in custody who is not, but wishes to be represented;*

(f) a person who is remanded in custody for the purpose of inquiries or a report being made.*

Generally an application must be made in the prescribed form and a statement of means submitted. These may be considered by a justices' clerk, a single justice or a magistrates' court who may make a legal aid order provided that they are satisfied both

(i) that the applicant's means are such that he requires assistance in meeting the legal costs of the case, *and*
(ii) that it is in the interests of justice that a legal aid order should be made.

In the circumstances marked* above and in the case of a person charged with murder the second requirement is deemed to be met, and the grant will depend solely on the applicant's financial resources. Where cases are proceeding to the crown court a through order should be made to cover the whole proceedings.

It should be noted that a magistrates' court may only make an order for the services of a Queen's Counsel with one junior counsel where the proceedings are a trial for murder and the order is made upon transfer for trial, or the prosecution is brought by the Serious Fraud Office and the order is made upon receiving the notice of transfer.

Application is made to the court and is considered by the justices' clerk or a member of his staff who may grant or refuse legal aid. In the case of an indictable offence where prescribed conditions are met, there is an appeal to an area committee of the Legal Aid Board. However, in all cases a renewed application may be made to the court where an officer of the court may grant the application or refer it to a justice of the peace or the court, in which case the application may be granted or refused as the justice or court considers appropriate.

Interests of justice

As to whether it is in the interests of justice that a legal aid order should be made, the Legal Aid Act 1988, s 22 provides that in proceedings by way of a trial the factors to be taken into account include:

(a) the offence is such that if proved it is likely that the court would impose a sentence which would deprive the accused of his liberty or lead to loss of his livelihood or serious damage to his reputation; or
(b) where there is a substantial question of law involved; or
(c) the accused may be unable to understand the proceedings or state his own case because of his inadequate knowledge of English, mental illness or other mental or physical disability; or
(d) the nature of the defence is such as to involve the tracing and interviewing of witnesses or expert cross-examination of a witness for the prosecution; or
(e) where it may be in the interests of a third party, eg the victim of a sexual offence who might be distressed at being cross-examined directly by the accused, or who might be spared an appearance in court if the accused is given proper legal advice as to his plea.

These criteria, which are used in the assessment of whether or not it is in the interests of justice that legal aid should be granted, are largely self-explanatory. A motorist who wishes to raise a plea of special reasons based on an allegation that a drink had been 'laced' would need an expert witness and would need to cross-examine witnesses to the incident. Such a driver should be granted legal aid (*R v Gravesham Magistrates Court, ex p Baker* (1997)). In *R v Liverpool City Magistrates* (1993) it was pointed out that 'expert' (d) above meant that the cross-examiner should be expert, it was not necessary that the witness should be an expert.

Guidance was also given on (a) above in that it was pointed out that the likelihood of a community sentence was not a sentence which deprived the accused of his liberty.

The applicant's means

The applicant must fill in and submit a statement of means and documentary evidence in support of the statement. Such evidence will normally be 3 months pay slips or proof that the applicant is in receipt of benefits (from DSS).

Such proof may be produced later to the court if it is not available at the time of application, eg the defendant is in custody.

However, where legal aid is granted on the basis that evidence in support of means will be produced later, and it is not forthcoming, the court may then withdraw the legal aid order.

A legal aid order may not be backdated but may be made after proceedings have been concluded in cases of urgency (*R v Highbury Corner, ex p Sonn* (1995)).

On receipt of the means form the justice's clerk or a delegated assissant will apply the regulations to determine fiancial eligibility:

(a) if the applicant is in receipt of income support, family credit or disability working allowance, he will be entitled to legal aid without contribution;
(b) if he is working his total net income and that of his spouse or partner is calculated;
(c) allowances are given against this income for dependants, council tax, housing, travelling and other expenses;
(d) if the resulting figure is £50 £or less the contribution is nil;
(e) if the resulting figure is more than £50, £49 (representing the income support allowance for a single 25 year old) is subtracted and the remaining figure divided by 3 to give the total weekly contribution.

An example illustrates the above procedure:

A man living with a partner and 2 children aged 10 and 16 years of age:

(1) Total net income		£230.00
Allowances for:		
Partner	£28.00	
Child 15	£24.75	
Child 10	£16.90	

Council tax £8.85			
Rent £50.00			
Travel £15.00			
(2) Total allowance			£143.50
(3) Disposable income			£86.50
(4) Minus £ 49.00	=	£37.50	
(5) Total weekly contribution			
((3) – (4) divide by 3)	=		£12.50

This contribution is made for the life of the case and will be increased by the amount of any capital in excess of £3000.

In essence a contribution of £1 is payable for each £3 (or part of £3) by which average disposable income exceeds the weekly limit but no conrtibution is payable where average disposable income does not exceed £50.

It should be noted that only the first £100,000 attributable to a mortgage is taken into account when deducting mortgage instalments from an applicant's income.

As the life of the case is indeterminate it is not possible to calculate the total amount that the applicant will be required to pay.

Legal aid subject to the contributions is offered to the applicant who may accept or refuse the offer.

If he accepts the offer he must pay the weekly contributions on a regular basis. Failure to do so may result in revocation of the order after notice.

If a legal aid order is revoked for non-payment of contributions any reapplication must be to the court of trial (*R v Liverpool Magistrates' Court, ex p Pender* (1993)).

At the final hearing. When the case has been heard, the bench should enquire of the clerk whether the defendant is liable to pay a contribution towards his legal aid. If so, any arrears can be dealt with there and then to avoid future enforcement action.

If the defendant is aquitted he may request remittal of any sum due to be paid and the repayment of any sums already paid.

Where an immediate custodial sentence is passed following conviction the liability to pay further contribution ceases.

Section ten

Remands in custody and bail

Remands in custody and on bail

'Remand'

When a case is adjourned to a fresh date the defendant may be remanded to ensure his attendance at the next hearing. The accused may be remanded in custody or released on bail. The prosecution will very often ask the court for a 'remand', when in fact it is seeking an adjournment. The other party to the case frequently does not object to the adjournment, but it should be remembered that the final decision rests with the court. Although the court may have been presented with a *fait accompli* where an agreement has previously been made between the parties, the magistrates should always be scrupulous to ensure that an adjournment is necessary. They should hear representations from both sides and make their decision judicially, taking all the relevant considerations into account. While it may not be possible to prevent an adjournment, the court may be able to avoid future adjournments. If magistrates do not keep a tight hold on the course of proceedings, it will not be surprising that undue delays occur in the administration of justice.

Remands take three forms:

Remand on unconditional bail. The accused is released with an obligation to surrender to the custody of the court on a certain day at a specified time. If he fails to do so, there are two consequences: the court can immediately issue a warrant for his arrest and he may be prosecuted for the criminal offence of failing to answer his bail.

Remand on conditional bail. The accused is on bail but with conditions attached to that bail, to ensure that he appears at court on the appointed day at the appropriate time or does not commit offences in the meantime or does not interfere with the witnesses in the case.

Remand in custody. Where bail is refused, the defendant is detained in prison or in police cells until his next appearance in court.

Juveniles. For remand of juveniles, see p 388.

When must the court remand?

Where the court is acting with a view to transfer for trial the accused must always be remanded on bail or in custody.

If the case is triable either way, the court must always remand where the accused was initially arrested by the police and brought to court in custody or bailed for his appearance, or he has previously been remanded in the proceedings.

Where the offence is purely summary, the court always has a discretion whether to remand or simply adjourn the case.

In the case of juveniles (under 17) the court may remand if it thinks it is necessary to do so in those cases where it must do so when the defendant is 17 or over.

Length of the remand – before conviction

In custody. A remand in custody is not normally for longer than 8 clear days, ie the day when the decision to remand is made and the day when the defendant is next due to appear in court, are excluded. Therefore a remand in custody may be from the Monday of one week to the Wednesday of the next.

There are three exceptions:

(a) If the defendant is to be kept in police cells, the maximum period is 3 clear days.
(b) Where the accused is already serving a custodial sentence and will not be released in the intervening period, he may be remanded for up to 28 days.
(c) The court may remand a defendant present before the court who has previously been remanded in custody for a period expiring when the next stage of the proceedings is reached or 28 days, whichever is the less. In exercising this power the court would have to have regard to the total length of time which the accused would spend in custody if it were to exercise the power. This would not affect the right of the defendant to apply for bail during this period.

On bail. Unless the accused consents, a remand on bail cannot be for more than 8 clear days. However, defendants always do consent to longer remands and that is why, as mentioned above, it is important for the magistrates to exercise control over the granting of adjournments. It should be remembered that bail is always granted to a fixed date and so it is not possible to adjourn a case *sine die* where the accused is remanded. An exception to this rule is a committal to the crown court although a plea and directions hearing may be specified.

Length of remand – after conviction

A remand after conviction (for further inquiries and pre-sentence reports) cannot be for longer than 3 weeks if in custody, or 4 weeks on bail.

Committal to the crown court

When magistrates commit proceedings to the crown court for trial (or commit for sentence) the court may order the accused to be kept in custody until his trial or it may grant him bail.

Remands in the absence of the accused

An application for a remand for not more than 8 clear days may in prescribed circumstances be heard in the absence of the accused. The conditions to be complied with before this is possible are as follows:

(a) the court is adjourning a case before conviction; and
(b) the accused is present before the court;
(c) he is legally represented before the court (although his solicitor need not necessarily be present in court).

The accused must be asked whether he consents to future remands being determined in his absence. If he does, the court may remand him for up to 3 occasions in his absence. This means that the defendant must be brought before the court every four weeks. If the accused withdraws his consent or for any reason ceases to be legally represented, arrangements will be made by the clerk to bring him before the court at the earliest opportunity, even though the period of his remand has not expired.

If the defendant has been remanded on bail or in custody and cannot appear because of accident or illness, the court may further remand him in absence. A court can always further remand in absence an accused who is on bail.

The decision whether to remand in custody or on bail

Presumption of liberty. The general principle is that an accused man has a right to be released on bail where he has not been convicted of the charge or where his case has been adjourned for pre-sentence reports. This means that the accused never has to apply for bail, it is up to the prosecution to object to his right to bail (although in practice the defence are referred to as making an application for bail). Therefore it is no reason for remanding an accused in custody that he has not applied for bail. However this right to bail does not apply to a committal to the crown court for sentence.

Exceptions to the right to bail. An accused can only be denied his right to bail if the court finds that there is an exception to that right. These exceptions are set out in Sch 1 to the Bail Act 1976. They differ according to whether or not the offence is punishable by imprisonment (whether or not the accused himself is liable to imprisonment because of his age etc).

A defendant need not be granted bail if he is charged with an either way or indictable offence and it appears to the court that he was on bail in criminal proceedings at the date of the offence.

Imprisonable offences. The exceptions to the right to bail are:

1 Where the court has substantial grounds for believing the accused would
   (a) fail to answer bail; or
   (b) commit further offences on bail; or
   (c) interfere with witnesses or otherwise obstruct the course of justice.

Each of the exceptions must be substantiated by a reason given by the court such as:

(i) the nature and seriousness of the offence or default (and the probable method of dealing with the accused for it);
(ii) the character, antecedents, associations and community ties of the defendant;
(iii) the accused's previous record when granted bail (eg committing offences on bail or absconding);
(iv) (except when remanding after conviction for a report) the strength of the evidence against the accused;
(v) any other relevant reasons.

2 Remand in custody for the accused's own protection (or in the case of a juvenile, welfare).

3 Where the accused is already in custody as a result of a prison sentence.
4 Where there has been insufficient time to gather information to make the bail decision.
5 Where the accused has absconded or breached the conditions of his bail in the same proceedings already.
6 Where the case has been adjourned for reports or inquiries and it is impracticable to gain the information or prepare reports without remanding the accused in custody.

Non-imprisonable offences. The exceptions to the right to bail are:

(a) it appears that the accused has breached his bail in previous criminal proceedings and in view of that the court believes that he would again fail to surrender to custody in these proceedings;
(b) remand in custody for the accused's own protection (or in the case of a juvenile, welfare);
(c) where the accused is already in custody as a result of a prison sentence;
(d) where the accused has absconded or breached the conditions of his bail in the same proceedings already.

General considerations

It is not common for a court to have to deal with a remand of a non-imprisonable case and it is even less common for the court to consider a remand in custody. Therefore the following remarks are confined to remands of imprisonable cases.

The usual grounds for the police objecting to bail are exceptions (a) (i)–(iii) above (failure to surrender, further offences or interference with the course of justice). It is worthwhile to examine these a little more closely.

Failure to surrender to custody. The accused may fail to surrender because he knows he will be convicted of a serious charge and will receive a custodial sentence. In considering this objection to the right to bail, the bench might have regard to the likely sentence that will be imposed, in which case the accused's record will be relevant. Then, the circumstances of the defendant: Is he a 'local' man? How long has he lived in the district? Does he have anywhere else to move to? Are all his friends and relations in the area? The court must also consider whether bail with a condition of finding sureties would not suffice instead of a remand in custody.

Further offences on bail. A defendant may consider that he will receive a custodial sentence and that he might as well be 'hung for a sheep as a lamb', in other words the final sentences he receives will not be materially affected whether he is sentenced for one or several offences. This is particularly the case with the 'professional' burglar or the youth with a penchant for taking the cars of other people without their consent.

Interference with the course of justice. In certain situations, a defendant released on bail would interfere with the course of justice. This has three main aspects. First, he might 'tip off' a co-accused who could then abscond or destroy evidence. Second, the co-accused might collaborate to concoct a consistent but false story. Third, the defendant might intimidate the prosecution witnesses, eg in disputes involving a domestic background. The court must consider whether conditions attached to bail would be sufficient to prevent this occurring, eg of non-association with co-accused, or with the prosecution witnesses.

Mistakes commonly made in finding these exceptions are that the bench fail to announce that they find substantial grounds for believing etc and that they announce reasons but no exceptions, eg the defendant is remanded in custody because of his character and antecedents and the nature and seriousness of the offence. These are reasons for finding one of the exceptions (a) (i)–(iii), but they are not in themselves exceptions to the right to bail.

Time limits. The Prosecution of Offences Act 1985, s 22 provides for restrictions on the period for which a person charged with an either way or purely indictable offence may be remanded in custody. The maximum period of a custodial remand is 70 days (84 in Birmingham) between his first appearance and the start of a summary trial or committal proceedings, as appropriate. Where, in the case of an either way offence, summary trial is decided upon within 56 days the summary trial must commence within 56 days of the first appearance. Time limits also apply to proceedings before the crown court.

At any time *before* the expiry of a time limit the magistrates' court may extend that limit if it is satisfied:

(a) that there is good and sufficient cause for doing so; and
(b) that the prosecution has acted with all due expedition.

Where a custody time limit has expired the accused must be released on bail with or without conditions.

Conditional bail

A custody sergeant at the police station may grant an accused conditional bail and may do so for the same reasons as a bench of magistrates who may feel that it cannot release the defendant on unconditional bail. It is only if conditional bail would be inadequate that custody should be contemplated.

Conditions are only to be attached to bail where it appears to the bench necessary to do so for the purpose of preventing the accused:

(a) failing to surrender to custody; or
(b) committing an offence while on bail; or
(c) interfering with witnesses or obstructing the course of justice.

Conditions may also be imposed to enable a pre-sentence report to be prepared. The court must give its reasons for imposing conditions on the bail.

Commonly imposed conditions are:

(a) residence (absconding);
(b) curfew (fresh offences);
(c) reporting to a police station (absconding);

(d) non-association with specified people (interference with the course of justice);
(e) sureties (absconding).

Other conditions may be imposed provided they are reasonable and are enforceable.

It must be emphasised that conditions are not to be imposed as a matter of course; they can only be imposed to prevent one of the occurrences mentioned above. If a condition is imposed it must relate to the mischief which is feared (a *guide* is given by the words in brackets above). Conditions must not be imposed which have no relevance to the reason given by the court, eg a surety because the bench fears fresh offences.

Conditions may also be imposed to require defendants to comply with hostel rules where residing at a bail or probation hostel on remand or for assessment.

Sureties. With one exception, mentioned below, no one has to deposit money or valuables to secure a person's release in remand proceedings. However, a third party may agree to stand as surety for an accused. A surety is a person who agrees to forfeit a sum of money fixed by the court (called recognizances and pronounced 'reconnaissances') if the accused fails to surrender to custody. A surety's obligations are to ensure that the accused surrenders to custody; he is not there to ensure that the accused complies with the conditions of his bail. The court should specify that the suretyship is to secure the accused's attendance at the next hearing or for each occasion to which the case may, from time to time, be adjourned.

In deciding whether to accept a person as a surety, the court should in particular have regard to:

(a) the surety's financial resources;
(b) his character and any previous convictions of his;
(c) his proximity (whether in point of kinship, place or otherwise) to the person for whom he is to be surety.

Forfeiting recognizances of a surety. If the accused fails to answer to his bail, the surety should be informed by the court that it is considering forfeiting his recognizance. Standing surety is a solemn obligation. The court will start from the basis that the whole amount is to be forfeited. The culpability of the surety will be investigated to see what steps he took to ensure the defendant's attendance. However, a surety should not forfeit his recognizance if he is not to blame for the defendant's failure to surrender when required to do so. When forfeiting recognizances the court must take into account the surety's ability to pay.

Depositing a security. An exception to the rule that an accused does not have to deposit money or valuables is where the court believes that the accused is unlikely to remain in Great Britain until the date of the adjourned hearing. The defendant may be British or an alien.

The usual security is money, but it could be a valuable item such as motor car, provided it is readily convertible into money.

The effectiveness of conditions. The usefulness of some conditions is questionable. A condition of reporting to the police at anything longer than 24-hour intervals is generally of little value and such a condition should be not imposed to make the accused more readily available for questioning. Nor should a condition be imposed for its nuisance value to the accused. A condition of depositing a passport is of little value, especially where the accused can travel within the E C without a passport.

Appeal by the prosecution

The Bail (Amendment) Act 1993 gives the Crown Prosecution Service the right to appeal to a High Court or crown court judge where a court grants bail to a person who is charged with or convicted of an offence punishable by imprisonment of 5 years or more, or an offence under s 12 (taking a conveyance without authority) or s 12A (aggravated vehicle taking) of the Theft Act 1968.

Where bail is refused

Making a further application. At the first hearing after that at which the court decided not to grant the defendant bail (which would have been the first time the case was remanded) he is entitled to apply for bail as of right. At any subsequent hearings the court need not hear any arguments as to fact or law which it has heard previously.

The court must, however, always consider the matter of bail on each occasion on which the case is remanded. As the liberty of the accused is at stake, it is suggested that any doubt whether to allow a fresh application should be resolved in the accused's favour.

Application to a judge in chambers. Where the magistrates have heard a full application and have refused bail, they will supply the accused with a certificate to that effect. He then has a right to make a bail application to a judge in chambers.

Bail in cases of murder, manslaughter and rape

In such cases where representations are made as to the exceptions to the right to bail referred to at (a)(i)–(iii) on p 457 and the court decides to grant bail it must state its reasons for doing so. Additionally a person charged with one of the above offences (or an attempt) shall not be granted bail if he has been previously convicted of such an offence and, in the case of murder or manslaughter, received a sentence of imprisonment or long-term detention.

Reconsideration of bail

Where a court or a constable has granted bail for an indictable or either way offence the prosecution may apply to have that decision reconsidered by the court who may:

(a) vary the conditions of bail;
(b) impose conditions on unconditional bail;

(c) withhold bail.

This may only be done on the basis of fresh information not previously available to the court or constable who granted bail.

Prosecution for failing to surrender to custody

The law is that the accused is released on bail with a duty to turn up at court on the appointed day at the appointed time. If he fails to do so the first consequence is that a warrant may be issued for his arrest. Secondly, he may be prosecuted for the criminal offence of failing to surrender to custody.

Where bail has been granted by a police officer for an accused to surrender either to a police station or a magistrates' court, any failure to surrender to custody should be initiated by charging the accused or laying an information. On the other hand, an accused who fails to answer to bail granted by the magistrates themselves should be brought before the court following his arrest. The court will then initiate proceedings of its own motion following an express invitation by the prosecutor. The prosecutor will conduct the proceedings and, where the matter is contested, call the evidence. Any trial should normally take place immediately following the disposal of the proceedings in respect of which bail was granted (*Practice Note* (1986)).

The offence is triable only summarily where bail was granted by magistrates and proceedings are begun by the court acting of its own motion. The accused must be asked whether he pleads guilty or not guilty. Where a prosecution is contemplated the clerk should be consulted to ensure the correct procedure is followed.

Defence. It is a defence to such a charge if he proves (that it is more probable than not) that he had a reasonable excuse for not answering his bail, or that having a reasonable excuse for failing to surrender to custody at the appointed time and place, he surrendered to custody at the appointed place as soon after the appointed time as was reasonably practicable. It is not a defence that the accused was not given a copy of the decision to grant him bail.

Penalty. A maximum penalty of 3 months imprisonment and a fine on level 5 in the magistrates' court or the accused may be committed for sentence to the crown court, where the maximum penalty is 12 months imprisonment and an unlimited fine.

Failing to comply with a condition. Failing to comply with a condition of bail is not an offence. It does mean, however, that a police officer can arrest the accused forthwith and bring him before the court. His failure to comply with the condition may in itself constitute an exception to the general 'right to bail'. If a defendant is arrested in breach of a bail condition the court should ask if he admits or denies the breach. If a denial is recorded the magistrates should hear evidence or a statement of the arresting officer's 'reasonable grounds' for arrest. If they are of the opinion that the defendant was in breach of his bail conditions he may be further remanded either in custody or on bail. There is no power to adjourn the denial of the breach (*Liverpool Justices* (1992)).

Bail pending appeal

The policy of the Court of Appeal has for long been against the granting of bail pending the hearing of an appeal against a custodial sentence, unless there are exceptional circumstances. The appellant's remedy is to apply for an expedited appeal. It is generally felt to be unsatisfactory that a person sentenced to custody is released in the hope of a successful appeal and is subsequently required to return to prison to serve his sentence. Therefore only exceptional circumstances will lead to the granting of bail (*R v Walton* (1979)). The court considering the application is not concerned with whether it would have imposed the same sentence, but only whether the sentence was reasonable. Where the sentence is clearly appropriate for the offence, then personal matters which are the basis for an appeal for clemency should not influence the court considering the bail application.

Disqualification of justices

When in the course of any bail application, a magistrate has been told of the accused's previous convictions, that magistrate may not hear the case if the accused pleads not guilty. There is no such restriction if he pleads guilty.

Summary of procedure at a remand hearing

1 Prosecution (or defence) applies for an adjournment. Bench decides whether to grant the application (length of adjournment may vary depending whether accused will be remanded in custody or on bail).
2 As the presumption is that an accused will be remanded on bail, the prosecution must put forward any exceptions to the right to bail. It is not necessary for evidence to be called and strict proof given. However, where an application for bail is to be made, it is desirable for the officer in the case to give evidence. See p 461 for cases of murder, rape and manslaughter.
3 Where the accused has had a previous application for bail refused, the court must consider whether he may put forward further arguments in support of bail.
4 The accused then makes his application for bail.
5 The bench consider whether there are any exceptions to the right to bail, ie:
   - can the accused be released on unconditional bail;
   - if not, would conditional bail suffice;
   - is there an exception to the right to bail?
6 The bench announces its decision
   (a) If the remand is in custody:
      (i) the chairman will specify the exception to the right to bail which applies together with the reasons for applying that exception where appropriate;
      (ii) the accused is given a record of the decision and a certificate of refusal of bail after a full hearing;
      (iii) the court may enquire whether the accused will consent to further applications being heard in his absence or having heard

representations from the parties, fix a date up to 28 days ahead, when it expects the next stage in the proceedings to take place.

(b) If the remand is on conditional bail, the chairman will announce the conditions and the purpose of those conditions. If sureties are required they may be taken in court or the accused remanded in custody until sureties are taken.

Decision to refuse bail

(exceptions (a) (i)–(iii), p 457)

You are refused bail in this case because we feel that there are substantial grounds for believing that if released on bail you would:

(fail to surrender to custody)
(commit an offence while on bail)
(interfere with witnesses or otherwise obstruct the course of justice)

and in reaching our decision we have had regard to:

(the nature and seriousness of the offence (and the probable method of dealing with you for it))
(your character, antecedents, associations and community ties)
(your record as respects the fulfilment of your obligations under previous grants of bail in criminal proceedings)
(the strength of the evidence of your having committed the offence)

You will therefore be remanded in custody to appear at this court on (date) **at** (time).

Decision to grant bail with conditions

The court grants bail in this case. You will be released with a duty to surrender to the custody of this court on (date) **at** (time)**. The bail will be subject to the following conditions:**

You are:

(to reside at (address) **in the meantime)**
(to remain indoors at that address between the hours of p.m. and a.m.)
(to report at police station between the hours of and on (specify days)**)**
(not to associate with the following persons)
(to provide surety(ies) in the sum of (each)**)**

The court considers it is necessary to impose the condition(s) to prevent you:

(failing to surrender to custody)
(committing an offence while on bail)
(interfering with witnesses or otherwise obstructing the course of justice)

Section eleven

Justices in the crown court

Justices in the crown court

The crown court is part of the Supreme Court of Judicature and exercises both civil and criminal jurisdiction. There are three kinds of professional judges: High Court judges, circuit judges and recorders. The most serious cases are dealt with by a High Court judge sitting alone but when circuit judges and recorders deal with committals for sentence or appeals they may sit with between one and four justices according to the type of case involved.

The following judges should be addressed in court as 'My Lord' (or 'My Lady' as the case may be):

(a) any circuit judge or recorder when he is sitting as a High Court judge;
(b) any judge in the Central Criminal Court;
(c) any circuit judge holding office as honorary Recorder of Liverpool or Manchester.

Subject to the above rule, the following judges should be addressed in court as 'Your Honour':

(a) a circuit judge;
(b) a retired circuit judge sitting as a deputy;
(c) a recorder;
(d) a deputy circuit judge.

When justices sit with a circuit judge or recorder, the justices are as much a part of the court as is the professional judge and the decision of the court is the decision of the majority of those on the bench. Only if there is an equality of votes does the judge or recorder have a second or casting vote. The judge or recorder must preside and his rulings on legal matters will bind the justices.

The rules which prescribe the number of justices who must sit in the crown court and their qualifications are complicated and liable to be changed by the Lord Chief Justice or the Lord Chancellor and such changes may affect all crown courts or only one. Moreover, where the parties agree the judge has a discretion to continue the case without justices.

Justices may deal with cases at the crown court even though the case arose in a part of the country for which they do not act as justices; for example, a justice for one county may sit at the crown court to hear an appeal from the decision of a court in a neighbouring county.

If the prisoner (technically all persons before the crown court are prisoners: those who have been bailed must surrender to custody at the beginning of the hearing and thus become prisoners) is found guilty then the bench decides what sentence to impose.

There is no jury present when the court deals with a person committed for sentence or when the court hears an appeal from the decision of a Magistrates' Court, Licensing Committee or Betting and Gaming Licensing Committee.

Procedure

The clerk of the court in the crown court wears a gown but does not perform the same functions as does the clerk to the justices in a magistrates' court. In particular, he does not act as legal adviser to the court, although in practice he may from time to time draw the judge's attention to some legal or procedural matter.

The proceedings begin with the arraignment of the prisoner if he is to stand trial or in other cases with the announcement of the case by the clerk of the court. When the prisoner is arraigned he is addressed in rather more formal terms than he would be when charged before a magistrates' court, but the arraignment is simply the charging of the prisoner and asking for his plea. The charge is called an indictment and if there are several offences alleged then each is called a count, so that one indictment may contain several counts.

If there is a guilty plea no jury is required. If any of the counts is denied and not withdrawn by the prosecution a jury is summoned. Justices no longer sit on trials following a not guilty plea but the following description is given for information. Each member of the jury takes the juror's oath separately because the prisoner may object to an individual sitting as a juror. The prisoner may object to a juror if he gives a reason for his objection. The bench will decide whether the reason is sufficient for dismissing the juror. The jury is then charged with the duty of deciding on the evidence the question of the prisoner's guilt or innocence. After this the trial proceeds in the same way as the hearing of a criminal charge in the magistrates' court until counsel have made their final speeches (the prosecution has a closing speech immediately before that of the defence) when the judge will sum up the evidence for the jury and instruct them, if necessary, on any legal points involved in the case. The clerk then gives the jury to the charge of the jury bailiff who not only ensures that they have no communication with anyone but also acts as their messenger to the court, so that, for example, he will warn the court that the jury has completed its deliberations and wishes to return, or that the jury wishes to have further guidance from the judge.

Frequently while a jury is 'out' on one case the court will occupy its time by dealing with another, perhaps a guilty plea or prisoner committed for sentence.

When the jury returns the foreman will be questioned by the clerk of the court and will be asked for its verdict on each count separately. When this has been done the jury may be discharged and it remains for the bench to decide the appropriate sentence if there has been a verdict of guilty to any count.

Sentencing

The maximum sentences which may be imposed at the crown court are generally greater than those which may be imposed in a magistrates' court. They are noted in the appropriate sections of this book. Imprisonment may not be imposed on persons under 21 years.

In certain circumstances (eg for breach of probation) a 'nominal sentence' of imprisonment for one day may be imposed.

Expenses

Justices who attend the crown court are entitled to be paid travelling, subsistence and loss of earnings allowances at the same rates applicable in the case of attending the magistrates' court. These rates are changed from time to time and can be obtained from the clerk to the justices.

Disqualification

A justice must not sit at the crown court on an appeal from the decision of a magistrates' court of which he was a member. Nor should he sit on the hearing of proceedings on committal for sentence under s 37 or s 38 of the Magistrates' Courts Act 1980 by a court of which he was a member. The same remarks apply to a case where a justice has considered an application for bail by a prisoner committed for sentence, or who has given notice of appeal. He may sit on an appeal from the decision of a licensing committee (ie liquor, betting or gaming) of which he is himself a member, provided he did not form part of the meeting of the committee whose decision is in question. Normally arrangements will already have been made between the crown court staff and justices' clerk's office which will ensure that a justice is not called to the crown court who is disqualified, but in any case of doubt the justice should inform the judge with whom he is sitting before the case begins.

Section twelve

The role of the justices' clerk

The justices' clerk

Most clerks to the justices continue to hold independent public office at the pleasure of the Magistrates' Courts Committee which appoints them. They may not be dismissed without the approval of the Lord Chancellor, who must in turn consider any representations made to him by the magistrates for the petty sessions concerned. Although newer justices' clerks are appointed on a contract they still hold the independent public office.

The justices' clerk must be distinguished from those of his assistants who on his behalf give advice to justices in court when the justices' clerk is not personally in attendance.

Functions of the justices' clerk

Some of the functions of the justices' clerk will be seen from the following extract from the Justices of the Peace Act 1997, which is not an exhaustive statement:

> 'The functions of a justices' clerk include giving advie to the justices to whom he is clerk, at their request advice about law, practice or procedure on questions arising in connection with the discharge ... of their or his functions as justices including questions arising when the clerk is not personally attending on the justices or justice. The clerk may at any time when he thinks he should do so, bring to the attention of the justices or justice any point of law, practice or procedure that is or may be involved in any question so arising.'

It should be noted that the term 'justices' clerk' is used in the Act where it is also defined so as to exclude a member of his staff.

Justices' chief executive

A justices' clerk may also be employed as a justices' chief executive. The functions of a justices' chief executive are to act as clerk to the Magistrates' Courts Committee and to carry out day-to-day administration for the area subject to the directions of the Committee.

Advice in court

Although the extract from the Justices of the Peace Act above refers solely to the justices' clerk himself, it is recognised that in practice he may delegate his advisory functions to court clerks who are either professionally qualified as barristers or solicitors or are qualified under rules prescribed by the Home Office. This is recognised by a Practice Direction on the role of the clerk from the Lord Chief Justice issued in July 1981, which states:

> '1 A justices' clerk is responsible to the justices for the performance of any of the functions set out below by any member of his staff acting as a

court clerk and may be called in to advise the justices even when he is not personally sitting with the justices as clerk to the court.

2 It shall be the responsibility of the justices' clerk to advise the justices as follows:
(a) on questions of law or of mixed law and fact;
(b) as to matters of practice and procedure.

3 If it appears to him necessary to do so, or he is so requested by the justices, the justices' clerk has the responsibility to:
(a) refresh the justices' memory as to any matter of evidence and to draw attention to any issues involved in the matters before the court;
(b) advise the justices generally on the range of penalties which the law allows them to impose and on any guidance relevant to the choice of penalty provided by the law, the decisions of the superior courts or other authorities.

If no request for advice has been made by the justices, the justices' clerk shall discharge his responsibility in court in the presence of the parties.

4 The way in which the justices' clerk should perform his functions should be stated as follows:
(a) The justices are entitled to the advice of their clerk when they retire in order that the clerk may fulfil his responsibility outlined above.
(b) Some justices prefer to take their own notes of evidence. There is, however, no obligation on them to do so. Whether they do so or not, there is nothing to prevent them from enlisting the aid of their clerk and his notes if they are in any doubt as to the evidence which has been given.
(c) If the justices wish to consult their clerk solely about the evidence or his notes of it, this should ordinarily, and certainly in simple cases, be done in open court. The object is to avoid any suspicion that the clerk has been involved in deciding issues of fact.

5 For the reasons stated in the Practice Direction of 1954 which remains in full force and effect, in domestic proceedings it is more likely than not that the justices will wish to consult their clerk. In particular, where rules of court require the reasons for their decision to be drawn up in consultation with the clerk, they will need to receive his advice for this purpose.

6 This Practice Direction is issued with the concurrence of the President of the Family Division.'

In court the clerk's duties are both advisory and executive. He may, if the justices so desire, perform those many tasks which ensure the smooth progress of the court's business. For example, if the justices so desire, he may decide the order in which cases are called, call cases on, identify, caution and charge defendants, take their pleas and put to them other offences for the court to take into consideration, he may deal with the swearing of witnesses, he may deal with such matters as explanation of probation and asking for the defendant's consent, giving alibi warnings in committal cases, taking recognizances which have been fixed by the bench, dealing with the arrangements for paying monetary penalties, questioning witnesses or defendants on the justices' behalf, including conducting means enquiries. When the clerk (or one of his assistants) performs these or any other similar tasks, he does so on behalf of the justices. There are at least three good reasons why the clerk should carry out most, if not all of these executive functions: his legal knowledge, experience and professional ethics will usually mean that he can do these things better than a lay justice can, there will be more uniformity of procedure if these functions are left to the clerk, and the less the chairman has to worry about procedural tasks, the more of his attention he can give to listening and decision making.

The extent to which the clerk exercises these tasks, however, varies from court to court and even in the same place it may change according to which chairman is sitting or whether the justices' clerk himself or one of his staff is in court. Whatever the clerk does he should be careful to avoid giving to the general public the impression that he and not the chairman is in charge of the court's affairs. The conduct of the court is always the responsibility of the chairman in consultation with his colleagues on the bench; but a wise chairman will usually leave the general conduct of business in court to the clerk.

Although there is nothing in the law which compels the clerk to give advice to his justices it is clear not only from everyday practice, but from the observations of judges in several cases, that he is expected to do so. He may do this while the justices remain in court or he may give them advice privately in their retiring room. The Lord Chief Justice has warned that justices who fail to take the clerk's advice on a legal point may be ordered to pay the costs of any resulting appeal. This warning arose in a case where justices insisted on finding 'special reasons' in spite of advice given to them in court by the clerk and later in writing.

While circumstances frequently occur which make it inadvisable to do so, the practice of giving advice in open court in a voice which the public can hear is generally to be recommended. If the justices retire the clerk should not retire with them as a matter of course: either the chairman should specifically and audibly invite him to join the justices or the clerk should remain in court and be seen to have been sent for.

If the justices retire it is generally better that the clerk should be with them. All too often justices are themselves unaware that a point has arisen in their discussion upon which they need advice, and unless the clerk is with them to hear their discussion he too will be unaware that they need advice. Moreover, if he is present during their discussion the clerk may be able to help by reminding them of parts of the evidence they may have overlooked, or by explaining the legal significance of particular evidence, or by correcting errors of recollection. In the event that the justices are later asked to state a case the clerk will find it a considerable advantage to have listened to the justices' discussion at the hearing. Once the clerk is satisfied that he can be of no further assistance to the justices he should return to his place in court.

If the justices do not send for the clerk when they retire, he is entitled to go to them to give them advice if he considers it necessary to do so, but will inform the parties as to what he is going to say to the justices.

Delegation

Apart from his duty to provide justices with advice when they sit in court, the justices' clerk may perform those judicial functions of a single justice which are prescribed in the Justices' Clerks Rules 1970, as amended. Amongst the more important judicial functions which a justice's clerk can perform are: the issue of a summons, a witness summons, a distress warrant or a warrant for arrest following a defendant's failure to appear at court so long as no objection is raised on behalf of the accused. The justice's clerk may adjourn a case and grant bail to an accused in his absence with the consent of the prosecution and in the same terms as previously imposed.

The clerk may take a plea, fix a trial date and conduct a transfer to crown court under MCA 1980, s 6(2) where the defendant is on bail. He may authorise a court clerk to exercise these functions and under the Children Act to conduct directions appointments and appoint guardians ad litem. He may delegate to members of his staff the power to grant and refuse legal aid in accordance with the Legal Aid Act and the regulations. Delegation should be by specific authorisation and in writing.

Section thirteen

Applications to a justice

It would probably surprise most magistrates to learn of all the various warrants and orders which a single justice may issue and documents they may sign both at the courthouse or at home. Fortunately it would be exceptional if any one magistrate found himself called upon to perform anything more than a small number of such duties away from the courthouse. This section does not catalogue all the magisterial functions but gives general advice and deals with some of the more common 'doorstep' applications.

It sometimes happens that the press will telephone a magistrate seeking an opinion or comment, especially if he is chairman of a bench or of a branch of the Magistrates' Association. It is unwise to deal with such a request immediately. In most cases the magistrate will refuse any comment at all, normally it would be appropriate to refer the enquiry to the clerk or to the chairman of the bench. Be very careful (having said, 'no comment', or words to that effect) that you are not drawn into a conversation isolated parts of which may make tomorrow's headlines. Words spoken conversationally can take on a whole new meaning when reduced to journalistic print. There will be times however when it may be proper to make some statement to the press. In such cases ask the caller to ring again in 30 minutes and use that time to discuss the matter with the clerk, the chairman or a colleague; this will help you to collect your own thoughts on the matter and then it might be helpful to make some written note.

You should invariably refuse to enter into any discussion of a case with any person who has been involved in it. A persistent telephone caller can be warned that he is liable to prosecution for making annoying telephone calls. A persistent anybody else should be told to put his complaint, or whatever, in a letter addressed to the clerk. If you receive any letters you should hand them to the clerk and not reply to them.

Children

(Emergency procedures under the Children Act 1989 are referred to in Section four.)

Warrants

A warrant is a document signed by a magistrate which authorises the person named in the warrant to carry out the action specified.

Signing a warrant is an extremely serious matter and a magistrate would be well advised always to refer the applicant to the courthouse where the application can be made in the presence of the justices' clerk. If that is not possible, the clerk or his deputy should be telephoned for his advice. It is only in cases of extreme urgency that a magistrate should contemplate issuing a warrant in the absence of the clerk.

The following notes are intended to give a broad description of the procedure. **They should not be taken to encourage the hearing of an application in the absence of a clerk.**

Some benches go as far as appointing an out-of-hours panel of volunteer magistrates who are given special training. Even so, in such cases a clerk is always contacted first about the proposed application.

For the purposes of this section warrants fall into two categories: warrants to enter premises (and, usually, search for goods which may then be seized); and warrants to arrest an individual.

1 Warrants to enter premises

1 The applicant

Usually a police officer. If it is not, the magistrate should check whether any authority is needed by the applicant, eg in the case of an official from the Gas Board (see below). As a sensible precaution, a police officer should be asked to produce his warrant card, and anyone else evidence of his identity, and where appropriate, his authority to bring proceedings.

2 Authority for issuing a warrant

A warrant of entry may only be issued where a statute gives authority to do so. When considering an application the magistrate should ask the applicant under what Act and section he is applying for a warrant.

Applications by the police generally fall into one of two categories:

Search for unlawful articles. These are powers of search for goods which generally it is an offence knowingly to possess, eg warrants to enter and search for:

(a) stolen goods – Theft Act 1968, s 26;
(b) drugs – Misuse of Drugs Act 1971, s 23;
(c) obscene articles – Obscene Publications Act 1959, s 3.

Search for evidence. Until the Police and Criminal Evidence Act 1984, there was no power to issue a warrant to search for *evidence*, eg of a murder, unless the object of the search was also an 'unlawful article' so that a warrant could be issued under the powers described above. Section 8 of the Act now provides a general power to search for evidence of an offence. However since the Act also gives the police considerable powers of search without a warrant in connection with the arrest of a defendant, an application for a warrant to search for evidence will very often entail the power to enter the premises of a possibly innocent third party to look for evidence implicating the accused.

Issuing a warrant to search for evidence (Police and Criminal Evidence Act 1984, s 8)

The application must be made by the police and the magistrate must have reasonable grounds for believing:

(a) that a serious arrestable offence has been committed; and
(b) that there is material on premises specified in the application which is likely to be of substantial value (whether by itself or together with other material) to the investigation of the offence; and
(c) that the material is likely to be relevant evidence; and
(d) that it does not consist of or include items subject to legal privilege, excluded material or special procedure material; and
(e) that any of the following applies:
  (i) that it is not practicable to communicate with any person entitled to grant entry to the premises;
  (ii) that it is practicable to communicate with a person entitled to grant access to the premises but it is not practicable to communicate with any person entitled to grant access to the evidence;
  (iii) that entry to the premises will not be granted unless a warrant is produced;
  (iv) that the purpose of a search may be frustrated or seriously prejudiced unless a constable arriving at the premises can secure immediate entry to them.

Reasonable grounds for believing. The magistrate himself must have reasonable grounds for believing etc and his judgment will be based on the information supplied by the officer. In the code of practice issued for guidance to the police, the officer must take reasonable steps to check that the information is accurate, recent and has not been provided maliciously or irresponsibly. An application may not be made on the basis of information from an anonymous source unless corroboration is sought. The identity of an informant need not be disclosed but the officer should be prepared to deal with any questions from the magistrate about the accuracy of previous information provided by that source or other related matters. 'Belief' is something more than suspicion and implies an acceptance that something is true even though formal, admissible evidence may be lacking. It may be helpful to consider the reference to this matter made when considering the offence of handling stolen goods at p 91.

Serious arrestable offence. Some offences are always in this category, eg murder or rape. Other arrestable offences are only serious where they lead or are likely to lead to, inter alia, death or serious injury or substantial financial loss. The clerk will be able to provide a complete list.

Relevant evidence means anything that would be admissible in evidence at a trial for the offence.

Legal privilege means in essence communications between a legal adviser and his client or communications between them and a third party in contemplation of legal proceedings. The clerk can supply a full definition.

Excluded and special procedure material. This includes material held in confidence such as personal or business records, human tissues or fluids taken for the purpose of diagnosis or treatment and journalistic material. A magistrate cannot issue a warrant in respect of excluded or special procedure material; application can only be made, where applicable, to a circuit judge.

May issue. Even where all the criteria have been fulfilled, the magistrate still has a discretion.

3 Procedure (for search warrants issued to the police for evidence under s 8 and under other statutes)

(1) The application may be made by a constable but it must have been authorised by an inspector or more senior officer, or in a case of urgency, the senior officer on duty. Where the officer is not known to the magistrate, a warrant card may be produced to establish identity.
(2) Except in a case of emergency, if there is reason to believe that a search might have an adverse effect on relations between the police and the community, the local Police Community Liaison Officer should have been consulted.
(3) The application must be supported by an information in writing stating:

(a) the enactment under which the application is made;
(b) as specifically as is reasonably practicable the premises to be searched and the object of the search; and
(c) the grounds on which the application is made (including, where the proposed search is to find evidence of an alleged offence, an indication of how the evidence relates to the investigation).

(4) The application may be made without notifying the person whose premises are to be searched but the constable must answer on oath any questions which the magistrate may ask him. Apart from questions designed to ensure that the grounds for the application have been made out, eg under s 26 of the Theft Act, the magistrate might usefully enquire whether the officer has had the same application previously refused by another magistrate. The police cannot 'shop around' for a magistrate willing to sign the warrant. A second application can only be made where it is based on additional grounds. Finally, there is a discretion whether to issue a warrant.
(5) The police will usually have prepared a warrant and two copies beforehand. If he is prepared to issue the warrant, the magistrate should read it carefully and check that it:

(a) specifies
 (i) the name of the person who applies for it;
 (ii) the date on which it is issued;
 (iii) the enactment under which it is issued; and
 (iv) the premises to be searched; and
(b) identifies, so far as is practicable, the articles or persons to be sought.

(6) The clerk should retain the information and the police must forward to him, after 1 month at the latest, the warrant either unexecuted or endorsed as to whether the articles or persons sought were found; and whether any articles were seized, other than the articles which were sought.

4 Procedure for warrants issued to persons other than police officers

The provisions outlined above might usefully be taken into account where relevant. For non-police warrants the information is laid on oath. The applicant will usually produce a prepared information and swear to it in the following words: 'I SWEAR BY ALMIGHTY GOD THAT THIS IS MY INFORMATION AND THAT THE CONTENTS THEREOF ARE TRUE TO THE BEST OF MY KNOWLEDGE AND BELIEF.' If he prefers it, he may substitute for the words, 'I swear by Almighty God . . .' the words, 'I solemnly and sincerely declare and affirm . . .'. If the wording on the information is not sufficient a further written statement should be appended to the information.

As a matter of practice the informant signs the information and the magistrate should retain this and forward it to the justices' clerk.

Warrants of entry for gas and electricity suppliers

The provisions are complex and are summarised below. It is good practice for all such applications to be considered at a courthouse in the presence of a clerk from whom advice may be obtained.

Applications may be made, for example, for entry to read a meter or to cut off the supply following non-payment of a bill. An electricity supplier may cut off the supply where the customer has not paid within 20 working days of a demand in writing and after 2 working days notice of the supplier's intention to do so. However this power is not available where there is a genuine dispute about the amount owed. (Note: this procedure only applies to a bill for electricity supplied and would not include monies owed on an article supplied by way of a credit sale such as a cooker. Nor is it relevant that there is a genuine dispute about the quality of service since the customer may use a separate procedure to obtain compensation.) The relevant periods where a gas supply is concerned are 28 days after the demand in writing and 7 days notice of intent to cut off the supply.

Right of entry. An officer of the supplier after one working day's notice (electricity) 24 hours notice (gas) may at all reasonable times, on production of some duly authenticated document showing his authority, enter the premises for the purpose of cutting off the supply. No notice is required for entry to read a meter except where a warrant is to be applied for.

Warrant of entry. No right of entry may be exercised except with the consent of the occupier of the premises or under the authority of a justices warrant (except in cases of emergency).

Requirements. There must be a sworn information in writing and the applicant must satisfy the justice

(a) that admission to the premises is reasonably required for the specified purpose;
(b) the applicant has a right of entry to the premises;

(c) the requirements of any relevant enactment have been complied with; and in particular
(d) the relevant notices have been given.

The justice might also ensure that

(e) there is no genuine dispute about the amount owed; and
(f) the amount owed is in respect of the supply of gas or electricity.

Code of practice. Gas and electricity suppliers operate a code of practice (of which the clerk of the justices may be able to supply a copy) under which it is undertaken to provide assistance to domestic customers to meet their bills and the suppliers may refrain from cutting off the supply from those who are particularly vulnerable during the winter months, nevertheless where default has occurred, the suppliers may resort to the procedure outlined above.

Duty to repair damage etc. Where a right of entry has been exercised the supplier must ensure that the premises concerned are left no less secure by reason of the entry and must make good or pay compensation for any damage caused in entering the premises or making them secure.

5 The warrant

If the magistrate is satisfied with the application he will sign the warrant (which will normally have been prepared in advance by the applicant). This is handed back to the applicant and is his authority to enter and search etc. A magistrate who has issued a search warrant should say nothing to anyone about it, not even to a member of his own family. This is so that no suspicion falls on him in the event that it may appear that the occupier of the premises was expecting a search.

6 Who may sign

Any magistrate may sign a search warrant provided he is not on the Supplemental List (ie retired from active work on the bench).

2 *Warrants of arrest*

Magistrates will frequently have encountered these during sittings at court, eg for failing to answer bail. The procedure is very similar to that for issuing warrants of entry. However, it is virtually inconceivable that it should be necessary to approach a magistrate at home. The Police and Criminal Evidence Act provides wide powers of arrest without warrant even for minor offences where there is doubt about the identity of the arrested person or an arrest is necessary to prevent harm to him or the public. Accordingly, a magistrate would be unwise to issue such a warrant unless he has the advice of his clerk. Such applications should, as a matter of practice, be heard at the courthouse.

Miscellaneous

Recognizance

A recognizance of a surety for bail should not be taken unless the proposed surety produces a certificate stating the amount and conditions of bail. The surety should be questioned so as to satisfy the magistrate that he has, or can easily obtain, the sum mentioned in the certificate. If the certificate states that a specific person is to be surety, evidence of identity should be required. The clerk or an officer in charge of a police station may take these recognizances and, in any case of doubt, the surety should be referred to one of these persons.

Certificate of good repute

A magistrate should not sign a certificate of good reputation or good character. If approached to do so he should refer the applicant to the clerk.

Passports

A magistrate should not endorse an application for a passport, nor sign the photograph therewith unless he knows the applicant sufficiently well to meet the criteria on the form.

Removal to suitable premises of persons in need of care and attention

(National Assistance Act 1948, s 47 and Amendment Act 1951, s 1)

The following provisions are for the purposes of securing the necessary care and attention for persons who

(a) are suffering from grave chronic disease or, being aged, infirm or physically incapacitated, are living in insanitary conditions; and
(b) are unable to devote to themselves, and are not receiving from other persons, proper care and attention.

Where the proper officer (formerly the medical officer of health) certifies in writing to the local authority that he is satisfied after thorough inquiry and consideration that in the interests of any such person residing in the local authority's area or for preventing injury to the health of, or serious nuisance to other persons, it is necessary to remove him from his residence, the local authority may apply to a court for an order of removal.

If the proper officer and another registered medical practitioner certify that in their opinion it is necessary in the interests of that person to remove him without delay, the local authority or the proper officer where duly authorised may make an application to a single justice having jurisdiction for the place where the person resides. The justice being satisfied on oral evidence under oath of the allegations in the certificate and that it is expedient so to do, may order his removal to a hospital where one is available or to some other place in, or within convenient distance of, the local authority area. If the justice thinks it necessary, the order can be made without notifying or hearing the person concerned.

Duration of the order. The order may be for a period of up to three weeks. After it has expired the local authority would have to make a full application to a court.

It should be noted, however, that as an emergency ex parte application can also be made to a court sitting in a courthouse, applications should normally be considered there except where circumstances dictate otherwise.

Statutory declarations

It is necessary to make sure that the clause at the end of the form is properly completed and dated. It is not necessary to read the document, nor need the magistrate be concerned to establish in his own mind the truth of the contents of it. His signature on the document simply attests that he was present and heard the maker of the document declare that the contents are true.

The words for a statutory declaration are:

> 'I, AB, DO SOLEMNLY AND SINCERELY DECLARE AND AFFIRM THAT THE CONTENTS OF THIS DECLARATION ARE TRUE TO THE BEST OF MY KNOWLEDGE AND BELIEF, AND I MAKE THIS SOLEMN DECLARATION CONSCIENTIOUSLY BELIEVING THE SAME TO BE TRUE AND BY VIRTUE OF THE PROVISIONS OF THE STATUTORY DECLARATIONS ACT 1835.'

The New Testament is not used for a statutory declaration.

Who may sign. Any magistrate, including those on the Supplemental List, may sign a statutory declaration.

Warrants to search for and remove mental patients

(Mental Health Act 1983, s 135)

A justice to whom it appears that there is reasonable cause to suspect that a person believed to be suffering from mental disorder:

(a) has been, or is being, ill-treated, neglected or kept otherwise than under proper control in any place within the jurisdiction of the justice; or
(b) being unable to care for himself, is living alone in any such place

may issue a warrant authorising his removal to a place of safety with a view to making an application under the Mental Health Act or other arrangements for his treatment or care.

Application is by way of an information laid on oath by a social worker specially approved by the local authority for the purposes of the Mental Health Act. The patient need not be named in the information.

Warrant authorises a constable to enter (if need be by force) any premises specified in the warrant and if thought fit to remove him to a place of safety.

Place of safety means residential accommodation provided by a local authority or a hospital, police station, mental nursing home, or residential home for mentally disturbed persons or any other suitable place where the occupier is willing to receive the patient.

Duration. The detention in a place of safety may not be for more than 72 hours.

Administration of oaths etc in certain probate business

Justices of the Peace are empowered by the Courts and Legal Services Act 1990, s 56 to administer oaths and take affidavits in non-contentious probate matters. The Judicial Studies Board has issued the following guidance for the assistance of magistrates' courts:

'(a) The oaths envisaged in this Act are those which are non-contentious and of a probate nature, ie, civil proceedings, and should not therefore be of great urgency requiring their administration out of court hours. Each court should therefore publish set hours during which these oaths will be administered.

(b) Justices should be discouraged from administering these oaths outside court hours and away from supervision by suitably qualified court staff.

(c) Justices should not administer oaths for documents which are to be used in court proceedings [including civil proceedings], and court staff should look at document headings with great care, to ensure that there is no court name or reference number thereon which might indicate a current court action.

(d) The wording of the oath to be taken is different from a court witness oath and is "I swear by Almighty God that the contents of this my [affidavit] [and the exhibits annexed thereto] are true".

(e) Be prepared for the oath to be sworn by members of all religions in the appropriate form – another reason why "out of hours oaths" should be discouraged.

(f) An interpreter may be needed and he should be sworn first, taking the appropriate oath.

(g) A deponent may wish to affirm, in which case he will do so in the appropriate form – again a reason for oaths to be administered in the court setting, as justices will not necessarily know the correct wording.

(h) Every alteration to the document has to be initialled by the administering justice.

(i) Any exhibit has to be dated and signed and must clearly indicate that it is the exhibit annexed to the affidavit produced and sworn by the deponent on that same occasion.

(j) The jurat or attestation shall state the date and place the oath or affidavit is taken or made [s 56[2]].

(k) No justice shall exercise the powers conferred in any proceedings in which he is interested [s 56[3]].

(l) In the event of any person being sufficiently handicapped to make it impossible for him or her to attend court to swear a document, arrangement could be made by a clerk to the justices for a justice and member of the court staff to attend upon that person at their home, or a mutually convenient place. This should not occur frequently, but should be provided for by courts.'

Index